ABOUT THE AUTHOR

RICHARD TREGASKIS is a reporter,
war correspondent, author,
motion picture and TV writer.

He began his chronicling of wars as
a Navy Correspondent during the Second
World War, both in Europe and Asia,
and produced such memorable works as
GUADALCANAL DIARY,* INVASION DIARY,*
and STRONGER THAN FEAR.

While covering the Nationalist-Communist war
in China, he wrote SEVEN LEAGUES TO PARADISE
and LAST PLANE TO SHANGHAI.* In 1962 he
wrote JOHN F. KENNEDY WAR HERO.

Mr. Tregaskis and his wife make
their home in Hawaii.

Published in Popular Library editions

Vietnam Diary

RICHARD TREGASKIS

POPULAR LIBRARY · NEW YORK

Ned L. Pines · President

Frank P. Lualdi · Publisher

POPULAR LIBRARY EDITION

Copyright © 1963 by Richard Tregaskis
Library of Congress Catalog Card Number: 63-21877

Published by arrangement with
Holt, Rinehart and Winston, Inc.
Holt, Rinehart and Winston edition published
in November, 1963
First printing: October, 1963
Second Printing: March, 1964

Published simultaneously in Canada by
Holt, Rinehart and Winston of Canada, Limited

PRINTED IN THE UNITED STATES OF AMERICA

Contents

Arrival   9

The Marines   19

The Army   147

A Leave in Hong Kong   189

D-Zone   201

Junk Fleet   215

D-Zone   225

The Swamps of Soctrang   239

The Special Forces and Strategic Hamlets   299

Christmas, a Battle, a Free Election   329

Index   377

DEDICATION:

To the men who gave their blood in the rice fields and jungly mountains of the Vietnam anti-Communist war; as of this writing, 50,000 Army of Vietnam soldiers, killed and wounded, and 1,050 Americans. May no man dishonor their bravery in this new kind of war—a war as critically important to our future as World War II or Korea.

Arrival

This is going to war, modern style—and comfortably thus far. I've been able to hitch a ride with a group of brass, heading down to Vietnam.

Most of these generals and colonels (and one ambassador) came up to Hawaii four days ago in this same aircraft, a big Boeing 707 model. ("Military model" means that it is a transport, freighter-style, with no windows—an aerial submarine, they say—a view of the outer world being cut off in the name of military austerity and functionalism. But inside there are reasonably comfortable seats.)

The brass came up for a conference with Defense Secretary Robert S. McNamara and staff (who jetted down from Washington, D.C., to meet them and the Pacific commander, Adm. Harry D. Felt). The conference lasted one day (yesterday)—one of a series, held every few months: the highest American command comes out to the Pacific to meet with the field commanders and deliberate on ways to win our running battle with the Communists in the hottest of the hot-war areas and our only shooting war—Vietnam.

Last night, the conference over and plans made for the conduct of the war against the Vietnam Reds for the next few weeks and months, Secretary McNamara and his staff roared off for Washington.

Today, at 12:30 P.M., the Southeast Asia military commanders took off in our big aerial submarine for Saigon and Bangkok. On board are Gen. Paul D. Harkins, chief of U.S. Military Assistance Command, Vietnam (USMACV), the

U.S. Ambassadors to Vietnam and Thailand, the chiefs of a half-dozen military sections in Vietnam (some hush-hush, like the Special Forces), and some plain hitchhikers like me trying to get to Vietnam on various assignments.

I was lucky enough to find a seat, my over-all objective being to get a firsthand, eyewitness look at the strange, off-beat, new-style war in which we find ourselves engaged in the miserable little jungle country called Vietnam, which our nation's leaders have decided is pivotal and critical in our Asian struggle with Communism. I am lucky to have military orders appropriate to my mission of writing a book about the war in Vietnam, and thus ride with such a distinguished array of brass—but within a few days I expect to be with people at the opposite end of the military scale, people who are engaged in combat against the Communist Viet Cong (VC).

I say it is a miserable little country because I have been there before, twice, and it would be dishonest to say that I enjoyed either time. The first time was in 1948, when the area was called French Indochina and a French Army, composed mostly of Germans and French African colonials, were battling to defeat the Indochina rebels. That war ended in 1954, when the French made peace with the Viet Minh at a Geneva parley, and Indochina was cut into four independent parts: Laos, Cambodia, and the two parts of Vietnam (the northern half a Communist state under Ho Chi-minh; the southern half eventually becoming a relatively free state and democracy under a Roman Catholic president, Ngo Dinh Diem).

Then, in 1957-58, I spent some unhappy months in the new Vietnamese republic, which was then feeling its oats as a self-determined nation free of French colonial control. The street names in Saigon had been changed from French to Vietnamese; for instance, the main drag, once called Rue Catinat, was renamed Duong Tu Do, or Liberty Street; the opera house, once a favorite target for rebel bombs when it was full of Frenchmen, was converted to a National Assembly or Congress. The gambling joints and opium dives that the French had countenanced (in fact, opium had been a lucrative French government monopoly) had been closed, but the new independent government was struggling to repair war damage and make the place fit for tourists again and they had too much to do. They were already fighting a guerrilla war against the Communists in the mountains and the swampy Delta country south of Saigon.

On that trip, when I went back to write some magazine articles about Vietnam, and I drove the length of that rough country in a jeep, it was hardly a model tourist mecca. The usual Southeast Asian diseases—sprue, hookworm, flatworm, roundworm, tapeworm, malaria, dysentery, tuberculosis—were well distributed, and so was the liberal coating of filth that keeps such things alive and flourishing.

I know from covering wars we Americans have been involved in (like World War II, Korea, China, Quemoy) that our GI's usually say whatever part of the world they are in is the worst in the world. Of course, they don't know, because nobody could claim our GI's have been everywhere in the world—not yet, anyhow.

Now that a large group of Americans have been sent to the war zone in Vietnam (more than 10,000 American military men and women), and I am going there, I expect to hear them say that Vietnam is the rear end of the world, and for once they will probably be right.

However, living in Vietnam should be quite a lot more bearable because, with all those 10,000 Americans in the country, there will be American food (even if it is C-rations) and water made drinkable by military lister bags.

The contrasts between going to war today and 20 years ago, when I went into Guadalcanal with the Marines, are striking. Then, it took weeks aboard transport ships to get our forces into position to attack the Japanese. We chugged into Tulagi Bay at 15 knots, all in one powerful force. Heavy cruisers and destroyers provided a massive naval bombardment; an umbrella of dive bombers and fighter planes from aircraft carriers covered our assault. The big attack came on that one day, August 7, 1942.

Today, there is no one big D-Day: every day is D-Day and the front is everywhere. Vietnam's long-continuing struggle against Communism lacks the punctuation of massive battles—but casualties (mostly Vietnamese) come just as certainly. As for our forces, some are moved into position by ship nowadays, but a large number are flown in and evacuated by plane: Military Air Transport jets like this one, clipping along over Pacific clouds at five miles a minute, or one of the fleets of charter planes flown by civilian crews and carrying American military men and women on contract flights with the Defense Department (since we are short of good air transports); others are brought into the war zone in the old propeller-driven airplanes, some of them dating from late World War II, the Berlin airlift, and Korean war days.

It may turn out that the guerrilla-type operations in this critical struggle with Communism will be more important to

11

our history and our future than even World War II. Gen. Eisenhower, who was cautious about our involvements in military campaigns abroad, and apparently more concerned with going down in history as a peaceful·president than anything else, said that if Vietnam should fall to the Communists, all of Southeast Asia would collapse like a house of cards.

President Kennedy, once inaugurated, lost no time acting on this proposition. In the fall of 1961 he sent his Military Adviser, Gen. Maxwell D. Taylor, down to assess the danger, dispatched some interim aid, and in January of 1962 created USMACV, under Gen. Paul Harkins.

Under Gen. Harkins, the American support and advisory forces grew from 7,000 to 9,000. In December, 1961, the first American helicopter outfit, the 57th Transportation (Helicopter) Company, arrived to bring the assist of vertical envelopment to the Vietnamese troops, lifting them into battle against the VC. Military men were enthusiastic: For the first time, helicopters in force were to be used against Red forces, with the potential of moving with lightninglike speed to get behind or onto the flank of the Communist guerrillas in their own territory—and also, hopefully, to halt the Communist advance, which was achieving some alarming successes both in the mountainous north and in the Delta area in the south.

Other helicopter units, American advisory units, and the antiguerrilla training outfits called Special Forces began to arrive in Vietnam. Our commitment in Southeast Asia was under way.

It's very possible that we may never have the nuclear super-conflict, the hydrogen-bomb donnybrook, of which we are running so scared that our fear seems to dominate every other consideration in life. This kind of highly expensive conflict seems unlikely as long as the Communists are sold on the bush-war kind of conflict, with which they have been achieving such spectacular results since the end of World War II (a quarter of the world's population has gone Communist). In simple terms: Why spend a million bucks for a big war when you can get what you want at a cheaper price, i.e., the revolutionary or bush war?

Our 707 is taking us to the latest of these bush wars, one distinguished by the fact that, as in Korea, we have decided to draw a line and say to the Communists: NO FARTHER.

It's a long pull to far-removed Vietnam: 6,000 miles from Hawaii and 11,000 miles, or just about halfway round the world, from New York. This plane will cover the distance

12

from Hawaii in 12 or 13 hours, and we should be in Saigon in time for dinner.

I asked Gen. Harkins' public information (PI) chief, Lt. Col. Jim Smith, to introduce me to Frederick E. Nolting, Jr., the U.S. Ambassador to Vietnam. The Ambassador, a mild-voiced man of 48 with the gentle demeanor of a scholar, explained the mechanism of the strange war in Vietnam. But what he said was quite aggressive. He gestured with clenched hands:

"There are two fists to our effort. There is the [Vietnamese government] striking force: trained and supplied by us—and most especially provided with mobility (the helicopters—and supplied with intelligence, which will put them in a position to find out where the hard core of the VC is and isolate them—and we have been doing this with increasing success.

"While one fist is attacking, the other is pacifying through the 'strategic hamlet' program, the clear-and-hold operation." He was referring to the Vietnamese government program, supported by the Americans to the tune of hundreds of millions of dollars, of fencing in and protecting newly freed villages—cleared, that is, of VC's—and making the villages, and the farming families in them, strong enough to resist further VC attacks.

I knew from my military sources in Hawaii that Secretary McNamara has always been one of the strongest champions of the strategic hamlet program in Vietnam as the most important method of driving out the Communists—and keeping them out. McNamara is supposed to have practically forced this new program through and made sure that the first strategic hamlets were built.

"The aim and result today," Ambassador Nolting went on, "is to cut the VC off from their resources—that is, the *people*—and gradually to isolate them. It's somewhat similar to Malaya [the 10-year-long British campaign against the Communist insurgents in the Malay territories, where villagers were removed from Communist territory and resettled in new strong points where they could live in peace and be protected by military forces]. But the system in Malaya was to move people to new locations. Here, the system is to give them their needs and the incentive for defending themselves."

I asked the Ambassador how far we have progressed with his two-fisted program for clearing out the VC and holding the territory.

"It's too early to say it's over the hump. But certainly the VC are somewhat worried about it. I think they're somewhat in a quandary about what to do."

When I asked about the strength of the enemy in the country, he answered quite precisely: "About 60 to 65 per cent of the population are estimated controlled by the government, 15 or 20 per cent noncommitted, and about 15 to 20 per cent controlled by the VC."

Since my principal interest on the trip to Vietnam is to write about Americans fighting there, I asked where the toughest engagements have been and where the bulk of the resistance has been found. Ambassador Nolting replied that the thickest concentration of VC strength has been in the Mekong Delta area south of Saigon, the rice basket of Vietnam. "There are supposed to be 9,000 to 11,000 VC troops in the Delta area," he said, "out of a total of perhaps 20,000 to 25,000 hard-core VC in the country as a whole.

"But the highlands of the north are vastly important too. Gen. Giap [the military genius of the Communists in their battle against the French] said that he who controls the highlands controls the country. Diem [Ngo Dinh Diem] said the same."

I stated my intention to visit both the Delta area and the high mountains to the north, and the ambassador smiled and said I should get a pretty good look at the hostilities, but that I should be prepared to duck, since both areas are dangerous.

I again sought out Col. Smith and asked for an interview with Gen. Harkins. The dapper PIO introduced me to the general, a tall, patient man with the impeccable bearing and uniform you would expect of a former commandant of the U.S. Military Academy at West Point and a long history as a corps (high headquarters) commander. He was too tired for an interview and I said I hoped he would have time to see me later. He smiled rather acidly and said, "Yes, I expect to be in Vietnam for some time."

I went back to my seat and talked to a spy type heading back to Vietnam to go on with his secretive work. Matter of fact, he is what you might call the head spy for operations in Vietnam, a large, well-spoken, engaging man with a good sense of humor and an immense dedication to and enthusiasm for his job.

Like Ambassador Nolting, he seemed to feel that there was reason for optimism about the progress of our war against the VC, because our side is clearing and holding new pieces of

Vietnam. "But we've got a lot to learn. We've never fought a guerrilla war on a national basis before. . . . We have to take the people away from the VC because they [the people] are the greatest single weapon . . . the first way of taking people away is by training and arming them. You don't take people away from the VC with high-flown slogans in Saigon, but . . . by having defenders in place. In addition, we are trying to do socio-economic things that are needed."

He said he was worried about the status of supposedly neutral Laos on Vietnam's western flank. It's well known that Russian planes are flying troops and supplies into Laos from Hanoi in North Vietnam, in violation of the Geneva agreement, which supposedly established Laos as a neutral.

"Do you think the Commies are concentrating their major effort on building up their position in Laos, and moving a lot of new strength into Vietnam from there?" I asked.

He didn't answer directly. "Laos will be a big blow if it goes . . . Laos is the strategic center of Southeast Asia, the key to Southeast Asia." But, he went on, "we are getting in some good licks against the Vietnamese Communists in the meantime, . . . and with our help, Ngo Dinh Diem may be able to get the VC really on the run before the Russians and Chinese build up too much strength in Laos . . .

"[If] the VC know the cards are stacked against them, they fight less well. Like a football team that's had a long string of losses, they're pretty down in the mouth."

It was dusk as we landed at Tan Son Nhut airfield outside Saigon. Moist, heavy, warm air met us as we climbed down the gangway, past a human chain of Vietnamese coolies unloading the baggage. I got a ride into town with Col. Smith, who commented: "Same old Saigon—same smell of mold." As we joined the thick auto traffic, I was forcibly reminded of the suffocating, oppressive heat of the city, the smell of spoilage.

In the city, the surge of traffic through the narrow streets was even heavier than it was the last time I was here. Streams of American, British, and French sedans and the still-dominant beat-up little Renault rear-engined cabs plowed through the streets with reckless disregard for others' safety—and their own. And there were the usual floods of Vespa and Lambretta motor bikes darting nervously into and around the traffic.

Downtown Saigon was brighter than I remembered it: there seemed to be whole new batteries of mauve-colored fluorescent street lights. Beyond the lights, however, were visible the same impressive concrete houses and government buildings built by the French—colonial versions of the old-style stone buildings of Paris, but executed in the characteristic orange-colored cement of the region.

The splash of neons in the heart of the downtown area seemed brighter than ever, with a new hotel, the Caravelle, across Le Loi Square from the venerable Hotel Continental Palace. New since I was here four and a half years ago, the Caravelle, a smartly lit, medium-sized hotel, would be undistinguished in any European or American city the size of Saigon (two million), but in Saigon it seems almost unbearably smart and modern.

Col. Smith's driver stopped the station wagon in front of the Caravelle, "the only hotel, but expensive," said Smith, and we unloaded my B-4 bag and rucksack.

I checked into my air-conditioned room with its blond veneer wood-work, angular fixtures supposedly modern in the European idiom, a closet, a bath with a bidet, a tub, and hot and cold water (!), a white telephone with French lettering, which indicated the origin of the hotel (it was built with money raised by Air France): *"Police, secours, pompiers, dérangements."* The interior of the hotel, like the outside, represented the height of luxury here in Saigon.

The hotel restaurant was on the 10th floor, its Top-of-the-Mark-type picture windows overlooking Saigon. The food wasn't bad, in a modified French colonial manner, but I ate cautiously, remembering the lessons taught me by that bitter but effective Asian teacher, the retching gut, on previous dysentery-ridden jaunts into Southeast Asia. I want to avoid the obvious hazards—there will be many more of the more unexpected kind coming up.

Thursday, October 11

Early this morning I was haunting Col. Smith's Public Information (PI) Office arranging for some transport up the north to Danang, where the Marine helicopter outfit is operating.

Smith's office is in a corner of Gen. Harkins' headquarters, a former French dwelling place in the *grand boulevard* section where the French colonial *grands segnieurs* used to live. It's a high-walled, apartment-type building of the inevitable concrete (white, in this case), with snappily uniformed American MP's on guard at the front gate. The American military offices of this high-command headquarters are spread across former living quarters in rambling fashion. Smith's

16

office digs, which are jammed into two back rooms that must have been servants' quarters at one point in history, are full of desks, file cases, and maps, like the other high-command offices of the building. They seem archaic and out of joint, but have one saving virtue in the oppressive Saigon humidity: air-conditioning.

Col. Smith's assisting officers, Cmdr. Gerald Zornow and Maj. Allan Galfund, gave me quick action on my request to go to Danang. They told me I can leave tomorrow on the Mule Train Air Force transport plane, which makes regular runs up north to bring supplies to the forces fighting VC guerrillas in the high jungles along the Cambodian and Laotian borders. Orders will be cut today in the adjutant's office, and I will leave tomorrow at 7 A.M. One of the PI officers will pick me up at the Caravelle at 6:45 and make sure I get to the right pickup point for the flight. That's the way to run a PI office!

Zornow spoke highly of the Marine helicopter outfit, called "Rathbun's Ridge Runners" after their CO, Lt. Col. Robert L. Rathbun (of Oakland, Calif.) and because they have the job of dropping Vietnamese troops in battle assaults in the rugged high mountains.

Zornow told me that the country where the Marines fly is "very hairy," meaning forbidding and difficult to land in. He mentioned a bad crash, in which seven Marines were killed, only five days ago, at Quang Ngai. Rescue operations had been almost impossible amid 100-foot trees and thick jungle tangle. It had taken the Vietnamese troops two hours to make their way 200 yards, and two days to get the bodies out.

Just this morning four of the dead Marines were loaded aboard a transport plane with a full military honor guard at Tan Son Nhut for shipment home. Three other bodies had already been sent, and the sole survivor of the crash, the pilot, is still in our American military hospital in Nhatrang with bad burns on face and arms. Smith, who went out to the airfield this morning, was apparently moved by the ceremony. "The transport pilot stood half an hour with his hand over his heart . . . and there was a squad of Marines on hand," he told me.

"The Marines are good boys," he added with a remarkable degree of respect, considering that he is an Air Force officer. I had always found them that way, from the first time I saw them on the way to Guadalcanal.

The Marines

Smith picked me up on time and by 7 A.M. we were threading our way through the assemblage of (former French) barracks buildings on the outskirts of Tan Son Nhut airfield. We found our way into an ancient French building as undistinguished and unfunctional as the MACV HQ, and checked with the well-worn American Air Force sergeant behind the desk. Soon we were rolling out onto the wide concrete plain of the airfield, picking our way along a line of dumpy C-123's, wheelbarrow-shaped cargo planes carrying the white-star insignia of the U.S. We pulled up next to No. 287, the aircraft scheduled to go to Danang this morning, and I was surprised to see how big this kind of beast is: a bulbous giant that can lift 15 tons of freight on its two powerful turbo-prop engines. These C-123 Loadmasters, Smith told me, are the main supply link of our military support operations in Vietnam. Since the roads are primitive and considerable territory is not yet cleared of VC's, we depend on these Air Force cargo planes, with an assist from some Army two-engine freighters called Caribous, to keep the far-flung fighting units supplied with all the impedimenta of modern war.

A bunch of crewmen in greasy fatigues were struggling to get a square crate into the open rear maw of the C-123. They were sweating and cussing in the oppressive early-morning heat of Saigon. A sturdy GI told us the aircraft would be taking off in 15 or 20 minutes. He was Airman First Class Jerry Morgan (of High Point, N.C.), serving as loadmaster on today's flight.

One of the pilots, a slim lieutenant named Louis Kirchdorfer (of Roseborough, N.C.), superintended while about a dozen GI's in fatigues and combat boots, with carbines and M-1's, loaded their barracks bags among the crates of the plane's cavernous interior. Most of them were Army Signal Corps people, heading for some secret assignment in Danang.

Lt. Kirchdorfer told me he has been here only a week, although his outfit, the Provisional Second Squadron of the 2d Air Division, Thirteenth Air Force, has been serving in Vietnam for almost five months. I asked him how he liked the life here.

"It's fine if I can fly," he said. "Otherwise, there's nothing to do."

I asked what he does if he can't fly on a certain day? What does he do to pass the time?

"Sleep," he said.

It quickly developed that Kirchdorfer, like many another Air Force flier, is in love with flying—probably would be unhappy if he couldn't fly, no matter what country he was stationed in. He's a graduate aeronautical engineer from North Carolina State University—not a bad background for a copilot of a C-123 in Vietnam.

The other (first) pilot, Lt. Marshall L. Johnson (of Crestline, Calif.), is comparatively a veteran. He came in with the original bunch of pilots of the Second Squadron in June. Since that time, four of the stubby 123's of the outfit have been hit by VC bullets, usually as they were dropping supplies by parachute to Vietnamese outposts surrounded by Communists. In early July, Johnson told me, one of the Second's C-123's plowed into a mountain near Ban Methuot to the north.

(Later I discovered that in that crash the pilot and copilot were injured. The two crewmen tried to get through the jungle to the nearest village, but soon got lost in the jungle thickets, then couldn't even find their way back to the aircraft until the next day. Meanwhile, a patrol of VC's reached the airplane, took what firearms they could find, but mysteriously didn't bother the injured pilots. All four Americans were eventually rescued by Vietnamese government troops. Since that time the C-123 pilots and crewmen have always gone flying armed to the teeth.)

Lt. Johnson signaled us to board the aircraft, and we found places among the canvas seats along each side of the cargo compartment (arranged for maximum discomfort in true military fashion, with a bar of tube steel running down the middle of each seat space). We followed the Air Force requirement of putting on parachutes before take-off, fastened seat belts as ordered, and listened in stolid and sweaty misery while the plane's navigator, Lt. Ed Rosane (of Pasco, Wash.), drilled us on the number of warning bells that would be sounded if we were to bail out, and what to do if we had a power failure on take-off: "Put your head between your knees because of flying glass." We couldn't have cared less about the possible danger of flying glass at that point.

At 8:20, with a great roar of engines, our ugly-duckling aircraft waddled toward the main long runway. The cabin looked like a bizarre junkyard, a storehouse of airplane parts with freight and passengers dumped willy-nilly inside: a cavernous tube of fuselage, with mazes of wiring, tubing, ducts, metal sheets, and rivets exposed everywhere, and the freight—cargo crates, tanks, huge containers of rations, spare airplane parts—dumped in with the passengers.

The plane reached the end of the runway, swung around, and lurched to a stop. We sat there waiting, sweating in harnesses and being gored by the tubing seats. I couldn't see out the windows as we took off, because the canvas seats put our backs against what windows there were. Never mind, I had one fair idea about traveling around Vietnam: It was going to be uncomfortable.

The crewmen adjusted to the discomforts of C-123 flight as if they had been through plenty of it. They hopped nimbly over the pile of cargo at the center of the fuselage and sacked out on various flat spaces as the plane gained altitude. Loadmaster Jerry Morgan had corralled a Medical Corps stretcher for sack-out purposes and, with a spare parachute for a pillow, extracted a pocketbook, *The Roots of Fury,* by Irving Shulman, from his pocket, lit a cigarette, and relaxed.

The Signal Corps GI next to me was an angular PFC named David Weiss (of Omro, Wis.), attached to the hush-hush radio communications outfit going up to Danang: "We're a little bit on the agency side . . . We don't talk very much about it."

Next to him was Sgt. Charles Parnell (of Lamperton, N.C.), a rugged-looking (battered nose, cauliflower ear) mechanic attached to the C-123 outfit, the Second Provisional Squadron. He was going to be dropped off at Quang Ngai, en route to Danang, to work on a C-123 stranded on that exposed landing strip in VC-dominated territory.

I had borrowed Lt. Rosane's headphones so that Johnson could talk to me by interphone despite the ear-dinning sound of those loud engines. He told me as we droned northward that this was going to be an "assault-type landing," meaning that because the landing strip at Quang Ngai is very short, emergency procedures for coming into such a cramped area have to be followed.

"The approach is a little lower . . . 60-degree flaps instead of 45 . . . reverse power . . . can come to a stop in 600 feet with 47-48 thousand pounds gross weight," he explained.

It was a typical rainy day in Vietnam, with very few breaks in the floor of cumulus clouds below us. At 10:20, I figured we were just about above Quang Ngai, because I heard copilot Kirchdorfer suggest, "How about going through that hunk of blue?"

Johnson, like the experienced senior pilot he is, said, "I'll go out to the coast and come back under it [the cloud cover]. It'll only be a couple of minutes." I guessed he was thinking that messing around in the clouds with all those mountains around can be rapidly fatal, as it has been for many pilots here.

"A bush war is going on right now," Johnson said as we came into Quang Ngai. "Two helicopters got shot down out there, about 20 miles west, about five weeks ago."

When the ramp opened and the dust settled, I could see the clumsy silver shape of another C-123 nearby. That would be the aircraft that Sgt. Morgan was going to repair.

A jeep came dashing toward us, with three Air Force men draped on it, all armed with pistols, bandoleers of ammunition, and sheath knives. Inside the plane, the sturdy Sgt. Parnell hurried to untie a squarish, yellow-painted metal stand from its cargo straps. Jerry Morgan sprang into fast action to help free the equipment, with an assist from a third crew member, husky, black-skinned Sgt. Willie Washington of Tallahassee, Fla. The gadget they were wrestling with was a starter motor for the downed C-123. If Parnell did a good job of installing that motor, the C-123 would be airborne and droning south to Saigon before sundown today, rescued from another precarious night in their narrow strip of outpost-airfield. It seemed evident from the general haste that this little strip was frequently under VC sniper fire and the unloading job had to be done quickly so that the second C-123 could get away before it, too, became disabled. You could see this urgency in every move of the men wrestling with the heavy aircraft equipment.

Nor could you miss the urgency with which Lt. Johnson gunned his engines as soon as the equipment was out, and shut the ramp doors as we taxied away. We speedily reached take-off position, wheeled around, and were off with a jerky blast of power, still sweating and wiping the dust out of our eyes.

I went forward to join the pilots as we flew along the seacoast under clear skies, riding over miles of handsome yellow sand beaches, deserted except for occasional clusters of houses and concentrations of fishermen's sampans shaped generally like the dories of New England. Most of the fishing boats were drawn up on the sand among the scrub trees of the beach front. A few were offshore, bobbing on the lucent aquamarine water. Where there were towns, there were also, invariably, large blanched squares of land, salt evaporating basins. Salt is great trading material in this part of the world.

Soon we were over a wide, sweeping bay and inland, a far-sweeping grid of houses and a few gray ribbons of surfaced roads: Danang. It had been a French naval base and resort town in Indochina days, when it was called Tourane.

We turned and moved up a widespread river valley and came out over a large airdrome. I went back to my seat again for the landing. We jerked to a stop on the Air Force side of the base, the ramp opened, and we passengers filed down the open ramp toward old French hangars beyond a plain of Marston mat—World War II pierced-steel planking. No doubt we had arrived too late to get any lunch today: Military flights seem invariably to be set up this way for passengers. But at least we had reached Danang.

I hitched a ride with an Army major to the Marine side of the airport. Also housed in the old French hangars and nickel-sized offices, which might be right for the French or the Vietnamese, the Marine headquarters seemed too small for Americans. In a lean-to office beside the hangar I met a lieutenant colonel whose name struck sympathetic memory chords. He was Don Foss, a cousin of a famed Marine flier I had known in Guadalcanal days, Capt. Joe Foss, who got the Congressional Medal of Honor for leading the Marine fighter planes defending Guadalcanal. Later, Joe Foss became governor of his state, South Dakota, and after that, commissioner of the American Football League.

Don Foss came from the same area, Sioux Falls, S.D., and somehow he looks like Joe—large and plain—although this Foss has followed a different branch of service within the Marine Corps. He's attached to a helicopter outfit and spends most of his flying time at the controls of the little observation and reconnaissance planes (called "L-19" in Army language, or "OE" in Marine-Navy talk) that do the scouting for the whirlybirds.

23

Foss drove me across the runway and over a wide expanse of meadows, through a little Vietnamese colony of former plantation houses and jerry-built shops for such tradesmen as grocers, tailors, bicycle dealers.

We turned into a big military compound behind barbed-wire barriers, where long barracks-type buildings of rough concrete were ranged. We pulled up in front of one and Foss helped me unload my gear.

Inside the building, there was a long hall, with cubicles on both sides, and a large bathroom, with a row of showers and a tile floor that has a huge "93" embedded in it. Foss explained that the bathroom had been built by the 93d Transportation (Army) Company, which had previously occupied the building. Then the 163d Marine Squadron came in and switched places with the 93d, which went to Soctrang, south of Saigon, where the Marines had been flying since arriving in Vietnam.

The change was a wise one, Foss said, because the Marine helicopters, the HUS's, have more power and can maneuver better in the highlands and mountains. The Army H-21's, which take longer to climb and can't carry as much load, are OK for air-phibious assaults in the flat Delta terrain.

The Marines have taken hold of the challenge both in the Delta and up here, Foss said. "They have proved this stuff from one end of the country to the other. . . . They are professional helicopter people.

"Troops would never have gotten in, down in the Delta or up here in the mountains, without them. The helicopters proved their worth . . . the troops back us up on this."

In the barracks, we met Maj. Aquilla "Razor" Blaydes (of Dallas, Tex.), a dark, saturnine man who is the operations officer of this Marine squadron.

"Have you got a flight out now?" Foss asked him, for my edification.

"I've got several."

"How many?"

"Fourteen."

I asked what the flights were and Blaydes answered:

"Administrative [carrying people around], resupply [carting food, ammunition, supplies], and an emergency medical evac."

"Did you make the emergency evac?" asked Foss.

"Yes," Blaydes replied. "Four stretcher cases—and ten walking [wounded] . . . —15 miles northwest of Tam Qui."

This afternoon before supper, I got a black-plague shot at the sick bay—complying with a regulation—and met one of the recent heroes of the outfit: Capt. Cy Herschberg (of New York, N.Y.).

A most unlikely physical type to be a hero (they usually are unlikely), Dr. Herschberg is tall, thin, slightly stooped, nearsighted, and bespectacled. His heroism consisted of being lowered 100 feet by sling from a helicopter into the Quang Ngai jungle to bring first aid to the eight badly burned Marines who cracked up six days ago.

I had heard in Saigon how Dr. Herschberg and a dental technician named Robert Stafford were lowered to the site of the crash; how they gave the injured men morphine, bandaged their severe burns, loaded them onto stretchers, and stayed with them through the night in VC territory until ground troops could cut their way through the jungle to reach them.

I made a mental note to talk to Herschberg and Stafford when they were not so busy. Tonight they were in the middle of sick call, giving out remedies for the complaints endemic to any military camp: cat fever ("cat" standing for catarrhal gastroenteritis), diarrhea and nausea, backaches, fungus infections.

At mess I also heard about the two Marines who have been wounded thus far in combat. Both were crew chief-gunners who were hit by rounds of enemy small-arms fire. One, a Kentucky boy named Billy Watson, is still on duty. He was out of action for only one day, with a slight wound in the behind. The other wounded-in-action, Lance Cpl. James Mansfield (of Oxford, Neb.) is in the hospital in Nhatrang. Ten days ago he took a VC bullet in the leg which has brought up some serious complications.

I was told there will be a chopper going down to Nhatrang tomorrow with the mission, among other things, of bringing mail to Mansfield and to Sinnott, the pilot who was the sole survivor of that recent Marine crash. I asked slim, olive-skinned Lt. Col. Rathbun, the CO of the squadron, if I could make the trip tomorrow and see Mansfield and the pilot. Rathbun said I could.

After dinner, I couldn't find Billy Watson anywhere in the camp, but Lt. Col. Alton "Tex" McCully (of Spur, Tex.), the executive officer, told me how Billy was wounded.

In the room which he shared with Don Foss, McCully illustrated with a pair of the armor pants used by the helicopter crewmen while flying over VC territory. (They also wear armor vests.)

Armor pants are made like a corset, with a zipper so that you can put the garment around your waist and then fasten the

25

zipper. When it's fastened, the plastic armor, covered with olive-drab cloth, becomes a snug groin protector and supposedly turns bullets or shell fragments.

Like a lot of people who wear the armor, McCully explained, Billy wanted to protect himself from fire coming from the most likely direction: below. So instead of wearing the armor, he had folded it over so there would be a double thickness, and had sat on it like a cushion.

It was a good thing he did that, Tex said, because "it went through two thicknesses of armor and just nicked him in the butt."

Saturday, October 13

This morning I woke up at 5 A.M. and found a mosquito inside the net over my bunk. It must have been inside all night and probably had been working me over. I let it bite my hand to see if it was the malarial type, which stands on its head when it bites. This one, fortunately, bit with its body flat.

Malaria is a big killer and disabler in Southeast Asia, though not so bad for us Americans, because we use DDT spray in our camps, sleep inside mosquito bars when we can, and take Chloroquin pills every week. (I noted the Marines have these purple antimalaria capsules on their tables.)

After breakfast, I got a jeep ride to the airfield with the four pilots flying down to Nhatrang. As we neared the runway, we saw that the Marine brood of choppers was already stirring. We had to stop at the runway while several of the whirlybirds thrummed into the air. Down the long line of parked HUS's, three or four were starting engines, and when we reached the ready room, a shack beside the hangar, the place was as busy as a railroad station in suburbia at 8:15 A.M.

Here, the pilots were getting their assignments from the duty officer who presided at the desk opposite the screen door. The assignments were mostly of the administrative kind, hauling small groups of people, ammunition, food, and supplies from one Vietnamese military post to another.

Some of these posts, I knew, would be deep inside VC territory or the vast areas not occupied by either side; accordingly, all of the Marine pilots wore side arms. Some sported picturesque bandoleers and handsome revolvers; a couple carried stubby Swedish K submachine guns. Almost all wore formidable-looking sheath knives.

The ready room itself was a standard briefing hut with maps on one wall and, on another side of the room, a long rack where the pilots' armor vests and pants were hung up like olive-drab ghosts. Another rack held the bubblelike crash helmets that all pilots wear.

The pilots were hovering around a large board on which the numbers of the aircraft were posted, and some were looking up on the maps the coordinates of the objectives they had to reach.

Pilots of the aircraft I was to go in were Capt. Jay Prather (of Dallas, Tex.) and Lt. Kenneth J. Babbs (of Mentor, Ohio). Both men were formidable specimens in their flying suits: Babbs was about six-feet-four; Prather about six; both had horrendous mustaches and were wearing long sheath knives as well as side arms and bullet-studded bandoleers. Our flight down to Nhatrang would probably be free of enemy snipers, but you never could tell in Vietnam; and if we had engine trouble and had to go down somewhere, we might have to pick our way through a lot of VC jungle before we could get out. I felt relatively unarmed, since the extent of my self-protective equipment was a short hunting knife I picked up a few years ago in Sweden.

Capt. Prather told me a quick story about a Marine chopper that recently took eight hits while taking a load of troops into an outpost. "They found out later the VC had an automatic weapon set up right in front of where the pilot landed. It was bore-sighted." But, he said, today's route down to the hospital at Nhatrang would probably be over water, if the weather was decent, so there would be nothing to worry about.

We stopped at the line shack where the records of the individual aircraft are kept on clipboards and the crew chiefs hang around. Pilots are assigned to different aircraft each day, but a crew chief stays with one particular whirlybird and is responsible for it.

Our aircraft today were Yankee Papa (YP) 71 and 76. ("YP" is the designation of the squadron, for purposes of quick identification, and "Yankee" and "Papa" are the new NATO words for the letters "Y" and "P.")

Our crew chief was patient, pipe-smoking, leather-faced Sgt. Dale T. Mitchell (of Springfield, Ohio), who looked as if he had personally gone through all the 188 years of Marine Corps history and gained wisdom from the experience: the kind of deliberate, sure-footed noncom whom young lieutenants treat with respect, if not awe.

Three other Marines showed up at YP 71; they had no real business going on the trip, they were simply rubberneck adventurers who had managed to get some time off duty and

27

wanted to go down to Nhatrang, which is a well-known sea-shore resort town as well as an important government military base.

Capt. Prather chewed out two of the rubbernecks for not having signed in at the line shack (the third man, Cpl. Le Grand Johnson of Beloit, Wis., had done so); then he looked the other way while the three climbed aboard.

We were off at 9:35, following the coast southward in bright daylight under clear blue sky. The kind of scene we passed over—mile after mile of bright sand and sea—would make a Florida real estate developer green with envy, but it was deserted except for hundreds of little slivers of fishing boats drawn up on the sand. What a pity that the longest stretch of perfect beaches I have seen anywhere in the world, with warm, clear, swimmable water to match, was going unused by thousands of busy American servicemen, whose interests were intensely directed toward another objective.

I was going to say something to Capt. Prather on the intercom about what Howard Johnson and the Florida Chamber of Commerce could do with this strip of beaches, when he spoke:

"See that mountain with the clouds on it—over on the right?" I noted a steep, conical peak covered with heavy green, thick-looking foliage, rising perhaps 10 miles inland. "That's where the helicopter crashed about a week ago—the one Sinnott was flying."

We came in at a landing strip in the thickly settled town of Quinhon to refuel and took off again quickly with still another 100 miles to go. It's nearly 300 miles from Danang to Nhatrang; you seem to fly forever along the seaboard of this long, narrow coastal country at the tip of Southeast Asia.

The bay at Nhatrang was beautiful: a long, clear, blue curve with a tawny border of sand and a broad boulevard running the length of it. The pattern of well-set white villas inland was a reminder of a once-determined French attempt to create a colonial Nice or Cannes on the China Sea. Last time I was there, it was in a sad state of disrepair, because the newly self-determined nation of Vietnam didn't share the French fondness for summer resorts, and the Vietnamese, even then being engaged in civil war, were in no position to promote tourism. Now that the war had developed into a huge international struggle, the condition of Nhatrang would presumably be worse than ever.

We saw the tents of the U.S. Army 8th Station Hospital

spread out over a patch of sand as we landed. After a quick GI lunch at the 8th mess hall (thoroughly horrible food), we found Mansfield and Sinnott.

They were both in the same tent, about three bunks apart. Sinnott, easily identified by the swollen and discolored burnt-tissue of his face and the arms and legs in heavy bandages, seemed to be still in a state of shock or pain or both, so I left him with Prather and Babbs for the time being.

Mansfield was identified by a cast and mountainous bandage on his left leg; a mild-faced youth, he was sweating in the tent heat but being patient about it all.

He said he had bucked bad luck the day he got shot. He had been struggling to get some flying in as a crew chief because he had always loved flying. His only job before going into the Marine Corps had been at the airfield at Holdredge, Neb. He had gained his private pilot's license, but when it came to becoming a Marine Corps pilot, "I couldn't hack the physical."

He had come to Vietnam as a mechanic on ground duty and had finally talked a crew chief who was going off duty into letting him fly. It was only a resupply mission, taking food to a Vietnamese outpost, not thought to be dangerous at all. "We had a bag of rice, six live chickens, and some dried fish—it was pretty foul-smelling.

"We thought the place was secure. I looked it over coming in; it seemed OK.

"We had two Vietnamese with us: one officer, and one operating a field radio. We touched down and they got out. I heard some firing. I saw the first man go down. He motioned to us to get up [take off]. I went up toward the front end of the troop compartment to get a rifle [an M-14 automatic]. I couldn't see where it [the firing] was coming from, but I thought if I could get a few rounds off there, it'd keep 'em down. Out minute I reached out for the rifle, the next minute I was sittin' on the deck facing the tail and I didn't have anything in my hand.

"I called in and said I'd been hit. By that time the pilot was taking off. Lt. Sandvoss was the copilot and he crawled down and cut the boot off and the sock. He stayed down with me while the pilot headed for home."

(Later, I talked to the copilot—Lt. Bert E. G. Sandvoss of Irvington, N.Y.—and the pilot of Mansfield's aircraft that day, Lt. Dorwin T. Blair of Cozad, Neb. Blair's account was a little more circumstantial than Mansfield's: "I had a flight of three birds. It was a new outpost and it didn't look too secure. So I told the other aircraft to stay up till I went down and looked it over.

("There was an Arvin [Army of Vietnam] lieutenant and an EM [enlisted man] with us. They got out of the plane. A lot of the troops on the outpost came running in toward us. The VC probably had their ambush set up for just that time. The Arvin had foxholes and people in them, but when the aircraft came in they left their foxholes and came toward the plane.

("The lieutenant was telling me to get out of there like this"—shoveling motions with both arms—"and I heard two shots. He grabbed his arm and I could see the blood running down. Then everything opened up. It sounded like a shooting gallery.

("I lifted off and Mansfield yelled over the intercom, 'I'm hit, sir.' I asked him where, and he said the leg. The copilot, Sandvoss, got down and he applied a pressure pack. I called the other aircraft and told 'em to have an ambulance standing by. I flew the chopper wide open all the way home.

("Mansfield was real calm after the copilot went down to him. He even told me after we landed, 'Thanks for the soft landing.' ")

I asked Mansfield about the wound and he pulled a boot and a bullet from under the bed. The boot, a high paratrooper type, had a hole at the top, in the front, and another in the back just above the heel. The bullet appeared to be of about .30 caliber, maybe an old French rifle.

"It hit up here, near the top of the boot; it went down my leg—I was crouching—it came out here. That bullet, I think it's about .28 caliber. I was lucky—it didn't flatten."

I took the bullet in my hand and saw what he meant. It was a steel-jacketed bullet, so that it didn't spread out or mushroom the way a soft-nose, or hollow-pointed, bullet might have done. If it had been that kind, it might have ripped the whole back of his leg apart.

As it was, the steel-jacketed bullet did enough damage. It smashed the fibula so that Mansfield will have to have a bone graft and a long course of treatment, so his recovery won't be complete for six to eight months. The surgeons came around to talk to Mansfield today and told him he had a Million Dollar Wound (one calling for a long convalescence at home before return to active duty).

I moved over toward Sinnott's bunk, and Lt. Babbs told

me in a low-voiced aside: "He still blames himself for the crackup."

I could see that Sinnott was still stunned and discomforted, probably both by recollections of the fiery crash and by the pain he was still feeling.

A film of insulating shock seemed to make it difficult for him to communicate. He did tell me that he had been able to talk to his wife in Euclid, Ohio, by trans-Pacific radio-telephone, the phone call paid for by the *Cleveland Press*.

"I talked to Nancy," he said. He said his kids are aged six months, 18 months, and three years.

I didn't want to press him with an inquiry into the crash, but after we had left the ward tent and were waiting in a steaming hot little reception tent for Capt. Prather to clear our return trip to Danang, the other three pilots of our aircraft were talking about the crash. Lt. Terry Jackson (of Pekin, Ill.) was saying: "Sure, he feels guilty, but the pilot always does. Accidents will happen."

The accident in this case was the kind that can happen any day in this wild, high, jungle terrain. Sinnott's chopper flew into a jungly valley that was solidly filled in with cloud, and he pranged into the side of a mountain. The fact that at the time he was suffering from vertigo, or disorientation, was beside the point: the thickness of the cloud made vertigo almost inevitable.

That was the substance of what the three pilots (Babbs, Jackson, and Lt. Dave Ross, of Cabool, Mo.) were saying about the crash and Lt. Sinnott's reaction to it.

Tonight, back at the Danang camp, there was no word about an assault mission into VC territory in the near future. But I noted that Bob Rathbun was hunched over maps spread out on his desk, conferring at some length with the two Marine officers who act as liaison links with the Vietnamese infantry outfits. As I walked by, they stopped talking, as if it were a top-secret matter they had been discussing.

Sunday, October 14

Tonight, before supper, I found out that there is a mission set up for tomorrow. Rathbun, who was out most of the day, flying in an OE (observation or reconnaissance plane), came in looking wan and pale (he's been battling a severe case of the drippy tummy but insisted on flying). He took off his bandoleer and pistol, and filled me in on what's to happen.

"We've got to change landing sites. They [the Vietna-

31

mese] wanted me to come in on a couple of little pinpoints. I can't operate that way. We'll work out some new sites."

Later, Rathbun was working out the new Landing Zones (LZ's) with a group of his officers in his room. He explained to me: "It's redeployment of troops—an administrative redeployment—set up for tomorrow. It'll be 18 aircraft," which sounds like a pretty extensive administrative redeployment. It also sounds suspiciously like a full-scale air-phibious attack, the kind I am anxious to go along on.

Having learned that Rathbun is a conservative type about his plans, I prepared my flying gear for a maximum effort. I loaded my 35-mm. camera with a fresh roll of film, packed camera and exposure meter and extra film into my haversack, with some emergency rations, filled my canteen with purified water, and clipped my sheath knife onto the belt of the new flying suit the Marines have dug up for me—all in the name of being ready in case the "administrative redevelopment" turns out to be a full-bore assault mission.

Earlier in the day, there was a feeling around the camp that a big mission was being prepared. The new chaplain, Lt. Richard P. Vinson (of Magee, Miss.) had a full house in the improvised chapel at the mess hall, his first divine service here.

Vinson is a dark, humble man with a hillbilly twang. His sermon, delivered before an altar improvised on benches at one end of the mess hall, revolved around the first six verses of I Corinthians and started with recollections of the "little bitty church" he once had in South Carolina. He progressed to the item that was perhaps most important in view of the rumbles of an upcoming mission: communion. Almost all of his audience came up to receive the wafer, wine, and blessing.

After the service, I talked to Vinson, who was berating himself for having given an inferior sermon the first time around. I told him it seemed like a very good one, and more important than my opinion was the verdict of his first assistant, a chopper pilot, Chief Warrant Officer (CWO) W. Larry Adamson (of Atlanta, Ga.), who had been first assistant under Vinson's predecessor, Chaplain Sam Baez. Adamson said, "I think Chaplain Vinson'll go over real well. He's got that country-boy way of speaking. We've got some real rebels here. I think he'll not only fill Sam's shoes but do better."

I stayed around a little while to talk to CWO Adamson, an earnest career Marine with a soft Southern drawl. Adamson evidently has been doing a lot of thinking about the killing the Marines have been doing here in the north and down south.

He said, "I know it's wrong to take a human life, whether

you do it in war or go out and blow off the top of a man's head. But there are mitigating circumstances—and Christ has promised forgiveness."

Adamson said he doesn't understand "the attitude of Orientals" toward killing and death. He told of one mission out of Soctrang when they brought some Arvin troops in for a landing in VC territory:

"I know these were supposed to be green troops, it was solid VC territory, and maybe they were nervous—but there was a Vietnamese woman with three children. She grabbed one up, the Arvin shot the two older ones and the kid in her arms, and shot her in the belly.

"Would we do that? We might kill the woman and the children accidentally, say in a bombing, but not . . . deliberately."

Later in the afternoon, I went down to Marble Mountain, one of the sights in the Danang vicinity, with the chaplain. There are five statues of Buddha in the caves, supposed to have been put up there by a former king of Annam who took shelter from his enemies in one of those caves and wanted to show his gratitude to a kind fate by erecting the buddhist shrines.

We drove in the chaplain's jeep to the foot of the mountain, a massive, steep block of calcite. Before the jeep came to a stop, we were accosted by a tiny infant of about four years, a frail imp in a black sharkskin shirt.

After bounding down the steep sand slope at the foot of the mountain he smilingly and shrilly advised us, "You see Buddha. I show you Buddha."

We engaged his services, and he was soon joined by an even smaller assistant who couldn't have been more than three and a half and who sang constantly, like a bird.

The head guide introduced himself as we trudged up the slope: Pointing to himself and still smiling his fey smile, he displayed his knowledge of English, picked up very much off the cuff:

"What your name—Chung."

I said: "My name is Dick."

"Zick." Chung tried to render the sound in Vietnamese.

The chaplain said: "My name is Dick too."

The boy: "Zick-too."

Monday, October 15

This morning Rathbun was bloodshot and attenuated, and he explained as concisely as ever: "I had cramps, diarrhea, and

33

the heaves last night—I had it several times in Soctrang, usually when I was on the country [eating native Vietnamese food]. They've got some fancy name for it." (He meant gastroenteritis.) Despite his illness, Rathbun didn't vary his plan to lead today's mission. He has led every assault mission carried out by the 163d since they came to Vietnam.

At breakfast, he indicated today's mission was going to be a hairy one after all. Razor Blaydes, the operations officer, asked him expectantly, "Just an administrative run today?"

Rathbun: "There's no such thing as an administrative run. You can get shot at." He was still enigmatic and his upset stomach seemed to make him even more cautious than ever.

At the briefing, however, we had the full details. "It'll be the 10th [Vietnamese] Ranger Battalion," he told the sturdy, bandoleered, and pistoled pilots in the ready room.

"There'll be nine troops apiece. They will have packs, M-1's, and other equipment, and so will be a little more than 150 pounds each."

He pointed to the first LZ for today's assault:

"It'll be 11 minutes in to the first Landing Zone. The [government] troops formerly in this area have been moved out, so it's likely that the VC will be moving back into this area.

"The second Landing Zone is a little bit west of the first." He indicated another area marked on the map in red and blue. "Be on your toes. It'll be an assault-type landing.

"If anybody gets any fire, don't hesitate to let your division leader know. He'll make the decision to go in or abort."

Rathbun's gunbelt hung low on his hips; he seemed to have no waistline left after his battle with gastroenteritis.

He stepped down, and a captain and a slim lieutenant gave intelligence and weather briefings. The gist was that two captured VC's had said there were two companies of VC in the area and that the weather would be overcast, with light showers.

There was a time check given by Razor Blaydes: "It's coming up on 9:11 in five seconds [holding up his watch]: Five—four—three—two—one—mark. . . .

"Taxi out at five zero [9:50]. Take off on the hour."

The pilots clustered around the map to have one last look. Rathbun was deep in conference with a Vietnamese pilot in a battered jungle hat and a mustachioed American Air Force lieutenant colonel in a flying suit. These two would be coordinating the air strike that would immediately precede our landing. Both were T-28 pilots and would be flying the slow fighters that would rocket, strafe, and bomb the LZ to diminish the ardor of any possible VC defenders.

Lt. Nguyen Tuyen, who had the rakish look of an American fighter pilot, wore a unit insignia displaying a tiger head at the center of a yellow, five-pointed star (the Vietnamese Air Force insignia). The American lieutenant colonel with the waxed, widespread mustache was blond and blue-eyed: Byron Kalin (of Livermore, Calif.).

The plane I was to board, according to Razor Blaydes, was No. 80, piloted by Lt. Eric Coady (of Harrington, Del.) and Capt. Frank Allgood (of Fort Scott, Kan.). Lugging our armor vests and pants and helmets, we trudged out to the double line of aircraft ranged on both sides of the long taxiway, and found No. 80.

Coady was an ideal Marine, six-feet-four, rugged-looking, handsome, muscular, personable, intelligent. If you went to Central Casting in Hollywood, and asked for a typical Marine officer, you would probably be issued Eric Coady.

Coady has a strong family link with the Marine Corps: his father, he told me, was with the 11th Marines on Guadalcanal and "had the course" of malaria, dengue, and all the other tropical cruds we encountered in the course of the South Pacific campaign in World War II.

The first pilot, Allgood, is an ideal Marine in a different way. He is older (in his mid-30's), shorter, and less heroically featured. He has a philosopher's face with a finely wrought pale forehead. But he has an engaging smile and a decisive manner.

At the aircraft, I met Lance Cpl. Roland Frech, the crew chief of YP 80, a neat, well-coordinated German (born in Germany but a naturalized American now), who also seemed a model of military appearance and effectiveness, and couldn't have been better type-cast as a crew chief on a fighting Marine chopper.

While stowing gear in the troop compartment, Frech told me that his father, a member of a German artillery outfit, the 121st Regiment, was killed at Stalingrad. His mother died after the war, and he came to Canada with an oil pipeline company. "After Canada, I went down to California and I landed up in the Marines."

Subsequently, Frech met and married an American girl in Norfolk, Va., where she lives now with their two-year-old daughter Kimberly.

Frech showed me the place on the steel doorsill of the plane where a bullet had hit. It was the same round that hit

Mansfield. Strange pieces of a tale falling into place: I was on the same aircraft aboard which Mansfield had flown when he took the bullet in the leg. Frech was the regular crew chief. He had been off duty when Mansfield made his first (and probably last) combat mission in Vietnam. I hoped it wasn't an omen that I was assigned to this ill-starred aircraft on my first helicopter assault mission with the Marines.

A truck came up next to our aircraft and dumped nine sturdy little Vietnamese troopers in steel helmets and battle gear, our load for the first lift. Troops were being dropped by American-made trucks all along the double line of choppers. At the same time, the drone of aircraft came from the Air Force section of the airdrome to the east, where the T-28's were taking off to begin their aerial strike of the LZ, in preparation for our air-phibious landing. Some of the saucy-looking little fighters were already circling the field overhead, standing by to form up for their raid.

At 9:48, Frech started the "putt-putt," the auxiliary power plant needed to start engines and the main rotor, and he motioned to the line of Vietnamese troopers, lined up at a respectful distance from the plane, to come aboard.

The troopers were small, probably less than five-feet-four on the average, but well equipped, with battle gear that looked worn and well cared for. They handled their arms competently: They looked young but experienced. I knew the 10th Ranger Battalion to be one of the best of the Arvin outfits.

They sat patiently in the rear of the belly compartment while Frech put on his bulbous orange crash helmet and got ready for take-off. Ahead of us, through a narrow opening, I could see the boondocker shoes of our pilots—the only evidence of the pilots visible from the troop compartment.

At 9:50 on the dot we taxied out across the steel-mesh plain and headed for the runway. We swung into a line of choppers that were turning at the runway signal near the control tower. Then, a minute or two before 10, we were airborne.

We circled the field once and headed west. Allgood was the leader of the Second Division (each division consists of six planes). Ahead of him, Bob Rathbun was in the first plane of the assault formation, leading the First Division. The operation was proceeding with a clocklike precision.

I saw the choppers ahead, fluttering dots against heavy gray cumulus clouds; the others were spread across the sky behind us as we thrummed inland over the rice-paddy land at the foot of the mountains.

In a few minutes the city of Danang had thinned behind

us and the green rice paddies in the valley of a wide river were growing fewer as the mountains began to heave up below us. In the valleys of the mountain spurs, wherever there was level land, there were wet, shining patterns of rice fields. I knew that we would be landing in such paddies as we took our three successive loads of Vietnamese Ranger troops into action against the VC.

Through my headphones I heard excited Vietnamese voices gabbling over the command channel—and references to "Black Tiger," the code word for the T-28 fighter-bombers.

The T-28's were bombing and strafing the first LZ, and at 10:08 I heard Rathbun calling Lt. Nguyen, the Vietnamese leader, and his counterpart, Col. Kalin, to warn them that the choppers were coming: ". . . all set. Okay, Tiger, I'm about 30 seconds out."

Frech took his M-14 automatic rifle from the front wall of the troop compartment and shoved a magazine into the breech. He clicked the first round into the chamber and fixed his long safety belt so that he could lean out of the door to fire if necessary.

We all knew the landing would be soon. Two of the little men in the steel helmets edged nervously to the small side windows and tried to look out. The hard-faced squad leader (who despite his grim features could have been only 20 or 21) sat down at Frech's feet beside the wide-open doorway, cocked his tommy gun, and craned out at the passing mountaintops.

I managed to get my armored vest zipper up—it was recalcitrant, as military gadgets so often are—and checked the position of the doubled-over armor pants I was sitting on. I remembered well the lesson of Billy Watson.

In this kind of moment, only minutes from a landing where we might easily get shot up, my mind raced through several hundred possibilities, all illustrated, most of the pictures dire and bloody.

Now we were coming in very low over tall trees and thick jungle and settling steeply at what still seemed to be maximum forward speed. The thrumming of our rotor and the roar of our engine seemed louder than ever, and as we came in past a hillside into a green valley, our nerves were reaching out for the much-feared and expected shot or fusillade of shots.

I saw a little tricklet of a stream as we came in close and, on the far side of the stream, a little twisted tree. In the blast of the rotor, the tall, lush green swamp grass swept back away from us as we moved in. The first man, a tiny individual with a

37

radio and tall whip aerial, stood in the door. Frech tapped his shoulder and then the eight others followed him, rapidly as a planeload of parachutists going out in a stick.

I had expected that the 10 or 12 seconds used up in the debarkation process would go slowly. Helicopter pilots said those seconds went like hours. But to me, trying to take pictures of the troops jumping out and watching the gale-swept grass for any sign of movement by a VC so that I could catch a photo of it, the time was only a blink.

Then, in what seemed one second, we began to lift out of the tall grass. Suddenly, Frech had whipped his M-14 barrel down and was leaning out the doorway, firing a long burst; bright shells were flipping out of the weapon, the muzzle rising and spitting fire: Brrrappppappppapp!

He had found a target down there on the ground, that was all I knew in the excitement of the moment. In the noise of the firing, I didn't know whether we were under fire or not. Anything could be happening.

Frech stopped firing and stepped back from the doorway. We were rising fast and a few seconds later we were hundreds of feet from the ground—and no more firing was audible. Frech was rubbing a sizable new red welt on his left forearm. Momentarily I thought he might have been nicked by some VC fire, but he made a comic grimace and indicated the bolt of his weapon. He had been leaning so far out of the aircraft to get his shot that his left arm had been in contact with the vibrating bolt.

I couldn't speak to him because I had no workable mike, and of course the noise of the chopper was so loud that I couldn't communicate by shouting. So I hastily wrote a note to him:

DID YOU HAVE A TARGET DOWN THERE?
He held up three fingers.
DID YOU HIT VCs?
He shook his head.
WAS THIS FIRST TIME YOU FIRE AT VCs?
He shook his head again and waved his hand as if to indicate that he had fired at VCs many times before.

He slipped another clip into his M-14 and kicked some of the empty shells out of the plane. I tried to get a look at the LZ, but it was already far out of sight—we were in a widespread formation of HUS's sloping down over the foothills toward the coastal plain of Danang. At 10:20 we landed at the airfield again, rolling up to the station marked with our number. There we stopped to pick up our second load of troops.

The leader of this squad was wearing the red beret of the Vietnamese paratroopers and carrying an old German Schmeisser. But all the other troopers wore steel helmets and were well equipped with M-1 rifles (the standard American infantry weapon, which looked huge when carried by the tiny Vietnamese). One of the troopers carried that marvelous infantry weapon, the BAR (which looked even more comically huge, being toted by such a small man).

At 10:32 we were taxiing out again and at 10:34 we were lifting off for our second LZ of the day. Again we went through the same panorama of sights, sounds, and breathless action.

I saw three of our choppers coming into the LZ, for some reason or other, from a direction opposite to ours. This time we must have landed later in the assault progression, because I saw a large number of steel-helmeted Vietnamese moving widely across the LZ.

This time there was no shooting. Frech kept his M-14 at the ready all during the liftoff, but he simply waved at the green-clad figures trudging along below.

We landed back at the Danang drome at 10:53, fueled, and were told by the tower to "hold the flight on the deck for one-half hour, because of an ordnance problem." It developed that there was some difficulty in rearming the T-28's for the next prelanding strike, and Rathbun called: "Request permission to shut down aircraft for 30 minutes in present position. We will shut down and restart in 30 minutes."

"Approved," said the voice from the Danang tower. So I took this opportunity to ask Frech what had happened at the first LZ, when he emptied the clip of his M-14.

"There were three of 'em [VC's] by that little creek —they had on those camouflage helmets. One was sittin' like this, with a rifle." Frech assumed a crouching position to illustrate.

Capt. Allgood interpolated: "If you see a camouflage helmet, you know they're regulars—hard-core VC."

When I asked Frech what effect his firing had on the enemy, he said, "I just thought I'd discourage 'em a little. I don't think I hit 'em. You know, we were goin' too fast." But it seemed remarkable that Frech could spot them and bring them under fire in such a short time, under such difficult circumstances.

Our third load of troops had been waiting to board the aircraft and at 11:32 they had the word to mount the bird, to do and/or die. The squad leader this time wore a camouflaged jungle hat and again the troops were steel-helmeted, well equipped, and well armed and wore the insignia of the 10th Ranger Battalion. As the choppers, each with the bold lettering MARINES on the side, were taxiing out, I heard a report from the command channel that there had been a new sighting of VC, apparently in the general area of our LZ's. I asked Allgood what, in his opinion, this meant.

"I imagine it was a patrol," he answered shortly. He was concentrating on take-off. We lifted from the ground at 11:44 and headed west again toward today's battle zone, which was only 10 minutes away, as today's helicopter flies.

The approach was again supercharged with the tense awareness that faceless little guerrillas hidden in the foliage down there could shoot up our particular aircraft with anything from a single homemade popgun to a section of heavy machine guns or a blasting battery of .57-mm. recoilless field pieces of the kind they have sometimes used against our helicopters in Vietnam.

Never knowing what was going to develop, your senses strained out like fragile antennae to anticipate any of the dire things that you knew *had* happened and could happen again at any moment. In effect, an uneventful mission required much the same kind of constant nervous alertness until its end as a mission on which everything happened from the first. In a way, the uneventful flights were more harrowing than the donnybrooks, and much less satisfactory.

By noon we were on the ground at the Danang drome, our last assault mission of the day finished. Until the debriefing back at the ready room, we didn't realize what had happened that day—or how close we in YP 80 had been to being pranged by antiaircraft fire from the first LZ. Fire, apparently directed at us, had burst behind us and to the rear, next to the aircraft of Lt. Frank "Ding Dong" Bell (of Mission Beach, Calif.). Probably the ack-ack had been from the three VC's whom Frech had spotted and taken under fire.

Bell, a tall, blond, pleasant young man with a ready smile, told us about it:

"We were over to your right and it went off right behind you. It probably was a rifle grenade. It went off with a big orange flash. A sliver of it came through my window and went into my flight suit, but it didn't get me." He held up the piece of jagged metal.

"The blast lifted the hard hat right off my crew chief's head."

(The crew chief, Cpl. Michael R. Shrouf, 22, of Oklahoma City, Okla., wasn't at the debriefing, but I talked to him later and he confirmed that the blast was like that of a rifle grenade. "That's what it was, a rifle grenade. It was a reddish-orange flash. It sure did lift up my hard hat. If I didn't have the strap on it, it probably would have tore the whole thing loose. Bell asked if I was hit. I tried to throw the mike switch to tell him I wasn't, and I couldn't find it. My hard hat was stuck up on my head."

(I asked how close the explosion had been to Bell's aircraft, and the earnest young crew chief said, "It was close: I'd say about six feet." But evidently there had been no damage to the aircraft, and nothing had hit except the steel sliver that struck the leg of Bell's flying suit.)

CWO Larry Adamson, the chaplain's assistant, had been flying in the last element in the formation today, and he saw the rifle grenade burst beside Bell's plane and also "a few others" across our formation. Apparently the VC's had been quick to respond with rifle-grenade fire despite the preliminary bombardment and rocket firing by the T-28's before our choppers went in with the troops. Probably it was a good thing that Frech, our crew chief on YP 80, had fired his long burst with the M-14 "to discourage 'em." Perhaps his firing had made the grenade firing less accurate. At any rate, no Americans had been hit.

The pilots in the ready room were kidding Ding Dong Bell about his narrow escape from a wound. They said he was squeezing his leg to make it bleed, so he could get the Purple Heart.

Apparently all the VC opposition came on the first assault mission. Nobody reported getting shot at in the second and third LZ's, and in general it had been a lucky day: no bullet holes in any of the aircraft.

The operation had gone with remarkable smoothness as far as the Marine choppers were concerned. The only holdup had been the slight delay in rearming the T-28's with machine guns and rocket ammunition.

This, incidentally, was Col. Rathbun's 88th assault mission since the 163d came to Vietnam. He said, "I'll have to get someone else to lead 'em [the assault missions]." But you could tell from his tone that he was kidding. He is already eligible for four Air Medals (which are supposed to be awarded at the rate of one for every 20 missions in Vietnam), and he no doubt will lead all the missions until the tour of his outfit in Vietnam is finished.

I asked Rathbun when he would get a report from the

Vietnamese on the land phase of today's operation. "Maybe in a few days we'll hear something about it," he said, "but they don't usually tell us much after we do our part. Besides, they [the Vietnamese troops] will be coming back on foot. It'll take a while before we get the word."

For the present, all I know about the ground operation is that it was an effort to sweep an area where the VC had been active, about 12 miles west of Danang, the nearest town being Phuoc Vhan, a pinpoint on the map.

Tonight, before dinner, I was invited to have a drink with Capt. Allgood, the first pilot of the aircraft in which I flew today. In the room were a group of pilots unbending from the day's air-phibious operation. The group included Razor Blaydes, the taciturn operations officer whose lean body, dark skin, black hair, and dark eyes substantiated the squadron legend that he has Apache blood (he doesn't); Maj. Ray "Pappy" Lemmons (of Pocohantas, Okla.), a huge redheaded hillbilly who has the largest number of helicopter flying hours in the squadron (2,400 hours); and Maj. Dave Webster, a Yale '51 graduate and especially qualified for his job as liaison officer because he speaks French, still the argot of most of the Vietnamese commanders.

Others came in and out to have a drink, but the attention centered on a good-natured argument between Razor and Pappy, who are apparently roommates and the best of friends (and mock enemies). This running mock struggle was much admired by the other officers, and Pappy and Razor played their parts to the hilt. (Pappy was swigging paregoric as a chaser for crème de menthe, since he had the drippy tummy.)

Razor was riding Pappy about his haircut, which followed the American military fashion of being cut so close that it was almost to the skin—the so-called "skin" haircut. In Pappy's case, since he has very red hair, the haircut has the effect of making his head look like a shaved turnip. Pappy had just been shorn, but Razor and the others insisted that the burly hillbilly needed a haircut very badly.

Pappy countered with an attack on Razor's alleged trouble with his knee. Pappy said he had an ailment too: a bad back—he couldn't even walk upright any more. With an imaginary pain, he clutched his lower back and limped his big wrestler's body across the room. Then he offered to wrestle with Razor and "really fix that knee," so he'd have to go back to Iwakuni (the Marine base in Japan).

Razor replied dead-pan that a pilot with the drippy tummy like Pappy's was a real menace to air navigation and that as operations officer he found it was his duty to keep Lemmons on the ground.

The fliers had brought a rattan chaise longue up from Soctrang. It was apparently the favorite chair of both Pappy and Razor and was called "the Fainting Chair" because you could collapse into it and it would support your whole body. At the moment it was occupied by Pappy, whose 240-pound bulk seemed to fill every curve of this Vietnamese-made contour-type chair.

Now Razor, pleading that his trick knee made him feel poorly, asked Pappy to run over to a nearby refrigerator to get another bottle of soda. As soon as the door closed behind Pappy, Razor slipped over and sat down in the Fainting Chair.

Pappy came back clutching the soda bottle, yelled protests at Razor's dirty trick, and Razor rapidly gave the chair back to him, saying, "Pappy's in worse shape than me."

Then Razor began a kidding attack on Pappy's "baby-san," the "baby-sans" being the Vietnamese women who clean up the barracks, do the laundry, and so forth.

Blaydes said Pappy's baby-san "weighs 65 pounds, her upper teeth go one way and her lowers go the other way—half of 'em are gold."

Pappy was equal to the assault: "Razor's in love again," he said.

Next, Pappy brought up a bright idea he had: He would buy one of the Japanese tape recorders you can get at low cost here in Asia, and this would help him to write letters to his young wife.

Blaydes said, "Right in the middle of the recording, we can yell, 'Hey, Pappy, stay away from those baby-sans!' so she can hear it."

"Yeah," said Pappy quickly. "Maybe that recorder wasn't such a good idea."

That was the way the party was going in Pappy Lemmons' and Dave Webster's room after the day's assault missions. Across the hall, Bob Rathbun's light was on, but he was doing some of the inevitable bookkeeping that a squadron commander of such a key outfit as this must turn out.

This night, he was busy not with plans for another airphibious assault but with an aftermath of the Quang Ngai crash of October 6—the one in which Sinnott had been the sole survivor. This aftermath was a plan to develop a new technique for rescuing choppers that have gone down in the high jungle: a rehearsal with new equipment like chain saws, a new type of litter, new first-aid equipment, etc. Probably tomorrow, Rathbun told me, a rescue squad will be trying some of the new techniques at Marble Mountain. Capt. Prather, who led the flight down to Nhatrang yesterday, will be in charge of the experiment.

Rathbun gave me a copy of his memorandum on the crash, with recommendations. Tomorrow I will make a study of the memo. Meanwhile, I am satisfied that there isn't going to be another assault mission tomorrow. There has been plenty of excitement for today.

Tuesday, October 16

This morning, when I went by Rathbun's room, he was working over photo and contour maps on his desk, and this time, since apparently I had passed what might be called the test of several assaults yesterday, he told me a few details in advance.

• "I just got a message from Corps—for another troop operation . . . The VC's have been going around this area collecting rice, paying off in chits [promises to pay]. It's harvest time.

"The planning for this one is more leisurely than usual. It's not a target of opportunity. I'm going out this afternoon and do a reconnaissance—see about landing sites."

When I asked if I could go along with him, he deliberated and then said yes. I learned a little about the target area. It centers around a coal mine to the west, an area thinly outposted and thinly held, and under frequent enemy fire.

He said the same troops will probably be used on this operation as on yesterday's. That means the operation probably won't be mounted until such time as the 10th Battalion can get back from the current operation, which might take three or four days, maybe even longer.

I knew the situation in which the Vietnamese Corps commanders must be—the same situation I had seen many times in World War II, where the commanders hesitated to commit untried outfits to new action and so they kept using the same battle-tested organizations, like the 1st, 34th, and 45th divisions and the 82d Airborne and the U.S. Ranger Battalions, over and over again. This gives certain selected outfits vast experience, and also knocks hell out of them until such time as new outfits can be brought into action.

I asked if there was any report yet on the ground phases of yesterday's operation. Rathbun said no, and "no indications where helicopters would be needed, like reinforcements or casualty lifts. If it were a bloody affair and we were taking a licking, we'd probably have urgent calls for helicopters to bring in reinforcements or evacuate casualties."

A little after one o'clock, Bob Rathbun briefed the other three pilots who would be flying with him on the two choppers doing the reconnaissance: Lts. Bill West (of San Mateo, Calif.), Fred Wibblesman (of Cincinnati, Ohio), Joe Martin (of Lufkin, Tex.).

I borrowed the body armor of an oversized Marine pilot who is on "R and R" (Rest and Recreation). I knew that we would be passing over a good deal of hostile territory on this reconnaissance, since we would have to pick feasible LZ's deep among the VC. Going deep and probably low into enemy territory, we might well need armor.

But after we flew up into the mountains past the confluence of two large rivers, and we knew we were getting close to the coal mine ("Right here is a large predominant mountain," Bob Rathbun had said as he pointed to the map in the briefing), heavy gray cumulus clouds were moving down from the high backbone of blue mountains inland, and visibility dropped sharply. We had to dodge around towering cloud masses to get glimpses of the LZ's Rathbun had marked out as possibilities. And any VC sharpshooters who wanted to bring us down would have had a hard time drawing a bead.

I borrowed a headset from the crew chief, redheaded Cpl. Daniel P. Phillips (of Jefferson City, Mo.), to sample the pilots' conversation:

"I want you to look at the green hill . . . those paddies." This was a reference to a high green mountain on the opposite side of the wide river. Over there, we could see the few buildings of the iron mine and the gleaming slag heap.

"That valley down there looks pretty good." I recognized Rathbun's voice.

"The high spots are what I would like, if we can follow areas in those."

I wondered briefly, with a slight chill, whether the VC, with a radio correctly tuned, might have been intercepting this interesting conversation. But I decided the conversation was only on intercom in this plane between West and Rathbun.

We turned in a wide circle and swung over the same lush mountains we had seen before the clouds descended. Soon we were back over the confluence of the two great olive-colored rivers, the lacing of trees, and the glassy green rice-paddy squares.

At 2:45 P.M. we were back at the Danang drome. Rathbun and Bill West had their photo maps heavily marked with red crayon to show the possible LZ's for the upcoming operation against the VC in the vicinity of the coal mine.

"Plenty of good landing zones in there," Bob said. "But there's no point in doing much more until we get some more word from Corps."

This, then, was the way in which LZ's for antiguerrilla operations were sought out and chosen. As Rathbun and I walked toward the hangar, he summed up our reconnaissance: "Peaceful, soft air, beautiful country. We're going to bring a lot of hell down there someday soon."

Back at quarters, I found the crew chief whom I had heard so much about since coming to Danang: Corp. Billy Watson (of Horsebranch, Ky.). Billy's wound had some humorous aspects. Any man who gets shot in the butt must take a certain amount of ribbing, especially when, as in this case, the wound was very slight.

Billy turned out to be a big, rawboned farmer, 25 years old, with a country manner and a drawl. Undoubtedly these things combined with a very serious manner to make him a perfect foil for jokesters. He told me about his background, certain features of which probably also lent themselves to the kidding he took from his squadron mates. But Billy's wry sense of humor was sometimes more than equal to them.

Watson came from a farming family, although he had worked as an auto and tractor mechanic. His home town was a source of much merriment among his squadron mates, but Billy had an answer to that kind of kidding. If some unwary wit sought to discomfort him by asking where Horsebranch, Ky., was, Billy would say:

"It's six miles from Dogwalk, seven–eight miles from Possum Trout, and six miles from Jugville. And the population just went down by one-half. A family moved away from there."

Before Billy would tell me more about the wound, he probed suspiciously into my purposes—perhaps he had taken such a riding about the wound that he grew wary whenever anyone asked about it.

"I don't want it in the paper now," he said, and added, "My folks are worried enough now." I reassured him that my story was for a book and that it wouldn't be printed for quite some time. Billy was reassured.

"We were takin' troops down to a little old town [Tra Vinh] supposed to be overrun by VC's. It was right at dusk. The country, it was not like it usually was, down there at

Soctrang. Everything down there is rice paddies, but this was close to timber: bushes and weeds.

"We made one trip that day [September 5]. We were takin' 12 troops. There must've been a big fight goin' on. When we landed and the troops got out, there were bodies layin' on the ground, five or six of 'em.

"We got hit right on take-off. We were about 50 feet off the deck, and the plane took a load, at least seven rounds.

"The engine caught one, the oil cell caught one, the fuel cell, the cabin, the tail cone; one was in a rotor blade, one through a strut. We'd have lost all our oil if we'd had any distance to go, but we were pretty close to base.

"I remember hearing the gunfire. Then I caught one and then I heard some more. It was more of a burning sensation than anything. Like when you play basketball and you slide 15 feet on the floor—like a floor burn.

"When it hit, it raised me out of the seat. It kept on burning. You couldn't do anything about it but sit there and let it burn.

"I told the pilot [Capt. Jerry Marvel] that I'd been hit. He told the colonel [Rathbun]. And the colonel had an ambulance standing by. The pilot asked how bad it was. I said it wasn't a fatal wound.

"I started lookin' to see how bad I was hurt and apply some first aid. I found that it [the bullet] wasn't in me. It was a good-sized welt, about the size of a half-dollar. The next day, it was about the size of a fist.

"I kept lookin' to see where it come from. It came right through the door. . . .

"When we got back to Soctrang, the doc looked at it but I didn't stay in the hospital. The major [Blaydes] said to take off a day. I been flyin' all that day."

Then, of course, the kidding started among his squadron mates, mainly centering around the question: Where would he wear his Purple Heart?

Billy could turn a barb aside, but the experience of the wound evidently affected him profoundly. Now, he said, when he goes out on a mission over VC territory, he has a weird feeling of the closeness of something he hadn't felt before.

"There's nothin' wrong with me. I been flying since that day. But I got a feelin'. Before, it couldn't be me. But now, it could be me."

I have heard lots of servicemen talk about this strange feeling of the imminence of death or injury, and I know it from my own experience. You might call it the Purple Heart syndrome, because it comes after a wound. At first, the natural assumption of the soldier is that the wounds will happen to anybody else but him, that he is not a statistic, and that somehow some unquestioned magic will keep him safe, no matter how bad the casualties get or how scared he is. Then comes the day of the realization, the shock of the wound, the disbelief, the pain. And very often, if he is not given to powerful flights of imagination, if he is not the imaginative type, more a man of deed than thought, the shock can be very profound. The idea is burned in letters of fire in his brain: *I can get hurt too.*

From this point on, frequently there emerges the very brave man, who keeps on taking the chances of being killed or hurt (on the average the chances of being hurt as compared to being killed run from 4 or 5 to 1 to 20 to 1, depending on the kind of war).

And Billy Watson was coming out a brave man. On September 5 he had flown 20 missions. Since then he has flown about 15 more with an increased awareness of the danger he and his fellow Marines are facing. The outfit expects to be in Vietnam until April or May of 1963, since the usual tour of duty here, for combatant as well as noncombatant troops, is one year. (In Vietnam, in a guerrilla war where the front can be anywhere, all troops can become combatant on a moment's notice.)

Now, said Billy, "One thing you can sure quote me on: 'I'll be glad to be back in the U.S.' You'll feel funny: Not havin' to sit there with a gun in your hand, watchin' everythin'."

Just before dinner, Capt. Lew Mills and Chaplain Vinson came in from Saigon with a DC-3 full of food and other supplies, and also the latest word from the American headquarters down there.

The food and supplies were mainly 3,500 pounds of frozen beef, and 200 cases of beer, to supplement the regular supplies flown in by the Air Force C-123's. The latest word was that a T-28 fighter and an L-20 with Americans aboard had gone down in an air-phibious operation in the Ban Methuot area. "They don't know if they were shot down or if it was just an accident," Mills said. "But they're sure as hell down." It seems that almost every day, along this troubled Vietnam front—which runs the whole length of the country—there is some such accident or war casualty.

Tonight at last I had a chance to scan Rathbun's report on the disastrous helicopter crash at Quang Ngai.

It was a lengthy report, but the initial paragraphs were a marvel of conciseness and functionalism:

HELICOPTER RESCUE REPORT		OPNAV FORM 3750-12
DATE OF EMERGENCY	6 Oct.	0920
Search commenced	0940	No radio contact
Arrival at scene	1010	
Time of actual rescue	0845	7 Oct.

Due to mountainous terrain and jungle growth no pickup site available. Bodies carried to suitable site and helo evacuated following day. . . .

This accident occurred in very difficult terrain to conduct rescue operations. The scene of the accident was in a steep mountainous area that was covered by dense jungle growth with tall trees. In addition the site was in a pocket or depression in the mountains, at the 1800 foot level. The only way to observe the crash site was to hover in very close and observe it through the hole that had been cut when it crashed. Hovering and hoist work were very precarious due to the above described conditions.

The Vietnamese troops on the ground which were providing security and conducting rescue operations had no means of clearing the area of trees. Therefore a chain saw, hand saw, axes, machetes, etc. are a must for a rescue team.

Later in the evening, I tried to reach Dr. Herschberg, who had played such a large part in the rescue, but he wasn't in his barracks room. Neither was Robert Stafford, the dental technician who had gone in with him on that first horrible night. The rescue team of Vietnamese Rangers couldn't get there until the next day. I asked Bob Rathbun about this phase of the accident operation, and he said:

"It's easy to do Monday-morning quarterbacking, but the Rangers who went in there had reports that the VC were going to move in and take the people. The Rangers had to worry about the VC, watch their security and all that, so they couldn't get in there fast enough and the people died during the night."

While I was with Rathbun, I took advantage of a little lull in his constant routine of flying and paperwork to ask him about his narrowest brushes with disaster in his 88 missions here.

"I've been shot up twice in Vietnam," he said. "Both times when we were down at Soctrang. The first time [August 18] I was literally shot down. I got a round in the gears and the oil flooded out and drenched the crew chief. We managed to land, with the plane wheeling around . . . got the tail onto a rice paddy dike.

"We got some security around the plane—Vietnamese troops—and our people came out and plugged the hole in the oil line so I could fly the aircraft back to Soctrang.

"The other time I got hit in the engine on take-off after delivering the troops [on an assault mission], and the engine was getting so noisy I thought it was going to fall out. But when I climbed and cut the throttle back, it leveled out. We got back to the base all right."

Harking back to his World War II days, Bob told me about the time in the South Pacific when he had tried to bail out of a Marine Corsair after it was shot up by a Zero. He had shot down two Zeros in the South Pacific air war in the Solomon Islands and was a competent fighter pilot. But the Zero, evidently flown by an expert, flopped onto his tail and scored hits all over the plane. Rathbun managed to lose the pursuer, but, his cockpit filled with smoke, he decided that his plane was on fire and that he would have to bail out. He was ready to hit the silk but his canopy jammed. Later he found his plane wasn't really on fire: some electrical trouble had produced the smoke. It cleared and he made his way back to base.

Rathbun said he has served 23 years in the Marines: five years in fighters, five years in transport planes, five years in helicopters, "and the rest in schools." He's already received 11 Air Medals, and whether he gets 4 more for his 88 missions thus far here in Vietnam is a matter of no consequence, he said.

I remarked that he didn't have to fly on all the missions, or on any of them, for that matter. As a squadron commander, he could easily let someone else lead the missions; but he has flown on every one, and thus flown more missions than anyone else on the squadron.

He said tersely: "That's what I'm trained for, that's what I wear a uniform for: So I hope my kids won't have to do it."

Rathbun has two sons, Robert Michael, who is 11 and Craig, 18 months. Snapshots of them in color are plentifully displayed all over his desk. Of Craig, a tiny towhead shown with Bob's wife, Bob said, "I'm gone for that one," meaning that this mite of humanity held especially potent strings to his heart. But he showed me two identical Vietnamese-made chests at one edge of his room: They were full of presents for both sons.

Rathbun, aged 41, is slim, handsome, moody, and brown-eyed. Like the other Americans I have met so far in Vietnam, he seems eminently qualified for his job—and looks the part.

He has been married since 1950. His wife, born Rose Lodge, was a West Virginia girl who had been a hostess for Capitol Airlines. He met her in Washington.

I asked what he would like his two sons to be, if he had his wish and they were not required to be military men.

"I don't want them to be doctors or lawyers or anything definite," he said. "That will be up to them. I just want them to have a good education—maybe at some good place like UCLA or USC." Even in one of the most dangerous of jobs, Rathbun seems to share the American ideal: better education for his kids.

I asked Rathbun if there was any word yet about the next assault mission, the one he had reconnaissanced today—or any word yet about the progress of the troops he and his squadron air-landed yesterday. He shook his head negatively, and added enigmatically, "It's hard to do things without all the tools." To me the meaning seemed clear. In this war, as in our other military struggles of this era, final decisions are up to the sovereign powers we are assisting against the Communists.

Wednesday, October 17

In the depth of the night, about 3 A.M., I heard the proud blast of artillery, coming from somewhere very close to our camp—very loud: *Barroomm! Barroomm!* I could hear the rustle of "outgoing mail," the shell shivering into the high sky. But the impact of the shell was inaudible. The target was probably on the other side of the mountain ridges, which rise on three sides of this town—north, west, and south.

There were three rounds, then nothing. When I saw Lew Mills in the washroom, I asked him what he thought was going on. Was it practice at this time of night? He said, "No, people." He remarked that the VC are pretty damn close to this town.

Any loud noises in the night hereabouts make the Marines jump. Attacks by guerrillas, the throwing of grenades, and full-fledged raids on outposts have been frequent. Mills told me about an outbreak of midnight .105-mm. fire from a government battery somewhere very near this camp, a couple of weeks ago. "You'd have thought it was in the building," he said. An overzealous major was on the phone immediately, he told me, to report "incoming mortar fire," and he had actually started to run around and wake people up, to alert them to a "surprise attack."

Later in the morning-night hours, another strange sound: the steady, breathing sound of heavy rain falling. With the predawn light the rain was still falling on the laundry strung out on cords outside our barracks-room windows.

Bob Rathbun said he dreads the appearance of the rainy season, which should be beginning in this part of Vietnam just about this time of year. "The pilots won't be able to fly," he said somberly. "They're tigers, and if they can't fly, there's a morale problem for them—and for the crew chiefs and mechanics too."

After breakfast, with the rain still pouring down in bucketfuls, even the routine resupply missions, bringing food and ammunition to the outposts, had to be scrubbed or were turned back by low-lying clouds.

I went over to the Vietnamese I Corps Area HQ, deeper in the city of Danang, and stopped at the American Military Advisory Group (MAAG) offices: a couple of cubicles on the second story of an old French military barracks. The building was now taken over *in toto* by Arvin.

I asked about the outcome of the assault made by the 10th Ranger Battalion three days ago. I was steered to the operations adviser on the MAAG staff, a gray-haired, immensely patient, and calm U.S. Army major (from Colorado Springs, Colo.), Robert S. Wagner.

"I haven't got the reports yet," he said. "I understand they killed one VC and captured a weapon." He must have felt disappointment at this apparently unsuccessful engagement, because he added, "We won't really know until the American advisers get back—and that'll be pretty soon." Then he added a word of explanation about the small VC casualty toll:

"You get 'em out in those rice paddies [in the flat Delta area] and you can run 'em down. Out here, a guy can make a turn and you've lost him.

"They [the VC] know the area. They know where the garbage can is and where the incinerator is. But the Arvins don't. They fall over the ashcan."

But, Wagner said, "The Arvin is now on the offensive and our MAAG operation is getting better. Also, we're getting better in our Ranger operation. That Ranger outfit [the 10th] has made five landings in the last couple of months. You saw how fast they got out of the choppers. And the choppers, how smoothly they work: in 20 minutes they're back for a turn-around, to pick up another load of troops."

Wagner is an old-time Army man with vast battle experience. In World War II, he started in an artillery outfit, volunteered for flight training, became a B-17 bomber pilot, flew 26 missions with the U.S. Fifteenth Air Force out of Foggia, Italy, and at war's end got out of the Army, he thought, for good. He worked for a construction outfit, Speck and Falk, building homes in western Pennsylvania, but when the Korean war broke in 1950, he went back into the Army. He was with the 32d Infantry Regiment of the Division, and in the flame of that fighting, he won a battlefield promotion to captain. Since then he has been a career soldier.

As operations adviser for I Corps Area, which includes the northern part of Vietnam from the Communist border, the 17th parallel, down south to and including Quang Ngai, Wagner carries a heavy responsibility. The most recent emergency he had to contend with was only yesterday, when a Vietnamese train was blown up by the VC, a mere 12 miles north of Danang, near Hai Van. "It blew the last four cars off the track, and one, over the charge, was wrecked. About a 50-pound charge—they knew what they were doing." Wagner's job, as operations adviser, was to get some Arvin troops on the scene rapidly, especially since the VC, with characteristic doggedness, had moved a propaganda squad into the wreckage and were lecturing the survivors of the train wreck about the advantages of "continuing the revolution" and throwing out the American imperialists. Wagner thought he might catch some. But by the time Arvin troops could be brought up, the VC had evaporated. In this case, if there had been a mobile reserve force of about 100 men ready in helicopters, they might have been able to fly in and catch the VC by surprise, but none was available.

It was still raining hard in Danang, so I stayed at I Corps HQ, hoping to visit with some of the U.S. Army people who have been doing dangerous work advising and assisting the Arvin troops against the VC.

At the MAAG mess and bar, I found two Americans who have been recommended for the Silver Star, the fifth-highest American military decoration and the highest on record among our fighting men in Vietnam.

They are Capts. Ray Vining (31, of Tacoma, Wash.) and Joseph A. Josh (33, of Decker, Ind.) who are pilots of a new helicopter outfit flying HU1A (Huey) jet-powered choppers. These new, swift helicopters have been detailed to the job of evacuating casualties and other medical emergencies for the U.S. 8th Station Hospital.

On August 30, planes of the 93d Helicopter Company were in the middle of a hot firefight in the vicinity of Quang Ngai.

Josh, a personable Italian-American (the family had shortened the name from Gioshio), happened to be looking in the direction of an Army H-21 at the moment it was shot down, apparently by a VC .57-mm. recoil-less rifle.

That was a wild day for the 93d, with 8 out of 12 ships hit on the first troop lift, 2 helicopters shot down, one of them piloted by the company CO, Maj. James E. Gray (of Fort Devens, Mass.). It was this aircraft, blasted by the .57, that Josh and Vining went down to rescue. With Gray as copilot was Lt. Lewis Stone (of Alexandria, Va.), Cpl. Billy Watkins (of Richmond, Calif.), the crew chief, and nine Arvin troops about to be put down in the troublesome LZ. It seemed that the choppers had landed right in the center of a hard-core VC battalion.

"I saw a big ball of smoke when the aircraft was hit," Josh said. "It went down fast. He was autorotating for about 5-6-7 seconds.

"I heard a radio report that an aircraft was on fire. I saw the ridge from which the fire was coming. The approach was a good approach, but the ridge was in the way.

"I was flying our aircraft from the copilot's seat. We decided to go in. The firing seemed to come from all around.

"It looked as if the whole side of Maj. Gray's aircraft had been blown in. We didn't know it then, but three of the troops were killed, and Watkins, Stone, and Maj. Gray had all been hurt."

The crew-cut Vining added, "I saw Maj. Gray standing up; the rest of 'em were in the grass. When we sat down with our aircraft, Lt. Stone was the first to get to us. He was the one who'd had the weapon shot out of his hand.

"The others came running over, except for Gray. He walked over. Gray had the crew chief by the arm."

I knew from the casualty report I had seen that Vining's and Josh's aircraft had been under heavy fire from the VC during their descent, pickup, and take-off. I asked how they accomplished their take-off with eight extra passengers in an aircraft designed basically for pilot and copilot and sometimes two observers.

Josh said, "It was hairy. And the take-off, that wasn't so

54

bad, except CG-wise." He meant that the aircraft's center of gravity was thrown way off by the extra load in the rear of the aircraft, and that this made flying the chopper a tricky business.

Once in the air, Josh and Vining made the trip back to the hospital without further incident, and the casualties got prompt medical treatment. Billy Watkins had steel fragments from the blast in his face and neck, and tendons in one hand had been cut so that it was useless. Despite this, he had managed to stamp out the fire and help the dazed and wounded Vietnamese out of the troop compartment.

Stone had been hit in the hand as he fired at the VC with a carbine. Gray had numerous cuts from the flying steel and a possible concussion, yet he helped Watkins to reach the rescuing plane. As a result of the action, Gray and Stone have been recommended for the Distinguished Flying Cross (D.F.C.).

In writing up the recommendations, Col. Bryce Denno, the senior American adviser in the Corps, labeled the rescue "one of the bravest acts I've ever seen," and Denno, a veteran of long service and wounds with the 1st Infantry Division in World War II, has plenty of experience to measure it by.

But whether the decorations will be given to the men is a moot question. The U.S. Congress, and the American people they represent, and sometimes the Administration, have been generally unwilling to recognize that Americans in Vietnam are at war and are being killed and wounded in very dangerous war jobs. It's now six weeks since this recommendation was made and not one official word has been heard by the men involved that day.

After talking to Josh and Vining, I found another officer who does a very dangerous job here and who was able to fill in another eyewitness piece in the story of the military operation I had seen started on the fifteenth.

This officer was Lt. Col. Byron Kalin, the T-28 (fighter) pilot, officially listed as adviser to the Vietnamese Air Force (VNAF). He was the same slim, mustachioed Air Force officer I had seen at the briefing before the mission, talking to his Vietnamese opposite number and Col. Rathbun, discussing the prelanding bombing, rocketing, and strafing of the LZ territory. In the absence of reports from the ground forces, Kalin's story now filled in some of the chinks about what had happened down there.

On that day, Kalin was assigned to a group of T-28's doing stand-by for close support.

"We got an immediate call for close support because they flushed out some VC up at the head of that valley where the LZ was.

"There were definitely VC there. The Butterfly [L-19 observation plane] reported he could see 'em. He called into ASOC [the flight direction center]—two T-28's were all locked and ready to go. We went to the target area, contacted Butterfly, and dumped ordnance on the target.

"Butterfly went in to check the results and he saw more VC. So he called for more support and they came in."

It was an impersonal, professional account, replete with such undramatic phrases as "target area" and "dumped ordnance." But, having made such runs in several parts of the world, I knew what it must have been like: diving in under low clouds toward jungly areas where VC might be waiting with antiaircraft weapons, holding the dive interminably so that the plane would be steady, a good platform for firing machine guns and rockets. And seeing with some satisfaction the fiery zips of tracers streaking into what seemed to be the right area of greenery, hoping that his fast-moving aircraft would pull out of its sharp dive in time, and pulling up too sharply, so his body struggled with stomach-rending g-forces and his vision grayed out.

I asked Kalin what he remembered of his passes that day, what he could see as he swept in to strafe and drop his fragmentation bombs.

"That mission was the worst we ever had," he said. "Because of the clouds, we had to come in very shallow, and lower, approximately 500 feet."

In terms of filling in what was happening down there in the LZ, Kalin's story was illuminating. "The Butterfly reported after the second strike that he could see what appeared to be some dead VC lying around. But we don't know whether they were dead or wounded which were being carried away. You know they usually do carry the dead and wounded away."

I asked Kalin how his part in these operations worked out: Did he get directions from the Vietnamese about what to do, or could he make his own decisions? He said:

"We fly the bird, I do the triggering—the only stipulation is that the Vietnamese [the man in the Butterfly L-19] must show me where to put it. All of the L-19 observers are English-speakers."

Col. Kalin told me he is one of four AAF pilots here who fly with the Vietnamese on their strikes. Like many of the Americans I have seen here, he is a man of vast experience in war. During World War II, he flew C-46 transport planes in Africa, India, and China. When the Korean war broke out in 1950, the Air Force needed fighter pilots, so Kalin managed to land a job flying F-80 jets with the 8th Fighter-Bomber Wing.

Earlier this year, when he had a chance to come to Vietnam, he talked it over with his wife back in California (his family raise lettuce and tomatoes back there): "I put it to her this way. I said, 'It's a year over in Vietnam without you [the usual tour of duty in Vietnam] or three years together in some foreign place we might not like.'" Kalin admitted he might have been tipping the scales a little in favor of Vietnam, so he could come out here.

He came to Danang "as adviser to Gen. Don [the Vietnamese Corps commander]. There was a shortage of Vietnamese pilots, so we got authority to check out and fly with the Vietnamese Air Force units. I've been flying for four months out of the six months I've been in the country. By now, I have 31 missions in."

I wished him good luck and asked him to intercede with the Vietnamese so I could get permission to fly T-28 missions and see for myself how they are. I shoved off and got a jeep ride back to the Marine barracks in the sluicing rain. If it keeps up like this, the assault mission I'm waiting for won't be happening for a while.

Thursday, October 18

The rain was still coming down in bucketfuls this morning, so I hung around the ready room where the Marine pilots lounged about on stand-by. They had to wait around for the assigned missions to places like Ben Jang, Lao Bao, and Hatan, in case the rain cleared. Also, some had the stand-by for possible casualty evacuations or other emergencies.

The pilots were reading pocketbooks or cat-napping on the wooden benches ranged around the room. It was a good chance to ask them about some of the adventures they have endured in the course of five months in action here in Vietnam.

One of the stand-by pilots today was Lt. William A. "Spring" Walsworth (of San Bernardino, Calif.), a modest and unassuming chap. It developed that he had been copilot with Capt. Jerry Marvel on September 5 at Tra Vinh, the day of assault operations which most pilots agree was the hairiest of all the squadron's history in Vietnam.

I asked about the nickname "Spring," and Walsworth explained that it came about because he had "fouled up on a detail once, and 'spring' meant 'spring-loaded to return to a fouled-up position.' " He said it was only one detail he fouled up, but "you know how it is, nicknames stick." He didn't specify what the "detail" was, but he indicated that on this particular day he had been celebrating when he should have been working. Let the mystery rest.

On the day of the Tra Vinh battle, he acquitted himself very capably. "That was the first time I'd been in an airplane that was hit," he said. "I'd made 20 or 25 missions before, and I'd been on missions where people next to me got hit. Marvel had picked up a lot of hits. Billy Watson's bird, No. 79, had picked up a lot of holes. They call it 'the Magnet.'

"This day, when we got shot up and I was flying with Marvel [in No. 79], we got six holes in the airplane. If we'd been a half-hour more from home, we'd never have made it back . . . Five birds got hit that day."

Walsworth remembered some of Watson's conversation on the interphone after he got hit:

"He [Watson] said, 'Captain, I been hit in the leg,' and Marvel asked him if it was serious, and Watson said he didn't think so. We got him back, and Marvel just walked out and got himself a beer. He didn't stop at the ready room"

Capt. David J. Moore, a burly pilot from Indianapolis, also remembered September 5 very well.

"We came back from an all-day administrative run," he said. "And they told us while we were still in the air to pick up troops, refuel, and go out. We were never shut down. There were 10 aircraft on that mission. It must have been a real tough battle down there on the ground. We could see the bodies."

A pink-cheeked second lieutenant named James S. Allen (of Lebanon, Conn.), agreeing that September 5 was the squadron's worst day of operations, said, "I almost landed on bodies when we came in."

Allen, who is so youthful in looks that you would probably believe it if you were told he was 16, added, "I'm the only one in the squadron who hasn't been hit."

"You sound disappointed," said Walsworth.

Allen neither denied nor confirmed this. He was cagey and serious. His apparent youth must have made him the butt of many jokes. Walsworth told me that Allen is one of the few second lieutenants in the outfit. "On October 18, it'll be one year since he got his wings." But, Walsworth said with some awe, somehow women flip over Allen.

The conversation in the ready room drifted to the time

when Col. Rathbun was shot down in the Soctrang area. The date was August 18, and Rathbun's plane was the first of the squadron helicopters to be hit. As usual, Rathbun was leading the formation when he got hit. He had dropped his troops in the LZ before he took the rounds that brought him down. (As Rathbun had told me, the plane was repaired in a rice paddy and he flew it back to base.)

Larry Adamson offered his recollection on the episode:

"The Skipper got word the night before that he'd been selected for bird [full] colonel. Next day he was shot down. So we made a bird, lost a bird, in 24 hours."

The pilots guffawed at the remembrance of the article in the Santa Ana *Register*, which reported the story: " 'The Colonel was reconnoitering Viet-Cong positions when a withering blast of fire brought his plane to the ground,' " one of the pilots mimicked.

Adamson added, "He took a round in the transmission and he said on the radio, 'I'm shutting down. I've lost my rudder control.' Then somehow the Skipper got the bird down in that rice paddy." Rathbun had been more modest in recounting his achievement in pilotage when bringing the helicopter in.

I left the pilots still hangar-flying and headed back to the barracks. The jeeps parked by the hangar were waterlogged; some had already been rigged with side curtains in anticipation of continuing rainfall. I dodged across the puddles of the compound and found Dr. Herschberg and Stafford in the sick bay, tending patients in the current gastrointestinal epidemic.

Between patients, I had a chance to talk to the 23-year-old Stafford, and he gave me a vivid account of the rescue operation after the bad Marine crash at Quang Ngai. As I had already gleaned from talking to others, the most tragic part of the story was that the badly burned men couldn't be reached with adequate medical supplies (specifically, water and glucose) until too late to save their lives. Stafford's story underlined this facet.

Stafford, a large, big-boned Hoosier (from Edinburg, Ind.), said there were five men alive when he was lowered by 100-foot steel cable from a Marine helicopter. The other three men had died in the crash and their bodies were still in the smoking wreckage of the aircraft. Four of the injured men had "second-degree burns all over their bodies. Sinnott was less badly burned."

Stafford was loud in his praises of the squadron flight surgeon, Lt. Gerald C. Griffin (of Dubuque, Iowa) who, although badly burned in the crash, with both legs broken and internal injuries, refused medical attention for himself until the others had been attended to. Also, he told Stafford how to take care of the others until Dr. Herschberg could be lowered to the crash scene, several hours later.

"I asked Dr. Griffin if he wanted morphine and he said he didn't want anything, to take care of the other people. Norton [Corpsman Gerald O. Norton of Moulton, Iowa] was lying about 10-15 feet below the others. He had his head propped up on rocks and his feet up, in a sort of shock position—his feet higher than his head.

"Dr. Griffin told me to keep him in that position. He said, 'He's been sitting up, don't let him lay down.'

"He [Norton] said, 'I want to lay down. I can't breathe.' He had been hurt inside some way; he was having a hard time breathing.

"Then I heard Lt. Sinnott holler something. I went up to him. He'd been hollering to some American advisers who were with the Vietnamese Rangers, coming through the jungle. I told Sinnott to save his breath. I hollered and guided them over.

"There were two [American] Army captains and a medic. They said they had somewhere around 20 or 25 Vietnamese Rangers with them."

Stafford didn't remember the names of either of the officers, but he recalled the name of the American medic: Nantz (Sgt. First Class (SFC) Hobart T. Nantz, Jr., of Harlan, Ky.). I found out later that one of the captains was Robert E. Deibel (30, of Boston, Mass.).

Stafford went on: "The medic [Nantz] gave water and morphine to Valentin [Lance Cpl. Miguel A. Valentin, Jr., of New York City], Dr. Griffin, and Lt. Sinnott. But there wasn't nearly enough water.

"From here on, I went up to talk to Norton. He was in pain, but I didn't know if I should give him morphine. Morphine suppresses your breathing. I asked Dr. Griffin. He said, 'Don't unless you absolutely have to.'

"The two officers went and looked over the wreckage, and the Vietnamese Rangers too. They found two bodies in the wreckage. [The dead were Lt. Michael J. Tunney of Pensacola, Fla.; Sgt. Herald W. Pendell of Macon, Ill.; and Cpl. Thomas E. Anderson of Seattle, Wash.] There were three— they probably never found the third.

"Then Dr. Herschberg was lowered down from the helicopter. And three stretchers—that's all we ever got. It was tough flying, hovering about those tall trees and lowering stuff. I turned over everything to Dr. Herschberg.

"We started carrying three of 'em [the injured] down—Norton, Hamilton [Sgt. Richard E. Hamilton of Dallas, Tex.], and Valentin. Sinnott walked down with help. Dr. Griffin stayed behind; he said he'd wait for the next load.

"The Vietnamese troops cleared a path—some of them used bayonets to clear a way to a little clearing about 50 yards down the slope. We were trying to carry the injured down to the foot of the hill where the choppers could pick them up in a clearing. They cleared a path about a foot wide. It took 15 minutes to carry Hamilton down. He was the largest of the bunch, over 200 pounds. I helped carry him down, myself and seven Vietnamese. We were walking on both sides of that narrow trail holding the litter.

"We took Valentin out of the stretcher. Dr. Herschberg took the stretcher up after Dr. Griffin. While he was doing this, I and the Vietnamese were trying to bandage the others as best as we could.

"Then we started making poncho litters [stretchers made from poncho waterproof sheets and branches]. It was Nantz's idea. We only made one.

"Dr. Griffin died in this little opening. We don't know exactly when. They had brought him down, and Nantz noticed that he wasn't breathing. Dr. Herschberg and Nantz tried to give him respiration. Herschberg said, 'He's gone.'

"We took Dr. Griffin off the stretcher and put Sinnott on it. I had been giving Dr. Griffin water, but he was taking the smallest sips—he knew it was very short—and he said, 'Give Hamilton some water.'

"We started down the mountain. Nantz was ahead. Herschberg was with Norton. I was back with Sinnott. It was tough going, especially carrying Hamilton, for the Vietnamese, small as they are. Dr. Herschberg decided he, Nantz, and I should go down the mountain, about 1800 [leaving the stretchers with the Vietnamese guards]. He wanted to find a radio with the troops farther down the mountain, so he could contact the helicopters.

"It was hard going down the ravine, there were kind of gorges there. The leeches got to us about halfway down the mountain. You wouldn't know it, but one would get your leg and you'd be walking in blood.

"We ran into some Vietnamese troops who had a radio. Nantz got in touch with the people at the foot of the mountain and asked for some supplies: blankets and IV [intravenous] stuff [glucose], water, and something to cut a clearing with. Dr. Herschberg decided to stay the rest of the night. One of the captains [Capt. Deibel] went down the mountain. He came back up and told us a doctor and two corpsmen were on their way.

"He said he saw flares down there. He thought they were VC flares trying to show where to move in to catch the helicopter [Marines] as they landed the people [a doctor and two corpsmen].

"Dr. Chiarenza [Dr. Angelo Chiarenza, of Brooklyn, N.Y., a Marine dentist] came up with the two corpsmen [Robert Ebeling, of Marion, Iowa, and Larry McGee of Albuquerque, N.M.]. It took them two hours to get up the slope to us in the dark. They were tired, carrying [four] blankets and IV injections, [six bottles of] dextran, a blood-volume expander. They had a few Arvins with them.

"Dr. Chiarenza asked where the patients were. We said farther up the mountain. He wanted to go right on up, so we all started. We couldn't see about five feet. We climbed for about an hour and a half—it was real rough. We got separated going up the slope. We finally had to give it up, from after 2 A.M. to a little after 5. We slept on the ground, with everybody laying with his feet on the trail.

"We got up the mountain before it was light. It was daybreak when we came upon Valentin. He was dead. We started on up. About 20 or 25 minutes up we found Norton. He was dead too.

"Then we went on up looking for Lt. Sinnott. We found him about 7 A.M. or close to it. He was in a little bit of pain. Chiarenza gave him a shot of morphine. We took a bottle of dextran, put it in a canteen, and let him drink it. Then we gave him a regular IV.

"We were trying to find Hamilton, but the Arvins told us he was dead. We knew that we needed water for Sinnott. Water is critical in burn cases because as the body fights burns, it takes water.

"McGee and I went down to a mud puddle we had passed on the way up the mountain. We filled up a canteen, and put iodine tablets in it. We took Lt. Sinnott down to the small clearing. We waited and waited. We didn't want to let go the smoke bomb in case the VC was looking for us. About seven o'clock, the helicopter was flying overhead. Sgt. Nantz shot off a smoke bomb. Col. Rathbun picked up Sinnott. Dr. Herschberg went up in the hoist. [He went up first.] A couple of tall trees were very dangerous. We got Sinnott into a hoist. Gave him another shot of morphine before we sent him up.

"They got the lieutenant [Sinnott] almost up into the helicopter and the hoist stopped. The crew chief [in the helicopter] got Sinnott by the back of the neck. He seemed to pass out. His arms dropped away from the hoist. Dr. Herschberg also reached out to get him.

"Then the copilot got the hoist to work. And we walked out—about three hours: Dr. Chiarenza, Sgt. Nantz, about six Arvin troops, and myself—about half an hour out, we ran into the Marine rescue party coming up, about 30 of them. They went on up the mountain to get all the bodies out. . . . The best thing I can call it is a lesson in life."

Friday, October 19

It rained hard all night, and this morning it had still not let up. Operations at the Marine camp were still on stand-by until such time as the rain should lift. So I caught a ride again to I Corps HQ to get what news I could. I was still on the trail of the story of what had happened on the ground after the airphibious assault of October 15.

This time I was able to find the three officer-advisers who had gone along with the 10th Ranger Battalion on that mission. They had walked back from that sweep operation with the Rangers and now could tell their eyewitness stories of what had happened.

In brief, not much had happened in terms of a military victory. The total of VC casualties seemed to be three killed and one wounded, and on our side, one of the Ranger Battalion had been wounded. As apparently often happens in this kind of counter-guerrilla action, most of the VC slipped away while the cumbersome mechanism of our combined air-land operation hung fire.

One of the American advisers, Lt. Edwin C. Brooks (of Dubuque, Iowa), was on his first action this time, and he happened to be next to the one Vietnamese Ranger who was hit.

"When we got there," the sturdy, crew-cut Brooks said, "three or four VC's began firing. One of the Vietnamese troopers was hit in the head. The next round landed right at the feet of an American sergeant who was with us, named Black [Glenell C. Black of Orlando, Fla.].

"The Vietnamese company commander brought fire to bear after the man was hit. Then they burned out a couple of known VC houses."

Brooks said he wasn't so disturbed by the firing as by the eerie feeling of hearing one of the VC's talking to the Ranger commander in an echoing, jungly valley.

"We thought that guy was tired of running and he wanted to give up. It turned out he wanted *us* to give up, or something.

"He said something like, 'We're your enemy and we don't like Diem.' He called him 'Diem My,' [meaning] American Diem.

"We moved along carefully because we heard there were foot traps along the trails. The VC dig holes and stick bamboo spikes in them so if you step into them you get a spike in your foot."

Brooks didn't seem dismayed by his baptism of fire, or even by his first experience with Vietnamese military rations, which are generally seasoned with a foul-smelling fish sauce called *nuoc mam*. "Once you get used to the smell, it isn't bad," he said.

Brooks has already proved himself adaptable to drastic changes in way of life. He had been a divinity student for a year after he got his B.A. at the University of Dubuque. Then he joined the Army, studied Turkish under Army auspices in preparation for expected duty in the Middle East, and after two years at Fort Riley, Kan., without a chance to go out of the country, he volunteered for duty in Vietnam.

From Capt. Deibel, the senior American adviser on the foray, I had the most coherent, clear-sighted account of what had happened.

Deibel is a pale, medium-sized man with glasses who seems physically undistinguished until you notice how well muscled he is and how vigorously he moves. He went to Boston (Mass.) Tech High in Dorchester, a southern district of the big city, and there he played football, continuing as a semi-pro for two years. His position was tackle.

He entered the Army as a private, but by studying in his spare time, he won his way to a commission despite his lack of a college education. Deibel, the father of five children—three boys and two girls—was sent to Vietnam out of Fort Jackson, S.C., at a time when his wife was to have a baby. "She'll swear I volunteered," he says with an eloquent smile, "although I told her different."

At the time of the crash at Quang Ngai, Deibel was the most active of all the American advisers on the scene in moving up and down that thickly forested mountainside to try to get help and supplies for the injured men. I was told that he probably lost a pint of blood when leeches got into his groin.

Not knowing it, he kept on. He was drenched in sweat and it was night, so he couldn't tell he was bleeding as he clawed his way through the jungle to bring succor to the badly wounded Marines.

Capt. Deibel puffed patiently on his pipe as he diagramed the ground phase of the latest air-phibious operation. He said there were six American advisers with the 10th Ranger Battalion.

"Just above LZ A [the day's first LZ] the first company had some resistance. That was the company where Lt. Brooks and Sgt. Black were the advisers.

"The company started up the slope. The Butterfly called in and said he was receiving fire from the high ground above the LZ.

"Brooks' company went up toward them and that was when the Vietnamese soldier was hit next to him and the round hit the ground in front of Sgt. Black.

"The company got into a firefight with VC up in that high ground. That was when they killed the two VC [and the VC talked to them in the echoing rocky chasm] and they burned the houses. Then they pulled back."

That, I could see, was the point where the T-28's were brought in to work over the high ground again. When the company moved forward again after the T-28 strafing, the VC had pulled out.

"You find 'em when you come in," said Deibel in summary, "but you know how that jungle combing is." And at the second LZ, the bag was also slight. "That was the 104th Company under Lt. Oze, the one that Lt. Frickie and Sgt. Orbry Davis were assigned to. They hit a few VC's and killed one. He seemed to be a regular, with a leather belt. He had 40 rounds of ammo and three grenades. He must have ditched his rifle, the way these characters usually do when they get cornered."

The plan, Deibel said, was for the second force to move in toward the first, to block any VC's the first force might have scared up. But that didn't produce any results. And when they walked through the area that the T-28's had worked over, they found no bodies. "You know how good their [the VC's] discipline is on getting dead and wounded out.

"On the third night, they [the Rangers] grabbed a VC. They tried to capture him. It was a kind of hand-to-hand struggle and the VC took off. They chopped him down with several BAR rounds in the head. He turned out to be a political type, with all the papers to identify him as a VC."

On this mission, Deibel said, he had traveled with the

headquarters of the battalion. "Sgt. Nantz [the medic] was with me, so if we got word of any of our people getting hurt, we could get help to them from battalion sources."

In this same group I met Lt. Edmond L. Frickie (29, of Paris, Ill.), a lean, hard-faced man and the only one of this bunch of advisors yet wounded in Vietnam. Frickie had the scar to go with the story of the wound: a long plow mark of roughened tissue prominent on the right side of his head, especially noticeable because of his skin haircut.

The wound happened four months ago on one of Frickie's early operations with the Vietnamese troops. He had finished his arduous training course at the Vietnamese Ranger training school at Trunglap. He had gone through Ranger training of the American variety and when he was on duty in Japan from 1953 to 1955, he had practiced judo and won his four-degree Black Belt for that kind of combat.

On the day of the wound: "We had taken our objective and moved out into a valley. As soon as we broke out, we got fire. I wound up behind a tree. I was just going to turn around and say something to the company commander when I got hit.

"It was just as if I got hit with a bare fist. I whirled around and hit the ground. It penetrated the scalp and hit the wood."

Despite Frickie's lightheartedness about the wound, the impact of the bullet (thought to be a homemade weapon of about .25 caliber) was considerable and could have caused a concussion in someone less tough. He was flown in to the U.S. Army 8th Station Hospital by helicopter, and the doctors operated on him the same evening. He stayed in the hospital for ten days after they had taken out the bullet, and "they wanted me to go on R and R to Bangkok. But I came back here . . ."

I asked him why, and I got the answer you'd expect of a good soldier, the answer I had heard many times from wounded men who had run away from a hospital and gone back to their dependable military buddies rather than face a replacement depot and hosts of strangers.

Frickie said simply, "You miss people after you hang around with them."

I could see that both Frickie and Deibel, who are the veterans among the advisers here, had that kind of fondness for their military work and the people they are involved with in it. Deibel spoke about the satisfaction of being out in the field with the Vietnamese troops, on an operation. "It's a lot more fun in the field than it'll ever be in Danang."

And Frickie hastened to add, "It's fun because that's what

our jobs are. To sit around here in Danang, we're not getting anything done."

Even with the sweating, the inevitable muck, dust, and blood of war, the Vietnamese rations, and sleeping in the rain with only a poncho—even with these deterrents, these two had a large enough dedication to refer to their jobs as fun. Deibel said in explanation, "They say it's because Frickie and I are kookie . . . but we know this is important.

"I think I've got the best job in the Corps Area, the best in Vietnam. . . . Just before you go into an operation, you wonder if you took care of everything—resupply, all the planning. You run it all down real quick in your mind, and you hope that this time we'll really get close to the VC. . . . You know how it is just before you come in with the choppers: the old adrenalin is really pumping—like just before the kickoff in a football game. We know the morale, the esprit, and the spirit —it will help if they get a good kill. . . . If we can get the VC in a position where they have to fight, they [the Vietnamese government troops] will beat 'em every time."

I asked Deibel if he intended to stay in the Army, and he said he thought so. "In civilian life, you don't meet people like you do in the Army. And you get around. I can't see driving on the same street every day and up the same driveway. I'd get bored with it."

I drove back to the Marine Camp with the third-ranking American military adviser in the Corps Area, Lt. Col. David P. McDuffie (of Brainerd, Minn.). McDuffie, a small, quick-moving paratrooper who has the same sense of urgent dedication that Frickie and Deibel have, spoke earnestly about the job we have to do here to beat the Communists.

As we drove through the downpour and plowed into a puddle so deep that the muddy water came up over the floorboard and we struggled ahead in low ratio, he said brightly, "There's a saying: 'We need a sense of urgency about counter-insurgency.' " Certainly, all of the Americans I have seen at their military work over here so far seem to have that sense of urgency.

Back at the Marine Camp, I learned that all flights had been canceled for today—nothing had even left the ground. The pilots and crewmen were restive: I saw some wrestling in the barracks, and another pilot was skipping rope like a fighter in a training camp. Rathbun was in Don Foss' room and they were pulling Foss' chest expander to see who was the strongest: Foss, Rathbun, or Tex McCully.

Saturday, October 20

The rain had let up somewhat by morning, so Rathbun took off on a flight that was evidently again over the coal-mine area, where I had flown with him. When he got back, I asked him if he thought the assault mission would come off tomorrow.

He shrugged. "Because of the rain, all the rivers are out of their banks and the maps aren't any good. And if we dropped troops now, they couldn't maneuver."

In the drizzly afternoon, I did some hangar-flying with CWO Adamson, Lt. Allen, and other young pilots, in the barracks. The general subject was the way in which helicopter flying up here in the north compares with operations when they were based further south, in Soctrang.

They all agreed that Soctrang was much more active and they lamented being here, where there is so much less assault activity, usually because of bad weather. It is just as Col. Rathbun had said: With the advent of the heavy rains, the pilots are involved in a morale problem.

Besides the rains and the cloud cover, the earnest, slow-speaking Adamson said, the mountainous jungle terrain makes a big difference in operating techniques.

"Down in Soctrang," said Adamson, "you'd just load up [the troops]. If you could get off, you'd fly. If you couldn't, you'd unload some people.

"Up here, it has to go according to plan. You have to calculate your fuel. The distances are the question. You can't put it [the airplane] down. There, you could put it down anywhere."

But even so, he said, there are some differences in favor of the fighting up here. "The troopers here are more eager to fight. [Besides that,] down there, [in] that rice-paddy country, that water was very deep.

"One day, Maj. Lemmons and I tried five times to put some troops down. Each time, that little lieutenant would go in over his head—holding his carbine over his head. He had sense enough so he'd bend his knees and he'd bounce up like a cork. Finally, Pappy landed on the other side of the canal, and the troops could get out."

Lt. Allen said, "Every day we flew. And that's where we got all our missions in. It looks as if we came in here after the 93d had all the good weather and all the missions. Now that they're in Soctrang, they're getting the good weather and the missions. We were down there in the rainy season, but down there you can fly even in the rain, because the terrain is so flat."

I tried to call through to the PI office in Saigon to see if I could get orders to go down to Soctrang and fly with the 93d. But the phone connection, made through one of the military circuits, ran true to form and I couldn't make the final link to Col. Smith's office.

I then stopped in Barracks 7 to yarn with some of the enlisted men (EM's) quartered there, and learned that they preferred Danang to Soctrang because here they don't have to live in tents the way they did down in the Delta area.

A large, muscular Negro, Cpl. Darwin L. Devers (of Buffalo, N.Y.), a helicopter mechanic, sitting at a table in a warm corner of the barracks, told me, "Up here, we got better working conditions, better working area, better barracks, a better liberty town—everything's just better."

Devers' friends, Lance Cpls. John T. Jordan (of Denver, Colo.) and Marion W. Lewis (of San Jose, Calif.), agreed with him. "Not so many frogs, not so many rats, not so many bugs as down there," Jordan added.

The boys kidded another of the group, Lance Cpl. Thonis J. Butreaux, a metalworker from the bayou country (Franklin, La.), about the fact that he naturally liked Soctrang because it's so wet. "He's used to swamps," said Jordan.

The conversation then turned to Devers, who at the age of 20 has eight children, four boys and four girls. This was a good subject for ribbing on an idle, rainy day, but it petered out and was replaced by something very close to all of them. the relative merits of the Marine's HUS's, and the Army's H-21's.

When I left, they were talking about hot rods. Lewis had "a Chevvy with a '48 Jimmie [GMC] mill in it, late plugs, an extension of the manifold." So it went on a wet night in the Marine camp. Practically any subject will do when the helicopters are idle.

Sunday, October 21

This morning the sun was shining for a change, but the effects of the first heavy rain of the season were still with us.

Out in front of the mess hall, which serves as a *pro-tem* church until the new chapel is ready (the Vietnamese are building it for their American allies), I saw Chaplain Vinson standing and squinting at the sun.

He seemed very glum, and explained: "With the rain, the

keys of the organ have all swelled up and if you play one, you play them all. I've got good recorded church music, but the electricity is off, so I can't play the tape recorder."

Somehow, the padre secured electrical current and played the recorder when services were called at 10:30.

This afternoon, the washed-out bridges in the neighborhood prevented a projected recreation party from reaching China Beach, eight miles from here. Some of the other kind of entertainment filled in: poker games and a little recreational drinking. Going into the pilots' barracks (the junior BOQ), I heard one jovial flier calling to another in a well-oiled voice:

"Come on, Pete, it's late. Let's get drunk and *be* somebody." The storm seems to have ended, and everybody expects that with the arrival of the sun, the assault mission, which has been expected, and undoubtedly dreaded too, will be on for tomorrow. So the atmosphere was a little loose in the camp this afternoon, and no one was inclined to clamp down on the poker games or a drink here and there.

But tonight, in the echoing hall of Bob Rathbun's barracks, where the Headquarters phone connections are, we heard Dave Webster, shouting as usual, on the line to Corps HQ.

"No ici. C'est Major Webster," he was yelling in pidgin French, evidently to someone who wanted to speak with Col. Rathbun. It seems that you usually have to shout into the phone, even for such a short distance as the one from here to Corps HQ. The common joke is that if you stepped outside and shouted at the same voice level, they would hear you over at Corps without a telephone.

After his French beginning, Webster evidently got someone on the phone who spoke English, and made it clear that Col. Rathbun wasn't there at the moment, and that he, Maj. Webster, the liaison officer, could take the message. Then the point of the call became clear: there was to be a 48-hour postponement in tomorrow morning's assault operation (presumably the air-phibious strike in the coal-mine area).

I talked to Webster about the import of the cancellation.

"I think they'll try to work out something tomorrow morning on a limited basis," he said. "At least there'll be the regular resupply, administrative, and medical evac missions, and maybe something bigger set up for Tuesday or so—that is, if the weather holds."

Word of the cancellation spread through the camp fast, and there was a general hullabaloo of jeeps and trucks to go to

Danang to run errands in town before the evening got too dark.

I got a ride into the little center of stores (mostly clothing, jewelry, and furniture, catering to the American Marines, Air Force, and Army people). I was in good company, traveling with Lt. Dave Marr (of Santa Barbara, Calif.) the only Vietnamese-speaking Marine in camp.

Dave is a slim blond youth who graduated from Dartmouth in the Class of 1959 and spent a year in the Army language school in Monterey cramming Vietnamese at the rate of 9 hours a day, five days a week, for a total of 2,500 hours of instruction. Now he converses easily with the townspeople, and they respond warmly to his mastery of the language, his pleasant personality, and his enthusiasm for things Vietnamese. It's too bad that language skills like his are so restricted, because the Chinese and Russian Communists are known to insist upon a good language preparation for the key people they send out to train the people who oppose us.

Aside from these general strategic considerations, I was glad that Dave Marr spoke such excellent Vietnamese. He helped me to get good buys on a shirt and a military cap, to be made by Danang craftsmen.

Since he is in such direct touch with the Vietnamese, and in fact officiates in all the high-level negotiations between the Marine commanders and the Vietnamese brass hereabouts, it was interesting to hear what he thought about the progress of our war here.

"The best you can say is that we're holding our own. The helicopter pilots see a lot of effort going into lifting troops in, then you hear of a couple of VC killed, a couple of Arvins killed or wounded. Then they withdraw." Of course, he was speaking of operations up here in the north.

I asked Marr what he thought about the rumbles of corruption among the officials of the Vietnamese government, and he said sensibly, "Some Americans say it's a corrupt government, and so we're wasting money and effort. But there's corruption in every government, including our own. Maybe it's most important to win the war."

Monday, October 22

This morning I went on a medical evac mission to Quang Ngai, with two choppers. But the evacuation turned out to be a sick Vietnamese lieutenant, not a battle casualty. He was

71

loaded into the other aircraft, flown by Lt. Ken Babbs. The bird I was flying with ended up hauling eight miscellaneous passengers, Vietnamese soldiers, one officer, and a slip of a girl in a woman's auxiliary uniform. The crew chief on our aircraft, Sgt. Dale Mitchell, said these Vietnamese WAC types are frequently on administrative flights.

I noticed as we sat down at the dusty helicopter pad near some metal-roofed Arvin buildings that the ambulance that came out to bring the sick man to the other bird also carried a woman in civilian clothes. She was apparently a wife, moving along with poppa to the hospital.

The other flights from Danang this morning were of the same kind: troop transfers, food-resupply missions to bases cut off from aerial drops by the rains for the last few days. Altogether a dull morning, but this afternoon things really began to jump.

We just about had time for a quick bite of chow, because word had come through that a big one, an assault mission, was laid on for this afternoon.

By 1:30, I was back at the ready room, where Bob Rathbun was going over a wall map with Col. Kalin, plotting the air-support phase of today's operation. It developed that today's mission would not be preceded by a T-28 strike. It was supposed to be a surprise—so no air preparation. But the T-28 flights would be airborne, ready for any emergency call in case a knot of VC opposition was encountered.

I heard Maj. Blaydes filling in Maj. Fred Klepsattel (of Boone, Ill.), who would be flying one of the Marine OE's on today's operation, beside a map board:

"Here's the village where they're doin' the talkin'. Gonna try to put 'em [the Arvin] in here, to stop 'em [the Communists] from takin' off into the hills. We got two LZ's."

I surmised from this that the VC in the area were conducting a propaganda session, a Communist version of what we would call a pep talk. The Communists are very fond of this kind of indoctrination, and will frequently give lectures at such unlikely places as at the scene of a road or train ambush. Such brash enterprise certainly deserves to be surprised and blasted by a quick raiding party of Arvin.

At 1:50, Maj. Blaydes called the roll of the pilots, and tersely filled them in on the assault plan.

"I'll go briefly over the frag [short for fragmentary order]. It's combat support: 240 troops [in our lift]. A delicate situation. About a company of VC. Some .60-mm. mortar."

Then Rathbun briefed, somewhat more explicitly: "These people are at a prayer meeting—propaganda type. They're supposed to be pretty good troops.

"We'll be coming down in the valley here [pointing to the map] past the coal mine. A lot of you are familiar with it."

Even I, with my short acquaintance with the Danang area, already felt familiar with it.

"Surprise is going to be our best tool in this operation. I want you to get in and out real fast."

There were the usual infinite details to go over. The troop pickup would be made at a soccer field near the district chief's headquarters. It was already known to some of the pilots. There was a time check, the customary count-down in seconds, so that the landing procedure would be smooth. Planes would be coming into the LZ at one-minute intervals. Serious, intent Maj. Webster unfolded a fresh photo-recon map of the area, and several willing pilots bent over to hold the map against the wall so all could see. A warlike throng of pilots, bristling with side arms and knives and with skin haircuts and walrus mustaches, crowded around the board where plane and section assignments were posted, finding what number aircraft and which division they were assigned to.

The first pilot of the aircraft I was to fly with was Lt. Joe Baranowski (of Bellville, Tex.) a huge, muscular man with an extravagant mustache. The crew chief was Sgt. Harvey L. Morton (of Oklahoma City, Okla.) a veteran Marine with an incipient reddish mustache. Morton's family was in the wholesale radio business, but he had been in the Marines for eight years, "seven years in the grunts," as he said, meaning he had spent that long as a ground pounder.

Morton's experience as a ground Marine showed now in the expert way in which he fitted the ammo. belt into his M-60 machine gun, one of the new 7.62-mm. (NATO) caliber, which hung on an ingenious swivel mount at one edge of the doorway to the troop compartment. One of the new gun-mounts being provided for the Marine crew chiefs, it replaces the M-14 automatic rifle, which uses the same caliber shells but is not as steady and precise and can't put out nearly as much steel. Eventually, all the Marine birds will be equipped with M-60's. Morton was lucky to get one of the early ones on his bird, but he said he hadn't yet fired it in anger.

Two Arvin lieutenants, little men whose names were Huc and Lac (Phan-Tien Huc and Huang Huu-Lac), climbed a-board our bird about 2:20. A minute later, Morton started the auxiliary plant that starts the engine and the main rotor and a few seconds later we were lifting off.

We fell into the rough formation of 10 choppers heading into towering gray rain clouds. I could see that most of the river banks were still flooded from the recent rain. I was sorry that this bird I was riding didn't have any extra headphones so that I could ask the pilots about the weather, the troop lift, the progress of the air cover that was to accompany us, etc. I would have to depend on hand signals and written messages to communicate with Morton.

By writing notes to the two little Vietnamese lieutenants, I found out, after some labor, that they were from the local 2d Division (Army of Vietnam). That was about all I had time for before we began to descend over an array of long buildings, which were evidently barracks, with a parade ground and soccer field (complete with goalposts) nearby.

By the edge of the field, troops were lined up in plane loads, waiting for the choppers. These were not the steel-helmeted, well-equipped 10th Ranger Battalion we had carried on the last assault missions but Self-Defense Corps (Militia, SDC) types.

While our rotors continued to churn, the troops dashed toward our choppers and scrambled aboard, evidently anxious to make an impression of military eagerness. Our two Vietnamese lieutenants got out and talked to a hard-bitten American adviser captain, who seemed to be superintending the loading operation.

I looked at our load of troops. They wore black uniforms, with red kerchiefs at their throats, evidently company identification. Some wore soft hats, half of them were bareheaded, though the squad leader had a plastic helmet liner. He also showed a possible Western orientation in the scraggly mustache he was cultivating.

One of the soldiers was barefoot, although he carried a pair of yellow rubber go-aheads, I guess for emergencies like walking over rocks. The only one of the troopers who didn't have a black uniform, he seemed out of place in green fatigues. As we lifted from the soccer field, I noted that he carried a blue blanket in a roll and a black mess pot strapped to his side. He had no headgear but carried a serviceable M-1 rifle and bayonet.

Our load of troops had good weapons, either U.S. M-1's or carbines, with the exception of one bareheaded trooper who carried a French submachine gun. Except for the barefoot soldier in the green uniform, they wore high black sneakers with cleated soles, something like the shoes we use on a basketball court. I've already discovered that this type of footgear is supposed to be much better than our heavy leather combat boots for trudging through paddies and wet jungle country.

Our rough line of choppers swung westward across the coastal plain, heading up a wide river valley still out of shape from the recent floods.

At 3:05 P.M., Morton flipped the bolt of his M-60, charging the gun with a cartridge. I guessed that he had been told by the pilots that we were getting close to our LZ, but 10 minutes later we were still at cruising altitude and seemed to be circling to the south of the coal-mine area.

When we curved north again toward the wide river, I knew for sure we were circling.

We could get the word to go into the LZ at any moment, so I got the zipper of my armor vest up and checked the position of the armor pants I was sitting on. Then, as the minutes passed and we were still circling, I began to worry about the surprise we were supposed to be springing on the VC propaganda types conducting their pep session down below. Surely they must have some misgivings by now, with 10 Marine choppers flopping around the neighborhood in large circles, even if the circles were not directly over the center of activity. A minute later, Morton spoke to the pilots on the intercom: he evidently was struck with the same thoughts and he shouted to me above the helicopter din:

"They don't have any air cover!" (He meant that we had no T-28's to guard us, so couldn't go ahead.)

I wrote on my notebook, and passed it to Morton: GOING BACK?

He pointed a finger up and moved his fist in a circular pattern, indicating that we would be hanging around the neighborhood. And my mind began again to run through the usual imaginings that come before a landing: Will the VC shoot into the troop compartment, as they have before, while the plane is settling down, or while it is stationary in the LZ and the troops are getting out? Will Morton's firing with the M-60 machine gun scare them off? Will they have shoved off because of our circling, or will they stay around just to have a shot at the choppers? Anxiety, in other words, came back with a rush.

At 3:25 we were still circling in a wide curve over the mountains to the south of the coal mine, and I figured we had been hanging around for a good half-hour.

Morton was trying to indicate something to the squad

leader in sign language. The American made a swooping movement with one hand, then flipped up the fingers of the other hand four times, probably indicating that it would be 20 minutes before we could go into the LZ.

The squad leader shook his head, as if in serious doubt. He looked out the open doorway of the chopper toward the coal-mine mountain to the north. He crouched there in the doorway, shaking his head as if to indicate that if the VC had been conducting a propaganda session down there, they would have been gone long since. I had to confess to the same feeling.

A soldier with a subdued, sad face (and no hat or helmet) hunkered down on the floor near the doorway and pointed toward the west, as if to indicate to an adenoidal soldier next to him that we were never going to make it.

But at almost the same moment, I heard the main rotor shift into a sharper, more urgent pitch. Morton made hand motions indicating to the squad leader that at last we were going to land. The time was 3:57, a good 45 minutes since we had started to circle the area.

At 3:58, we were sloping down toward the coal-mine mountain and the bend of the big, wide river. But we circled once more, turning slowly under the towering rain clouds that were moving in from the northeast. At 4:07 we were coming in very low over thickly wooded hills and rice paddies scattered along the bends of a mountain river. At 4:09 we settled into a paddy field, a rush of warm air from the ground hitting our faces. It seemed strange that this rice meadow, which had looked so green and lush from the air, was so brown at close inspection: a field of crenelated chocolate mud tufted with rice plants.

We hit the ground with a surprisingly hard bump, considering that it was mud and water. In that breathless moment when our load of uniformed boys were charging out the door, splashing into slimy, hip-deep mud, I saw other Marine choppers squatting in the muck, the troops jumping out of them. Then, the last red-kerchiefed trooper out, our engine roared and our rotor groaned as we began to lift. I tried to take pictures, but the plane pitched as we rushed forward and upward with maximum effort. As the squad fanned across the paddy below us, I saw a herd of gray water buffalo, huge beasts deep in the mud of the next paddy. They seemed to hesitate a moment in the terror of the helicopter sounds sweeping over them and rushing figures of soldiers suddenly moving near them— then they bolted as if on a signal and splashed at a wild gallop toward the next paddy.

Morton, his eyes slitted as he crouched over his M-60, ready for any hostile surprise, tightened his hands on the gun grips. There were large splashes along the ragged river bank to our right: beasts and perhaps people plunging into the water.

But there were no rifle shots, no rattling of machine guns. Soon we were again at cruising altitude, some 1,500 feet. I pointed back to the ground and wrote a question for Morton in my notebook:

"WHAT YOU SEE ALONG RIVER BANK?"

He wrote: "PEOPLE JUMPING INTO THE RIVER."

There had been no evident trouble in the LZ, none of the choppers was down, as far as Morton knew. And there were no radio reports of trouble on the ground, of any distress calls as yet. We headed back east toward the soccer field to pick up our next load of troops.

They were waiting for us, divided neatly into helicopter loads. The U.S. captain who was acting as adviser to these SDC troops was doing his job well. At some kind of signal, the men began to run smartly toward us.

Our new load included two men in dressy officers' caps. One was a lieutenant, a plumpish, intellectual type with tinted prescription glasses, and his assistant, who was evidently a kind of secretary.

This time all our troopers were bareheaded but well armed, like the last lot, with carbines and M-1's. One carried that master weapon of the squad, the BAR.

At 4:45, we were settling over tall trees, approaching a field of mocha-colored mud and rice stubble. But this time the rice hadn't yet been harvested: The fields looked much greener, even when you were close in.

The moment of suspense was coming up: the seconds when the chopper is most vulnerable, slowing to a halt—and the moment of maximum danger when it is actually *at* a halt (for about 10 or 11 seconds).

At 4:46 our black-uniformed soldiers were slipping out of the chopper, assisted briskly by Morton.

The troops waded bravely into the waist-deep mud. There was no firing to be heard. Then as the last of them were piling out of the plane, Morton motioned to the Vietnamese lieutenant and his assistant to go. The lieutenant smiled somewhat nervously and indicated that he and his apprentice would stay. In that second, Baranowski gunned the engine to maximum boost and pitch and we lifted from the mud with a nervous shudder. It was too late for the lieutenant and his assistant to get out at that point anyhow, unless they wanted to try a parachute jump without parachute. Pilots are jealous of every second on the ground when they hit the LZ, and anyone who wants to get out had better act quickly.

I wondered if our surprise party had completely missed the boat. I could see the black-clad troops we had dropped setting up a good-looking skirmish line along a dike in the rice field—but there were no visible signs of firing, no puffs of smoke, no zips of tracers, no rattle of guns.

We seemed to be at cruising altitude pretty rapidly and in a couple of minutes I saw a sign that our troop lifts for the day had probably ended: Morton flipped the steel ammo. belt out of the breech of his M-60 and, aiming carefully downward, fired the bullet that remained in the chamber. That was writing *finis* to the assault story.

Back at the airdrome, it seemed in retrospect that today's assaults were a big bust. There had been a serious holdup in laying on air support—in fact, it never had been properly arranged—and long before the helicopters could be brought in, the VC's and their propaganda school had vanished.

Dave Webster, summed up the day's events very concisely: "No contact. They flew. They flew the coop."

When I asked Rathbun tonight about the assault mission that is supposed to take place tomorrow, he replied tartly, "I'm supposed to do a reconnaissance tomorrow morning—and hopefully have the mission at one o'clock."

I said, "It's a lot to expect you to reconnoiter a mission in the morning and lead a strike in the afternoon."

He shrugged. "They have to learn about helicopters."

At dinner, the CO of the Marine task unit 79.3.5, Col. Julius W. "Buck" Ireland (of Baltimore, Md.), suddenly appeared. He had come back from Japan, and had been flying on today's assault missions. He was talking about the SDC troops we hauled into a battle engagement today.

"Those troopers had quite a lot of spirit," he said, "except one that I carried who lost his nerve. He was so scared he —— his pants and smelled up the plane. But he got out all right."

Later in the evening, the electric lights went out again—this still seems to be kind of residual effect from the recent floods—and the usual rash of flashlights, lanterns and candles appeared. I saw Padre Vinson sprawled out in his room, reading by the light of altar candles.

Across the hall, there were candles burning in one room and I could hear a mouth organ and strains of "Lili Marlene." As I moved toward the sound, the voices changed to "Home on the Range." In the room, I found Capt. Jay Prather, and Drs. Herschberg and Chiarenza.

The group had stuck candles in bottles, and the scene, with the harmonica sounds and the flickering soft light on the candlewax, was romantic. At last, the yellowish electric lights went on again, but the boys in Prather's room turned them off.

Dr. Herschberg, as he flipped the switch, said, "We just had it made, so why spoil it." The electric lights in the building went off again in a few minutes anyhow.

Tuesday, October 23

This morning I called the Saigon PI office to ask if I could get orders to the Delta area. This time I reached Cmdr. Zornow through the miscellaneous odd noises of the Starcom (military) phone system. He said if I wanted to come down to Saigon this week end, I could go on down to Soctrang, the seat of the 93d Transportation Company.

Then I went down to the ready room, where it seemed an assault mission was being prepared—the one Rathbun had spoken about yesterday. The pilots were on stand-by and Rathbun was in the middle of intensive conversations with Ranger advisers Frickie and Brooks, for it was to be another 10th Ranger Battalion strike. But after nearly five hours of stand-by and many alarums and excursions, Maj. Blaydes finally told the pilots: "Ok, get your gear out of the planes. At 4:40, we'll have the final word." The final word, of course, was to scrub the mission, and it came at 4:40, as promised.

As I was hanging up my armor suit in the ready room, Bob Rathbun was doing the same. *"C'est la guerre,"* he said. Aborted missions after prolonged tension are a big part of any war—any kind of war.

Tonight I secured the afteraction reports of the squadron and found documentary evidence that their war was much wilder down in the Delta than it has been up here, despite the fact that the weather was rainy there too.

Down there, the 163d had its first hit on August 8, when a bullet went through a flap of an OE. After August 18, when the first helicopter—Rathbun's—was hit, the hits came with alarming frequency: three planes on the 19th, three on the 21st (Babbs, Baranowski, Gunter, Baker, Korman), one on September 2, one on the 4th, and three on the 5th.

To me the remarkable thing was that with all the holes in the 163d aircraft, only two men were hit—only one of them seriously wounded—and none killed, from the days when they were so closely embattled, down in the Delta. Only nine aircraft have been hit since the squadron started partial operation here in late August. Missions have been far fewer, but seven lives were lost in the crash of October 6.

I knock wood for the 163d, and hope that their good luck continues, that they have no more casualties.

Wednesday, October 24

This morning was another bright, clear day, but no assault mission was mounted. With the pilots on stand-by in the ready room, it was a good time for a bull session and I got into a discussion with Eric Coady, Jim Allen, and blond, tense Lt. William T. McFall (of Wichita Falls, Tex.) about the Birch Society. McFall said he thought the Birch anti-Communist league was worth while "because it helps bring attention to the issue [Communism]."

I said yes, but the Kennedy Administration has done a lot more to call attention to this issue—helped us to know our enemy, and has brought action to bear on the issue (like the action of the Marine helicopters in Vietnam); but for Kennedy, we wouldn't be in action in Vietnam, or in Cuba, where the naval blockade is now on.

McFall said, "Yes, I've been grateful. I was a scholarship student in college and I want my kids to enjoy freedom as I have." (McFall has one child so far, a son.)

McFall thought we should have used a blocking force in our last helicopter assault mission: "Otherwise, they just fade away."

Allen was busy oiling his new Swedish K submachine gun, one of the most popular of the side arms carried by the pilots, although hard to come by. Allen had secured his by dint of some "classified" trading method. (He swapped a fancy knife for it.)

The expected mission didn't come through before lunch, and when I got back afterward, a flight of six helicopters had taken off to bring Vietnamese troops into an embattled outpost —the stand-by was over. However, the rain clouds came rolling in at about that time and the six birds came back to base without having fulfilled their mission.

I stopped at the Marine hangar where the mechanics were working over some new armor plate (aluminum) being installed on the HUS's. I talked to one of the most veteran of the crew chiefs, a tawny, muscular Samoan named Cpl. Vitale

Sooto (pronounced "So-to"). Besides having flown on about 50 missions, Sooto, a descendant of Samoan royalty, is one of the most popular of the enlisted men, a kind of model for the younger men—except on the rare times when he decides to celebrate.

Maj. Lew Cignotti (of Naugatuck, Conn., with a wife and three kids in Wilmington, Del.), the vastly capable chief of maintenance in this Marine outfit, gave me the word about Sooto's "celebrations": "That's why he's been busted up and down in rank. Usually [when he celebrates], his temper snaps and he socks somebody.

"Once, somebody got him with a chair from behind and ended it, but usually—well, he's a pretty big boy.

"Sooto always builds a circle of young kids around him. He's just as nice as pie to them. But sometimes when the booze is available, he blows it. Just bang, he socks somebody!"

I was more interested at the moment to find out why the Marines have such a superb maintenance record. It is well known in Vietnam that they manage to keep many more helicopters flying than the Army transportation companies. For one thing, the Marines have much more numerous and better equipped maintenance sections in their squadrons. I pointed out to Cignotti that I had heard that an Army company is lucky to have 8 birds out of 18 ready to fly, whereas a Marine squadron consistently mounts 22 out of 24.

I know how hard Cignotti works to maintain his record, and when I asked him about it, he said directly, "I've got good NCO's." I said I knew it was also important to have good officer leadership. The mustached Cignotti smiled: "Treat 'em like a man and they act like a man. If you have to baby 'em—don't fool with 'em."

Thursday, October 25

This morning, when Col. Rathbun asked me what my plans were, I told him I intended to go down to Soctrang and spend some time with the 93d. Razor Blaydes, who was there too, said that sounded like a good idea; but, he added with his usual dry humor, "I wouldn't recommend flying with the Army. Might cut down on your longevity."

I checked with Col. Kalin to see if any T-28 strikes were impending today—I'm hoping to make one or more missions with the fighter-bombers—but Kalin said nothing doing as far as he knew.

I went by the ready room to check with the pink-cheeked

Lt. Jim Allen, the duty officer there for the day. He showed me his clipboard, which was thick with frags., different types of flights laid on for today, like resupply, transfer for personnel, medical evacuation, etc.

"Plenty of administrative flights," he said. "Take your pick."

I skimmed through the list of frags. and settled on one to an outpost frags. close to the Laotian border. I noted that Baranowski was flying one of the flight of four choppers taking long-overdue supplies to Taluong, which is way out in the high, wild jungle and recently inaccessible because of the thick clouds and rainstorms.

"They've been starving," Baranowski said. "If we can get in there, they'll be real grateful. It's just an outpost, not a command post. I haven't been there yet."

Clutching armor vest and pants, canteen, notebook, haversack with rations, bug repellent, camera, film, and, most important of all on any trip hereabouts, "no go" pills handy for the emergency of drippy tummy, which can overcome you at any moment in Vietnam, I trudged out to YP 87, Baranowski's bird. The copilot was Lt. Bob Fritzler (of Windsor, Colo.).

Besides our load of crates of food and ammunition, we carried a Vietnamese soldier, a dapper type with a red Ranger beret, American-type jump boots, and a well-cut, handmade noncom's uniform.

We lifted off about 8:40 and were soon flying over an unbelievable wilderness of jungle mountains, huge, bright shapes of green with tongues of clouds in the valleys. Sometimes the cloud deposits were strewn like huge white lenses over the valley floors. Some of the steep mountain streams were bubbling with white where rapids steamed. And not a sign of human life anywhere in this high vastness.

The crew chief was S/Sgt William F. Goodson (of Louisville, Ky.), a Marine obviously well qualified by experience. He seemed as enthralled as I with the magnificent, eerie scenery below us. It was unnerving to see the country growing wilder moment by moment, with never a place to put the plane down in those dense trees if there should be an engine failure.

At 9:10, we were still flying, so close now to the tall trees that we could see the graceful long length of them studded close together, and there seemed to be even more of those cloud-strewn valleys. On every side, it seemed as if nearly everything was higher than we were and all the mountains around us were looking down at us.

Soon we were coming down lower, over a tin-roofed

outpost scarred into the greenery beside a river with wide white rapids. There was a short, orange-colored dirt road hacked into the mountainside, and a do-it-yourself bamboo fence. But we were still too high to see any figures of men yet. Goodson snapped the bolt of his M-60 machine gun and I knew we were ready for our run in to a landing.

But before we could land, we plunged into a solid cloud. We churned on into it, seeming to turn blindly, and at last we came out over a totally different part of the valley. In a minute, still turning, we passed over a roaring white waterfall perhaps 80 feet high and plunged back into the cloud. I hoped that while we were still in this soup, Baranowski and Fritzler would somehow find our way around the obstacles that loomed up on all sides. This situation was apparently similar to the one Lt. Sinnott faced when he had that tragic accident at Quang Ngai.

After circling several times, going in and out of clouds, we managed to find a hole in the sky and, in a few minutes we were landing near the tall bamboo fences that marked the perimeter of the outpost. Goodson crouched over his machine gun, looking sharp for the slightest hostile move beyond the fence.

A flood of wild-haired Arvin soldiers poured toward us, thronging up to our doorway with hands out. They were muddy, gaunt, and hungry-looking. They were very excited and one of them reached out eagerly to shake our hands as we slid the crates of rations toward the door. These people were just about out of food: no wonder they were so happy to see us.

While the Arvins were unloading the food supplies, Baranowski kept his engine and rotor running for rapid take-off, and Goodson kept a sharp lookout for any unfriendly movement out there.

In as few seconds—it seemed—as it took to discharge troops on an assault landing, the supplies for Taluong were unloaded, a battered Arvin trooper in crusty greens, with yellow mud on his boots, climbed aboard for transport back to civilization, and we lifted from the Taluong landing spot in full pitch.

But instead of heading back down the escalator of mountains we had climbed to get up here, we turned north—and instead of going down the slopes toward home, we kept heading into mountains and across cloudy valleys that seemed to be higher than before. Apparently Baranowski and Fritzler had decided to get out of this backwoods sector by bucking the worst of it for a few minutes longer, streaking across the northern boundary of the Republic of Vietnam, and coming back to the sea. However, we still had some increasingly high ridges to climb, with our straining HUS's fighting manfully to hold altitude over the jungle. I wondered if we had the power to make it, and I was sure of one thing: If we had to go down in this stuff, we would certainly have had it for keeps.

I think we all heaved an internal sigh of relief when a little before 10:00, we saw a mild, low hilly area ahead, with slanting rays of sun ranged across it. We had reached our escape corridor. From there until we reached Hué, the northern capital on the South China Sea, the flying seemed a lot more relaxed. The mountains were lower, the jungle was less relentless and had occasional open spots, and it seemed a short time before we were flying over rice paddies and occasional clusters of houses. We were getting back to civilization. At about 10:30, we were over the large lump of land betwen Hué and China Beach, that magnificent sweep of coastline six or seven miles long. The grid of streets marking the city of Danang came into view: We were home again.

Once we were on the ground, I hurried around to the front of the plane to see the two pilots as they wearily extricated themselves from their high seats and climbed down, mission accomplished for today—at least thus far today.

I had some vague idea of the problems those two had been wrestling with for the last two hours. Taluong, besides being a new outpost in the most frightening upcountry of Vietnam, is stuck right in the middle of the main net of the Ho Chi-Minh trail, where VC reinforcements come in from the north. It was always an adventure to find the outpost, and the severest test of pilots' nerve and off-the-cuff blind flying.

Fritzler, another large, heavily mustached type, was stretching and rubbing red eyes. I said, "That one looked kind of hairy."

He grinned wearily. "It was."

I was ready to go back to the barracks and relax, but as I headed toward the ready room, Maj. Blaydes hailed me. "Got an emergency evac," he said.

Nerve-frazzled as I was, I certainly didn't feel like another few hours of flying over jungle and VC-sniper territory. But if there was anything going on out there, I didn't want to miss the story.

He said there was some fighting going on in the Tung Son vicinity, where we last dropped the troops near the coal mine, and some Arvin casualties had to be evacuated.

I started for the helicopter indicated, but Blaydes stopped

me again to suggest: "Better get some more flak gear. Still shooting out there."

I picked up pants and vest and trudged over to the planes, where some arms and ammo. were being loaded.

The pilot, Capt. Sam Horton (from Pageland, S.C.) and M/Sgt George J. Peart (of Santa Ana, Calif.), the line chief, both had heavy, reddish-blond walrus-type mustaches. The other pilot was the red headed Texan, Lt. McFall.

If the VC had shot down and captured the four of us this day, they would probably have marveled about the four strange types in the aircraft: all four of us large, at least twice as big as any Vietnamese in captivity, three with reddish-blond hair and mustaches, the fourth, McFall, with the reddest hair of the four.

Peart, the crew chief of our plane, YP 87, is irreplaceable as the squadron's line chief. He is one of the most venerable of the enlisted men (aged 36) and six times a father, yet he insists on flying combat missions all the time (and I have been told by the commanders that his flying is marvelous for the morale of the younger men).

Peart started the putt-putt, we taxied out, and a few minutes later, at 11:24, we lifted off, with the other bird, YP 94, tailing us.

But the supposed emergency evac—like many another emergency helicopter mission mounted by the 163d every day —never reached the place where the casualties were supposed to be picked up. We didn't get shot down or even shot at, and the VC didn't get the nice bag of four large-sized blond men they might have had if things had gone differently and they had been on the ball with their antiaircraft fire today.

We were forced down by blinding dark clouds and sluicing rain and detoured into the job of hauling some Arvins and some cases of grenades from one point to another. By that time the mountain valley where we were supposed to pick up the wounded was hopelessly socked in. The Arvins decided to abandon the magic-carpet device of the helicopters and fall back on their old reliable method, the truck, rolled into wilds as far as possible.

So we hauled a district chief named Phuoc and his military aide, a Vietnamese captain, and a large bag of rice into a military post, where he was much saluted and bowed to. Then we hauled him back to his district capital of Hiep Duc. It was all very close to the seacoast and very tame, and we were back at the Danang drome by 3:30. My second emergency evac had been a washout like the first, but I knew that my experience wasn't typical. Almost every day some of the Marine chopper pilots go in, frequently into very dangerous and forbidding territory, to carry out the battle-wounded.

Tonight was drizzly and dark, but strings of colored lights like Christmas decorations blazed all over the Vietnamese barracks near the Marine camp. Tomorrow will be Vietnamese Independence Day, the anniversary of the day in 1955 when Ngo Dinh Diem threw out Bao Dai, the French puppet, and set up a free Vietnam.

The Vietnamese were already partying tonight, and all day tomorrow will have receptions, parades, and meetings, including some of the top American helicopter people and military advisers from Danang.

Also tonight there was quite a deal of merriment on a very independent basis at the Marine camp; the new Officers' Club ("Slop Chute" some of the boys call it) was opened for the first time. It's a concrete house with open (screened) sides and a well-stocked bar where scotch is a quarter a drink. There's a hi-fi record player and "small chow," like canned nuts, dispensed by a combination of Vietnamese and American volunteer bartenders.

It's a good layout, and apparently one much needed here. Col. Rathbun, coming out of the club about midnight, said he was sure of this, and added, "I appreciate a chance to see how the attitudes of the boys are."

"What does your spot check of attitudes show?" I asked him.

"I came out full of thought about their leadership," he said deliberately.

"It's capable, competent, responsive." I thought that was as concise and direct a tribute as I could imagine.

I had a few minutes with Rathbun before we turned in, and he was in a candid, reflective mood.

I asked him why he went on leading every assault mission himself. He said, "Sometimes I think about it. Why should I stick my neck out? What's there to gain from it? Nothing but a big goose egg, on personal terms.

"I love my family, I love my wife. I have it hacked in selection. I've been selected for full colonel.

"Should I do it for the Air Medals? I had 11 Air Medals when I came here, so if I keep on leading the missions, at the end of my tour I'll have 15 instead of 11.

"But it's self-respect. That's what it comes down to. . . . I owe responsibility to those boys, and I owe it, the way I said, because I wear the uniform and it's what I'm supposed to do."

I chose that moment to ask Rathbun a question that sometimes opens up layer after layer of character structure when you are trying to find out what makes a man tick.

"What do you want from life?" is the question, and its bluntness sometimes has a marvelous effect. At first, the interviewee usually bristles and remarks that you must be kidding. But then the full impact of the question hits, and the fact that it goes to very fundamental issues begins to register. If you can get an answer at this point, sometimes you get brilliant illuminations.

Rathbun said, "I put the highest value on family life. I want my kids to have respect for the family.

"Love is having things in common. It's wanting to do things for the other person because they mean more than the things you do for yourself. Mainly, the thing I want for myself is for my family to respect me, that's one thing you can have in life." So it all seemed to be tying together, the internal structure of Robert L. Rathbun, the things that made him go: He wanted to respect himself as a military man, a man devoted to doing his job well, so that his troops, and his family would also respect him. Not at all a bad personal goal in life for a fine Marine officer and commander.

Friday, October 26

Today, being the No. 1 national holiday of the Vietnamese, there seemed to be a general moratorium on offensive action, and except for a fly-by of six helicopters in connection with a parade in Danang, there were no missions for the chopper boys.

The town was clogged with parade traffic. There were thousands of blue-uniformed Republican Youth lined up at roadblocks waiting for word to move. There were cloth signs hung up at intersections saying things like: *Long Live President Diem* and *The 26th Is the People's Victory Day;* I got those translations from Dave Marr, the interpreter, who went into town with me this morning.

Fortunately, the sun was out bright and hot. Mosquito bites and other skin irritations in our spate of wet weather (and unfailing tropical heat) have a way of rapidly turning into infected blisters hereabouts. And sun helps to heal them. Some of us stripped down to shorts and jogged along the mud road that led to the Vietnamese camp.

This afternoon Col. Ireland, the task unit commander, announced that liberty to town was secured, meaning all permissions to go to town were canceled. Col. Ralph Davis, the camp commandant, said this was being done to avoid the danger of involvement in incidents provoked by the VC on this sensitive day, a day when it would be especially impolitic for Americans to be blown up by bombs or hand grenades, manhandled, shot, or otherwise roughed up.

So the traffic of Marines to their places of relaxation was heavy: to the Officers' Club (O Club) the EM's beer parlor in the officers' dining room after dinner, the sergeants' bar in Barracks 13. At the Officers' Club, I found Lew Cignotti, Razor Blaydes, Bob Rick (the liaison officer at I Corps), Chaplain Vinson (sipping a coke), and Pappy Lemmons, all of them engaged in a hangar-flying session.

Pappy and Razor were spinning tales of World War II, Chaplain Vinson had the Korean war to draw on, Rick and Cignotti had this war only.

I edged the conversation a little toward Vietnam and the fashion of war that we are probably going to be following for the next 20 years as we struggle with the Communists. This kind of war, I was saying, is unique in that we are in the business of helping small nations to fight against Communists and, by beating the Communists, to keep their countries relatively free. Now, in this era of nationalism, as former colonies become independent, we have to convince the new nations that self-determination and the vote are better than the police state and the single-party system. We have to sell the new nations on the proposition not only that our system is better but that it's worth risking death and injury for.

Blaydes (who is one of the most eager beavers of this outfit but wouldn't ever admit it) said enigmatically, "Maybe we're not convincing them [the Vietnamese]—except maybe a kill-crazy division commander." He was referring to a divisional commander down in the Soctrang area, whom I had heard the Marines talk about before.

Pappy Lemmons wasn't so sure. He said, "They have to use this [here he brandished a fist as big as an eye round of beef]. Maybe it's not exactly our way, but . . ." He left the sentence unfinished, but his meaning seemed clear: that the fight with the Communists is a death struggle against a bitter and relentless enemy.

At about this point, the electricity went out again, we lit some Coleman lanterns, and the singing started, as it usually does by candlelight. A bunch of young pilots who evidently had some experience singing together, for they had something like professional finish, sang "The Jolly Coachman," and "I

Want to Go Home." The latter seemed nostalgic and almost haunting, here on the evening of Independence Day in Vietnam, in the Asian tropics 10,000 miles away from the homes of our men here.

Saturday, October 27

This morning I found there were a dozen miscellaneous helicopter flights going out, but no assault missions in the predictable future.

The duty officer with the frag board was Capt. Sam Horton. "Nothing much exciting," he said, thumbing through the frags. "There's one resupply: four choppers going to rotate 250 troops and 10,850 pounds of rice. That'll take all day. Then there are six planes hauling cargo all morning—25,000 pounds. To Trabang and Bato.

"There's one medical evac, already gone, to an outpost 15 miles northwest of Quang Ngai. Four men wounded there— maybe sniper fire. There's still one more resupply: two choppers going to Ben Giang—2,200 pounds of rice and fowl, pigs, and vegetables. And there are three OE's going out on reconnaissance. Up near Quang Tri on the northern border.

"Oh, there's one more thing. An HU1A is down at Quang Ngai—lost its stabilizer bar and autorotated into the field. The Bell representative is going to go down to fix it up."

The latter item interested me, because the HU1A is a new jet-powered Army helicopter, just being introduced to the Vietnamese war. It is one of the new helicopter weapons which we should have had many years ago for just such types of war as this—but we dragged our feet because we overemphasized the nuclear bomb at the expense of other war weapons.

Sam said there was a plane going down there in about 15 minutes. I said I wanted to go.

Meanwhile, I had a chance to talk to Razor Blaydes, bright-eyed and bushy-tailed this morning even after the strenuous night with Lemmons, Webster, and the others at the Slop Chute last night. The Blaydes-Lemmons bull session had gone on long after the club had closed at 1 A.M. They had celebrated Vietnamese Independence Day until 4 A.M., and had been continuing the hangar-flying and bull session when I left last night. I asked Blaydes if they had settled important issues.

He said, "We decided the medical and signal people have to be taught."

"How about teaching the people politically?" I asked.

"The average Vietnamese has nothing," he said, indirectly answering the question. "He has a little rice. He has a buffalo that belongs to his village. And wife and children.

"They're different from us—about things like taking care of wounded. Sometimes we have a hard time getting 'em to call for helicopters to evacuate the wounded. If they're wounded and you're carrying 'em back, you never hear a peep out of 'em.

"These Vietnamese are amazing people. I've seen 'em gut-shot, head-shot. They don't feel it at all—or if they feel it, they don't show it."

At any rate, I believe Maj. Blaydes was trying to say that Asians have to be measured by different standards from those of Americans and Europeans, that a different scale of values has to be set up before you can make any judgment of the way the new American method of war is being employed.

I said I thought human beings were basically the same in their appetites, wants, and fears, with a few local differences. Fundamentally, men want women and security, women want men and security, all are afraid of death and injury—and those who have lived under a dictatorship prefer self-determination and free government if they can achieve it.

In other words, we were about to reopen last night's bull session—probably with as little precision as last night—when I recalled the HU1A forced down at Quang Ngai and the imminence of the flight down there.

The choppers going down there had already left, but I hitched a ride with an Army plane also going down, a De Havilland Otter. The mission of the Otter, the Army pilot told me, was to pick up the two HU1A pilots and two tech representatives from Bell Aircraft who were already there.

We had to swing over the seacoast of Danang for a few minutes to drop off four American Special Forces troopers who were going to make a practice parachute jump. The Special Forces people are supposed to keep up with their parachute jumps as a measure of physical fitness.

We circled over the coast while the jumpers sat on the floor by the door. Three looked like seasoned, steady types. The fourth was much younger, a kind of Dead End Kid out of *West Side Story*. He talked a lot and kept kneading the pack of the man next to him. The man being kneaded was very patient about it all.

On the first pass, the jump master crouched in the windy door, then he and the second man stepped out into the prop blast and disappeared, and with each exit, the young, nervous one let out a yell.

The Dead End kid was all upset as he and the other remaining jumper struggled to pull the flopping, rattling static lines into the plane. The jumpers were going out with the usual lines that pulled the chutes from their packs. It seemed as if the young jumper could scarcely contain himself. Perhaps it was one of his early jumps.

The plane circled back and it was the turn of the last two to exit. The quiet one stepped out carefully, his body whipping successfully aft and the chute opening smoothly.

Then the kid gulped, stepped into the doorway, and waited for the moment. Would he yell as he went out, fulfilling the classic need of a paratrooper to shout, "Geronimo!" or some other lung-emptying cry as he goes out the door? He did, a good, wailing yell as he sailed aft. The crew chief of the Otter, Specialist Fourth Class (Sp/4) James Purcell (of Hickman, Ky.) pulled in the last two flopping static lines. I reflected on the obvious liking that paratroopers, Rangers, Special Forces, and other elite soldiers have for the final gesture of defiance in their young lives, which is flinging themselves out of aircraft in defiance of the most fatal law of nature, gravity; a kind of offering of themselves in a death wish to show their carelessness with life and health.

At 4:05 P.M. we got to the dusty Quang Ngai airfield and taxied up to the end of the runway where the HU1A sat. The figures of helmeted Arvin troops were spread liberally on the far side of the runway, this airport being none too secure from VC action and the HU1A, our newest kind of helicopter, being an especially valuable prize. Evidently an emergency detachment of a couple of companies had been thrown in to keep the aircraft safe from enemy capture. The pup tents of the soldiers dotted the meadowland out as far as the beginning of the jungle, probably a quarter of a mile, and undoubtedly security forces were deep into the edge of that jungle. I hoped so.

We found one of the pilots, muddy and weary, beside the aircraft, while a Bell representative, in sport shirt and Wellington boots, clambered over the top of the fuselage, examining the offending rotor where the stabilizer bar had come loose.

I was most interested in the aircraft, a huge overgrown dragonfly with a bulb-shaped fuselage and a long, sticklike tail boom. On top of the fuselage was the awkward stovepipe of a jet engine, with all sorts of odd, potato-shaped metal housings for the gears and collector mechanisms that power the main rotor, and a standard button-shaped jet exhaust.

The advantages of this new kind of bird are already well known in this helicopter-oriented war: mainly, greater smoothness and power, less maintenance and more speed.

The first bunch of HU1A's—aerial ambulances—came in about a month ago. Since then, another group have arrived equipped with forward-firing rockets and machine guns. According to the reports, they have been doing a good job of supporting the air-phibious landings of the Army helicopters down in the southern part of Vietnam. There is a still newer and more powerful model, the HU1B, which is supposed to be coming in to Vietnam pretty soon, and this should be especially fascinating to follow in action.

The HU1A here on the airstrip at Quang Ngai was one of the very early models, assigned to aerial ambulance and liaison work, and unarmed.

Capt. Sam MacReynolds (of Paris, Ark.) had been standing vigil over the aircraft since it went down yesterday. The other pilot, Capt. Dick Center (of Madison, Wis.), had been flown out earlier in the day.

"We [he obviously meant he] stayed up during the night trying to get the thing set. We were afraid the VC would get it [the HU1A]. The Arvin assigned 200 troops to guard it." MacReynolds, who spoke with the hillbilly accent appropriate to his farmer's background, explained that at the time of the accident, he and Center were making a reconnaissance flight over the flooded area of the north to see how badly damaged the bridges were over the rivers and inlets between Quang Ngai and Danang. Flying with them were five engineers, two Vietnamese and three Americans, who were to make notes of flood damage.

Then the accident happened.

"The stabilizer bar flew off, and it set up a terrific off-balance. We thought the thing was going to shake itself to pieces." The stabilizer bar is a short metal projection at the center of the rotor, which automatically smoothes out the roughnesses of rotation. With the stabilizer bar gone, the pilots had to hold the vibrating control stick of the aircraft by brute force.

"I was trying to shut off a detent switch so I could shut off the throttle. But it was vibrating so, I couldn't get my finger in there to cut off the switch. Center and I both had hold of the cyclic control stick with both hands. Holding it was like trying to hold a pig when you're going to castrate him. You get hold of his feet, and boy, what a struggle.

"We both held on for dear life and autorotated the bird in

—in 2 minutes and 20 or 30 seconds. It was real rough. The aircraft wanted to roll over 40 degrees, and downward 20 degrees. But somehow, with both of us hanging on, we got it down."

I asked Tom Harris (of Saunderstown, R.I.), the sportily dressed technical representative from Bell Aircraft, how he thought the accident could have come about. He got a special glint in his light-colored eyes and said, "Somebody didn't torque down the stabilizer bar, that was all. This is the first time this kind of accident has happened, except for once, in the States." Whoever was at fault in the matter of not torquing down the stabilizer bar, it easily could have cost the lives of seven men.

By this time a squad of new mechanics had been brought into the Quang Ngai scene by other aircraft, and they were setting about the business of repairing the damage. But it was clear that the plane wasn't going to be flown out under its own power tonight. Capt. Galen Murphy (of Maplehill, Kan.), pilot of the Otter, said we would therefore take off and head back for Danang.

We loaded aboard the aircraft, led by Capt. MacReynolds and Sp./4 Jim Purcell. Also on board: the two tech representatives, Tom Harris of Bell and an older, bespectacled man from Lycoming Engines, Sam Jordanides (of Ansonia, Conn.), and John Patterson (of Fayetteville, Ark.), a Red Cross official who had apparently come along from Quang Ngai out of curiosity about the HU1A. I had seen Patterson sitting up in the copilot's seat during the trip down here, and hadn't realized until this moment that he was a representative of the American Red Cross.

Aboard the Otter, MacReynolds relaxed in what must have seemed like a fantastically comfortable chair after his two-day ordeal at Quang Ngai, and was asleep practically as soon as we were airborne.

I had a chance to talk to the plumpish, personable Patterson, the first Red Cross representative I have seen thus far in the Vietnam war.

Patterson told me that his main preoccupation in Vietnam has been with emergency leaves—in other words, leaves for American military men in Vietnam who must go back home for emergencies such as deaths and serious illnesses in their families.

"My job is to validate the emergency leaves," Patterson said. "I figure we're running about 60 to 65 leaves a month, and they all have to be checked out and expedited. You've got to expect that many, when after all we have more than 10,000 men here."

It was nearly 6 P.M. when I hiked over from the Army side of the Danang airfield to the Marine part. However, it still wasn't too late to put in a Starcom call to Saigon, to chivvy Col. Smith, the PIO, a little bit about my desire to make a trip down south to the area of fiercest fighting. I asked him about official permission to make a flight with a T-28 fighter plane on a mission up here in Danang, and said I also wanted to fly with the new American HU1A fighter helicopters, the new outfit equipped with forward-firing machine guns and rockets.

Col. Smith said that he was going out with a party of influential Vietnamese tonight, and promised to pursue the various projects, especially the T-28 mission—an encouraging enough answer. After dinner, in the barracks where I live, I met a new arrival, Capt. Jim Harp (of Philadelphia, Pa.), who was being entertained in Jay Prather's room. He had just been given two bullets, which, by tradition, are presented to a new arrival with the following advice, delivered by a Marine of long experience in the Danang billet: "If I had all that time to serve with this outfit, I'd shoot myself." The second bullet is included in case he misses with the first. Harp, the new arrival, said that he was going to shine up the bullets for the next man and carry on the tradition.

Sunday, October 28

The weather wasn't very forbearing this morning. It was drizzly, and Bob Rathbun's reconnaissance flight to run up LZ's for another air-phibious operation washed out because of the horrible clouds.

Today was a good time to run through some personal maintenance, since there were no flights going out. I went into town with Rathbun and Jay Prather, both of them being intent on picking up new furniture for their rooms. Rathbun got new slats for his bed which he had ordered some time ago: hand-made, of Philippine mahogany, for about $3. Prather ordered a desk, also of Philippine mahogany, which will also be hand-made and delivered for about $10. We kidded Prather about the famous story of the Marine who ordered a chiffonier from one of the local contractors and gave the carpenter-cabinet-maker the measurements in every possible direction, only to find that when the article was delivered, the only possible use for it would be in a dollhouse. The Marine had given the measurement in millimeters instead of centimeters, and the cabinet-maker had carried out instructions. Prather, a canny, veteran Marine with many travels in strange ports behind him, wouldn't be apt to make such a mistake.

Tonight Bob Rathbun was sick again with "Ho Chi-Minh's Revenge," which afflicts all of us under primitive foreign conditions. He missed his dinner, and couldn't even manage to sip the coffee that Col. Ireland brought him from the mess table.

I tried to give him some of my antibiotic pills. He said he didn't want to take any medicine, even if it was given to him by the flight surgeon, because if the medicine had any sedatives in it, he might be grounded—and he didn't want that. Even now, on the umpteenth go-round with drippy tummy, Rathbun's principal fear was that he might miss the self-appointed duty of leading the mission.

Monday, October 29

No assault mission again today, so I used the time to catch up on a vital bit of research with the Marine choppers: what it feels like to go on what the Marines call the Pig ——— Run. They say that they carry three important things in their choppers: VIP's, VID's, and VIC's. The VIP's— Very Important Pigs— are probably most important in the opinion of the Vietnamese, although VID's, meaning "Ducks," and C's, "Chickens," are also high in the Vietnamese standard of values.

The pilot I elected to fly with today was, again, walrus-mustached Sam Horton, with Sgt. George Carr (of Pueblo, Colo.) as crew chief. Copilot was Lt. Faustin Wirkus (of La Gonave, Haiti, and Falls Church, Va.).

Horton's load for today was 15 pigs and 4 troops, and our destination was Mang Buk, a very remote montagnard outpost close to the Laotian border.

Fortunately, the porcine freight didn't come aboard for quite some time, and as if to insulate us somewhat from the olfactory shock, Carr had decorated the cabin with a large, bright-colored Varga girl from *Playboy*. At 7:30 A.M. an Army truck pulled up beside us with the pigs in bamboo containers, and the four troopers who would be accompanying them. I helped Carr and the four troopers muscle the containers into our troop compartment while the pigs squawled loudly. It soon became apparent that they were going to augment their already-unpleasant smell with fresh deposits all during the trip. The troopers also added to the odoriferous impact in our cargo compartment: They had apparently recently dined on foods redolent of garlic and *nuoc mam*, the favorite Vietnamese dressing for any food item. Furthermore, they carried garlic buds with them in little string sacks.

The troopers, parking their tommy guns against the bulkhead, took their places on the floor of the cabin just forward of the pigs. At 8:09 our engine was turning over and the rotor had started, but we were still waiting for the word to go, and the waves of scent from the cabin assailed us with increasing power. At 8:10 I heard the crew chief clearing with Horton: "All set below, sir." Our take-off time was supposed to be 8:15; with the precision usual for the 163d, we rolled out to the runway and lifted off at 8:19.

The pig odor seemed to grow stronger, if anything, as we left the ground. It was apparently powerful enough to somewhat affect even the Vietnamese trooper next to me, for he took out a small can of Tiger Balm, the favorite patent nostrum of Asia, and put some of the greasy stuff on his nostrils and temples.

We were heading south and west and apparently in the direction of Quang Ngai, where we would pick up some fuel for our jaunt to the far-inland Mang Buk.

The two pilots were concerned, the way they always are in this rainy weather, about getting in to the objective. "We ought to be able to get in there if this stuff stays real high like this," Wirkus said.

"Yeah, pretty favorable this morning."

We were flying over VC territory on the way to Quang Ngai, and Sgt. Carr unlimbered one of the two M-14's at the front end of the cabin for any possible action. Amid the self-augmenting odor barrage of the pig cargo, I found some refreshment in the Varga girl figure, a redhead with a minimal drape of black lace.

Within 10 minutes the ground was obscured by rolling clouds, and in moments we were riding over solid gray cloud bank. There was one other difficulty—always unforeseen difficulties in any operational flight under such primitive conditions—I heard Horton calling the flight leader: "Two-dash-zero, this is Three-dash-zero. We've got an unusual gas burner. I've got about an hour left."

I heard the characteristic voice of Razor Blaydes, who was leading today's formation: "I'll take the flight back and refuel at Quang Ngai. We're going to come back and get underneath the overcast."

We turned and began to break out of the clouds, although

the sky still seemed to be about six-tenths cloud cover. I saw a wide river underneath us, and heard the usual conversation between the field at Quang Ngai and Blaydes:

"What's your location now?"

"I have your field in sight." That would be Blaydes' voice. We were letting down over green animal lumps of hills and the ground warmth was flitting into the cabin, intensifying the natural graces of the pig scent. At 9:46 we were about to touch down beside the HU1A I had seen yesterday.

We taxied up beside a large plastic fuel tank and Sgt. Carr told the ground crewmen while the engines were shutting down, "OK, we want about 1,300 pounds."

But as we waited, another impediment developed. Coming back from his negotiations with the ground crewmen, Carr told us about a problem with the fuel pump on the ground.

By now, the Quang Ngai locals had heaved into sight on bicycles, with little flystands loaded with soda pop, and were vending their vividly orange and green beverages. The usual crowd of Vietnamese urchins had appeared at a respectful distance from our aircraft, and in the hot ground blast the pig smell wasn't getting any better. I had a pain in my ears from all the maneuvering in and out of the clouds, and was trying to swallow it away.

I figured we had been hauling our passengers—troops and pigs—in the belly for about an hour and a half. With the fuel shortage, the engine trouble, the fuel-pump difficulty, and the bad weather we had encountered on the way to Mang Buk, the VIP lift for today wasn't working out very well. Carry, back from wrestling unsuccessfully with the fuel pump, sniffed the air disdainfully in the cabin and confided, "Boy, I know one thing—when I get home I'm going out of the pig business." Our two pilots had descended from the cockpit to try to solve our difficulties, and were waiting for final word from Razor Blaydes. Lt. Wirkus came up with a concise pronouncement on the odors of the troop compartment: "Pig ———— and garlic."

Sam Horton, returning from a conversation with Blaydes, confided, "He's got a seriously wounded at Baja. So let's unload the bird here and we can pick up the wounded and take him back to Danang." That seemed to be the new direction. The troops unloaded the pigs, Sgt. Carr produced a broom from somewhere and swept out the pig droppings and the garlic buds.

Thoroughly sensitized by the pig odor, I decided to stay with Sam Horton's bird for the trip to the outpost where we would pick up the seriously wounded Vietnamese trooper. By this time the ground crewmen had repaired the fuel pump—the trouble had been water ·in the storage tank—and we loaded up with fuel for the next lap of the trip. It was unbelievable luxury to be able to take off with a clean-swept, relatively odorless compartment.

Apparently we were over thick VC territory, because Carr unlimbered the M-14 and sat tensely with it, watching every move out of the door as we made knots westward. At 11 A.M. we came down over the obvious outskirts of a military post stuck in the jungle, descending over foxholes and several layers of bamboo fence. A knot of bedraggled Vietnamese troopers were waiting for us, and an American MAAG captain stepped forward the minute we touched down in the maelstrom of dust. With the engine still running and the rotor ticking over, Carr jumped out of the cabin to talk to the captain and quickly jumped back up again to pass on the word to the pilots through the intercom system. "They sent him [the casualty] out by road," he reported.

"How long ago?"

"About 15 minutes ago. He called Maj. Moore—he's already on the way." Sam Horton didn't waste time in this apparently unhealthy spot. "We'll get out of here then," he said and we lifted from the ground with the inevitable shower of dirt and swirling dust.

We headed back toward Quang Ngai again and, landing there, found that the other choppers had already returned from Mang Buk, having delivered their load of pigs and troops. Maj. Blaydes summed up the flight up to the mountain stronghold: "I'll never eat another pig. I gagged all the way to Mang Buk."

Now it seemed that the other choppers, having fulfilled their mission, were going to have another go at hauling the remaining two planeloads of freight, which had been temporarily deposited at Quang Ngai, up to what Razor Blaydes called "The Hill," Mang Buk.

Then there was still another change of plans—today's resupply mission was getting to be a shambles—as one of the planes under Major Blaydes command was detached and sent with a wingman to pick up Gen. Harkins, who was making an unexpected tour of the area today. In the shuffle, I left Horton's and Wirkus' gas burner and changed over to an aircraft that was going to carry some of the remaining freight back up to Mang Buk. Two aircraft, Nos. 82 and 92, were going to make the flight, and I boarded No. 92, which I noticed was labeled, *The Mistake*, up near the pilots' compartment. Mistake or not, it was preferable to ride in that aircraft, because No. 82 was going to carry the 15 pigs we had carried as far as Quang Ngai and I wanted no more of them if I could avoid it.

We didn't know what our load in YP 92 was going to be until a truck pulled up beside us, and when the tailgate was lowered we saw a horrifying sight: ranged inside were 24 cans of *nuoc mam*. Sgt. Jack W. Dulaney (of Fort Meade, S.D.), the crew chief, shared my attitude about this delightful cargo. As we helped to load the five-gallon cans of the stuff, marked *Nuoc* in red paint, Dulaney commented, "Boy, that's some stinkin' damn stuff, isn't it?" But as we moved out toward the center of the landing strip for take-off, I was struck with the thought that it was a great improvement over the pigs as cargo, because at least it didn't perpetually augment its smell as it went along.

This load of cargo had another advantage in that the two Vietnamese troopers who had climbed aboard to fly with us to Mang Buk didn't carry garlic buds or garlic ordor with them this time. Furthermore, the cabin of No. 92, like Sgt. Carr's, was well decorated with leg art from some *Playboy*-type publication—this one a blond beauty with very effective flanks and slim waist and a rip in the middle of her body, where perhaps somebody had stacked a gun against her.

Again we headed west over the big, spooky mountains and picked our way over cascades of gray rain clouds. Soon the jungly peaks were begining to thrust up on all sides of us, and in fact seemed to be trying to climb through the door. Eventually we hit on Mang Buk, scar tissue of a base carved in the jungle, with fresh clearings among the tall trees and rings of bamboo fences encircling the buildings. As we settled in for a landing, a fat-bellied C-123 came zooming in over another part of the outpost and disappeared steeply into a valley. At the last minute before it sank out of sight, I saw shadowy shapes of cargo tumbling from the rear end: a low-altitude supply drop, without parachutes. This, coupled with our own sizable Marine resupply mission here earlier in the day, indicated that the supply situation in this remote outpost must have been desperate, seriously attenuated by the recent heavy rains.

Our pilot, Lt. Miles Gordon Gunter (of Aransas Pass, Tex.), kept his engine running while the Vietnamese troops, spying the silvery cans of *nuoc* sauce, clambered over the wide-open doorway. The two Arvin troopers who had come with us assisted with the unloading, and Jack Dulaney pitched into the job with vigor. He confided, "I want to get away from that stuff."

"That stuff," which is such a shock to the nervous systems of newly arriving Americans in Vietnam, is about as familiar in Vietnam as catsup is in the States. It seems even more prominent, since it doesn't have any competition, the way catsup has to compete with Worcestershire and A-1 and Tabasco in the U.S.

Nuoc mam is prepared in large vats, like salt-drying basins. First, the manufacturers grind up fish and let it ferment through a gamut of stinks and degrees of spoilage. The grade-A *nuoc mam* is fermented for a year, cheaper grades are drained off earlier. Then, it is tapped as a clear liquid—supposedly full of vitamins, if you can hold your nose long enough to get it down.

A sturdy-looking Special Forces noncom, wearing the characteristic dark green beret, appeared to help us with the unloading of the comestibles. We barely had time enough to find out that he was S/Sgt William Carrier (of Portland, Ore.) before Gunter gunned our engine and we started to rise with nervous speed over the tall bamboo fences, this being an insecure area, to state the proposition mildly.

Stopping at Quang Ngai to pick up some fuel, we found that several of the Marine choppers were still here, including Maj. Blaydes' YP 94.

I bummed a ride back to Danang with the same trio with whom I had started today's flight. This time we had two extra passengers: a well-shaped female correspondent of *Newsweek* magazine, Beverly Deepe, who had come up from Saigon with Gen. Harkins' airlift; and Col. Dave McDuffie, from I Corps HQ, who was acting as a sort of conducting officer for Miss Deepe.

I queried the colonel on the status of my request to make a flight with a T-28 mission, and sure enough, since he was senior man in charge of PI (he was posted on the doings of all correspondents in the Corps), he had received word that the Vietnamese government had approved my request. However, he said that they had specified I'd have to make the flight out of Nhatrang. I didn't know the reason for this, but I did know that Nhatrang is a training base for T-28 operations, and surmised that the Vietnamese government people were trying to restrict me to some kind of a training flight instead of an operational one. I told McDuffie as much, and asked if he thought I could stretch this permission so that I'd be able to make a flight out of Danang and go strafing and bombing with Col. Kalin. He said he would see what he could figure out.

There was one further bit of business aboard the northbound chopper. I've become attached enough to the Marines at the helicopter base so that I didn't want them to miss a chance to entertain a visiting correspondent of the more interesting sex, especially a glamorous one with the more generous curves of the Western world, and the round eyes which are also such a novelty, and therefore so much in demand in this part of the world. I presumed on my slight acquaintance with Miss Deepe and invented a story to the effect that Col. Ireland, whom I was sure she had met, had authorized me especially to invite her to come and inspect the new Marine Officers' Club at the helicopter base. I said that Col. Ireland wanted her to be his special guest this evening. Miss Deepe declined, but finally agreed to come to the O Club tomorrow night, after she had run down some news stories she was searching for at I Corps area. I hoped the Marines would reward me for my valor in their behalf, if the miracle of a round-eye female visit ever came to pass.

Back at the Danang base, I found other ambitious social doings in preparation for the O Club tonight. A group of the young officers had apparently been preparing for an elaborate improvised ceremony for several days running. The butt of this endeavor was Lt. George Clark (of Marshall Wis.), a communicator, who is never ordered to fly in the choppers. It seemed that Clark, who frequently beleaguered the pilots to be taken along on an adventurous mission, was told that he couldn't go because of Max Gross.

"Max Gross" is pilot shorthand for the absolute weight limit allowed on a helicopter when it takes off. A pilot refusing Clark was stating that he was at that absolute weight limit, therefore he couldn't carry another passenger. The pilots honored Clark's good intentions, and wanted to indicate to him that they did, but they also wanted to ride him a little.

So for several days they had been collecting props. Capt. Prather, one of Clark's roommates, had been doing most of the foraging. He had gathered together an old crash helmet, a tachometer, and an airspeed meter from a derelict Army aircraft; a homemade pair of overgrown pilot's wings, with a pair of boondocker Marine shoes embossed at the center, to indicate that Clark was actually more of a "grunt" than an aviator (these wings had been designed by Angelo Chiarenza); a strap of the type one encounters standing up in the New York subway, to indicate that Clark was a nonproductive "strap-hanger"; and at last, a certificate, properly embossed, indicating that he was a certified strap-hanger and that known by his alias, Max Gross, he was recognized as a true nonproductive crew member. The crowning touch was the name, printed in luminous letters across the front of the crash helmet: ALIAS MAX GROSS.

When the mementos of Clark's strap-hanging status were given to him tonight, there was another bit of business carried out by the officers: a farewell for Dr. Chiarenza, who has been transferred to the Brooklyn Navy Yard and will be leaving tomorrow morning. The new dentist, Dr. Lee Bowen, was already on deck for his duties, taking part in the festivities. In Chiarenza's honor, the officers had shaped a banner from a bedsheet, lettered with the following message, printed with a laundry-marking pen: SO LONG TO ANGIE, THE BEST GODDAMNED DENTIST THE COMBAT MARINES EVER HAD.

"He's a good little ——————," said Clark in tribute.

Tuesday, October 30

This morning, I checked the frags and found that the most interesting helicopter mission of the day apparently was to be another afternoon flight up to Mang Buk, which is still short of supplies. I arranged to go on it, then stopped in to visit with Dave Marr, the outfit's towheaded interpreter.

I found him perusing a Vietnamese novel entitled *Afternoon Leaves*, which he said is a romance, in accordance with the Vietnamese penchant for writing about man-woman love.

"It's about a girl who is pregnant and they don't know who is responsible. It's not too different from the novels in the United States," Dave said.

When I came in, he was being served a cup of tea by his room girl, whom the boys call Gladys (her real name is Kimh, meaning "glass," but in the confusion of explaining to his roommates what the name meant, Marr settled for Gladys). WO George W. Baker (of Pine Bluff, Ark.), one of the roommates, was complaining this morning that Dave's knowledge of Vietnamese gave him an unfair advantage: he is showered with all kinds of privileges (like cups of tea) at the slightest provocation.

"That's why he's got all the skivvy drawers in the building," Baker said, "whenever there's any doubt about who the skivvy drawers belong to, they are always given to Marr."

Right now, sipping his green tea, reading his stylish Vietnamese novel, comfortably attired in a T-shirt and shorts, sitting beneath the display of *Playboy*-type art that graces his walls, as it does the walls of most of the young officers' quarters, Marr was a picture of military contentment, Vietnamese style.

Down at the field this afternoon, I found the roads were swirling with yellowish dust. Now, with the sun out, the other face of war showed: if not mud, there was dust—nothing in between.

I climbed aboard the chopper being flown today by Maj. "Pappy" Lemmons, with Lt. Richard Baker (of Pomca City, Okla.) as copilot. Our crew chief, superintending the loading of 800 pounds of rice, in huge sacks, in the cargo compartment, was Sgt. Duane Larson (of Albert City, Iowa). For today's trip, I came equipped with trading materials: two Boy Scout knives. Mang Buk, being a remote post, has a name among Marines as a source of authentic crossbows and other aborigine souvenirs. I had been told that you could get a good crossbow for a standard Scout knife—and was determined to arrange this if we stayed on the ground long enough.

We were off the ground at 1:30, carrying the rice and a Special Forces lieutenant, complete with green beret, named John Dunlop (of Saugus, Mass.).

With the skies clear today, it seemed quite easy to find our way to the Vietnamese outback. With only a few white tongues of clouds in the valleys, the mountains seemed considerably less sinister. The gas pumps at Quang Ngai were working well today, so our touch-down was brief. When we reached the terrifying high jungle, we had little difficulty in locating the stronghold at Mang Buk.

This time, we were going to have a few minutes on the ground—thus, I might be able to talk to some of the American advisers stationed with the troops here, and see how they had been making out with VC raids and snipers.

When we shut down our engines, Pappy said we would have perhaps 20 minutes to roam around the post before taking off again. So I sought out the first American I could see on the ground, a Capt. Louis Weiner, from Chicago, who somehow managed to achieve a Brooks Brothers look even in fatigue greens and combat boots. He seemed a lot more like an attorney, even in backwoods clothes, than a frontier adviser in the Vietnam jungle. I found out as we talked that he had studied accounting at Roosevelt College in Chicago—"just what I need up here," he added.

Weiner said that he had been here four weeks, and that really it wasn't such bad duty at all. Previously he had been an adviser at another base called Ashau.

This area, he said, "is cooler, it's a lot cleaner and there are less bugs, leeches, flies, mosquitoes, and those odd-looking green, yellow, and blue monsters we had at Ashau.

"And best of all, the rats are better. There [at Ashau] we had to leave the Coleman lanterns on all night to keep the rats away. One night a rat bit me on the big toe. They were using our living quarters as a runway."

I asked Weiner if the Mang Buk garrison had had some contact with the VC recently. He said: "Last Sunday, there was some shooting—a kind of raid. But no casualties, at least on our side."

I was watching our two helicopters very zealously, since I didn't want to be left behind in this nowhere outpost—and a group of Arvin troops were gathering beside the birds, apparently getting ready to be taken back to Danang or Quang Ngai. But apparently I still had time enough to wander through the village and see if I could scare up some souvenirs.

I soon found a small Vietnamese trooper-tradesman who somewhat diffidently was offering two montagnard crossbows for sale to any visiting Americans. I hauled out my two penknives and offered them as bargaining material in exchange for the privilege of examining one of the crossbows. They were of two different grades: one, made of polished heavyweight dark wood with a strong bowstring, would have been a fit decoration for a living room wall; the other, much lighter in weight and smaller, had a somewhat puny string.

The little Vietnamese tradesman, whose alert impersonality would have been a credit to any Middle Eastern market place, indicated in no uncertain terms that the best I could do in the way of a deal was to give him both knives in return for the lesser of the two bows. I told him that I wasn't interested on those terms and, with the aplomb of an Arab merchant, he turned away with a not-quite final hand wave of conclusion—interrupted, as if abstracted by something he had seen accidentally. Turning back to me, he pointed to my Swedish sheath knife, a valuable item of good *rostfri* steel with a laminated leather handle and an aluminum hilt. That, he indicated, he would consider as trading material in return for his good crossbow.

I was not about to part with my treasured side arm, and indicated this as well as I could in pantomime. The little uniformed trader acknowledged, and rapidly hauled away with his bows.

The experience tied in with what I had heard about the trading situation in Mang Buk. When the first Marines began to fly in to the outpost and the first infantry advisers and Special Forces soldiers reported for duty there, they could win the best crossbow with the slightest of trading material: a Hong Kong-made cigarette lighter. After a while, this currency wore thin as the montagnards realized that cigarette lighters had a very short lifespan without an accompanying supply of lighter fluid. Then knives began to be popular, and the latest wrinkle was the high demand for hunting knives or K-bar service knives, of considerably more value than Boy Scout knives. Now, it seemed, the Vietnamese troopers, like my friend with the two crossbows, had taken the business away from the montagnards. The lowland Vietnamese, racially akin to the Chinese and much cannier than the aboriginal mountainfolk, are good tradesmen.

Noticing that Lt. Baker, Lemmons' copilot, was waving a finger in the air, indicating that take-off was imminent, I hurried back to the plane and found five Vietnamese troopers and one American MAAG adviser type climbing aboard our aircraft.

When we lifted from the ground, I was able to "talk" to the American by passing my notebook back and forth between us.

In this way, I found out that he was SFC Robert N. Farner (of New Philadelphia, Ohio) and that he had come up here for only two days to repair some small arms belonging to the Arvin troops. He was stationed at Danang, and apparently both he and the Vietnamese troopers who were flying out with us had been brought up to do this ordnance repair work. The Arvin troopers all wore the shoulder patch showing a bomb and the number 81, indicating that they were in the 81st Support Company.

I asked Farner what he had seen of VC activity here at Mang Buk, and he answered: "NONE. I DIDN'T ARRIVE TILL MON. A.M."

I used the same method of communication with Sgt. Larson and found out the bare essentials about him: He is 27 years old, is married, and has two children back in Albert City, Iowa: Rhonda Dee, age 5, and Rachelle Rene, 19 months.

This method of communication was tedious and time-consuming; furthermore, the heavy tremor of the main rotor made it difficult to write. The letters in my notebook looked as if they had been fashioned by an octogenarian with cerebral palsy. (I am having difficulty with notes I've made on the helicopter missions. I find I have to read them over the same night they are made, or I sometimes lose a word.)

The extent of my remaining notebook conversation with Larson before we got back to Danang was my comment:

"WE HAULED 24 5-GAL CANS OF NUOC MAM TO MANG BUK YESTERDAY."

I added the comment, "STINKO!" and Larson nodded his head emphatically.

Tonight a big event transpired at the O Club. Beverly Deepe, the glamorous correspondent, honored her promise to show up as the guest of Col. Ireland and was on hand with round eyes, curves in the right places, and wearing a dress! The officers, usually quite boisterous after a full day of flying, seemed constrained. Possibly they were awed by the sudden appearance of feminine beauty, and undoubtedly were somewhat restricted by the fact that she was Col. Ireland's guest. They sang mild songs in her honor, "Hey Nonny Nonny No" and "The Jolly Coachman."

It was a tame evening. Col. Rathbun introduced Miss Deepe to the assembled officers. She looked somewhat prim and wore her glasses, and left at about 11 P.M. to go into Danang, where she was to stay at a hotel.

I overheard a bit of conversation about the name of the Officers' Club. So far no name has been applied to it except the general designation of O Club. One of the officers respectfully suggested that it be called Buck's Club, after Col. Buck Ireland. Another, less polite, suggested that it be called Wetkos Club.

"What's that mean?" asked another.

"It means, 'We eat that kind of —————!' " explained the other.

But the main nickname for the O Club continues to be Slop Chute, a fairly descriptive term, even though this one seems to be remarkably orderly. The only disorder associated with the place thus far has been one small accident, which occurred when a couple of guests, coming out the front door in the dead of night, turned too sharply to the left and ran into some coils of barbed wire, which caused a few contusions.

Wednesday, October 31

I scanned the frags this morning and decided to go out on a different kind of Marine mission today: a reconnaissance flight in an OE. I checked with Maj. Klepsattel, who has been flying these reconnaissance missions practically every day, and got his permission to make the flight. He said he was going to fly over "a couple of VC training areas inland of Quang Ngai." That sounded interesting enough.

I knew that the OE pilots are supposed to have what the rotary-wing boys call "the hard rides," meaning that in flying over the seemingly endless miles of tall trees and dense jungle, the OE has even less of a chance to make an emergency landing than the helicopter. The helicopter can at least come down vertically, whereas the straight-wing observation plane needs a landing run and, even at minimum speed, is moving 35 or 45 miles an hour in a forward direction when it touches the ground.

Therefore, the hazards of flying over the jungle in this light, single-engined aircraft are considerable. In the words of one helicopter pilot, Ken Babbs, "Pilots are worried not about enemy action but about having to go down somewhere, and the straight-wing boys have a lot tougher shake in this line than we do." But there is room for respect for both kinds of courage: that needed to fly helicopters in assault landings and that needed to make long, harrowing drags in straight-winged OE's over enemy territory in search of intelligence.

I walked over to one of the OE's with Klepsattel and was checked out by him on the emergency procedures in case we did have to go into the trees.

I would be riding in the back seat, and he indicated to me several packages of emergency equipment we would use if we had to make a forced landing. One included two suits of black clothing, which he said would enable us to "blend in with the landscape." However, I couldn't envision my six-foot-six self blending very easily into any Vietnamese landscape, even with the blackest of clothing.

There was also a grease gun, a .45-caliber submachine gun, which I could use if we had to go down and got embroiled with VC. Klepsattel also helped me adjust my parachute, and instructed me: "If the engine should quit or if we get knocked out, or if we haven't got a place to land, we bail out. I open the door and dive out first, this way." He demonstrated how he would open the frail fabric side door of the plane. "But we probably won't have to."

I knew what Klepsattel meant. Pilots flying over this terrain keep mental catalogues of all possibly reachable emergency fields traversed during the previous 20 minutes, just in case they need a place to glide to in a hurry.

Klepsattel had been through one engine failure in an OE on Okinawa. It had happened just after take-off from the Marine field and he had no choice except to pick out the softest-looking ground he could find and mush his way in among the trees. He didn't have enough altitude to turn and get back to the airfield. He emerged from the crash barely alive, with a wide assortment of broken bones and a bad back, internal injuries, and other miscellaneous hurts. Nevertheless, he rapidly recovered and went back to full duty, flying OE's in long reconnaissance flights over impossible jungle territory.

At 8:29, Klepsattel fired up his engine, and we taxied out toward the runway. The other OE attached to the squadron at the moment was taking off just ahead of us, bound for a similar reconnaissance mission but in another direction.

As we waited for clearance from the tower, I surveyed my view in various directions. Directly ahead, Klepsattel's sturdy neck with parachute straps. A large open window ahead and to the right. At my right knee, the grease gun, the VHF radio dials at my left. And underneath my seat, a small pancake of armor in gray fabric. There must always be armor for these flights over the VC. The extent of their armament might be a homemade popgun; it could also be a .57-mm. recoil-less rifle, Chinese made.

We took off at 8:33 and headed south along the coast, a pleasant blast of warm air coming in the open window. With the armor shield in my seat, I couldn't sit up quite straight, but the protection was worth the discomfort. I heard Vietnamese conversation on the radio command channel, the language sounding, as it always does, like baby talk.

We went due south along the coast a short distance, and then cut inland over thrusting mountains and thick, scudding clouds.

Klepsattel said on the intercom, "This is the area we're supposed to check, and it's socked in completely, about six-tenths clouds, so we're going to go farther down south. There's supposed to be a battalion concentration in there." Klepsattel lifted a plastic-covered map and pointed to a square marked with red crayon. "I've got to fly over that Viet-Cong area."

I looked for something distinctive in that huge green muscle of mountains below, but it seemed to be all of a piece. We droned on for what seemed hours, and I guessed from our low altitude that we had gone beyond the VC rectangle marked in red crayon. But I was wrong. We hadn't even reached Quang Ngai. Since our first objective was heavily obscured and we had to go on to alternates, our trip was just beginning.

As we flew over the now-familiar site of the helicopter crash on the side of the mountain north of Quang Ngai, Klepsattel pointed out the lush paddy fields and the ranks of old French houses that marked the city. Soon we turned southwest, heading toward the high mountains again, and I hated to see the paddy fields slipping behind. They are always pleasant emergency landing areas.

We were in the higher mountain region now, and Klepsattel pointed out another red rectangle on his map. As I located it, I could see three T-28's, our perky little fighter planes, with the yellow Vietnamese government star on the side, cruising over the area, apparently looking for something to shoot at.

Klepsattel pointed out a couple of Vietnamese artillery positions, a film of smoke rising from them. Apparently this was an embattled area, with the Arvin troops closing in on a VC stronghold. As we passed, another type of aircraft—an all-metal observation and liaison aircraft—also circled the area, probably cueing our artillery on the accuracy of their fire. "Probably that's a Special Forces L-28," Klepsattel said.

But we still hadn't come upon any of the VC concentrations that we were supposed to be reconnoitering.

"Just ahead is the area which is supposed to be a VC training area," Klepsattel said. "It's about 3,500 feet high. We can't even see it from here, its about a thousand feet above us." He pointed out a road winding up the side of a mountain that disappeared into the clouds. As usual in this part of Vietnam, the weather was on the side of the guerrillas, shielding them from our aerial observations.

"I'm going to sneak down this valley from the other side," Klepsattel said, "and see if we can see this training camp from the other side of it."

We slid over a couple of forested divides and up a valley among rough, cloud-topped mountains. Our altimeter showed 5,000 feet: We were about 1,000 feet above the mountains, but to the right peaks towered several hundred feet higher.

Heading north, we passed over a mountaintop outpost surrounded by the usual tall bamboo fences and, in this case, a circular mud ditch. Klepsattel said it was a Vietnamese outpost, but as we dipped down low over it, not a soul was in sight.

"We've been supporting that outpost by airlift," he said. "Nobody there now, though." Evidently the Arvin troops had been withdrawn from this exposed position.

From this approach, we could get a better view of the VC concentration area and the road, which now I could see was simply a dirt track running up the mountainside. However, there was no open camp or outpost area marking the VC concentration, as there had been at the point of the former Arvin outpost. With absolute air supremacy in the hands of the Vietnamese and their American allies, the VC can't afford to set up any camps apparent from airplanes, even in the deepest jungle.

Klepsattel pointed to the red area on his map: "We're just south of Tam Qui [now called Quanh Tinh]: they know we saw 'em." Klepsattel was making a note in some sort of a logbook. He has sharper eyes for this kind of reconnaissance than I. Our main objective achieved, we turned toward the coastline, where at least we would be closer to a paddy field if an emergency landing became necessary.

We passed over Route 1, principal road of Vietnam, the narrow black-top strip built by the French along the length of the seacoast. It was now only partially useful to truck traffic, and that only when heavily protected by truckloads of troops and armed vehicles.

At 11:28, we were back on the ground, taxiing in to the Marine area. Klepsattel expertly swung the little aircraft into a parking spot, and chopped the engine. I breathed a silent thanks to the aircraft engine manufacturers who have provided us with such a good power plant and the mechanics who keep it that way. We dragged our weary bones out the side entrance of the fragile aircraft. My stomach, as usual in this low-altitude flying in light aircraft, was slightly uneasy, but at least we were back in one piece.

Klepsattel looked absently at the fuselage and the center section of the wing, his tired eyes skimming over it in search of bullet holes.

"Probably we had many shots fired at us today," he said. "But no holes."

We got back to the barracks area in time for lunch. Afterward, seeing Frank Allgood in flying gear, complete with revolver and cartridge belt, I asked him what was up for the afternoon. He said that he would be flying reconnaissance to prepare for a T-28 strike.

I stopped by the room of the camp commandant, Lt. Col. Ralph Davis, the genial Oklahoman who is in effect the mayor of our Marine town, and asked if he knew of anything sensational coming up in current Marine planning. He said one such item is the first R and R trip to Hong Kong. It will probably be undertaken this week end by the "Trans-Paddy Airways," the remodeled DC-3 that serves as the principal air-freight and passenger transport for the Marines here. In the absence of any further word on an assault mission, my requested orders to the 93d at Soctrang, or official sanction for flying T-28 missions, I was strongly tempted to request permission to make this R and R (servicemen rendered it "Rape and Ruin") trip. Hong Kong has always had some of the wildness and fun of Paris about it, and in our current war involvement in Vietnam, it is supposed to have become the Paris of the Pacific area. But I wanted to check through a few more possible avenues of military action hereabouts before embarking on this delightful bit of Hong Kong dalliance.

At the brightly lit hangar I fell in with Lt. Ken Babbs, who waxed nostalgic about the active shooting war in which the Marines took part in the Soctrang area—and how tame this northern involvement seems by comparison.

"You should have been down there, where we worked hard and had a sense of accomplishment. It was like war. Up here, there's a liberty town, you don't work so hard, everybody is on his own, and things kind of fall apart. That's why we have a little morale problem.

"Down there, you have pretty solid VC areas, where you can assume everybody is an enemy. You know, the 362 [the 362d Squadron, which preceded this outfit into Vietnam] were wild men. One chopper would go first, and when the people would go running, the second plane would spray 'em.

"Hanoi Hannah, who used to be on the air Fridays at nine o'clock with a news commentary in English, used to complain about what she called 'The Marine Butchers of the 362.' She used to say that they ate human liver for breakfast, and when the 163d came in, she welcomed us and said everyone [meaning the Communists] hoped they would be more humanitarian."

Tonight I heard rumbles that a large-scale air-phibious operation will be coming up pretty soon. In the frags for tomorrow, there's a reconnaissance to be undertaken by Col. Rathbun in the coal-mine area—a sore spot of VC activity about 15 miles to the west of Danang. It seems as if this is going to be a big one, because the rumor is that the 10th Ranger Battalion, the crack air-phibious troop outfit of this area, is going to be used in the operation. The Hong Kong R and R trip can wait for a little while.

Thursday, November 1

This morning when I caught a ride down to the line with Maj. Blaydes, I seized the chance to continue the bull session of the other night. I felt that his ideas had been stimulating and showed a refreshing kind of ruggedness and independence of thought, the kind of American hard-headedness and eagerness for truth that has always stood us in good stead through, and an affinity for the struggles of the common man that may still win us the victory in our world-wide struggle with Communism.

"What would you do to win this campaign?" I asked him.

Blaydes (cannily): "How much authority do I have?"

I: "No declaration of war by the U.S." This restriction, of course, is the first requirement of the modern kind of war, the Leninistic or limited kind invented by the Communists.

Blaydes (without hesitation): "I'd mobilize the Vietnamese. There's no reason why they shouldn't be completely mobilized. Then I'd drive over to the Laos border, come back and clean up."

I: "That would take a lot of strength."

Blaydes: "We have it."

I: "What would you do to grab the high ground?" One of the well-known difficulties with using helicopters to capture jungly high ground is that you generally have to land your troops in the valleys (since the mountaintops are inevitably heavily overgrown) and then the troops have to go up the slopes on foot, in the old, time-worn way of the infantry; and this is a tough proposition. A few able troops on a mountaintop can inflict hard casualties on much larger numbers of men coming up the slopes.

Blaydes: "There are ways." I knew he had in mind various methods of getting observation over the enemy—some of them still on the secret list—one of them being the use of observation planes (like the L-19's) to spot enemy movements and to control artillery and strafing and rocketing attacks against them.

"The main thing is to get the strength out," he added, and that did sound like the first requirement, whether you are going to drive the VC out of the swampy ricelands south of Saigon or route them from the dense jungle of the highlands.

"There are a lot of new Arvin troop outfits being formed and trained," I suggested.

"That's right." He nodded and said nothing more, but the thought unsaid was, "Maybe not fast enough."

Down at the line, I saw a group of Special Forces troops, in green berets and camouflaged jungle hats, and checked with the OOD to find out where they were going, and whether I could go along.

It seemed that they were heading out to a lightly held area called Quanh Tinh, and possibly another outpost or two in the same area if the weather permitted, to see how much the locals could be organized against the determined VC efforts there.

The American troopers on the plane were a Capt. Ambert Chase (of Moundsville, W. Va.), Lt. Wade Lovings (of Marion, S.C.), and four strapping sergeants: Lester Levreault (of South Hadley, Mass.), Charles Heaukulani (of Hawaii), Alfred Harrison (of Columbus, Ohio), and Howard Heathman (of Wichita, Kan.). With them was a very Americanized Vietnamese interpreter named Thanh (aged 20 and called Johnny), who wore a rakish campaign hat in the best go-to-hell style (one side of the brim pinned up) and who seemed to speak "American" with a New York accent. There was another, more conservative, Vietnamese interpreter, Nguyen Ngoc-Minh, 22.

I talked to the tall Capt. Chase about this mission while we were waiting for take-off.

"This is only a survey," he said. "We're going to assess the place." Exactly how he was going to make his assessment, Chase didn't explain, except to say that two of his crew were medics, they had the Special Forces medical training, and that they "can do anything, debride bullet wounds, do operations. I feel completely safe with them."

I know the mechanism of the Special Forces teams: They usually number about a dozen men, some trained in medical aid, some in demolition and the handling of explosives, some experts in weapons, some communications experts—and all given a basic indoctrination in the skills of the other specialists in their teams so they can fill in if one of them is put out of action.

These teams go into primitive outpost areas and train the local inhabitants in the use of modern military weapons and demolition equipment and show them how to make raids and patrols and set up defenses as well as prepare ambushes. The Special Forces are keystones in the new kind of armies we are preparing.

We took off at 8:35, and I didn't have a chance to talk to the Special Forces people until after the short flight down the coastal plain was over and we had landed in a meadow at Quanh Tinh.

Heathman and Harrison filled me in a little bit on the background of the place while the Marine chopper was shut down and the Special Forces detachment waited for some

Vietnamese troopers supposed to meet them there. A bicycle brigade of cautious civilians had turned up across the river and were surveying us cautiously from afar.

"This is the only part of this province that's secure so far," Heathman said. "We've pushed 'em [the VC] all the way south from Danang, this far. And this place is secure because of the Arvin troopers here."

Apparently the Special Forces boys were planning an over-all effort to push the VC still farther south, to clear this whole province and a lot more than that.

"If we succeed," said Harrison modestly, "we'll push 'em clear across the Laotian border." Here was an SFC who had the same hope and the same intent that Maj. Blaydes had.

The Special Forces group, the vanguard of a full detachment that would probably be coming down here to do their good work in the next few days, now spotted the Vietnamese troopers they were waiting for. After a protracted conversation between the Americans and the Vietnamese troopers, it was decided that the Green-beret (Special Forces) types would stay a couple of days here.

When I asked the husky Harrison where they'd stay, he said good-naturedly, "We'll just flop out somewhere."

By this time (10:15) the Marine pilots and crew chief, Capt. Bob Finn, Lt. Ed Anderson (of Mt. Kisco, N.Y.), and Sgt. J. D. Jones (of Garden Grove, Calif.), were getting restive with their vulnerable bird sitting in the only allegedly secure part of a fought-over province. The minute the Special Forces plans were finalized, Jones kicked on his putt-putt and at 10:19 we were homewardbound.

Back at the Marine camp, I sought out Maj. Dave Webster to find out if Col. Rathbun had turned up any LZ's in the coal-mine area that would be acceptable both to him (as workable for his choppers) and to the Vietnamese troop commanders.

"A big one is coming up all right," Webster said. "But it won't be tomorrow. Col. Rathbun selected some landing sites from his reconnaissance this morning. They were a long way from what the Corps planned.

"They [the Vietnamese Corps people] asked for a further recce this afternoon. But Rathbun won't buy it. He won't get stampeded into settling for LZ's where his boys might get clobbered. So he's going to make another reconnaissance tomorrow morning, and that'll give time to pick out better LZ's and set up a good T-28 strike and artillery preparation for Saturday. The mission will probably be on that day."

I could see one reason for Rathbun's chronic upset stomach, beyond the obvious one. There is a great nervous strain in battling a foreign (and sovereign) military authority who are ignorant about the kind of warfare you are teaching them and helping them with—especially when you are also risking the lives of your American specialists, who must help with the critical part of the operation. More credit to Rathbun that he has the determination not only to stick to his military principles but also to risk his own neck on their validity by leading every assault mission. But this is probably also rough on his digestion, to put it mildly.

The principle of helicopter warfare involved here—Rathbun has mentioned it to me several times—is that you can't just put your finger on a map and say, "I want the helicopters to put the troops in there." You have to consider the approach, landing, and exit, and all the ways in which the choppers can be shot down by enemy ground fire during each phase of the assault procedure. Also, you have to consider all the preparations that have to be coordinated before the choppers can bring troops in, such as softening up the opposition just before the landing to cut the chances of casualties to a minimum. As Rathbun sometimes says, "They [the Vietnamese] have a lot to learn about helicopters."

Near Dave Webster's room, I met a new arrival, a lean Irishman with a New Yorkish accent, Lt. Lew O'Neil (of Queens, N.Y.), who is a representative of the outfit that will replace the 163d Squadron and Task Unit 79.3.5 in January or February. This new squadron, the 162d, is currently aboard the carrier the USS *Oriskany* in Hong Kong. O'Neil, who seems a savvy, well-coordinated type, is here on temporary duty to get the lay of the land, fly some missions, and then report to the 162d.

There is a constant progression of new Marine, Navy, Army, and Air Force outfits coming to the Vietnam battleground. There may be 12,000 American servicemen in this country at this moment, but next year at this time, probably 30,000 will have served hitches here, because of the rotation of units.

While visiting Dave Webster, I also stopped to see Capt. Prather, who lives nearby. Jay had told me he wanted to show me some 35-mm. color slides he had made of Vietnamese kids. These kids, in my experience, are invariably cheerful, smiling, and personable, and the American servicemen seem much taken with them.

Prather's slides were of winsome infants at China Beach,

and they were all cunning little bugs. He explained an obvious fact about those pictures: "I find they always turn out to be little girls about four years old." He was referring shyly to the fact that he has one such of his own back in Dallas: her name is Robin.

Friday, November 2

I spent the morning going over what the squadron calls its "Hit Parade," the record of all of the antiaircraft fire taken since it first came to Vietnam. My conclusion was mainly that the squadron had a total of more than 60 hits and that the most frantic pace was struck during the month of August, the time some of the pilots called "the Big Push" down in the Delta area.

Maj. Webster told me this afternoon that the assault is definitely on for tomorrow. The briefing will be this afternoon. "There goes my Hong Kong trip," I said.

"Maybe you can do both," he suggested. "Fly the missions in the morning and still make the trip to Hong Kong in the afternoon." However, assault missions have No. 1 priority for me.

Even though many of the pilots already know about the imminence of a mission tomorrow, the routine duties of camp have to go on—even shopping, a minimum amount of which has to be done, even in a military camp at the front. I went into town with Pappy Lemmons and two new arrivals from the Marine base at Iwakuni in Japan. Since the new men would be here only a few days on temporary duty, Pappy showed them a couple of shops where they could buy necessities for themselves and curios for their womenfolk. Pappy himself was looking for an exotic item much in demand among the servicemen here: a tiger claw set in a gold mount. Vietnam has splendid tigers (being one of the few countries where they flourish), and the business of supplying tiger claws and teeth to jewelers to be made up into charms and necklaces continues despite the war. But Pappy was detoured from the tiger-claw objective and took a fancy instead to a display of uncut stones in one of the many stores catering to American servicemen in Danang's main street.

We came back to camp long before sundown. Pappy never did make up his mind on a purchase of stones, tiger claws, or even a flashlight or one of the green baseball caps that some of the merchants make up for members of the squadron, with the number "163" on the front. He is as anxious to get a proper night's sleep and be in good shape for tomorrow's ordeal as any of us.

Saturday, November 3

I was awake at 4:30 and over to the mess for breakfast a half-hour later. Before 6 A.M. we were on our way down to the flight line with gear ready, including emergency rations and canteens full of water.

After calling the roll in the ready room, Razor Blaydes pointed out the LZ's and gave coordinates to the pilots.

"The basic mission is to take 540 people, the Ranger Battalion, into this one LZ.

"This Ranger Battalion will make a sweep to the west of 14–15 miles. . . . We'll be coming through this pass near the coal mine. Maj. Beuch [Maj. Bill R. Beuch of Laughton, Okla.], a MAAG officer, secured 14, 15 rounds of VC fire here—automatic weapons—so we'll take it careful.

"We'll taxi at 20, take off at 8:25. We'll be at LZ 4 at 9:05.

"The weather's a problem. There will be a weather report by eight o'clock . . . radio check and procedures you all know. . . and downed aircraft procedures."

Col. Rathbun took his place beside the large map: "Looks like we've got a pretty fair run in. We're going to take the wide-open route in. The LZ is up to the north here . . .

"I would like to take six planes in with me . . . that would be Frank [Capt. Allgood]. One-minute separation . . . Maj. Lemmons will be right behind. The LZ is a big flat area. We'll straddle a little stream here."

Blaydes gave a time check in his usual staccato way: "In 20 seconds it'll be 20 after—10 seconds—5—4—3—2—1— mark."

Rathbun added, "In the first load I'd like to have troops on board by 8 o'clock. Okay—crank 'em up at 8 o'clock."

At first I got aboard Rathbun's aircraft, which today was YP 71. But after a check with Sgt. James Dailey (of San Jose, Calif.), the crew chief, I found out that Rathbun's plane didn't have any extra phone jack or earphones, so moved on to No. 74, being flown today by Capt. Sam Horton and Lt. Ed Anderson. There's an extra phone outlet in that chopper, so I'll be able to hear the calls on the command frequencies and get a better understanding of what's going on during the mission.

I climbed into the troop compartment with the crew chief, Cpl. George Hartsock (of Iowa City, Iowa), who was going over the idiosyncrasies of the plane with the other corporal who shares the duty: Carlton Davenport (of Portsmouth, Va.).

Davenport, who wouldn't be on flying duty until the end of the month, said, "Now you can't fly missions until you're on flight pay—since that guy got shot." He meant that since Cpl. James Mansfield had been badly wounded at a time when he wasn't on flight pay, the authorities now insist on that prerequisite before assigning crewmen to missions.

At 0800, our 10 troopers came charging aboard with steel hats and carbines. Hartsock seemed jumpy. He signaled to the four soldiers standing at the back of the compartment to sit down. He started the putt-putt, the engine choked and sputtered, and at last the rotor began to whirl. As Blaydes had prophesied, the weather report began to come in about this time. And it was bad: "The LZ is still clobbered in. The approach route is still clobbered in."

At 8:08 we started to taxi.

"Six-dash-three-zero-from One-dash-three. Are you winding up now? . . . Six-dash-three is not turned up yet." The usual chatter of the moment before take-off.

As we gained altitude: "Six-dash-three to One-dash-three . . . I've got a rough-running engine."

"Okay, go ahead, drop out."

At 8:14, the king-sized copilot of our aircraft, Ed Anderson, asked Hartsock to pass up the grease gun from the troop compartment. I helped with that project, since Anderson was sitting directly above my head, and the slot, opening on a low view of his boondocker shoes, was directly in front of my face. I passed up the .45-caliber weapon to him.

There was a little restive chatter between Horton and Anderson up front: "You had a little trouble getting off."

"Yeah, I got a load down there." That would be Anderson passing conversation about Sam Horton's take-off, which had been a little hesitant.

A bit more conversation about the thick ground fog, which lay over the rice lands in white shreds.

"Like a blanket of snow."

"Yeah."

The plane I had chosen to fly with was the second plane of the Second Division, led by Capt. Allgood. You can never tell where firing will erupt in the course of a landing of an assault column like this. In any case, from the middle of the column, you would be fairly sure to have an over-all view of what was happening in the front, the back, and the middle.

Through the usual confusion of command-channel talk

there came a stream of Vietnamese babble, which sounded excited. As usual, Anderson and Horton tried to pick some sense out of the conversation.

"What'd he say?"

"The colonel said he expected the weather'd be cleared up by H-Hour, and this guy said he'd drop all of his bombs and goodies on time." What I had missed was some exchange between Rathbun and the T-28 fighters that were going to prepare the way for our landing. Probably out there with the T-28's was Col. Kalin, who was usually with the advance elements.

Then we heard the meteorologist cutting in with a weather report: "It's breaking. Right now you can get in from the south."

The Vietnamese troopers must have sensed that a landing was imminent, because the little man next to me slipped a clip into his carbine, and two others craned to look out the window.

We were flying over ribs of clouds as the mountains rose higher beneath us. Anderson said on the intercom: "Well, at least we've got pretty good concealment from the ground."

Now I heard Rathbun's clear voice on the command channel: "Black Tiger, this is One-zero-one." (Black Tiger was the call of the T-28's today, and One-zero-one was Rathbun's identification.)

"This is Black Tiger. Right now we are over the LZ."

"OK, I will give you a call five minutes before." That was Rathbun, making sure, as usual, that the T-28's finished their strafing and bombing and rocketing work over the LZ before the first helicopters appeared on the scene.

The troops in the compartment were stirring and picking up their weapons. They must have recognized something on the ground—possibly the steep mountains around the coal mine.

"Black Tiger, I am approximately five minutes from target."

And a sassy fighter pilot's voice, with a Vietnamese accent: "Okay-doka."

Then came the scramble of excited voices, most of them Vietnamese, as the pilots worked over the LZ with bombs and machine guns. From the confusion, one American voice stuck out: "I have one bomb left."

"OK, No. 3, go ahead."

Something had changed in our main rotor pitch, our aircraft was vibrating pronouncedly: I knew it was about time to shift into maximum pitch for our run into the target. Hartsock confirmed this by flipping the first cartridge into the chamber of his M-60 machine gun.

"One-zero-one approximately one minute from target. I am approximately one minute from the target."

"OK, I have you in sight."

Suddenly we were running out of clouds, the green spread of mountains beneath us. There could be no doubt about our being in maximum pitch as we slipped rapidly down a mountainside toward a steep pass. The troopers were standing up to get ready to go out the door—bless them for their training. I heard Rathbun's voice on the command frequency: "OK, this is One-zero-one. I came in too fast to the east to be able to make that landing. I'm going around once more."

We kept going straight in, and the troops crowded around the door as Hartsock nervously swept the ground with his M-60.

I saw our choppers moving in a couple of directions—and at the same moment I heard a few staccato shots, which seemed to be at a distance. It could have been enemy fire—or even an accidental burst from one of our own guns. Our ears strained for the sound of more small arms. Hartsock was manhandling the troopers out of the doorway, shoving them into the marsh grass. The seconds ticked away very slowly until the last one was out.

As we were lifting from the paddy, I heard a call and recognized Allgood's voice: "One-zero [Rathbun], this is Three-zero. We took a little fire just as we lifted off from the river." Looking down and behind, I could see now that our troops had landed close to a river, and were now deploying along the bank and some dikes in the rice fields next to it. At that second I jumped at a tumultuous sound: a long, angry outburst of automatic-weapons fire.

"Five-dash-zero from One-zero. Are you out OK?"

"Affirmative."

"Looks like you've got a big hit." That, I thought I recognized as Anderson's voice: Perhaps he was reporting on a hit scored on Allgood.

I looked through the port-side window to see Allgood's plane, No. 85, which was flying perhaps 70 yards ahead of us and to our left, but I couldn't see any damage from this angle.

Straining to catch some comment on the command frequency that might illuminate the shooting, and the reported damage. I heard: "Our choppers return at this time to home plate"—an order from Rathbun to his birds.

Then I heard a little interphone conversation between Anderson and Horton: "Those guys are gettin' to be better shots."

Anderson said, "Third Division leader [Allgood] got hit . . . it shattered his windshield . . . it looks like it came in here and went out down here . . . looks like flak."

I looked out the window again at YP 85 and still couldn't see any damage from this rear angle. I could see though that the crew chief, sitting in the door, and the pilot on this side, who would be Allgood, seemed to be OK. I listened for further radio calls indicating trouble, but nothing more was forthcoming.

At 9:34, our formation was strung out on the approaches to our airfield. We came in and landed and pulled up to our assigned station without any hitch, and took aboard our second load of 10th Ranger Battalion troops.

Over the earphones I heard Horton call to the crew chief: "Hartsock, better take a quick run around the plane—see if we've got any holes." Hartsock disconnected his helmet, jumped out to make his inspection, and was back in a few moments: "It's OK, sir."

We were off again at 9:43. The clouds seemed a little lighter than on the first run. Rathbun was right on the ball looking out for his boys: "Hello, Tango Tiger, this is One-zero-one. I request new strike, just west of the mountain. I request you strike both sides of the river just west of the canyon."

I listened for an answer, but the only response was a confused gabble of voices speaking Vietnamese, with a very high level of static. Even Rathbun seemed to be having trouble understanding it: "The T-28 transmission is no good. It's breaking up."

As we hove over the first mountains of the coal-mine area, Rathbun repeated his call: "One-zero requesting strike west of the north-south river."

Again there was an answering voice, which seemed to be Vietnamese, speaking with broken and excited tones.

I disconnected from my phones for a minute to look ahead through the port-side window, and saw what appeared to be strings of smoke rising from the mountains near the coal mine.

When I picked up my phones again: "Tango Tiger, this is

121

One-zero-one. Four minutes from target. Request strike as briefed."

There was still trouble going on in the LZ, I gathered from the radio.

"One-zero to Three-zero. Which side you receive fire from?" (That would be Rathbun calling Allgood.)

"The right side." ·

"This is One-zero. We'll favor that side." Then, in a few seconds: "One-zero. One minute to landing."

Now, from our own interphone, Anderson called the crew chief: "OK, Hartsock, we're going to the river."

"Yes, sir."

One of the pilots called: "OK, Hartsock, watch out for that right side. They've been getting fire from that side."

With a thud and a shaking crash, we landed among the wet rows of rice plants. Instantly Hartsock was goosing the Vietnamese troopers out of the plane, and I heard one of the pilots, probably Horton: "Boy, that was some landing."

The troops were jumping splashily into the muck of the paddy and hurrying for cover behind a dike at the edge of it. I saw four or five columns of thin white smoke rising on the hill to the north—probably a relic of the last softening-up attempt on the LZ before we came in.

I heard our engines scream, and the plane struggled and shuddered, as if unable to rise.

I heard some firing: a cascade of small arms, individual rifle shots, and some submachine guns and BAR's.

"We broke something, it looks like." That was Anderson, but the moment he spoke, our bird seemed to gain strength and leaped from the ground.

Apparently, on the command frequency, I heard someone talking about shutting down his rotor, then a call from Rathbun: "This is One-zero. Cover those aircraft on the deck." He was instructing the T-28's to orbit over some of our aircraft, which had apparently been shot down on this landing.

"This is One dash Zero. I have two aircraft in a downed condition in the Landing Zone. We request you keep air cover for security until we can get some troops in."

I asked the pilots of our aircraft, "Do you know which birds went down?"

Horton answered, "I think one of them was Six-zero. Maybe the other one was out of Five-zero." Six-zero would be the last element of our string of aircraft, the one commanded by Pappy Lemmons.

Craning to look back through the door toward our LZ's, I

noted an OE circling high over the mountains, and a couple of T-28's zipping around at maximum speed.

Our aircraft, No. 74, seemed to have a damaged landing gear. We had a call from a nearby aircraft, saying that our tail wheel might be damaged. Our pilots asked Hartsock to take a look out the window and check the tail wheel. He called back: "It's muddy but unbroken." We had made our landing at a terrific rate, and hit the tailwheel hard, but it appeared to be twisted only because it was so thoroughly covered with mud.

Another aircraft was having landing-gear trouble. "Yankee Papa Eight-zero—advise you of a flat tail wheel."

I listened in while our pilots commented on the latest damage: "That would be Col. McCully," Anderson said. Apparently he and Horton were still considering which planes were lost in the LZ. Anderson said, "The 6th Division is all together. I guess there is one missing between four and five."

Rathbun, still trying to arrange action to protect his two downed birds, put in a call for "a Vietnamese English-speaking officer who is familiar with tactical situation, to determine if two aircraft can be recovered." Next, he called to Panama Control and reported, "The flight is returning to base now. The crews have been picked up." Then, ever the efficient commander: "One-zero. Request additional HUS's standing by for the next lift."

Andy said on the intercom, "Boy, this has been a wild day." At 10:45 we were home again. Sam Horton was giving instructions on the intercom: "Hartsock, when we get this bird on the ground, I want you to check it over real good."

This time we would stop for refueling before picking up our third load of troops. According to the plan, this third lift was considered to be a nonassault lift, because by this time the LZ's were presumed to be secure. But the way things had been happening today, you couldn't tell.

While waiting our turn in the line-up of choppers getting fuel, I realized I'd have to decide whether to cut away from the flight now if I wanted to make the R and R trip to Hong Kong. I jumped out and hurried over to the ready room to check on the DC-3 flight. It was going out on schedule—at this moment loading up people not engaged in today's mission—and if I wanted to go, I'd have to get aboard in the next five minutes.

At the ready room I saw Lt. Frank Bell, who told me in passing, "It's me again. I got hit in the transmission. We lost all our oil." He had been in the fourth element, and his had been the aircraft that had been shot down.

The other downed aircraft, I gathered on the run, had

cracked up on landing. Lt. Ed Madigan, who had been copilot aboard the first of the squadron's helicopters to go down, had been copilot on this ship. The other pilot was Eric Coady.

Madigan was still upset about the crash. I asked him if he had broken his landing gear coming in to the LZ. He said nervously, "I don't know what happened." I crossed the ready room toward the flight line, figuring that YP 74 would be refueled and ready to go by now.

I had made up my mind to stay with the outfit during the completion of the day's assault missions.

I met Bob Rathbun, rapidly checking up on damage along the line of planes, and learned that he, too, had decided to stay with the outfit and lead the last lift, even though he had planned to make the Hong Kong trip. "I can't ship off with two of my birds down," he said simply.

Hurrying down the line of refueled aircraft, I saw Allgood's chopper, very clearly marked with a bullet hole in the windshield.

I stopped to talk to Allgood. "You should have been with us this time," he joked.

I asked him if he heard the bullet snap as it came through. He said, "I heard all kinds of things. I guess it snapped. Glass shattered—I guess a cupful of glass flying around the cockpit."

Aircraft were beginning to move down the taxi strip, so I hurried on, found Horton's aircraft, and climbed aboard. Hartsock hadn't found any damage in his inspection and the plane was heading for the next station to pick up its third load of troops: ten men and an efficient-looking squad leader.

I noticed that Allgood's plane was among the choppers that were taxiing out and that he was sitting in his position on the right side of the cockpit. Apparently, the bullet hole in the windshield wasn't enough to deter him, his copilot, Lt. Austen Bates (of Phoenix, Ariz.), or the crew chief, Sgt. Harvey Morton. Since the aircraft had not been otherwise damaged and since these were able and eager Marines, they were going to fly it on the last lift of the day, all else be damned.

Airborne once more, we soon reached the coal-mine vicinity again, and Rathbun was calling the T-28's to warn of our approach. "Hello, Tiger Flight. This is Ledger One-zero. Scheduled to land in a few minutes . . . I will contact you before I start in."

Hartsock charged his M-60 again as we circled over the LZ and then started in over the trees.

Horton said on the intercom, "OK, Hartsock, we'll make

the terrain in about one minute." In a moment we saw one of the downed Marine aircraft, belly-deep in a rice pond.

"They really did a job on that aircraft, didn't they?" one of the pilots said, and almost in the same breath: "Hartsock, look sharp," for we were settling into the middle of a rice paddy, and even though the LZ defense periphery extended for a mile or two, you never could tell when you might draw a stray round.

As our last three troopers were going out, we saw three other soldiers staggering toward us, leaning on each other. One was limping very pronouncedly, dragging a leg behind him. Two had steel helmets but no guns; the third one was bareheaded, still clutching a tommy gun. The pilots kept the aircraft on the ground until Hartsock and I hauled them aboard and dumped them on the floor, puddles of water forming around them. Then we roared into full throttle and lifted from the mud.

I noticed that the hatless man was also shoeless and had a bandage around one ankle. The other two appeared to be shocked and stunned, but no bandages showed. The one with the bad leg seemed most frightened, as if his mind just couldn't percolate under the severe shock of the realization of what had happened to *him*; as if the unimagined horror of being hurt in combat was simply overwhelming. I remembered what Razor Blaydes had said about how the Vietnamese wounded seemed impassive and unemotional. This certainly was not true of these three frightened men from the Ranger Battalion.

Anderson inquired of Hartsock by interphone: "We got three wounded aboard?"

"Yes, sir."

"Are they bad?"

"No, sir, not bad."

Hartsock ripped open a field ration and passed out cigarettes from the small box inside. I gave them the candy.

I heard Horton calling in to Danang tower: "This is Two-two. I have three WIA's [Wounded-in-Action] aboard—I have casualties to go to the hospital."

Allgood, the Element leader, also called in, helping to prepare the way for the arrival of our three wounded: "This is Eight-five. Eight-five. I have a helicopter with wounded."

In a few moments the Danang tower instructed us to take the wounded to the landing field near Danang Hospital for ambulance pickup. The time was 12:48.

We flew toward the coast, passed over a line of metal-roofed buildings, and cranked down into an area which evidently was the helicopter pad, for an ambulance with a large Red Cross trundled out toward it as we came in.

As Hartsock and I helped the three injured men out of the aircraft, it occurred to me that I didn't know what their injuries were and, with the language barrier what it is, probably would never know. But Hartsock's off-the-cuff analysis was probably correct: they weren't badly wounded. Also, it was possible that their injuries weren't caused by enemy gunfire.

I had a chance to check up on that when we got back to the Marine field and passed through the ready room. Eric Coady and Madigan told me that their troops had been shaken up when their landing gear collapsed. One of the troopers had been clonked on the head by the rotor as the plane tipped over. Lts. Blair and O'Neil, the two pilots whose aircraft had picked up Coady and Madigan, confirmed this.

Lts. Ding Dong Bell and Dick Chapman (of Los Angeles, Calif.), whose aircraft had been shot down by enemy small-arms fire in the LZ, were still around the ready room, the center of an attentive group of pilots.

Ding Dong: "We heard something hit, the aircraft shuddered, then the crew chief screamed that it was leaking."

Chapman added, "Bell said, 'Take it, Dick, It'll go.' "

Bell picked up the narrative: "Then we got out. Didn't you see us fighting across that open field?"

"You sure looked naked," one of the audience agreed.

Allgood had left the ready room, and I found him over at his quarters in the Marine barracks. He still seemed calm and alert, despite the near-miss. I asked him about his feelings when the bullet hit, and he said:

"I thought I had it, because I was watching that part of the windshield when the round came through. There must have been a cupful of glass flying around. I went to the doctor after the other two lifts, and the doc washed out my eyes. But he couldn't see any glass in them."

I asked him what he thought about the net results of the assault operation of October 15, when I had flown in his plane and the net result from that air-phibious operation had been three VC's killed and one wounded.

"For that kind of operation," he said, "where they pulled in the T-28's, we should have had 12 AD-6's [A bigger, more formidable ground-support airplane] with rockets and bombs —they would have blasted the top off that ridge, really would have blasted them out." There was plenty of fight in Frank Allgood.

Incidentally, Allgood was born the son of farming parents, at Fulton, Kan. Neither parent had a high school education, but he managed to get a college degree at Springfield and then went to Kansas University for his M.A. in teaching. He taught a year, but his heart wasn't in it. Once, at the age of 16 and 17, he had worked in the oil fields near Teapot Dome, Mont. "That was a man's country," he said. "It was an experience I was very glad to have. You were not supposed to show fear on those high rigs." The memory of that experience had stayed with him, made him yearn for a career of action. He had gone on to the Marine Corps in 1953. "I got to Korea, but the war was over," he said. "I missed the Korean war," he added with evident regret.

At lunch I picked up another facet of the story of today's air-phibious operation. Don Klepsattel, with whom I had flown the mission on an OE the other day, had been observing during today's assault.

"I saw the two birds go in," he said. "The first was the Coady and Madigan chopper. It slewed around and I thought it was going to turn over. Then the other one went in—I didn't see much of a security guard around it."

After lunch, I asked Rathbun if he was going to go in after the two birds. "It's being done now," he told me. "You can't wait a minute. Dark's coming on. You've got to go in and shoot it." I guess he meant fix up the birds so they can be flown out.

I also asked him about that static-filled conversation I had overheard between him and the Vietnamese T-28's, when he was trying very insistently to get them to strike the area to the right of the LZ, where we were getting some VC fire. (That was the time he had said that the radio transmissions from the Vietnamese were "breaking up.")

I read the annoyance in his face as he thought about it, and then his self-control took over. "Don't get me started on that."

Later, I talked to Lt. Col. Bob Losse (of St. Louis, Mo.), who at the moment was chocolate-colored mud up to his thighs and his boots were dripping from wading around in the paddy. He had flown in with Maj. Cignotti, the chief of maintenance, to assist the repair crew working on the two downed birds. The shot-up chopper had been repaired successfully and was now back at the base.

Col. Losse is not attached to the Marine outfit here. He came down from Japan on temporary duty to check up on the communications facilities, and the trip into the LZ, with its attendant muddying, was a volunteer service.

He said, "The mechanics worked like heck and repaired the plane with the hole in the transmission. The one with the broken strut is still there.

"The Vietnamese troops are thick around the aircraft for at least a thousand yards. They said the VC had been trying to hit the aircraft all day, but there is no firefight going on." He added that there had been some mortar fire on the southern edge of the LZ area, according to reports that filtered into the vicinity of the downed aircraft. But in general, the loss of the aircraft has changed the plans of the Vietnamese for a sweep to the west. They had to leave a heavy security force around the two aircraft, to prevent their being damaged or captured by the VC.

I saw Rathbun and Blaydes in Rathbun's room later in the afternoon. Razor said he had heard reports from the Vietnamese that the troopers in the assault landing killed two VC's— and the latest gossip was that the round that hit the Bell— Chapman chopper was of small caliber and high velocity. (The bullet splattered when it hit the transmission deck.) This led to the usual crop of rumors that the VC might have some new high-velocity arms similar to our M-14's or M-60's. I have seen many captured VC rifles and pistols in the rooms of the squadron people here, but all of them thus far have been homemade weapons, fashioned out of lengths of pipe or tubing, with crude trigger and bolt mechanisms. The Arvin authorities, of course, pick up the workable modern arms captured from the VC for their own use, so only the homemade weapons are available to the pilots as souvenirs. But judging from the aft-eraction reports I've seen and from what I've heard from the pilots and advisers, the VC have a pretty motley collection of homemade arms, only slightly augmented by what they can capture from the Arvin troops or bring in from China by coolie-back.

I asked Blaydes his opinion on this. "That's the way it is," he said. "Some guy up there has a popgun—so we splatter the place with T-28's."

There is no doubt that we do have a tremendous advantage over the VC, not only in our helicopter techniques, but in our abundance of firepower.

Rathbun and Blaydes were working over a photo-map of the same area where we landed troops this morning, developing a plan to bring in a striking force to one flank of the VC position, in an attempt to close a pincer movement on the VC flank—that is, if the VC flank can be discovered.

"You have to find them first," Rathbun said. "They're pretty good at the fast fade-out."

Sunday, November 4

A check with the frags at the ready room this morning showed that the second of the two aircraft downed yesterday was still in the LZ under heavy security guard. The efforts of the repair crew to fix the broken landing gear hadn't worked out. On their second flight into the LZ, weather had kept them from landing.

Clouds, still hanging heavily over the mountains, were an effective curtain to the west. The pilots were lounging around the ready room, ready to go, but all flights were put on stand-by, pending improvement of the weather.

Maj. Cignotti was on pins and needles to repair the damaged chopper. "We've got to get in before three," he said. "We'll need three hours to fix that strut."

Beside the OD's desk at the entrance to the ready room stood the bullet-pierced windshield from Frank Allgood's aircraft, YP 85. Frank was claiming the glass pane as a war souvenir, and no one would contend with him on that issue. The panel had already been replaced by a windshield from "Ciggy's Junk Yard."

A major from I Corps MAAG was on hand and standing by for an action—evidently the same flanking maneuver that Rathbun and Blaydes had been plotting last night. The major was Bill R. Beuch, whom Blaydes had mentioned in his briefing yesterday as having been shot at when flying through the coalmine pass months ago.

Beuch relayed the latest action report from the troopers who had been landed in that LZ yesterday: "As of 1400 yesterday, there were two killed and two wounded [he meant Communists] and some of our people got hurt."

Maj. Beuch had flown into the LZ with Cignotti's planes yesterday when they repaired the shot-down aircraft. He described the sniper fire directed at the planes by the VC's during the time he was there. One round hit the ground near the disabled Marine plane during that afternoon: "I heard it hit and saw it kick up the ground. It fell about 30 feet away. I'd say that guy [the sniper] was at maximum range for that rifle."

I had the chance to talk to some of the pilots and crewmen who were waiting around on stand-by, and fill in the chinks of yesterday's action. One of them was Cpl. Bob J. Loftin (of Port Arthur, Tex.), crew chief on YP 89, which picked up Madigan and Coady after their bird cracked up. Loftin said:

"I saw those guys [Communists] firing. It was on the second trip, when we were coming in from east to west. It was right beside the river, on the right side, a group of about 10 to 15 around the edge of a clearing. I could see some of the muzzle blasts. I'd say they were mostly wearing black, and some had dirty green uniforms, or some off-the-wall color. I'd say they were a way off from where we were—about 300–400 yards. I heard the firing. But it didn't sound like automatic fire."

In this, our second, landing yesterday, the plane in which I was riding had been ahead of the shooting: the fire had hit Bell's plane two elements behind us. In the first landing, we had been closer to the action: The round had hit Allgood's plane, leading our element, only 60 or 70 yards ahead of us.

Talking to Loftin, I found that he was no exception to the general rule that the crew chiefs are married and familied. His wife's name is Barbara, and he has two kids, a boy, two, and a girl, three. He said he has 23 assault missions to his credit since he came to Vietnam.

At 8:30, Maj. Blaydes announced to the ready room: "OK, all flights except Six-zero, stand by in your flight gear in your rooms." In other words, the weather was so bad that most of the pilots could stand their alert in their barracks rooms.

By 11 A.M., the weather situation was so bad that the weather flight (Six-zero) still had not taken off. Cignotti was still standing by in the hopes of taking a flight in to repair the remaining Marine chopper downed in the LZ, but chances still looked grim.

I went back to the barracks and fell into a bull session with Allgood, who now had his war souvenir standing up against his wall.

Strangely enough, he said practically the same thing Blaydes had offered as a way of winning the war: "I'd get a lot of Marine airpower in and bring the troops up and seal off the border, and then work backward." Not a bad solution, assuming that he had the trained manpower to do the job.

Monday, November 5

There was no change in the coud cover this morning, and it was still drizzling. I bummed a ride down the line with Razor

Blaydes and Harvey Jensen, and we splashed belly down in an impromptu lake near the barracks, the jeep floorboard-deep and immobilized in the water. We were pulled out by a truck in short order.

The weather still had all flights on stand-by, including the flanking movement Blaydes and Rathbun have been working on. The plan of that assault mission is to lift 120 men onto the flank of the VC estimated positions near the coal mine. (Cignotti's plan to fly in and repair the Madigan-Coady plane so it could be flown out of the area also was on weather-stand-by status.)

I talked to Dave Webster while waiting for some action, and asked his opinion on the way in which we should prosecute this Vietnamese war. Webster's position and experience and judgment are pertinent, because he works every day with the Vietnamese people over at Corps, and has to arrange liaison for the American Marines involved. This strongly colors his views.

Webster, who majored in history at Yale, is a most literate and intelligent man and has told me about his ambitions to write. At the urging of his wife, he has just signed up for a $400 course that teaches writing by mail. (He was killed in a helicopter crash in January, 1963.) Webster's answer to my question, "What in your opinion should we do to expedite our campaign?" reflected his immediate background and experience in Vietnam: "We should do it their way. If we try to do it our way, we'll have friction and won't get it done anyhow."

The mission to carry a company of Ranger Battalion men into that flanking surprise attack on the VC's was scrubbed because of the weather. But Cignotti's flight of two ships finally took off, despite the weather.

I got aboard one of those aircraft, climbing into the troop compartment with a cargo of rescue equipment and tools, and there found Sgt. Robert T. Keasler (of Grand Prairie, Tex.). Lts. Keith K. Kerr (of Purcell, Okla.) and Ed Madigan were the pilots of the plane I rode. Cignotti and his maintenance and repair associates were riding in the other aircraft.

The flight was uneventful. We dropped off the repair party and didn't draw any fire—indeed, the LZ seemed quite calm and peaceable. We were back at the Danang field by midafternoon. The two birds would have to remain on stand-by to go back later to pick up Cignotti and his crew in case they weren't able to complete their repairs before sundown, But the repair boys did their job, and the bird was able to fly back under its own power.

Tonight, at the mess hall, there was a special cake made for COLONEL JULIUS W. IRELAND OF TASK UNIT 97. It commemorated the departure of the commanding officer of this outfit, who was being promoted to a higher command in Okinawa.

The colonel brought some of the cake over to the O Club and made a speech. He spoke easily and well: "I'm new to helicopters, but I've been flying left-hand seat with some of the world's best helicopter pilots, here in Vietnam, and I'll be coming back about once a month from my new command, MAG 16, and I'll expect to put in some more left-seat time here."

The new commanding officer of the outfit will be Col. Tex McCully.

At the party for Col. Ireland, Bob Rathbun was kidding McCully about the authority he would now have: "Now that you're going to command the Task Unit, I expect to be wickered out of the Hong Kong R and R trip."

McCully was noncommittal at first, but Rathbun needled him further, saying that he had talked to McCully about it earlier and he knew from what McCully had said that Tex would never stay here at Danang and let the squadron commander go to Hong Kong. This time Tex said, "Damn right."

Tuesday, November 6

Checking with Corps this morning, I found out that the last air-phibious operation, beginning last Saturday, has been more successful than the previous series of assaults undertaken by the Marine choppers on October 15.

This time, according to Maj. Wagner, the American operations adviser at I Corps, the Arvin discovered a couple of supply dumps that belonged to the VC and near there killed three VC, captured two prisoners, and recovered two trip grenades set up as booby traps, which fortunately were not detonated. In the fighting in that vicinity, one of the Arvin troopers was wounded and one of our automatic rifles was captured by the VC.

In the ration dump we captured 600 kilograms of rice, 500 kilograms of salt, and 15 cans of kerosene.

But as usual, the bulk of the enemy had escaped and, apparently, carried away some wounded with them.

"A central problem is that of intelligence and counterintelligence," said Wagner. "The big problem is to locate the enemy and prevent them from fading away.

"We must know where the Army is: the secret bases, the recent infiltration routes, the rear areas. We now have much of the information."

Maj. Wagner introduced me to the Vietnamese Deputy Chief of Operations in this Corps Area, Maj. Nguyen Van Hieu, a slight, alert, well-scrubbed individual whom Wagner, in an aside to me, characterized as "very bright." The Vietnamese operations chief spoke highly of the strategic hamlet program: "In each tactical area, the Army is responsible for support, barbed wire, and weapons, and we are making progress. Elections are being held in many of the strategic hamlets."

Maj. Wagner said the VC offensive operations in this area recently have been small-scale. "Since June, we haven't run into VC concentrations of battalion strength, but they're now in the stage of building cadres for offensive operations. The first [Communist] phase is to get recruits and build up their armies, the second phase is to have advance bases near the lowlands, and the third phase is to take over the lowlands.

"Quang Ngai is the major objective of the VC in this Corps Area. At Quang Ngai, the mountains come almost to the coast; that is, on the north and south side of Quang Ngai. The Quang Ngai vicinity is giving us the most trouble right now."

I asked Wagner what the greatest need of the Corps Area was in terms of equipment, and he replied, "We could use three or four squadrons of helicopters." I was glad to see that he had the same zeal for our new magic weapon that I had seen among the Marine pilots.

"We need a reserve, a reserve striking force, helicopter-trained, so we can commit them fast. We need quicker reaction time." He added that the hardest tactical situation in the overall Vietnam campaign right now is in the Delta area.

"Our situation here, compared to the southern part of Vietnam, is not nearly as critical as, for instance, in Camau or Soctrang. Compared with that area, the VC up here is very far away."

I took advantage of this visit to Corps HQ to put through a call to the PIO at Saigon. After the usual protracted struggle, I reached Cmdr. Zornow in that office and had some cheering news: I'm all set to go down to the 93d Transportation Company at Soctrang. Furthermore, I'm now cleared by the Vietnamese government to make T-28 missions, up here in Danang or in other parts of Vietnam.

As soon as I could, I checked with T-28 pilot Byron Kalin, who said no strike missions were scheduled for today but there might be something tomorrow.

Wednesday, November 7

This morning I checked with Kalin, who as yet had no definite word that T-28 missions had been scheduled for today. I then went over to Corps HQ to begin the cumbersome military arrangements for the flight down to Saigon.

While at Corps, I heard that Brooks, Deibel, and Frickie, the three American adviser officers who usually go out with the 10th Ranger Battalion, had just come back from their most recent foray against the VC.

I sought them out at their billet, the Unity Hotel, a former French pension, and found them still with mud on their boots from the long hike back. Deibel, the former pro-football player from Boston, said, "The VC had really worked over that first town with propaganda. They had signs about the mercenary Americans, and 'My Diem' [American Diem] written everywhere with chalk. They also said, the way they always do, that the Americans are *cobans*, meaning 'no good.' "

Frickie, the specialist in hand-to-hand combat, told about the VC his outfit caught in the first village. "The VC's were trying to get out of that village. There were three VC killed there, and we got one POW.

"The next day we sent another patrol and had another contact. We captured one guy and another got away. The guy who got away dropped a bag with photos of Ho Chi-Minh and other VC people in his outfit, and a letter from Hanoi and also one of introduction with a VC stamp on it, identifying him with a photograph and stating his rank and training.

"From the first day's POW's, we got a rucksack. It had an OD blouse in it. But no weapons. Those guys all hide their guns, throw 'em away."

Deibel said the Commie guerrillas get into their black suits and say, " 'We're not VC. We're laborers, not fighters.' " He added that the job of guarding the two downed choppers had taken a lot of troops away from the offensive operation they had planned. "When we got that sniper fire on the first day, we saw some movement about two-thirds of the way up the mountain above it. It might have been where the fire was coming from. We blasted them with machine guns and didn't get any more [fire].

"It sure was a big relief when the last helicopter took off. We were afraid they [the VC] were going to bring mortar fire on them. They [the VC] sure missed a bet with that last chop-

134

per. On the third day all we ever got was a couple of rounds in the rear."

Our little conversation was interrupted by news that a train, heading north out of Danang toward Hué, had been blown up by the VC. I rushed back to Corps HQ, got a jeep ride back to the Marine flight line, but missed the troop lift that was being sent up to aid the dynamited train.

I cussed myself out for having missed a story, although I soon learned that the Marine lift got to the train too late to see any trace of the VC.

The Marines who took the troop lift in came back from the mission, and six helicopters were on stand-by in case another troop lift should be needed or the scene of the train wreck suddenly erupted into action again. In the ready room, some of the pilots who had made the mission were still standing by.

One of the pilots, still shaken up by the experience, was Lt. John Calvert, of Buford, S.C.:

"We were at Hoa-My, giving some SDC troops practice in loading and unloading the birds. Then we got the call to take 48 troops up to that beach. It was kind of like a 'Tiger Force' ["Tiger Force" is the designation for a small reserve striking force of the kind mentioned by Maj. Wagner yesterday], but it was their first action, and they were SDC troops.

"We landed on the beach about ten yards away. We could see the second car of the train blown up. It looked as if it was blown in half. It was a cattle-type car, all busted up, but it was still on the track.

"The passengers were spread out as if they were defending themselves from the hills inland of the tracks. Right at the place where the train was blown up, the bridge was out too, or beat up anyhow. There were three armored cars on the track which had come up from someplace. There was one dead man, a civilian, on a stretcher beside the train [it turned out later that the so-called 'dead' man was not mortally wounded]. There were also two WIA's that I didn't see. There were about 30 or 40 people around the train. The VC's must have come down from the high ground on the inland side of the train track.

"We didn't have much chance to look around. It was just a quick landing and then: get out."

Lt. Miles Gunter was moved by what he had seen at the site of the train wreck too: "Did you see his legs? One leg was almost completely severed. It was almost like he got run over by the train. He had his legs splinted and he had wounds in the face, his teeth knocked out. He must have got a plank right in the face. There were three dead. That one woman shot by the VC in the head, and there were three WIA's."

I got still another account from a MAAG adviser from Corps HQ who had gone up with the Marine lift and was still around the flight line: Capt. Maxwell R. Thurman, a bespectacled, fast-speaking, sharp-minded infantry officer (from High Point, N.C.). With him now was Maj. Wagner, who had also made the trip up to the site of the ambush.

Thurman gave the best account of what had happened: "The charge went off underneath the car right behind the engine. The train had an engine and eight cars.

"There was only one radio in the train, and that was in the car that got blown up. They must have had good intelligence.

"The radio was a TR-20, belonging to USOM [United States Overseas Mission]. The car was wrecked; they [the VC] probably put about 30 pounds of dynamite underneath it, and the radio went with it. There was no radio communication, so the VC came down and started lecturing the people about VC objectives.

"The VC got the passengers out and gave them a propaganda lecture. That woman. I personally saw her with a hole in the back of her head. Dead. The story is that she got shot by the VC when she wouldn't do as they wanted. It looked as if they were trying to collect some money from the passengers. Then there was that Arvin sergeant with leg wounds. [That sounded like the 'dead' man I had heard about before.] There were a lot of Arvin soldiers riding on passes on the train.

"There were probably about 30 VC. The Tiger Force [the mobile reserve that the Marines took in] is chasing 'em now."

Maj. Wagner, calm and deliberative as always, said, "That Tiger Force idea worked well. It was a kind of impromptu Tiger Force, but it could have worked well if we had got there a little bit earlier. They [the Vietnamese HQ people] were trying to send the armored train in with the armored cars. But once they got there, the Tiger Force did fine."

I said that today's development, even though the time schedule was a little bit mixed up and delayed, was good confirmation of what he had been saying yesterday and that the idea of a mobile striking force, alert for emergency action wherever needed, was vindicated today. That's the way these principles are being worked out, by trial and error.

At 4:40, the news was passed to the pilots on stand-by

around the ready room: "Secure the staff now." The alert for the day was over.

Tonight, at the O Club, some of the officers were continuing the discussion of the advantages of having a quick-acting small force standing by with the choppers for emergency commitment. Maj. Webster was loud in the praises of this "concept of instant retaliation," but he added that we need better radio communication and liaison to get the troops to the objective more quickly.

Youthful Lt. Allen agreed, and cited his own experience in the airlift that was sent up to the train wreck today: "We were sitting around today for 20 minutes at Hoa-My and we saw those armored cars go on up on the tracks while we were waiting. We could have been up there a lot sooner, and we might have caught those VC while they were still lecturing the passengers."

Thursday, November 8

This morning in the ready room I found out from OOD Joe Baranowski that there wasn't much doing so far in the way of missions: "There are a lot of little frags . . . some resupply, one bunch of five aircraft going to Mang Buk and stopping at Quang Ngai, where there's also a lift of 4,000 pounds of cargo and four passengers into the coal-mine area, and two aircraft going to Miet Xa with passengers and freight."

I was debating what to do when a call came through from Col. McDuffie at I Corps HQ to say I should stand by for a possible T-28 mission. But by lunchtime, nothing had developed, the weather was still holding up scheduled Marine flights to the outposts, and the T-28's had received no further orders.

I went back to the barracks and started talking to Rathbun about the favorite subject of the officers hereabouts: how our side can win this war. He said, "One of the main things is you have to have the support of the people, we have to do that." I told him that at Corps HQ, Wagner and his opposite number, Nguyen Van Hieu, had been trying to get some of the static and useless outposts disbanded and some troops made into a mobile reserve. I also told him that Wagner had suggested that he'd like to have three or four helicopter companies in this Corps instead of one. I also mentioned that junior strategists at the O Club were talking about the firehouse concept of a Tiger Force standing by with the helicopters all the time.

Rathbun had evidently been giving this idea some thought, for he came up with a quick answer: "You can't make the operation that big. You immobilize troops that way, anyhow."

At this point, I had another telephone call from McDuffie. I was to get down to the Air Force hangar immediately about the flight. I knew what he meant by the cryptic reference: the T-28's were going to be flying right away.

At the hangar I located the T-28 operations office. There I met the American who would be flying on today's mission with two Vietnamese pilots. He was rugged-looking, grizzled Lt. Col. Herbert R. Mann (of Lawton, Okla.). The two Vietnamese were slips of men, Lt. Ng Huy-Cuong, aged 27, and Lt. Vu Dam Thuong, 24. Both were wearing gray flying suits and, like the T-28 pilot I had seen at close range, they looked very Americanized. They wore American-style insignia: a tiger, in this case set in a yellow star, instead of American white, to indicate that it was a Vietnamese rather than an American outfit. They also wore a patch identifying their unit, which was a Disney-type caricature of a wolf, with the word *Lobo*. Both had trained in the United States, at Reese A.F.B. (Tex.) and Spence A.F.B. (Ga.).

Col. Mann was a fighter-pilot veteran of both World War II, and Korea, scarred with experience, but still looking fit. We piled into his jeep, lugging parachutes, which he flung on the hood as we started out for the planes. He explained the habit of carrying the chutes on the hood of the jeep: "I've done it in three wars: with the P-51's in World War II, F-80's in Korea, and here for 18 months." Mann briefly explained today's mission as we rolled toward the line of racy-looking T-28's at one end of the Air Force area: "The target for today is some VC concentrations. Inland of Quang Ngai."

Mann explained the Vietnamese operations rule I already knew about: I would have to fly with a Vietnamese pilot. The Vietnamese Air Force (VNAF) didn't want two Americans in one T-28. That would make operations seem excessively American.

As we came abreast of the planes, I saw that they carried an insignia very much like AAF insignia: the white star in a blue circle—but in this case there were yellow bars across the circle to indicate Vietnamese affiliation. The planes looked very primitive compared to modern jet fighters, but also very dashing—something like the fighters of World War II or the Spanish Civil War. We got out and climbed into our chutes, and Mann helped me to adjust the seat of the plane in which I'd be riding.

I was to fly with Lt. Huy, the leader of the flight, with Col. Mann on one wing and Lt. Dam on the other. Mann said to me as I slid down in the seat behind Lt. Huy: "He's a qualified flight leader." Vietnamese armorers were checking the fangs of our little tiger aircraft: four rocket pods, roughly the shape of bombs, hung from the wings of each T-28. And there were muzzles of .50-caliber machine guns in each wing.

We lost no time: The afternoon was already advanced and we would have to be back here before dark. We started engines at 3:20 and inside two minutes were taxiing out toward the runway. We whipped off the ground and snapped toward the coastline, my plane leading the formation. Flying at 150 miles an hour at 300 feet, we made a gentle curve to the right, toward the south and Quang Ngai.

It was a bright, clear day as we flew along China Beach, but ahead to the south and inland lay towering gray mountains of rain clouds. Here, it was perfect flying weather, and the racy little planes with their skittish maneuverability were all that an old-time fighter pilot could ask for.

These T-28's are the Navy model of old Air Force trainers, the type used at the time of the Korean war, except that these have a slightly more powerful engine. Roughly the same engine, incidentally, as that used in the Marine helicopters; but since the T-28's are so much lighter and built for maneuverability, they are very perky little aircraft.

At 3:44 we turned away from the beach and headed inland toward the high-piled, dirty clouds and mounds of mountains rising into them. Then, within two minutes, we seemed to be right on the deck between the clouds and the mountains and speeding into thickening masses of mist as we climbed.

I tried to talk to Lt. Huy on the interphone, but his English wasn't equal to any involved conversation on an airplane radio. I'd wanted to find out a little more about our mission, but I rapidly gave up. Soon I would be seeing for myself. At least I could see well—the tall Plexiglas canopy was clear in every direction except directly ahead, where Huy's bulbous crash helmet stuck up.

The air was bumpy, our planes slewed around, we dashed through scuds of clouds and over mountain ridges thick with dark green jungle. Then, almost without warning, we were riding down ridge and curving over a steep valley. Now I knew we must be on something like the run into the target area, because the rattle of our engine was much louder and my airspeed meter showed that we were verging on 200 knots, which is getting pretty close to maximum for these antiquated planes.

Suddenly we did a pinwheel turn, Huy stood the aircraft up on a wing-tip and flung it around like the arm of a compass, apparently in a move to confuse any possible observers on the ground. A moment later we charged down a green ravine toward a forest river at the foot of the mountain. In the noise and excitement, and the g's of our dive (our airspeed indicator was showing 225 knots), I couldn't see any target ahead— nothing but the massed pompoms of green trees and, ahead, the jungle stream with a strip of sand on one bank. But no people, no houses, no target that I could identify as such. However, the pilot must have had houses for his target, because in a second I heard our rockets go *charrmmpp*—like a soft chord of thunder.

Huy manhandled the plane into a steep climb. The thick jungle that we had been charging straight into turned up on edge and slid behind, and we saw the rain clouds ahead. I knew we were pulling g's, because my vision grew dark, my neck snapped, and the camera I was holding up to get pictures to the rear suddenly became three times its weight and I was having trouble holding onto it.

We were circling as well as climbing at full throttle, and I tried to train the camera back to cover the other two aircraft, which were following us in single-file runs down the slope toward the target. I could see the second plane (probably Col. Mann) firing its rockets as it swept down that steep grade; the pencils of white smoke rising strangely straight up; and the tiny pirouetting shape of the aircraft.

Then, the third T-28, its white wings pinwheeling into a sharp turn, was charging down the slope. Trails of white smoke arched slowly in front of him into the green muscle of the hill. I knew the first strings of smoke must have come from the ground: a fire caused by rockets from the second plane?

That was the first of our targets. We had another one lined up. We headed west in the thin layer of air between the low-hanging clouds and the thrusting mountains, and at about four o'clock, under hanging shreds of gray cloud, we were circling over a bend in a river. Bony mountain ridges trailed in several directions, pelted with that thick hide of green jungle.

We spun around on our wingtip again, and I saw the throttle handle in my dual controls go forward as the pilot accelerated. In a second we had flipped over and were in a steep diving run, at maximum speed, toward the sharp bend in the river. There were some houses on the slope just above it: evidently our target. Beyond them, I could see the bank rising sharply into a high ridge. This was going to be a hard pull-up, if we were to avoid pranging into the mountainside.

I watched the head of Lt. Huy, the crash helmet cocked forward over his controls, and I could see from the position of my control stick that he was intending to make a low pass over the houses, holding his dive so that the plane would be a steady gun platform.

Suddenly I heard the *chunng* of the rockets and saw the long, furry streaks reach out toward the river bend. But before I could see them hit, we were pulling up very sharply. The jungle-green slope abruptly changed to gray cloud as we flung into a wing-over.

We circled back toward the high ground above the river to the south, still flying at full throttle, and went into another vertical bank and sharp pirouette. As we started into our second pass on this target behind the third plane, I saw his rockets streaking like long white claws in front of him, curving into the forest near the houses at the bend of the river.

As we roared in again, I saw the blink of firing down below from among the houses. An orange flash appeared among the trees just above the river; at the same moment I picked out a couple of houses in a clearing nearby. We were swooping down with such *Götterdämmerung* clatter and vibration that I didn't have time to estimate what kind of houses they were or if they were our target. The orange flash winked again, and once again. We were getting enemy fire.

This time there was no *chunng* of rockets going out: this was a machine-gun pass. I heard the surprisingly slow pace of our .50's: *Bap-bap-bap, bap-bap, bapapp!* In a second we had gone over the houses and were pulling up sharply. Gray clouds, which had suddenly appeared in front of our nose, were sliding off to one side, half of them replaced with greenery as we spun around on a vertically banked wingtip.

Having felt some severe g stresses while handling the camera, I grasped it for dear life and tried to train it on the second T-28 as it roared down the slope toward the houses. But in the stress of the sharp turn, the camera rode low, feeling at least as heavy as the last time. In the welter of camera and camera-case straps, mike cord, parachute straps, and the large notebook I was trying to balance without dropping my pen into the recesses of the cockpit, I couldn't seem to bring the camera into position for a picture. In a few seconds we were making another sharp turn in the other direction—presumably to throw off the people who were firing at us from the ground —and the whole river bend area fell out of sight. We zoomed over the top of the nearest ridge, still at full, protesting throttle, turned again, and once more came charging down the slope. I still hadn't seen any human figures down there, but smoke was rising from the tall trees near the houses—probably the result of the rockets or the machine-gun fire that we three 28's had been pouring into the area.

We swooped into our third pass on this target and I hoped it would be our last. One steep, maximum-speed dive into a deep valley, with a 3- or 4-g pull-up after the pass, would be enough. But more than one was wearing, to say the least.

I watched my dual controls as Huy held us in our deep dive. The stick was jammed forward, the throttle knob in the same position to ensure maximum speed, the stick moving nervously from side to side as the pilot trimmed his plane for the strafing run. His helmet was tilted forward as he lined up his plane on the circular gunsight in front of his face. But this time it was the rockets that fired, not the machine guns. Because we were pulling up very sharply, I didn't see the rockets curving away from us—or even see the houses.

We climbed up in the sky this time, heading north and west and holding a straight course for a few seconds after the initial turn. Before we put a mountaintop between us and the bend of the river and the other T-28's, I remember thinking that at last the mission was over and we would be heading back home. But we no sooner got over the ridge top and into the next valley than we were turning again. I could pick up no clue from the excited conversation I heard on the command channel (it was in Vietnamese), but it was very clear that we were going back for at least one more pass. And a rather shocking fact about this kind of aerial warfare was beginning to dawn on me: Here, because ground opposition was light, compared to World War II or Korea, it was possible to make many more passes over an enemy target. In the other two wars, it had been a supreme effort and risk to penetrate enemy defenses, drive in to the target under heavy ack-ack fire, and get your bombs out without being shot down. And after dropping the bombs, you still had a long exit route, sometimes besieged by enemy fighters, before you could get home. You certainly hadn't hung around long in the target area: it was too dangerous.

Here, the situation was quite different. Even when there was antiaircraft fire, like the flashes we had seen from the ground, you had the obligation to stay airborne over the target area and come back many times to make sure that you got hits.

That was exactly what we were doing now. Again I tried to locate the houses, again I waited for sound of the guns or the rockets (each pass involved firing either rockets or guns, not both), which somehow is always a shock to the nerves.

We made four, five, six passes, the other two planes tailing in behind us each time. And each time there was the same tension, the same knotting in the chest as we committed ourselves to the run, then swept up in a wild violent wing-over to escape possible antiaircraft fire. But there was no more ground firing. I remember thinking that we probably effectively discouraged them with our second pass.

We made our sixth pass at 4:09 P.M., this time with the popping .50-caliber machine guns. Then we headed straight north and held our flight course: Had we made our last run for today? I hoped so. But we circled once more, making an even wider course than before, and headed back toward the target houses again.

By this time the other two aircraft had completed their passes, and I could see no sign of smoke from the ground. Presumably, all three of us were out of rockets and just about out of .50-caliber machine-gun ammunition.

At last, it seemed that our mission was going to be over. Huy continued to gain altitude and headed north and inland into a low-dripping gray cloud, which swallowed us quickly. Because the T-28's use such primitive navigation techniques, Huy had to keep his formation in sight all the time, so he wouldn't lose them. He dove sharply to escape the cloud and chopped back his throttle, waiting for the other two planes to catch up.

Soon they came up on our wings, and we were heading in the direction of home, scooting through low-flying islands of clouds that bounced us considerably. Beneath us, the high mountain ridges were close, but Huy wanted to fly below the clouds to keep contact. The two T-28's were tucked in close beside us; frequently the adjoining wingtip was riding in the notch between our wing and tail.

We headed east out of the high-mountain zone toward the coastal plain. Poking our way up through a belt of high clouds, we flew above them, at 7,000 feet. When we came down again, the mountains were definitely lower and we could make out the white strip of the beach along the South China Sea. Now I knew our mission was over, and Huy looked back at me inquisitively, apparently trying to see if the violent maneuvering up there had upset my stomach. He asked a question that I couldn't quite read, even on a second go-round: His accent was a little too thick, especially on the interphone. He smiled slightly and extended a finger, whirling it in a spiral pattern, apparently to indicate that everything was OK and that we were heading home.

The restful stretch of white sand and the clear aquamarine water were a very welcome change after the steep dives and turns, the machine-gun and rocket firing, up in the jungly mountains. At 4:28, we reached the long curve of Danang Bay, and minutes later we came swooping in for a landing, making the same kind of violent, hot-rod turn that I had almost become used to in the course of this afternoon's business.

A wave of heat and nausea swept over me, but as we touched down, Lt. Huy cranked back the canopy and a flood of fresh air burst over us. In a few seconds, I wearily extricated myself from the cockpit and joined Col. Mann and Lt. Dam in a jeep parked nearby. They had already looked over their planes for bullet holes. None there.

On the way to the T-28 operations HQ, I asked Mann and Dam if they had seen any firing during their passes over the last target, and Dam said, "Yes. They firing straight to me. Very fast—*da-da-da*."

In one of the operations rooms Mann introduced me to the debriefing officer, a young lieutenant, Allen Gray (of South Orange, N.J.) who was wearing a gray flying suit.

Somewhat in the manner of schoolteacher on a lectern, Gray unfolded a sheet of questions and began to interrogate us about the mission. Col. Mann was the most articulate, of course, since the debriefing officer evidently spoke no Vietnamese.

Mann said that, on the first target, one of the six houses blew up as he made his rocketing pass. That would account for the smoke we saw. "It was an explosion similar to that caused by highly volatile fuel. It was a ball of fire, about twice the size of the house."

Lt. Gray led us on as rapidly as possible: "OK, where's the next place?"

"A VC concentration," Mann said.

In giving a description of the area, Mann spoke about two rope bridges, which I had completely failed to see. They must have been below the target area. All the pilots talked about the houses there, and little Lt. Dam had a chance to talk about the enemy fire he had seen as he made his second pass into the target area: "Before I start to fire, to shoot the gun, they shoot me."

Dam, still very excited about the firing, told his story at least three times, even including the imagined sounds of the firing that he glimpsed winking at him from the trees: "*da-da-da*—coming straight to me, very fast."

Lt. Gray, concerned with more objective reactions, went through his list of questions: "Any people, caves, trucks, fortifications?" And fixing the pinpoint targets we had been after on the map: "Read off the pinpoint to me . . . what speed were you traveling at the time? . . . in this target area, or down here, did you see any helicopter landing areas or possible landing strips?" Gray was assiduous in amassing intelligence, and Lt. Dam, somewhat handicapped by his lack of English, was still telling his story: "I start to fire, but before I fire, they shoot me."

When we folded up our session, I walked out with Col. Mann, who seemed satisfied that this had been a successful raid: "We had an explosion—and that probably indicated that we hit a gasoline-storage area, or at least a fuel area. We had a good explosion and some deterrent fire from the ground—quite an eventful mission. Sometimes we have nothing."

Mann drove me back toward the Marine hangar in his jeep. I asked him about his family, always a productive topic of conversation among the veteran soldiers of Vietnam. How did his long separation—he had said earlier that he has been here in Vietnam 18 months—sit with his family? Obviously he had extended beyond the usual one-year tour of duty here. How, I asked, did his wife like that?

"My wife is a captain in the Air Force at Clark [Clark A.F.B., in the Philippines], so it's no hardship. I have seen her once since I came here, and I'll see her again."

One saving grace in his domestic situation, Mann said, was that he and his wife have no children.

He told me, as Col. Kalin had before, that the AAF officers here in Danang had come as advisers, but "they [the VNAF] were short of pilots, so we sold them on our program." Which meant that the American pilots were filling in as pilots on bombing, strafing, and rocketing missions against the VC. The only limitation was that the flight leaders of attacking formations had to be Vietnamese.

Tonight at dinner I told some of my Marine buddies that tomorrow I will be leaving to fly down to Soctrang and have a look at the Army's helicopter operation. My friends assured me that I was taking my life in my hands by attempting to make missions with the Army. It was one thing, they said, to fly with a combat outfit that had been trained for assault operations, like the Marine helicopter squadrons. But the Army —that was something else. One of the boys said, "The Army guys try hard, they're pretty able people—but they have a half-ass airplane and half-ass maintenance, so naturally they have a half-ass operation."

Whatever the operation, I'll be getting a firsthand look at it pretty soon. Tonight I went through the dismal job of packing up the weighty impedimenta of a war correspondent in Vietnam: rucksack, air mattress, canteen, knives, camera equipment and typewriter, green fatigue clothes and flying suit, extra shoes, and the really fundamental equipment: my big diary, pens, foot powder to guard against fungus, spoon and can opener, bug repellent, toilet paper, and a supply of no-go pills. Of all of these bits of equipment, probably the most basic are the no-go pills, because in a country where the "go" viruses are exceptionally plentiful, the kind of control no-go pills can give you is irreplaceable if you are going to be doing a lot of flying.

The Army

This morning I got a ride down to Air Force headquarters at the field with Chaplain Vinson, our soft-spoken padre who had a distinguished record in the Navy, in the Korean war, before he entered the ministry. The chaplain gained the Silver Star for running a landing boat into the Inchon beachhead under heavy enemy fire.

Now his previous military experience helped as we threaded our way through deep mud puddles. Each time the jeep seemed about to shudder to a stop, he down-shifted expertly, and we slithered through. He commented, "I've driven more Diesel engines than I've given sermons."

I knew the story of Vinson's becoming a minister. During the Inchon landing he had been acting as coxswain of a landing boat, and had stood up for a moment to look at some obstacle forward of the boat, when a Communist gunner had swept the rear, killing and wounding several of the troops, missing Vinson. He had reflected on that experience and wondered why his life had been spared. It was this reflection which had turned him toward the ministry.

Chaplain Vinson dropped me at the C-123 part of the Air Force hangar, and I booked in with the next flight going to Saigon.

There was the usual delay about picking up an Air Force flight. This small section of the hangar had been set up as a kind of impromptu terminal. Therefore, 15 or 20 servicemen lounged about with their barracks bags, waiting for the next lift to Saigon. Behind the counter there were the usual weary enlisted men, bored with their noncombat job. At last I got through to the sergeant in charge and was told there would be some wait before I could get on the next southbound C-123.

I was told that there was a tent somewhere in the area where passengers could wait. I found this club of sorts in the third row of tents a couple of hundred yards from the hangar. I managed to find a place to sit and even a cup of warmish coffee. There I met a tall, graying, erect colonel named Wirt Corrie (of Crewe, Va.), who introduced himself as "the mayor of tent city," a modest way of saying that he was the senior Air Force officer in this installation and the boss of Cols. Kalin and Mann and the other T-28 pilots for whom I have learned so much respect.

Col. Corrie spoke proudly of the American combat pilots working for him: "The thing I am trying to insist on is that they send me only highly qualified people . . . I try to spread them around to as many kinds of duties as possible so they can sit around the table when they get back . . . I think the President announced this as a way of life. It's as important for us to train as the Vietnamese."

Corrie explained that he meant the pilots who came here would automatically become experts on the kind of small anti-Communist war we seem destined to fight. "I am a sort of a counterinsurgency expert. I guess a lot of us will be occupied with this for a lot of years.

"My approach to this—air. It's making a big difference here. I think it is *the* weapon."

He spoke enthusiastically about the T-28: "The beauty about this aircraft is the big wing, and the turning radius allows us to work in the valleys. The T-28 is a trainer with a little extra power . . . this war allows slow flying: you don't have opposition."

I asked him about the opposition we encountered on yesterday's mission, and he said, "The VC ordinarily don't fire unless they are spotted. When you see fire, it's a sign that you have spotted them." Col. Corrie praised the Vietnamese T-28 pilots: "They learn fast. At first they needed guidance in leading flights, but they catch on. They fly quite well and they shoot beautifully. They operate well against ground targets."

He chuckled. "Some of the VNAF pilots have sort of gone Hollywood. But it is good for them. They're eating American food and putting on weight."

Back at the C-123 section of the hangar, I found that one of those birds was getting ready to take off. I joined the passen-

148

ger load of nine Vietnamese medics and one AAF enlisted man. As the crew chief said, it was "a light load only."

We struggled into parachutes, were briefed on emergency procedures in the event of engine failure or bail-out over the jungles, and settled back into the lumpy canvas seats with the assurance of a noisy ride and no lunch. Fortunately, by this time I had learned my lesson about traveling in the 123 and had brought along a can of salted nuts, which I shared with the Vietnamese soldiers on either side, while the crew members ate their box lunches at a distance.

We landed in Saigon at 1:15, naturally too late to get any food—but then, you can't expect military transport to provide anything like the comforts of an airline. However, the PIO made up for that somewhat by sending out a station wagon to pick me up and take me to the BOQ.

My friends at the PI office, Smith, Zornow, and Galfund, told me that I probably couldn't get orders cut to go down to Soctrang until Monday, which meant if I went by Air Force transport, I would probably have to wait until at least the following day to go. But Galfund said he thought he might be able to arrange transport with the Army, which is less formal than the Air Force about transportation arrangements. Meanwhile, Galfund was telling me about a recent casualty in the new HU1A (called "Huey") outfit that has come to Vietnam. Last Saturday, this outfit lost their first man, a gunner killed near Vinh Long; and in the same engagement one of their officers was hit in the heart and saved a fatal wound by his armor vest. I decided that while I am waiting for transport to Soctrang, I will try to reach this Huey outfit, which is based at Tan Son Nhut airfield, here in Saigon, and talk to some of their people.

Saturday, November 10

I went by the PI office early this morning and got Maj. Galfund to go out to Tan Son Nhut with me. You need a military escort to get into the side of Tan Son Nhut where the Huey outfit is quartered.

On the way out to the airfield, Galfund told me that the trip to Soctrang is definitely laid on for Monday, and that he will be going down there with me. It will be nice to have company on an assignment, especially Galfund, who had a distinguished combat record with the infantry both in World War II and in Korea. Galfund is a wiry, graying, tough-talking New

Yorker who earned a Silver Star during the European campaign in World War II.

We found the Hueys, unmistakable with their huge two-bladed rotors, lined up near a maintenance hangar. The planes looked, and are, practically new. The first jet-powered helicopters to reach Vietnam, they carry interesting machine guns and rocket tubes mounted beside the fuselage—Army fighter helicopters.

We were met by the CO of the Huey company, Maj. Robert E. Runkle (of Fort Scott, Kan.), a tall, lean officer with light blue-gray eyes. He drove us over to the tent camp of the Huey company, which is known officially as the Utility Tactical Transport Company (Helicopter) (UTT). I told Runkle that I wanted to do a story on Johnnie Lee, the gunner who was killed a week ago, and on the officer who had been hit in the heart and not been hurt. Runkle said he would introduce me to the people who flew with Lee, and also to Capt. Steine, who had had such a narrow escape.

The Huey tent camp was barely that: wall tents set up over board platforms, with mosquito bars visible inside, like blocks set up on thin-legged Army cots.

"We'll be in screened tents in about a week," Runkle said. "It'll save a few people at roll call—they might otherwise get carried away by mosquitoes."

On the subject of the outfit's first casualties, the major was cool and steady: "It's a shame when something like that happens. But a man would be a fool if he thought it wasn't going to happen."

Runkle was a combat veteran of the Korean war, where he served in a rifle company and was decorated. When I asked him what decorations he had received, he said, "The Bronze Star, the Purple Heart, and scared."

We had lunch at Runkle's tent: lamb, green peas, ice cream, and pie. "The best food in the area," Runkle said, and it was the kind of treatment that a combat outfit like his deserves. He said his new outfit has flown 60 to 65 missions in less than a month. This is possible because the pilots mut fly as many as three or four missions a day. Runkle said that he has flown 25 missions since he came here and the pilots in general have had from 15 to 40 or 45.

The CO said that the fighter helicopter of the Huey type is an innovation in warfare, but that it seems to be working out very well—these jet-powered helicopters are giving a good account of themselves. When they fly along to escort the troop-carrying H-21 choppers, the enemy ground fire tends to diminish. "The most successful missions have been where there were VC, but they chose not to fire because the Hueys were there."

Despite his combat experience, the recent casualties seemed to prey on Runkle's mind. "This is so ironic. I tried to prepare my people. Quite logically, we expected a couple of injuries before a fatality. It might be a year before another. Or it might be on today's mission."

Maj. Runkle introduced us to Maj. Ivan Slavich (of San Francisco, Calif.), his executive officer. Slavich will be taking over the company on the 25th of this month, when Runkle goes back to the States to pass on some of his know-how to Army aviation units. Slavich, a clean-cut, well-scrubbed, and erect former Marine, was also a combat veteran in the Korean conflict. Runkle said, "Those of us who had combat experience —we've built it into them [the others] to be real conservative." He explained that he meant they would have to expect casualties, since this is the only Huey outfit functioning and they would be flying on practically every major assault mission with the various troop-carrying helicopter outfits, like the 93d, the 33d, and the 57th.

About that mission of last Saturday, which cost the outfit their first casualties, Runkle said, "We had pretty heavy opposition. We figured there was at least one automatic weapon. Two pilots saw automatic tracers, but we don't get shot at on every mission, by a long shot. Quite honestly, I can't say I've ever been fired at—and Slavich, once or twice. . . . Sometimes there is not a round fired."

A young, blue-eyed officer came into the tent: it was Capt. Joel R. Steine (of Warrenton, Ga.). Steine is one of those good-natured, smiling types to whom everything seems to happen and who always manages to carry off his adventures with an air of insouciance.

He said the firing last Saturday broke out at the second LZ of the day's assault operation. "The H-21's reported fire from this area, and we made a pass. On that first pass we picked up one round through the roof. It knocked some soundproofing loose—it was floating around the area.

"On the second pass, I'd been firing for about three seconds when this round came through the windshield and through the instrument panel and ended up hitting me. It knocked the breath out of me. It was like getting hit with the dull end of an ax.

"My copilot, a MAAG lieutenant colonel named Blackman, took over the controls. I did a rapid damage assessment, found no damage, and took the controls back.

"It was the same area in which Johnnie Lee was killed. He was hit approximately one minute after I was. Mr. Wright [CWO Richard H. "Pappy" Wright of Augusta, Ill.] was his pilot. Lee was the gunner.

"The [Wright] aircraft was behind me. We heard on the radio—Mr. Wright reported—that he had a wounded on board.

"There was a lot of firing going on, and we were receiving a lot of firing. You can tell by the sound when they are close: they snap. The noise was so great, I don't remember hearing the sound of my machine guns."

Steine said he was astounded to pull the bullet out of the pocket of his armor vest. It was a .30-caliber bullet, and a smooth-bore, which didn't get through to his flesh. He said he went back to fly five more missions after that one. He flew eight missions all together that day. Yesterday, he said, he flew some more missions and the enormity of his narrow escape had dawned on him. "You should have seen me yesterday. I had on two armor vests, 40 pounds of armor."

Steine said that he had written to his parents—his father owns a clothing store in Warrenton—and that he had been able to call through to them by trans-Pacific telephone yesterday.

"I went down to ITT and placed a call, and got right through to my father. Being sort of hard of hearing, and being's he likes to have a couple before dinner, he said, 'I hear your voice, I know you're well. I'll let you speak to your mother.'

"She said they'd just received my letter and they were talking about it. She said that the papers had run a story about a captain being hit in the heart, and they said that it was in this unit, but didn't give the name. She said that she had had a premonition."

Another officer came in to Runkle's tent. It was the grizzled CWO, Pappy Wright, the most veteran pilot in the outfit, with 3,000 hours in helicopters to his credit. About Johnnie Lee's death he said:

"We were escorting the second lift into LZ No. 2 and making our second pass, when we got some automatic weapons. We could hear them. Johnnie called and said he'd been hit. I thought he'd said the bird had been hit, but the blood came up. I asked the Arvin [the Hueys are required by the Vietnamese military to carry a Vietnamese Army representative on every flight] to do something. He took one look and said no—he turned thumbs down. Lee was still alive and still conscious when we carried him off the aircraft, but he died right about then. I guess he died of shock."

Pappy Wright was no stranger to action and casualties. He, too, had served in the Army in Korea, after first having served in the Navy as a PBM gunner.

Wright told how Johnnie Lee had been wounded: "He was sitting on a folded groin protector, but the bullet just missed it. It hit him in the big artery of the leg."

As we left Runkle's tent to go back to Saigon, I asked him if he was going to recommend Steine for the Purple Heart. Runkle said, "In view of the fact that Lee was killed, Steine doesn't want the Purple Heart. He got what he wanted out of it: nothing." Runkle gave us his jeep to get back to town, and before we left, I asked him if I could do some flying with the Hueys. He said it would be tough, because normally they carry two pilots, the gunner, and the Vietnamese observer, but that he might be able to figure out some way in which it could be done.

Seeing us off, he said, "The armed helicopter is proving to be more effective than even I hoped for. I think they [armed helicopters] have a tremendous field in counterguerrilla operations."

Maj. Runkle's driver, PFC Robert Hanna (of St. Louis, Mo.), drove us into town, and on the way I asked him what sort of a man Runkle is, and what he thinks of Runkle as a person. He answered simply, "We love him."

Back in town at the BOQ, a former French apartment building, I was reminded that, unlike the Marines at Danang, the people of this high headquarters in the capital city close their military operation down for the week end, beginning Saturday noon. If you talk to the Americans hereabouts on the subject, they point out that Ngo Dinh Diem is a Roman Catholic and naturally observes Sunday as a day of rest, so why shouldn't they? Nevertheless, it's somewhat tough to take this change if you're used to living with people who figure that this is a seven-day-a-week war and that the main difference between Sunday and the other days is that you might also have church services.

I went up to the terrace on top of the Brink Building, where there is a bar and a small jazz band that plays on Saturday nights beside a dance floor, and where the Americans are allowed to bring their wives and girl friends for drinks. It's all very civilized, except that no dancing is allowed under a recently passed Vietnamese "morality law," which forbids dancing as unbecoming the conduct of war. However, it seems that there should be other ways of indicating one's willingness to fight.

Sunday, November 11

Today, which used to be called Armistice Day, was for me a day of rest in Saigon. It was the kind of a day you must have once in a while for personal maintenance and related chores.

But I did have a chance to get a kind of preview of what the campaigning will be like down in the Delta country. In the Brink mess I met two young officers who had spent months in the Plain of Reeds to the south quite recently. They were Capts. Earl Starboard (of Big Lake, Minn.) and Bob Scofield (of Tacoma, Wash.).

Scofield is very husky-looking, with the kind of musculature one gains from weight-lifting. A graduate of West Point in 1953, he lifts weights at the gymnasium downtown, and coaches football. Starboard is small and wiry, with a slight mustache.

Scofield said that he had made many operations with Vietnamese troops in the south, and three times had fallen into the VC mantraps. Mantraps are pits, lined with spikes and covered over with greenery, which the Communists set for Vietnamese troops on the trails. In each case, Scofield had fallen in only part of the way and had been able to hold onto the edge of the trap, so that he wasn't hurt.

Starboard counted 22 operations he had made in the embattled Delta area with the Vietnamese Seventh Regiment. He said his first firefight was in May, when "we caught the VC with a river behind them, and the battalion commanders cut across corner and trapped 'em."

But Starboard pointed out that the fighting in the south often has some of the same frustrating overtones as the anti-guerrilla activity in the north. "You have to land right on top of them, or they disappear. The first 50 meters the guy's a VC. The second 50 meters, he's thrown his weapons away. By the time he's gone 200 meters, he's a peaceful farmer. The big, successful operations we've had down here have been when we landed on top of 'em."

The Vietnamese soldiers are "good troops," Scofield said; "they're stoical, they don't complain, they'll follow their leaders—God help them!—and they have a lot of resistance."

Scofield, who lost 43 pounds during the time he served as

adviser to the Tenth Regiment of the 7th Division, said he was never sick when he was out with the troops. "I only got the drizzlies when I got back because the food seemed rich. Out there in the field they ate *nuoc mam*, rabbit—which probably was cat—and dog."

Starboard said that in the matter of uniform, he soon learned that the main thing was to have an extra pair of shoes. "I took one extra pair of boots and a change of underwear and socks, and a jungle hammock and a Vietnamese poncho, a plastic square for driving rain. I got so I could carry all this in a map case." Starboard said he agreed with Scofield that the Vietnamese were "damn good troops."

Tonight I was busy again with assembling all of my gear for the next move. The plan now is that Allan Galfund will be leaving tomorrow afternoon at 1:20.

Monday, November 12

Galfund and I got aboard an Army Caribou, a Canadian-made troop transport, and the trip down to Soctrang was short and pleasurable. We didn't even have to wear parachutes, and that particular design, the Caribou, is a lot more habitable than the prickly C-123's.

Within an hour we were over Soctrang—a spreading of houses over a juncture of rivers, with canals cutting the ground between. Close to the town we saw the black-top strip of the airfield, with helicopters lined up along both sides of the runway, their rotors like clustered flower petals. There was a large hangar, which appeared to be of French manufacture, and rows of concrete buildings, barracks. As we came in for a landing, I could see the airfield was surrounded by green swamp and a thick gauntlet of barbed wire, with security gates and guards. This was the famous helicopter base, center of the toughest American fighting in Vietnam, once home of the Marine choppers, now the base of the 93d (Army) Soctrang Tigers.

As we taxied up to the operations building, a CWO named Willie Ruf hurried out to greet us.

Ruf said, "Too bad you didn't come yesterday. We had a good one this morning."

I asked if anyone got hit and he smiled and said, "No, not on our side. There were VC all over the place. One guy I see with his rifle up, I figure I'm going to get it. Just then an HU1A let go with a rocket. The rifle went one way and arms and legs were all over the place."

Ruf took us over to the quarters of the CO, Capt. Chuck Benedict (of Independence, Kan.). Benedict, a patient, bright man with a battered face, pugnacious jaw, and the easygoing manner of an enlisted man, said that Ruf was right—the day's mission had been something. "There were VC flags all over the place—and a lot of people running. And it looked like pretty good bag. All the reports aren't in yet, but so far we heard of 8 KIA's [Killed-in-Actions] and 14 POW's." Benedict had also seen the episode described by Ruf. "Ruf saw three VC's run into a hut. There was a Huey hovering right next to him and he let 'em have it: a rocket right through the front door."

We went around to the O Club, a bare, new concrete building with a bar and a line of well-tenanted stools, gray leatherette lounge chairs (Vietnamese-made) and cocktail tables. On one wall was a collection of VC souvenirs, homemade rifles, the drive shaft of the helicopter in which Maj. Gray had been flying when he was shot down, a VC flag, and some VC camouflage helmets. There was also a chart showing the number of our aircraft hit and shot down: the list was formidable.

This O Club required a minimum in the way of dress. Many of the men wore T-shirts and shorts or merely bathing suits, with chests bare and rubber go-ahead slippers on bare feet—altogether a sensible costume for this festering, wet tropical climate.

Sunbrowned, muscular Capt. Don Toth (of Pen Argyle, Pa.), maintenance officer of the squadron, showed me the squadron mascot, a puppy called "Tiger." He was of indeterminate breed, what we would call a Heinz Terrier back home, and he was clumsily cunning, with huge paws, innocent eyes, and a shaggy light brown coat. Toth said that Tiger has had 10 missions, flying with the 93d on 10 air-phibious operations.

"He's on his way to his first Air Medal," Toth said "but he probably never will get it. I wish they'd either give 'em [Air Medals] or just say never mind. None of this business of putting in for it after twenty-five missions."

Apparently the question of Purple Hearts has been much in the minds of these pilots, who have had the largest number of wounded of any of the helicopter outfits in Vietnam. Toth introduced me to the only one of the pilots so far who has been put in for two Purple Hearts, CWO Edward Gilmore (of Pekin, Ill.). Gilmore had his last wound at Tay Ninh.

That action, Toth was telling me, erupted when the Hueys were first fired upon, about two weeks ago.

"We had an aircraft down with a bad engine, the VC's

started to overrun us. We had T-28's and Hueys operating around there, and they went right into the VC.

"There were about 20 VC troops moving out of the woods. The Hueys came in to point-blank range. Three of the VC's got up. The Huey gunners got the three.

"Our troops were backing away from the wooded area, and our gunners were firing. There were tracers all over the place. We hovered to get maximum effect. It was a real donny-brook and that's when Gilmore got it—but it wasn't too bad, as you can see. He's all right now."

Gilmore said that the hairiest operation he could remember was when the 93d was up in Danang and two birds were shot down, lost. That was the operation called Lam Son II.

"The area had been worked over by the AD-6's of the Vietnamese Air Force. They had hit the area, but they hit the ridges instead of the Landing Zone. Intelligence proved later that the VC had previous information about our operation. They had their positions all prepared for automatic weapons.

"The particular area where I landed they had arranged in defilade.

"We got hit in the drive shaft. It set up a big vibration.

"The two choppers that got hit and had to land came down in an area that was untenable. Four other birds were disabled in the LZ, but got out.

"One of the gunners on the aircraft flown by CWO Don McPeak took seven hits. A sp/7 named Benson, a crew chief acting as gunner, took two bullets in the leg. He was evacuated to the States.

"And the ship flown by Maj. Gray and Lt. Stone was shot down, and both of them were wounded, as well as the crewchief, Billy Watkins—35 holes in their drive shaft."

I had heard this story before, from the people up at I Corps. It was strange that it should persist in the memory of the pilots of the 93d, too, as their hairiest mission.

Gilmore added modestly that he had been copilot in the aircraft flown by Don McPeak, the one that took the seven hits and in which Benson took the bullets in his leg.

"It was automatic fire. It hit the rotor blades, the transmission—five went into the fuselage—everybody in the aircraft got hit by flying shrapnel."

That had been Gilmore's first wound.

Another aircraft, No. 032, flown by Capt. Bertram Leach and Lt. Harold Bergdahl, a former commercial artist now a pilot, took a round through the windshield. "The round hit in front of Bergdahl—it nearly hit Leach—and went down the drive shaft and knocked out the servos. That meant the pilots had to manhandle the aircraft—it was like when the power steering goes out in a car. But they got the aircraft back to Quang Ngai."

Capt. Don Toth said the two downed aircraft in that operation had been Nos. 662 and 350, but of the others hit, "One took a round in the fuel cell, and others got rounds in their blades."

It was strange that the Marines up in Danang looked back with homesickness on the actions they had left behind in Soctrang as the hairiest of their careers, whereas the 93d remembered some missions in present-day Marine territory as their roughest.

The pilots got into a bull session about their worst missions, the discussion provoked when one of them said:

"They're all about the same; it's just the ones where you get hit or lose somebody that are the worst ones."

Don Toth recalled one hair-raising mission the 93d had taken part in three weeks ago.

"We dropped off our first load of troops and went back for another. If the area was secured, there was supposed to be a red panel out.

"We couldn't tell. We went in, and found out. The first ships got shot up. In the first airplane—that was Mr. Kibler's [CWO Robert Kibler of Erie, Pa.]—the crew chief got hit. The second aircraft caught a load. The oil cooler and servos got shot out, and they couldn't get off the ground. The crew chief was killed—he got hit by two rounds, one in the heart and one in the back.

"At the same time an L-19, flown by a captain, was shot through the control cables. The VC, they just popped up from everywhere, shooting.

"I saw three or four taking pot shots at us. I saw one guy shooting at our aircraft, out in the open, before he got it. That VC was on a suicide run, it seemed to me. He couldn't get out.

"On that same mission, two VC's jumped up and our first sergeant got both of 'em with his carbine.

"In that action, we had our fourth aircraft destroyed, and the Hueys fired 20,000 rounds of .30-caliber and 180 rockets, the pilots told us."

The bull session and drinking session was still going on, every bar stool in the place occupied, all the chairs at the little tables taken, when Capt. Toth took me along to the barracks to show me my quarters. He told me as we walked in the blistering heat of the dazzling tropical afternoon, "We've had five wounded so far," he said. "The hell of it is, when you come back, they say, 'Where've you been?' and you say, 'Vietnam,' and they say, 'Where's that? What state is it in?'" Toth said there will be a mission again tomorrow, with a briefing at operations tonight.

There was still enough light left for a game of volley ball as we made our way to the operations building. A clamorous group of ground crewmen, and some pilots who aren't going to be flying on tomorrow's mission, were jumping for the ball at a net strung just outside the concrete building. The door was open because of the sweltering heat.

Inside, a group of 30-odd pilots sat on chairs or the concrete floor or leaned on the counter of the ops room, while Chuck Benedict did some of the briefing in front of a large situation map.

He was pointing to the map and talking over the din of the boys playing volleyball outside: ". . . the first five ships land in the north side of the objective. The second five on the south. On the second lift, we split again: the first four on the right, the second four on the left. . . . These [the enemy] are Territorials, the equivalent of the SDC among the Arvins. [He meant that the VC opponents we will be encountering tomorrow will be more like the Vietnamese government SDC than their regular Arvin troops.] Their TO [Table of Organization] is only two BAR's for a company. The rest of 'em have spears, crossbows, homemade rifles, and all the rest."

One of the pilots spoke up from the floor: "You can still get a Purple Heart from one of those BAR's." Benedict nodded soberly and went on: "The Hueys will want clock position for fire." I was cheered to know that the HU1A's will be protecting us in the landing maneuver.

Someone asked, "Are they going to be daisy-chaining over us?"

"They are," said Benedict, with a big smile, indicating he felt as I did about having the support. He went on: "Take-off is at seven o'clock. We'll be there at 7:53. Crank engines at 6:50."

After the briefing, I walked to quarters with Benedict, who confirmed that he was always cheered by the presence of the Hueys. "I don't feel too good when we're going in. You know the VC are there, or you wouldn't be going in." The newly arrived major who will be taking over as CO of this squadron, Paul Ewing (of La Crosse, Wis.), agreed. "We're learning how to do this," he said. "We're a little bit handicapped by maintenance and lack of aircraft. You need three companies to get sixteen planes. But after all, we're writing the book here. We've got a lot to learn. It's the first time helicopters have been used like this."

At the light pole in front of the barracks—a heavy tropical night had fallen—I saw a vibrating cloud of specks suspended in the yellow electric glow. When I got closer, I saw what the cloud was: swarms of green bugs, about as big as gnats, which clustered wherever light showed.

CWO Richard B. Adams (of Leominster, Mass.) had the cubicle next to mine in the barracks. I asked him about the bugs. He said, "Sometimes in the morning they're a half-inch deep in the washbasins. Sometimes it's green bugs, sometimes black, sometimes it's crickets."

I complained that these mill around blindly without any apparent method, bombard your hair and fly up your nose and into your mouth. He smiled tolerantly: "They don't hurt you, they just harass you."

Nevertheless, the bugs are a big pain, and I rapidly discovered that they also have a knack of getting through the mesh of your mosquito net.

The fact that there is a shower building here in the camp took some of the curse off the bug assault, especially since some farsighted soul had turned off most of the lights in the washroom vicinity and the insects were not hovering in such great numbers. I bathed myself first in water, then in repellent, borrowed a bug bomb from Adams, and saturated my sack with DDT before climbing in.

Tuesday, November 13

Getting up about 4:30, I was pleased to see that the bugs had retreated. Those little pests had kept me awake a good deal during the night, despite the precautions I had taken before getting into bed. There were several hundred dead ones in the sack and on the floor, but no fresh attacking waves.

In the washroom, Adams' prediction had come true: There was a liberal coating of dead green bugs in every washbasin. However, there was water to wash them away, plenty of it, in contrast with the situation in the Marine camp at Danang, where the water supply was always temperamental.

Maj. Galfund and I were assigned to aircraft No. 690, pilots to be Capt. Toth and WO John Walsh (of Wayne, Penna.), whom we had met last night. Both are capable, levelheaded officers with steady nerves—as we discovered in the course of the day's operations.

Galfund and I found our aircraft just as the first yellow gleams of dawn were illuminating the lines of sway-backed choppers ranged on either side of the runway. There was a light on in the cabin of our ship, and the crew chief was working over an Army clerical form with Don Toth. In the long, barnlike cabin, a little brown beast wobbled on unsteady legs, his eyes more pitiful than ever: Tiger, the outfit's mascot.

Toth was saying that Tiger had been through a bad night (probably not as nervous a night as a lot of the human beings involved in today's mission, who knew what was in store for them).

"He [Tiger] got into some hot sauce last night and foamed at the mouth. But he seems to be all right now."

The crew chief and the gunner were busy with preflight chores. The crew chief on these H-21's tends the rear door, at the left. The gunner has a station at the forward doorway, on the right side, where a .30-caliber machine gun is mounted on a steel bar.

In this case, the crew chief was Sp/5 Ted Taylor (32, of Hutchinson, Kan.) and the gunner PFC Burl McDonald (20, of Pixley, Calif.). The older man had the weightier job.

Toth and Walsh walked along the side of the aircraft, giving it a good-natured once-over. "I guess it'll go," Walsh said. "All the parts are here."

Toth responded in the same spirit: "I counted six blades. A good airplane."

We climbed aboard, got into our armor vests, and placed our armor pants as seat padding. Galfund and I sat on a row of canvas-covered seats opposite the machine gun manned by McDonald at the front of the troop compartment. The seats were not bad, more comfortable than the C-123's, and at least there were a set of earphones and an intercom jack nearby, so we could hear the radio calls.

The main impression in this barn of an airplane was of size. It seemed much larger than the Marine helicopters, but I knew that the troop-carrying capacity was the same and the power of the engines a little less. This aircraft had gone into production in 1951, and undoubtedly some of the aircraft in this Army company dated back nearly that far. The line of broken-back "flying bananas" that were supplying helicopter transportation for today's assault looked hopelessly awkward and antiquated. In its time, the H-21 was a marvel and it made wonderful things possible in infantry tactics, but it should have been long since replaced by a newer type of helicopter like the HUS or, if we had really bent our brains to the problem, by a ducted fan, a jet-powered aircraft that can take off vertically, hover, make all kinds of speeds from reverse to 400 mph forward, and land vertically as well. Such aircraft are at last available in the experimental stage, but right now we are stuck with flying bananas in Vietnam.

At 6:58, our two rotors began to revolve, the huge, slow-turning windmills shaking our big bird as they gained speed. At 7:04 we rolled out a little bit toward the center of the wide runway, and were airborne. This bird felt completely different from the Marine choppers, mainly in that it seemed relatively powerless. Even without any troops aboard, one had the feeling that this H-21 chopper was straining to get into the air.

The longer sweep of cabin with its two doors and the fact that the pilot and copilot are visible through a wide-open cockpit door gives an impression of spaciousness that is lacking in the chunkier, more compact Marine helicopters.

I looked out the forward door, past the downy-faced gunner whose crash helmet carried the name MAC on the back, in red letters. He was smoking nervously. At the rear door, the older of our two crewmen, Ted Taylor, was calmly watching the paddies go by.

I heard some conversation on the interphone about Tiger, the little sad-eyed mascot of the outfit. Evidently Toth and Walsh had stashed the little beast somewhere forward. Walsh was saying to someone on the radio, "We've got Tiger." And I heard another voice, a worried fellow pilot in another aircraft: "The little bugger better not fall out."

Mile after mile, we passed over sheets of shimmering green rice land, mostly under water, diagramed by ditches and canals. The H-21's, strung out in a kind of loose Indian file (the Marines flew in relatively neat two's), were heading for Can Tho airfield, a staging area built out in a swamp near a marsh town where we would be meeting other helicopters coming down from the north. With these choppers from the 57th Transportation Company in Saigon, we would have 16 helicopters available for today's assault.

At 7:32, we came in for a landing over a little strip of gray-topped runway, with some old French country houses nearby: ugly orange-colored concrete blocks with tile roofs. As our wheels touched down, I could see that a couple of L-19's had already landed, and five helicopter shapes were already parked beside the runway. They were the wasp-waisted, bulbous-headed Hueys, their rotors like two-bladed antennae, from Bob Runkle's UTT company. There was a headquarters tent set up near a lagoon, and several companies of Vietnamese troops, in American green uniforms and helmets, clustered along the edge of the pond.

We pulled over to one side of the runway and Toth shut down the engine. Other birds from the 93d were squatting down like chickens, their clattering rotors and engines sending mountainous dust clouds flying. While we were waiting for the rest of the choppers to arrive, I had a chance to talk to Taylor and to McDonald. Taylor is rugged-looking, with a rough face, and he seems to have plenty of savvy about this war in the swamps. He was wearing jungle boots—as he said, "If you wear regular boots, they get wet and they swell up. These dry out. If you wear regular GI boots, you get sores on your feet." Taylor, who had a hillbilly accent, told me that he had worked in a steel mill at Pueblo, Colo. back in 1948. He'd worked in a blast furnace for a while. Now he has 13 years in the Service.

He talked to Mac gently, as a veteran to a neophyte, instructing him about a smoke bomb—a cardboard container with metal ends. He took one from a rack on the bulkhead of the plane. "You know what to do with this smoke?" Mac said no.

Taylor said, "If we get hit, don't ask nobody, just pull the pin and let it go. Pull it quick." The purpose of this smoke bomb, he explained, was to warn the other birds that one of the 93d's helicopters was going down, and to serve notice that the crew had to be rescued.

I asked young, plump-faced, blue-eyed Mac about his background. "I worked as a clerk back in California. But I like this flying. I've been here eight months and been on eight missions." Taylor said wearily, "I must have a thousand." Mac was clearly aware of his inexperience in the gunning art, and seemed very eager to learn.

Mac is one of four children and has a half-brother in Germany; his father grows oranges, alfalfa and cotton.

The various aircraft required for our air-phibious operation were arriving. First, a couple of specks swiftly materialized in the sunny sky, then two more: saucy little T-28 fighters, which, with the Hueys, would convoy us to the LZ's. The T-28 pilots buzzed the field, right on the deck, and pulled up in sharp wing-overs, then made fast landings—true Hot-Shot Charlies.

At 8:52 we saw a line of dots coming from the north: the helicopters of the 57th Company. They wheeled in and squatted in dust clouds, the same breed of sway-backed H-21 as the 93d.

I followed Toth and Walsh up to the lead ship of our

formation, where pilots from our outfit and the 57th were gathering for briefing.

Capt. Ray Delahanty, the operations officer, was holding up a military map against the Plexiglas nose of the chopper. He spoke about some changes in landing procedure, then gave us the critical intelligence about expected enemy resistance: "There's about a company in there, in black, as always. You know if they stand still, they've got the word and don't expect to be shot at. But if they start running chase 'em."

There was a bit of byplay after the briefing as one of the American Military Advisers (a captain) came over from the headquarters tent and put a hand-embroidered patch on the chest of one of the 57th pilots. The captain was Richard A. Jones (of Berkeley, Calif.), a lean, hard-bitten blond man whose uniform testified to his experience in the swamps: a small pack high up on his back to keep it out of the mud, jungle boots with canvas shanks and rubber-cleated soles, a steel helmet covered with a camouflage net; and he was carrying a Swedish K submachine gun, which I had already learned from the Marines is a very savvy weapon to carry.

Now, he pinned the patch, which carried the legend, SAIGON COMMANDO, on the shirt of a baldheaded, chunky helicopter pilot, Capt. Tom W. West (of Hiram Falls, N.Y.). The patch was intended to satirize the fact that the 57th is stationed close to Saigon and therefore the men are exposed to the blandishments of the big city.

Tom West, one of the veteran pilots of the 57th and a West Point graduate, pretended to be very moved by the presentation. He started to sob and wiped his eyes with a flak vest, saying, "Ah, you shouldn't 'a' done it." The episode got a laugh —it was the kind of comic relief needed in a tense moment like the one beginning an assault mission into VC territory.

We tramped back to the airplane and I noted that Toth, who had once been a teacher, spoke paternally to the new gunner McDonald: "We're going to be the last one on the flight. Look on the outside. Everything on the inside will be taken care of by the Hueys. If a guy jumps up in front of you, don't ask for his name, just get 'im."

In a few minutes, the troops, which had been standing by near our choppers, moved toward the doors and climbed aboard. They were well uniformed, with steel helmets and camouflage nets, jungle boots and M-1's. The squad in our aircraft had a radio, and their faces seemed older and harder than some of the SDC troops I had seen up north.

At 8:40 we were off, and the feebleness of the H-21's was even more apparent. We had quite a long run along the landing strip before we could get up enough lift to clear the ground.

We headed west over a wide, muddy river and Mac zealously worked a cartridge into the breech of his machine gun and fired four or five rounds into the water to set up his gun for action. Then he pulled on his armor pants and crouched over the gun, even though it was not yet time to go down to the deck for our approach. The Army favors this kind of right-on-the-deck approach as being safer from the point of view of antiaircraft fire. The Marines follow a different theory, claiming that, higher up, they are visble for a longer time to a ground marksman but make much more difficult targets.

A few miles beyond the river, we abruptly descended and started flying at 25 or 30 feet, skimming over the tops of the watery fields. At the same moment, the engine started groaning and shouting at higher speed, and we felt the increased vibration of maximum pitch. We were evidently starting our run in.

Toth and Walsh bent concentratedly over the controls. We were rushing along at bloody great speed, lifting over every line of trees to duck down to the deck on the other side. As we swept over groups of farmhouses—thatch-roofed, mud-floored dwellings in clusters among the rice paddies—McDonald swiveled his .30-caliber at every passing house, ditch, and rice field, anxious to be prepared for any sudden hostility.

This "contour flying" was a roller coaster: one minute sweeping so low over the fields that it seemed we would clip off the top of the rice plants, the next minute skimming the tops of the palms—sometimes there were thuds as our landing gear hit tree branches. All you could do was hang on and hope, but the speed was exciting; a kick.

Mac was very alert, bobbing and weaving like a boxer. You could see that he kept a spear-sharp eye on every rice field, but so far, nothing down there was moving.

This contour flying went on for 5-10 minutes and it seemed as if we were never going to reach our LZ. Then, suddenly, the plane seemed to slow, as if brakes were being applied, and our aircraft was jumping over a ditch and splashing into a paddy. Near us sat a barnlike farmhouse, dark, spooky, and empty, and beyond it another ditch. The only sign of life was the flapping take-off of a black bird, which rose from the ditch behind the house.

The troops, clumsy as football players in their heavy gear, started bundling out of the aircraft. In the H-21, it was the crew chief's job to shoo them out the rear door of the compartment while the gunner, at the forward door, kept an alert eye and a ready machine gun on the surrounding territory.

I went down the cabin to make pictures of the little men jumping out, clutching the M-1's that made them seem even smaller. They were flopping without hesitation into hip-deep water, struggling toward a dike that rose some 50 feet away. For such little fellows, they strode manfully enough through the muddy water, among the stubs of rice plants. They held their weapons above the water as they wrenched their muscles forward through what was evidently deep mud. They had to turn their bodies for each step.

The last trooper out, the engines roared and we began to lift slowly from the paddy. I went forward where Mac was still crouching over his gun, sweeping it from side to side to cover any possible movement below us. As we gained six or seven feet of altitude, there was still no movement in the field or on the spot of ground around the farmhouse.

We scooted across the paddy toward a row of palms, and, looking back, I saw the other ungainly birds coming in behind us, their widespread landing wheels splashing into the water. On the other side of the ditch, another bird was discharging troops, and I could see the men struggling to move across the paddy toward a brown, dry path that ran along the edge of the field. Some of the other troops had already gained this relatively dry spot and were moving along it toward a dusty road probably three feet wide—no more than a donkey track at best. Still there were no sounds of shooting, no movements that could be identified as enemy activity.

Our chopper plowed ahead, vaulting a couple of fields before gaining altitude. Then, with a rush of speed, we climbed and turned and fell in with a line of helicopters now heading east. At 9:13, I spotted the Can Tho airfield below.

I looked at Mac. He had strapped his machine gun into a stowage position and was sitting on the floor, rubbing his smooth chin as if he had a beard. There was a glassy look in his blue eyes, as if he had been thoroughly threaded and worked out by the experience of the landing.

Three minutes later, as we approached the runway, I could see the troops lined up in neat loads, waiting for us.

Walsh was on the interphone: "If the second objective is as far away as the first one, we're going to be out of fuel." And Toth said to the crew chief, "Taylor, check the tank, would you?"

Toth brought the chopper neatly to his assigned station

and we sat there with rotors idling while our new load, 11 sturdy little men, scrambled aboard. They were well-armed with M-1's, two tommy guns, automatic carbines, one shotgun, and a BAR, its 12-pound bulk dwarfing the man who struggled with it. Again there was a radio man; he came up to the head of the cabin and knowledgeably picked a box to sit on near McDonald's machine-gun mount, as if he was thoroughly familiar with the geography of the H-21 helicopter. Mac gave him a friendly pat on the top of the helmet, and the trooper smiled and stuck his tommy-gun barrel out the door opening.

The radio command channel was saying in my headphones, "One minute till take-off."

After we had gained altitude, someone was talking (I assumed it was Walsh): "Are we going into a different area this time?" Toth said, "Yes, . . . no troops in the area." What he meant was that, like the last landing, this would be an assault into VC territory and that there were no Arvin or friendly troops in there. As if to emphasize the point, two T-28's swept by our door, graceful as gulls, and curved almost at right angles to our course, sweeping over the squares of rice paddies and turning at the far end to weave back in our direction. It was the kind of fighter-escort maneuver that the Navy calls "Thach Weave." It was comforting that these speedy little fighters and the hornetlike Huey fighter helicopters were going in with us.

I watched the Vietnamese trooper sitting next to me, holding an M-1 that seemed about as big as he, with hand grenades taped high up on his harness to keep them out of the wet. He was wearing a steel helmet with a neat camouflage net; and while I watched, he took off the helmet and attached his wrist watch to a strap inside so that it would be kept reasonably dry, no matter how deep the water into which he would plunge on landing. In short, he seemed knowledgeable and experienced, like the other troops we had been carrying here.

The radio on the command channel said "Turning left 90 degrees . . . drop to final now."

We turned, and with the word about "final," we dived down to contour altitude, 20 or 25 feet above the rice paddies, and began our run into the LZ. Mac charged his gun, and crouched behind it, tense as a spring while he pointed his barrel at the beginning and end of every rice paddy that we flew over, and covered every farmhouse (strangely enough, they were all apparently unoccupied): He wasn't about to be caught unprepared if a VC should suddenly open up from somewhere down there on the ground.

We swept on at breathless speed, and I watched over Toth's shoulder, fascinated, as each wall of trees loomed up and, at the last minute, dropped out of sight, sky taking its place as we skimmed over the treetops. The roller-coaster dash was as thrilling as before.

Once or twice we saw black-clad figures, apparently farmers. But these men had got the word: When they saw us passing, they stood stock still.

Abruptly, the single-file line of choppers ahead of us started settling into a field, and our own chopper shuddered and staggered as we began to sit down in a wet paddy among tufted rows of rice plants. Moments later we were struggling for altitude as three or four other choppers settled down behind us. The green-clad troops seemed to be spread far and wide across the stretch of paddy, but, as before, there was no audible shooting, and not one native figure in black could be seen. The operation looked like the same kind of ghost hunt I had followed in the Danang area.

There was one big difference down here: The fighter helicopters. A thin-waisted Huey went swooping by like a giant dragonfly as we lifted from the paddy, and as we turned, another one passed.

I began to wonder if this day's work was going to be like the type of air-phibious operation that Maj. Runkle found so satisfactory: where Viet Cong are known to be in the LZ, but they are too afraid of the Hueys to open fire on any of the helicopters.

I knew what was indicated next—refueling—before we picked up our third load of troops, and we heard a radio call related to this situation: "This is Mail Call, all helicopters refuel—1,000 pounds."

After we touched down, at 9:55, Taylor came up to talk to McDonald. "Sure ain't much happening," he said.

Mac said devoutly, "I'm glad."

A fuel truck was moving down the line of choppers, stopping to pump gas. Again there was another briefing of pilots at the head of the column of aircraft. Toth returned from it and said that some word about the earlier assault landings of the day had come back from Division HQ: "They got a confirmed 10 VC killed, in the second landing." So despite the apparent tranquillity of the place, the VC had been there, and the fear of our aerial strength had kept them from firing until our troops were on the ground and they could be engaged on more even terms.

I asked Toth what was next.

"We go on one more assault mission, then we got an Eagle flight," he said. Our day's work, it seemed, was a long way from finished. And the peak of excitement was still to come—though we didn't know it at that point.

Toth, Walsh, and I sat in the sparse shade of the helicopter while the fuel truck was working its way toward us. The crewmen were already cracking out some cans of C-rations. It was only 10:15, but it seemed as if a long day had already passed and it was more than time for a bite of lunch. Maj. Galfund decided to change aircraft on the next assault mission, and shifted over to the helicopter of Richard "Black Cloud" Adams, so-called because the choppers he flew had been hit more often than any other in the company.

I got a quick fill-in on Walsh and Toth while we were waiting for the fuel truck. Walsh said his folks came to Santa Monica, Calif., in 1955, and he had had some training in fixed-wing aircraft with the RCAF before going into the American Army. Toth, a former paratrooper in the 101st Airborne in World War II, went to pilot's training in 1949, got out of the service long enough to study for a degree in teaching at Stroudsberg State Teachers College (Pa.), and then went back to the service in 1957 and to helicopter school. He served for a time in Special Air Missions, taking VIP's on courtesy flights. It must have been a job for which he was naturally fitted, because he is tactful and deferential and keeps himself immaculately groomed even in the taxing environment of "Bugville" (the nickname the 93d gave to the Soctrang base). At 41, Toth is the oldest pilot in the outfit, but you would be inclined to estimate his age as 10 years younger, for he keeps himself looking very fit. A couple of the pilots have already told me that they hope they are as fit as Toth when they're 35, let alone 40.

At 10:39, a jeep rolled down the line of choppers, tooting his horn. It was the signal to get ready to go. We climbed aboard our old bird, and our Arvin troops followed suit. In their green uniforms, wearing green cloth caps, the 11 men looked chillingly like the Chinese soldiers we had fought in Korea.

At 10:47, two of our escorting T-28's took off with their usual hot-rod rush, and five minutes later we rolled out to the center of the runway. Toth goosed the engine to full throttle, and we lumbered along, lifted slightly into the air, and the pilot picked up our rear end, like a fireman hitching up his suspenders, to gain momentum so that we could hike over the trees at the end of the field. We circled up to join the column of flying bananas assembling upstairs for the third air-phibious assault of the day.

At 11:10, our column swept low over the paddy fields and we began our contour flying at high rotor pitch. I was thankful that we had a good pilot with fast reactions at the controls, and a faithful, if loud, engine, which chugged along without stuttering or stumbling.

As we neared the LZ, the Hueys were passing us on both sides, orbiting in two directions, and staying very near. Moving around the compartment to make pictures of the troops, I missed an interphone conversation that must have warned our gunner of the presence of VC troops in the field below. Someone was shooting at us from ahead, and when I looked at Mac he had whipped his gun to the right to fire down the length of a ditch. The bullets spat out, the shell casings clattered to the floor, the gun pop-pop-popped. I saw the bullets splashing water in the ditch among the lush greenery, but no sign of human movement.

In a second, the ditch and splashes and whatever enemy activity there had been were behind us, and, lifting over a line of trees, we sank down into the chocolate-colored mud of a rice paddy, our rotor blades turning up a local squall in the water as Taylor shoved our cloth-capped soldiers out the rear door. I went back to the door to watch them go and, beyond them, saw part of our parade of flying bananas squatting down in the field to our left, the troops fanning out from them with impressive speed. Three Hueys were shuttling back and forth overhead during the seconds we were on the ground.

As we were climbing up into the sky again, one of our pilots called by interphone to Taylor: "You don't happen to know what Mac fired at?"

"A VC."

"Bet he missed 'im."

There seemed to be plenty of activity in this LZ. I saw a puff of white smoke to our right, where an L-19 was circling: That would be a marker dropped to show the T-28 fighters where VC were firing from.

Quickly three T-28's peeled off and swept down on this corner of paddy where the smoke bomb had been dropped. One T-28 made a pass, there was a flash underneath it and a streak of white smoke, and as we moved away, I saw three or four planes circling over the area, and fresh geysers of white—sizable ones, indicating bombs—rising from the rich green paddy. (Later I discovered that B-26 bombers had also been called in and that one of them had been shot up but managed to make it back to base.)

On the way back, I heard bits of extraneous conversation on the radio channel: some talk about an H-21 that was having trouble with its landing gear and was going to make a forced landing in the swamp near the staging area, and the voice of a helicopter crewman (pilot or gunner or crew chief) lamenting that "I never bring a camera along when something happens."

As we circled over the Can Tho airstrip, we heard radio calls still concerned with the helicopter that was having trouble. Since it couldn't land on the runway with a broken landing-gear strut, someone had contrived the bright idea of dumping a sandpile in the middle of the runway. But someone else had another idea: The chopper could sit down between two jeeps, letting their steel bodies take up the shock. At last it was decided to put the ship down, as originally suggested, in the swamp.

At 11:47 we landed and Toth expertly wheeled the bird off to the side. As soon as we shut down our engine, he was on McDonald's neck for what he called a "popping" performance with the machine gun when we were being fired at.

It developed that Don had seen a black-clad VC banging away at us on our landing approach, and "we took some rounds—heard it go by. The guy was shooting at us from about three o'clock," Toth explained to me, and in the same breath went back to Mac. "You got 980 rounds," Don told him, "but I might as well fire at him with my .45. Your gun was just popping, instead of going like a machine gun."

Mac tried to explain: "There was a guy with a black coat as we were lettin' down, but I didn't see any gun. I fired a couple of rounds though." Taylor said, "There were a lot of people over on the left that shouldn't be there—just sitting there."

Then Walsh added his comment, which seemed to be diametrically opposed to Don Toth's: "I don't want to discourage you, but because they're out there, they're not necessarily VC's."

It was a remarkable spectacle, the poor gunner being chewed out by one pilot for not shooting enough and by the other pilot for shooting too much. Such is the confusion of guerrilla war, and the temperament of the men fighting it, after their nerves have been stretched taut by tensions of fighting an elusive and frequently clever foe. But to 20-year-old McDonald, the criticism was a heavy blow. You could see him making up his mind that By-God-Next-Time he was going to give them hell down there in the fields and put up with whatever criticism he might incur for firing too much and too soon.

Don Toth started for a pilots' briefing, and I walked over with him, stopping on the way to talk to Chuck Benedict. He commented that the day's most recent mission had been hairy: "Don't like 'em like that last one," he said. "I could see machine-gun fire splashing in front of me. We were the third aircraft behind you. There were five planes behind us. But no hits."

I missed briefing, but Toth filled me in about it: "There are two aircraft going to take a blocking force in here"—he pointed to his map—"and we're going in here. About here is where the VC fired at the L-19 and the B-26. They got fire from about a company of VC with automatic weapons. They knocked out one of the B-26 engines. The Eagle flight is canceled, but we're going to run the troops in for this blocking force."

As we hurried back to the aircraft, Don stopped to read a short lecture to McDonald, this time in paternal tones: "You'll really have to watch out this time. The VC have automatic weapons. It's all right if you have to fire." A jeep went down the line of helicopters and the driver yelled, "Four minutes—four minutes to take-off."

I saw Mac talking to his gun, swinging it nervously by the grips: "Don't you pop this time."

At 1:19, our fourth load of troops came aboard the Toth-Walsh chopper. This load was like the last, except that it included a dandified individual with a walking stick—apparently a well-placed officer.

This time the Hueys flew very close to us, like convoying dragonflies, shuttling back and forth as if to indicate that this was going to be a very hazardous mission and they were going to be completely alert and dependable. Our fledgling gunner, Mac, showed the same determination—even before we went down to the deck for our contour approach to the target, he was crouching, wheeling, and snapping the gun from one side to the other to follow any possible target.

But as frequently happens in a war, a big build-up was followed by a definitive letdown. As the troops moved smoothly out of our squatting chopper, a line of choppers was coming in on our right, other troops were spreading across the fields—and there was no sign of the enemy firing we expected. We lifted and headed for home, still without giving Mac a chance to fire. There were no reports among the pilots of any hostile action until after we had all landed at Can Tho and Black Cloud Adams told us there had been some excitement when he landed with his troops.

"Just as the troops were debarking, *Da-da-dadadadada!* There were splashes in the water ahead of me. They also fired at the plane behind me. Then the Hueys saw the firing and circled around and blasted the village—you remember that village at three o'clock." I had to admit that I had missed this bit of action. But that's the way it is in this or any kind of war that I have known: You can be right on top of action, but you might not be aware of it because your positioning is poor.

Altogether, this had been an exciting day, and many of us had learned a lot, including gunner McDonald and me. My first experience in flying with the H-21 helicopters had shown me the vast differences between fighting in the wet Delta country of the south and fighting in the high jungle mountains of the north. I have learned tremendous respect for the ability and courage of the men fighting in both areas.

There is another air-phibious assault set up for tomorrow morning. Grimy and dusty, Al Galtund and I got back to Soctrang just in time, it seemed, to have supper and check in at the operations room for the briefing to tomorrow's mission.

Before the briefing, Paul Ewing, breaking in as the new CO of the 93d, said that the current operations out of Can Tho have brought in a pretty good bag: three VC KIA's and two enemy BAR's captured (he meant an enemy equivalent of our BAR's, made in China), at a cost of 11 Arvin WIA's. That may not be too high a price for three Communist killed, but the blood of the Vietnamese government troops is certainly flowing.

Capt. Delahanty gave the pilots a general fill-in on today's operation. He said that our attack near the town of Vinh Vinh had hit into VC territory that was so remote that the people living there didn't even know about the government of Ngo Dinh Diem. He pointed to the area on the map, a stretch criss-crossed by rivers and canals, with no marked roads, and it was easy to see how such a place could exist in ignorance of the outside world.

The company's only Negro officer, Capt. John Falls, briefed us on tomorrow's mission. No doubt aware of his conspicuous position among the officers, Falls spoke with a very precise diction and seemed to chose his words carefully, although he confessed he can't spell the names of a lot of the Vietnamese towns like Tam Hiep, which he called "Tom Hip." Falls said that tomorrow's mission is going to be staging out of

Tam Hiep, and that it will be led by the 57th, since most of the aircraft will be from that outfit. (In today's mission, the 93d led, because it supplied most of the aircraft.) On tomorrow's attack missions, "We are supplying four aircraft, the 33d [which bases out of Bien Hoa, north of Saigon] will supply six, and the 57th, eight." Again, three helicopter companies will be needed to supply enough choppers for the air-phibious assault. The Army helicopter outfits simply don't have the maintenance facilities they need to keep their birds in shape.

Capt. Falls pointed out tomorrow's objective area on the map; it developed that this, too, was a remote locale, although in a different direction, almost in the southern suburbs of Saigon. Very few details were given about the lifts except to indicate where the LZ's will be. The 57th Helicopter Company will presumably give us a full briefing tomorrow morning when we reach the staging area.

After the briefing we went over to the O Club to wash away some of the gritty feeling of day's operation. The pilots, clad in T-shirts and shorts or bathing suits weren't too numerous. This was the third day of sustained air-phibious operations, and a lot of the fliers were more interested in sleep, in getting ready for tomorrow's missions, than they were even in booze. However, those who were on deck for O Club merriment were vocal, and Connie, the little Vietnamese girl who assisted with the bartending, seemed to liven things up.

She had come back after a couple of days off, and was serving with two volunteer pilot-bartenders. A most unsmiling kind of Vietnamese, she seems to lack the Vietnamese feminine charm and grace, but she is well constructed, and in blouse and checkered pedal-pushers, is a pleasant change for eyes tired from squinting into rice ditches on the lookout for VC snipers. Connie seems to have a figure on the order of 30-18-28, which would be approximately the dimensions of the Vietnamese Venus. She has a snarling, surly face, apparently chosen because it helps to keep amorous 93d Lotharios at arm's length, and she has responded quickly to American training. She is quick to react to a drunk, or any other American whose expression doesn't please her, with a sure-fire American squelch: "——— you, Jack."

I met the pilot with whom I'll be flying tomorrow, Bob Kibler, a handsome, blond, scrubbed young man who has the largest number of combat hours in Vietnam of any of the pilots in the 93d, about 300 hours. Kibler likes Soctrang better than Danang, because the strain of flying up north over practically impenetrable jungle and high mountains, with rain clouds everywhere, had been very wearing.

"It took a thousand pounds off our backs when we came down here. There, you look for the best area [if you have to make a forced landing] and the best area is with 50-foot trees instead of 150-foot trees. You look for little draws where you can get the fuselage in, never mind the rest. You expect to wipe off the blades, but if you can get the fuselage in somewhere, you're lucky. We got there in the wet season, January. It was solid overcast. If it wasn't raining at the airfield, you could go down the road for a mile and it was raining. Many things you had to worry about up there, you don't have to worry about here."

But helicopters are tricky birds to operate with in any kind of terrain, Kibler said. "There is a lot to watch out for, you can't goof off. One minute you're flying along fine, the next minute, *whammo*." Kibler said that the typical radio transmission among the helicopter pilots is: "What the ————! Over."

Tonight, every light in the camp supported a cone of milling black-bodied gnats, which have the same habits as their green brothers. I sprayed my mosquito bar and my sack with Dick Adams' DDT bomb, but many of them made their way through interstices of the mosquito net, and are still doing so as I try to write my notes. The furnacelike heat of the tropical night is bad enough, here in the swamps, without this bonus annoyance.

Wednesday, November 14

I was up at 4:30 again; it wasn't a bad morning at all: the moon was bright and the air had cooled off somewhat.

Galfund and I, dragging our armor vests and pants, crossed the still-dark field looking for Kibler's plane. The pilots were only lumps of heads in front of the red lights of the instrument panel and I had to get the cabin light on to make notes of the names of the crew chief and gunner: Sgt. Toney March (of Lexington, Ky.), a huge Negro with his cap on backward, and Sp/6 Philip Norris (of Owensboro, Ky.). I hadn't known it till now, but the other pilot with Kibler was Capt. Falls, who had briefed us last night about this mission.

As the first greenish gleams of light illuminated the lines of sausage-like H-21's on both sides of our field, Sgt. March tripped our putt-putt engine, and in a few seconds our big rotors began to grind. About six o'clock we lifted off. There was a long flight over rice-paddy country as we churned northward. By the time we reached Tam Hiep, many aircraft had gathered there. We joined the flowerlike shapes of the H-21's, the dartlike, trim-waisted Hueys, and big-winged L-19's, parked near several knots of troops—a vast, impressive spread of military power.

An American Ranger adviser, a blond warrior formidable in his standard antiguerrilla gear, immediately stomped out to our plane. Noticing the presence of some extra Americans, he said to Al and me, "If any Arvin troops have to be knocked off, you go first. We're already overloaded." Allan Galfund agreeably suggested that we split up, but the adviser seemed not to hear. He was a trifle overofficious.

Anyhow, we did have to split up, and I was assigned to the next helicopter in the line. I checked in with the crew chief, Sp/6 Arthur Hensley (of Forsythe, Ind.), and the gunner, PFC James Harper (of Elva, Ala.).

At 7:20, our troops clambered aboard: the Civil Guard type, not as well equipped as the troops of the 21st Division we had carried yesterday. They had only plastic helmet liners, unmatched uniforms given some uniformity by red scarves, and an assortment of footgear—some GI boots, some sneakers. But their arms at least seemed good: carbines, a BAR, and Tommy guns.

I discovered that the pilots were CWO Art M. Albritton (of Sarasota, Fla.) and CWO Sidney B. Shows (of Mendenhall, Miss.).

After a short run to the target area, we dived down to the deck and began the usual hurdle race. We didn't seem to be flying quite so low as we had been yesterday, but it was still low enough to boost your heartbeat astronomically.

I watched the gunner, Jim Harper, wheeling and dealing: squatting, crouching, swinging his gun on every close-passing house or rice ditch or figure, his body twisting like a cat's, his finger nervously on the trigger.

We squeaked over farmhouses where there was wash on the line, and once passed over one farm so low that red dust rose behind us, stirred up by our fans. We were startled to see it—dust seems like the last thing to expect when you're over a stretch of wet paddy, although somehow, we always seemed to come back from these missions covered with grime.

We were following the leader, as we had done before, and the paddy chase seemed to go on endlessly over slick, shimmering fields and canal towns, but at last, at 8:04, we landed in a rice field next to a farmhouse and a weathered and wet-look-ing sort of barn made out of strips of thatch and bamboo. There was no sign of life in the open, barn-like structure.

Hensley ushered our Civil Guard troops out the back door; they not nearly as certain in their movements as the regular Arvin troops we had carried yesterday. I saw one jump and fall flat on his face. He still clutched his rifle, pulled his legs up under him, and somehow again began to struggle through the waist-deep water toward the divider at the edge of the paddy, his back and arms now gleaming with chocolate-colored mud.

We climbed over the trees and headed toward the base at Tam Hiep. I got on the interphone and asked Albritton and Shows if they had heard any firing or any reports of any firing. They said no.

Back at the staging area, the pilots assembled near one of the H-21's for a post-mortem about the mission. A major from the 57th, Darwin Beauchamp (of Hemet, Calif.), map in hand, was talking to the clustered pilots: "All in all, the mission went very well."

CWO Bob Kibler, standing next to me, echoed, "It went very smoothly."

After the debriefing, we were told we would be on stand-by, waiting for the next lift. The crews lounged in the angular shade of the troop-carrying choppers, and Al Galfund, back from a visit to the command jeep, told me: "Col. Vann will brief you." I had heard that Col. Vann (of El Paso, Tex.) is a fairhaired boy among the American advisers and that his op-posite number in the Vietnamese Army, Col. Cao, is a fireball in the Arvin command. Cao heads up the 7th Infantry Division, whom we were assisting with helicopter transport today.

Galfund led us to the sparse shadow of the radio jeep, where Col. Vann was standing next to the radio operator. He turned out to be a wiry, quick-moving, blondish man with glinting red hair on his forearms. He was wearing fatigue greens and rubber-treaded jungle boots with fold-over puttee-type tops. He has the rapid (almost harsh), decisive manner which in my experience characterizes a good field commander.

The colonel, who came originally from Norfolk, Va., said that his army training has been in the business administration-accounting field—but you might well say that his work here is just the opposite: a fighting field command.

He gave us a quick, concise rundown of today's operation, pointing out the position of all of our units on a military map:

"Our only concern now is that the enemy is in there. It's an operation that we've been waiting for for some time. [There are] two Ranger companies and six Guard companies." He unfolded his map on the hood of the jeep and put the overlay, marked in red and blue pencil, on top of it so that we could see where all of the troop units are and where they will be maneuvering for the next day or two.

"[Here] we are 30 clicks [kilometers] from the area of operations, which is 15 kilometers south of Saigon." He pointed out the operations area at the tip of a river delta south of the junction of the Saigon River and one that he identified as the Vaico. "It's strange territory. We haven't got in there before."

He showed us where the Ranger and Civil Guard companies have landed.

He made it clear that we still have the job of carrying two additional companies to the assault area and that the ultimate stratagem is to move the troops around so that eventually we will block off a concentration of VC. The last planned movement is to airlift another force and put them in on the flank so that the VC's will be pinned in on two sides. He said that in this area, so close to Saigon, the VC have had things pretty much their own way, and that it's about time we should chop them up a little. This sounded like a sensible way to use helicopters—to fling unexpected flanking movements upon the enemy with lightning speed.

"They've [the Communists] been encircling Saigon from the south," he said. "This area has always been safe to them [the VC], but by moving troops in by a river force and helicopters, we have the opportunity to cut them off. If we know their intentions, we can get them. We've already proved that: in the operation of September 2nd, we caught them and killed 278."

I asked Galfund if he could set it up for us to talk to Col. Cao, who, at 36, is probably No. 1 man among Ngo Dinh Diem's field commanders. He endeared himself to the President of Vietnam at the time of the revolutionary attempt to overthrow Ngo in 1959, when Cao's troops drove the rebels out of Saigon.

Galfund said he would do his best, and meanwhile I went to take as much ease as possible with some of the crewmen lying in the shade of their aircraft.

It was peaceful there by the river with the crickets chirping. I sat next to a big Negro gunner from Brooklyn, N.Y.,

Isaac "Ike" Grayson. I asked him about differences between duty here, in the Soctrang vicinity, and duty in mountainous Danang.

"Anywhere in South Vietnam it's about the same," he said. "But at Soctrang the facility is better. At Danang, you couldn't count on water. Down here, you can take a shower at night."

I asked Grayson about Soctrang and Danang as liberty towns. "I wouldn't call that [Soctrang] a liberty town. It's got one main street and two bars."

Al Galfund took Mert Perry (the Time-Life correspondent) and me up to Col. Vann, who in turn took us over to see his Vietnamese opposite number. Col. Cao, standing in green fatigues at the front of his troops, was a small, stocky figure, impressive in his sureness. Judging from his decisive manner and his mental sharpness. I would estimate that he, like Col. Vann, is a good field commander.

Vann, introducing us, said that Cao has been a division commander since the age of 31, and added that Cao's division has killed five-twelfths of the VC killed in Vietnam. Vann said that Cao is a writer too, the author of three books: "about the military operations in Vietnam and an autobiography of part of his life."

Later, Mert Perry told me that Col. Cao is given to thinking of himself as the new Napoleon, and that the book tells how he grew and gained dimension in battle. Mert also told me that Cao wanted a map room built for him exactly like Napoleon's, with the war map on a certain wall. Everything went well in constructing the room, and the smallest details were being duplicated, until someone suddenly opened one of the doors into it, and it was discovered that the door opened right in the middle of the map. Cao recovered his dignity by having the room redesigned.

When Mert once asked Cao about the reason for his success as a military commander, Cao said, "Leadership," pointing to himself.

We had a chance to talk briefly to the colonel and I asked him, "What would be the first thing you would want here if you could have anything you wanted?"

Cao said, "Closer contact among the peoples of the world, so they can better understand each other." Then he added, "Your question was a general question, I answered it generally." I said yes, but more specifically, what would he want for his troops? He said simply, "More choppers [he pronounced it "shoppers"]." Col. Vann hastened to add, "Many division commanders would like to have helicopter companies attached to their divisions."

Vann and Col. Cao hustled off to some military conference, and we rejoined the crewmen who were still waiting for action. In this guerrilla-type war, as in any other I've seen, a great deal of time seems to be spent in waiting, but waiting in such a state of readiness that it's difficult to do anything except to wait.

I took advantage of the idle time to scout around for the Hueys' parking place, and there I found Maj. Bob Runkle, the commanding officer of that outfit. He talked to me while keeping a wary eye on a big tanker truck that was fueling his birds. The truck backed fairly close to one of his precious Hueys and he let out a yell that halted it. Then he chewed out his sergeant: "Don't you *ever* let a truck back around the birds without somebody to watch it."

Runkle spoke about the success of Huey operations here:

"We don't pretend we know all about the birds or how to use them, but they seem to be very effective. They've had a tremendous effect on the morale of the H-21's. We've been operating every day and getting good results . . . we've given more than we've taken." He said that even in the short time the Hueys have been operating here, they have proved to be a great weapon for this kind of warfare: "They have one big advantage over faster aircraft, including the T-28's. We can get right down there with 'em [the troop-carrying H-21's]. No one else can."

With no instructions as yet about our operation, the crewmen began breaking out rations—the crew of the Harper-Hensley aircraft being no exception. I learned that they had even found a way to heat up the cans of cold C-ration by sticking them on top of a can filled with gasoline and set afire. They suggested that I go over to Kibler's aircraft, since he was carrying the rations for today, and pick up something from the local Duncan Hines.

The franks and beans, the most desired ration, were all gone—as were the chicken and the hamburgers, so I ended up with a choice of beef and potatoes or ham and potatoes. I knew what they were: lovely cold grease. However, the biscuit ration that went with them isn't bad, especially when eaten with the little flat tin of peanut butter that is included. And there was a five-gallon cooler of cold water beside the chopper, which made the whole meal quite acceptable.

Rations were short today, because the 57th had made a

mistake in the cases they brought. What the supply officer thought were two cases of C-rations, turned out to be boxes containing cans of DDT. The men of the 57th came over to the 93d and asked for a share of our rations.

After chow, one of our pilots, lazing in the slim shade of a helicopter blade, commented ironically that there was one way to precipitate action this afternoon: "All we have to do is lie down and they'll call us."

They talked about Tiger, the company's little meek-eyed, roly-poly mascot, who at that moment was attempting to get some nourishment from chewing the toe of my sneaker. Kibler said, "He's eaten bits of franks, potatoes, beef, candy and crackers. Might as well try your shoe."

The talk turned to animals, about cats and dogs. Someone said he didn't like cats, and Kibler said he did: "Cats are like women. They can be so full of sweetness and light and love you up when they want something. But don't bother them if they don't feel like it." This invoked reminiscences of attractive women, and some not so attractive. The conversation then moved over to the Hueys and their fearsome armament of rockets and machine guns. "You press the fire button and all hell breaks loose," one pilot ruminated.

"You hit the fire button and wipe out all the birds ahead of you," offered another.

"Yeah," said Kibler, imagining himself in a situation, " 'I'm the new flight leader.' "

The irony was extended: " 'Flight leader, coming in for a landing, pressed the fire button by accident,' " said Kibler, writing himself a scenario: "*Scheww!* No more holdups from the control tower. 'Oops—just wiped out the control tower—still having trouble with this thing.' "

It might have been interesting, this dramatic projection of a Huey pilot with a touchy gun switch, but a jeep swept down the runway, the driver honking the horn insistently.

We hurried aboard the birds, cranked up, and this time it seemed that we weren't going to load up here. The mission was to go to LZ, pick up some troops, and move them to another area where they'd be a blocking force to hem in some VC.

We were off at 12:10, and it seemed only a few minutes before we were sitting down in a paddy just beyond a house. This one was full of Vietnamese women and kids who peeked at us through the door.

This was a secure area, at least in theory, and as we came in we could see green-uniformed Arvin troops at several parts of the fields, and one squad very close to the paddy we came down in. The soldiers, pushing against the rotor blast and the mud, struggled across the field toward our rear door. The water in this paddy seemed deeper than I had yet seen it. As they reached the doorway, Hensley reached out to pull up the first of the line, and nearly fell out in the effort. Mocha-colored up to his waist, the trooper slid across the steel floor, and a sudden puddle of water followed him as the crew chief went back to lift the next man aboard.

The soldiers were being hauled in, slipping and sliding when they reached the slippery floor, which was now coated with chocolate-colored mud and awash with water. But they kept coming, driven by the awareness that assault helicopter operations have to be carried on at a breakneck pace. Wet clothing, muddy boots, clips of ammunition, and the guns that seemed too large for them to carry made the struggle to get aboard very hard for these troopers. The machine gunner had the hardest struggle, for he had wrapped ammunition belts around the barrel of his weapon, so that it must have weighed 35 or 40 pounds. I noticed that they were wearing worn, ragged uniforms, and one had a green fatigue shirt and some sort of dark trousers below.

We lifted with our soggy load, streaked over more paddy fields, and plopped down again, disgorging our troops into another deep green mixture of water, rice stalks, and mud. I hoped that this planned flanking movement would work, that some VC's would be caught in the supposed pincer movement.

Our empty aircraft lifted with relative ease, but the pilots held it close to the deck, as if we were carrying a planeload of troops into an assault.

We picked up another batch of soldiers, as ungainly and long-suffering as the last lot, but better-equipped. We went through the same routine getting them aboard, and then headed for our LZ.

After we safely deposited our load of troopers, I thought we surely must be through for the day, but it seemed we were a long way from it. We headed back to Tam Hiep, where we were put on stand-by again. More waiting in the scanty shade of the helicopters. Cols. Vann and Cao were making maximum use of the magical American wings.

Albritton and Shows went off to another briefing, and came back shortly. Albritton told us what our orders were: "Pick 'em up and take 'em to the road, the CP. It's another case of FFL [Follow the Flight Leader]."

At 2:28 the Hueys were off, and we followed a few minutes later, quite jaunty in performance because there were no troops aboard, and headed generally north. We came down into a paddy, but this time there was one difference—there was a narrow dirt road, almost a red color, close to the paddy. As we came in, we saw troops running along it: Arvin troops.

A group of 12 soldiers, their green uniforms darkened by rice-field muck and sweat, dashed from the road toward our plane, struggling as if for dear life. Hensley got his exercise helping them slither aboard, and Harper, the gunner, tapped me on the shoulder and pointed out the left side window of the aircraft. There we could see a group of men in black—black scraps of clothes shiny with wet—carrying another man in black who was wounded, his arm streaked with gore. I noted that two of the group of people near him had their arms tied behind them; a few feet away, an Arvin trooper with a tommy gun stood guard. These were VC prisoners, carrying one of their number who had been shot.

They carried their wounded fellow trooper with a bizarre disregard for his comfort, as if he were cordwood or a twisting of heavy blankets. They struggled down the road and finally stopped, exhausted. Setting their wounded compatriot down like loosely connected baggage, they left him tilted on his pelvis in the red-orange dust of the road, like a side of beef.

But they weren't going to load him on our chopper. We had more than a full load with our 12 troopers. The POW's were heading for the next helicopter in line. Apparently the captured VC were off to division headquarters at Tam Hiep for military interrogation.

At 2:59, Albritton gunned his engines and the heavy bird shuddered and rocked and lifted clear of the paddy.

Only four minutes later we sat down near a small donkey track, a red streak running through a paddy, with another road, wider and more civilized, near it. We helped the sodden troops out and left them to carry out their flanking movement as we chugged southward once more.

This was the fifth lift of troops we had made today, and, weary as I was, I was glad that our magical weapon was being used to the ultimate. But when it became evident that we were going to make still another troop lift, nerves and sinews began to rebel, almost audibly. Yet there were no palpable complaints from Messrs. Albritton, Shows, Harper, and Hensley. We turned back north, chugged back over the endless, wet, green swath of paddies and palm trees.

At 3:15 we were squatting down in another field beside a strip of road. A squad of troops came scrambling down the divider next to the road, and splashed their way into the paddy.

Now we could see that this water was deeper. Some of the soldiers were wet up to their chests. Although they had to turn their bodies with each step to wrench their legs out of the muck, they still moved eagerly, apparently anxious to reach the vehicle that was going to pick them up and take them somewhere away from here. Checking with Albritton and Shows, I found out that we were taking this load back to the vicinity of the CP.

I looked at our squad of troops, their green uniforms black and slick with water and sweat, their shoes coated with cocoa-colored mud, and I thought they deserved at least this: to be picked up by our helicopter magic carpet and taken back to a position of relative safety. These SDC troops seemed younger and more poorly uniformed than the Arvin soldiers we had carried earlier today. The troops in this lift wore yellow scarves, and four of them were bareheaded.

Soon we were over the wide red dirt road that I remembered from the previous stop at the CP. The bedraggled-looking troopers splashed into the paddy and made for that dusty road as if it were something warm and homey. As they climbed up the steep embankment, I saw, beyond them, a group of prisoners moving along, their feet bare, their black outfits tattered, wet. There were five of them in this group and, as last time, they were carrying a wounded man.

A couple of them also had their arms tied behind them with ropes, and an Arvin soldier stood over them with an automatic carbine. And again they were carting their wounded fellow VC as if he were a limp sack of potatoes or rice.

After flying in the direction of Tam Hiep for 15 minutes, I permitted myself to hope that this was the end of the day's activities.

But from the way that Albritton and the other pilots taxied their birds over to parking places beside the runway, it was clear that we were not yet free to go back home—not even now. We were still on stand-by. The time was 3:45, and it had been a long day, considering that we had started before dawn this morning. I climbed down and flung myself on the ground to catch whatever rest I could. I had plenty of company. Up and down the runway, crewmen were prostrate underneath the rotors of their aircraft.

One of the crewmen who came to visit with our bunch was a tall, towheaded, baby-faced gunner named PFC Robert Eiler (of Conneaut Lake, Pa.).

Eiler was talking about a captured VC gun he had seen carried back aboard his chopper by one of the Arvin troopers.

184

The interesting thing about it was that it was an automatic weapon, what he called a "BAR type," and it was apparently of Chinese manufacture.

"An Arvin had it. He let me look at it, but he wouldn't let me keep it."

He explained that the Arvins get a reward for VC weapons they turn in, and the highest bounty is paid for automatic weapons.

Eiler said that the weapon had a slightly larger shell than the BAR, and "it had some kind of funny writing on it."

I asked if it was Russian and he said he didn't know Russian from Chinese: it could have been either, but it did have numbers on it—it was machine-made and of non-American make. From all reports, it looked as if the Arvin troops, in this day of rapid helicopter movement and flanking attacks, were getting some results. The scuttlebutt running around in the divisional command post is that so far 10 VC's have been killed and a dozen captured.

At last there was a cry in the distance, including the key words ". . . go home." With a rush, we were back in the birds and rapidly heading over a string of rivers and endless paddy fields, which in the afternoon light shone like burnished silver. At 4:45, we saw the whorl-like pattern of muddy rivers that marked Soctrang.

Back on the field, we wearily headed for the operations hut lugging our armor vests. After a day like this, one thing seemed to have No. 1 priority: to get something wet at the bar. The air was still baking hot and dusty—and there was a new, unpleasant complication at the moment: our water supply had temporarily gone bad. There was some stoppage in the water tank near the operations room, and I saw a group of four Vietnamese workmen chopping into the concrete lid of the tank with axes. That seemed like a crude way to solve the problem, but as hot as it was, I would have approved any method of expediting renewal of our water supply.

Tonight, after chow, the O Club was howling: it seems that there will be no assault mission tomorrow, and a little relaxation was more than overdue. I decided to fly back to Saigon tomorrow and do a little checking up on another form of relaxation: the Marine R and R flight to Hong Kong.

Maj. Paul Ewing, the new CO of the outfit, drummed on his glass with a knife, and said he had an announcement to make. He got up and read a promotion letter to WO/3 John Cooney, who has been promoted to the next step up in rank. More than half of the pilots of the 93d, and in all of the Army

185

chopper outfits here, are warrant officers: meaning generally that they started as enlisted men, and worked their way to officer status.

Cooney has the largest amount of helicopter time of any of the pilots here at the 93d, perhaps even in all of the Army aviation. He has more than 5,000 hours of chopper time, and Ewing read the letter with an eye to the fact that promotions come slowly for warrant officers. At last Cooney had achieved the top warrant rank, WO/4.

Whatever the reason, the pilots cheered, clapped, and booed gleefully when the letter about Cooney's promotion was read, and they sang what I have already learned is one of their two or three favorite songs here in Soctrang:

> "For he's a jolly good fellow,
> For he's a jolly good fellow,
> For he's a jolly good fellow,
> Which nobody can deny—Bull————."

Thursday, November 15

This morning an Otter, a small Army transport, came in early, but there wasn't room for Galfund and me on this lift to Saigon. It was jammed full of people from the 93d being rotated home. EM's who had served their term of duty in Vietnam were being replaced by new arrivals from the States, and naturally, these people had priority on any seats available.

About 11 o'clock, a DC-3 (C-47 in Army and Air Force terminology) came in. It was a beat-up old clunker, probably a veteran of many World War II flights, and it carried the longitudinal yellow stripes of the VNAF on its fuselage and the VNAF yellow star—which made it look like a kind of off-color American air transport.

The pilots were Hollywood types, the way the VNAF fliers often are: good-looking, dashing hot-rocks, wearing dark glasses, who told us that they would be taking off at three o'clock, and that in the meantime they'd like to go into Soctrang. Evidently they had girl friends in the town, their plea fell on sympathetic ears, and they won a ride without delay.

The plane had come on an official mission, the pilots' visit to their friends in Soctrang only a by-product. The mission was to transport four enlisted men and a captain of the AAF to Soctrang. Their job: recovering some 50-caliber machine guns jettisoned by the B-26 when it was shot up on Tuesday's mission. I remembered the episode, though I hadn't heard that the

B-26 crew lightened their aircraft by cropping such critical material in uncertain territory. The American captain, a rakish fly-boy type, said that his job was to recover the machine guns, which, as far as he knew, had been dropped in four feet of water in enemy territory. "We have an Anthis-gram to recover the stuff," he said, referring to the fact that directives from the AAF commander in Vietnam (Brig. Gen. Rollen H. Anthis) had a slightly dictatorial character sometimes.

The captain set about getting an H-21 from the 93d Company to carry him out to the approximate area where the .50-calibers were dropped. The Air Force was very clearly perturbed about the possible loss of such valuable weapons. These machine guns, having a range of 7,000 yards, could effectively shoot many of our helicopters out of the sky, if they fell into the hands of the VC.

While the captain and his four cohorts were arranging transportation, we climbed aboard the stuffy C-47, a veritable breadloaf oven in the hot sun. We sat and sweated in the cafeteria-tray-type seats arranged on both sides of the cabin.

On this lift, 11 more EM's were being sent back home on rotation. They came aboard, with their B-bags, joyous about at last escaping from Bugville. They had come to Vietnam with the initial group of the 93d, in January of 1962. They were getting home a little head of schedule. Actually, their term of service was supposed to be a rounded year, but in this case their reliefs had come in, so they were enjoying a two-month grace period.

A quick check, as we droned north toward Saigon, showed that of the 11 enlisted men on the plane, there was one gunner who had flown assault missions. He was Sp/3 Sam De-Loune (22, of Thibodeaux, La.), a machinist and welder who had flown missions as a gunner. Like the others on this lift, he was going home for a 30-day leave before being assigned to new duty.

Near him sat a redheaded Sp/4 named Clyde Chaffin (of Ferndale, Mich.), who hoped to surprise his family by being home for Thanksgiving, when they didn't expect him until Christmas. Unlike the other men going on leave, Chaffin isn't married, so he is going home to his parents. His father is an executive planning engineer at Ford Motor Company.

"It'll be cold," Clyde said with obvious satisfaction. "I'll just have time for a cup of coffee, and then we'll eat turkey."

As we came near the wide-spreading metropolis of Saigon, there was a general outcry among the T-shirted passengers. They had seen a white Pan American jet taxiing across the airfield. Someone said, starry-eyed, "That's· what'll take us." He was wishfully projecting good fortune for himself and the others: the good fortune that on military orders they might be able to travel to the States on a Pan Am jet, on a subcontract arrangement. A small percentage of people traveling on military orders have such good fortune.

But Sp/5 Robert Calhoun (25, of Hattiesburg, Miss.), an electrician, wasn't so sanguine: "We'll get a DC-6—if we're lucky."

We made a fast landing at Tan Son Nhut airfield under the hot-shot guidance of our Vietnamese pilot, and one of our willing passengers cried out with a mock British accent: "Hurrah—we made it."

We taxied over to the military side of the airfield, at an impractical distance from any transportation to the city. Galfund struggled to get to a telephone and arranged some sort of wheels for the forsaken EM's, while they sat in the sun near the aircraft. Soon the transportation matter was straightened out, the 11 men were loaded on a truck with their bags, and Galfund and I bummed a ride into the PI office. It seems there is a temporary shortage of housing accommodations in Saigon—replacements are always coming in and swelling the rolls of Americans in Saigon to the breaking point—and I ended up on an Army cot in the living room of Cmdr. Zornow's quarters in the Brink BOQ.

I learned that there's been a holdup in some maintenance work on the Marine Corps transport which is scheduled to make the Hong Kong hop, and take-off probably won't be until Sunday. However, that Marine transport, an R4D, will be coming down to Saigon on Saturday to pick up some freight, so I'll be able to hitch a ride back to Danang, and go on from there to Hong Kong with the Marines on Sunday. Happy R and R days!

A Leave
in Hong Kong

Friday, November 16

I spent almost all day trying to get U.S. currency for the trip to Hong Kong and currently am feeling that I'm lucky it didn't take me all week. After a lot of red tape and running around, I finally reached the cashier's office and took my place in line with other Americans waiting for their chance to get dollars. A well-fed Vietnamese clerk examined my check very carefully and deliberately got together my $75, informing me that it was the maximum amount I could get, unless I were married and had a wife and/or children in Vietnam, in which case I could get $100. I also learned I'd have to go through the same routine before I could get any more money next month. I thanked him and went on my way, not any wiser but much more tired.

Fortunately, I had some highly qualified help from Vice-Consul Rogers in unraveling another accumulated bit of red tape: a visa problem. The Vietnamese government had given me a one-entry permit to come into the country and had limited it to 30 days. I now needed a permit that would allow me to re-enter the country after the Hong Kong visit. Rogers knew how to carve his way through Vietnamese jungles of regulation and requirement, and he got me the necessary documentation. I went to bed exhausted, satisfied that being a Saigon Commando and battling the tangled threads of military red tape was fully as strenuous, if not as dangerous, as being out in the field among the VC.

Saturday, November 17

I had a call from the PIO this morning saying that I had better be ready to catch the R4D on a moment's notice. I was also told that Maj. Bob Runkle, CO of the Hueys, had cracked up at Tan Son Nhut airfield while carrying an Army general on some kind of evaluation tour. The general's aide had been slightly hurt, but the general, Runkle, and his crewmen had miraculously escaped injury. The bird, however, was reduced to junk.

At 11:45, while I was packing my bags, Cmdr. Zornow called to tell me to be at the military part of Tan Son Nhut airfield in time for a one-o'clock take-off.

The crew of the "Trans-Paddy Airways" was standing by at the airfield, waiting for the senior officer, Col. George Linnimeier, the new executive officer of the Marine task unit at Danang, to get back from Saigon. The victuals and other supplies, like beer, were all safely loaded into the plane. Also aboard was a big load of Armalite AR-15's.

The Armalite is the latest wrinkle in submachine guns. It's an Army weapon which the Marine Corps, with their usual astuteness in picking up Army rejects that are valuable, has snagged for helicopter use. It is very lightweight, very accurate, and, although the slug it fires is only about the size of a .22-caliber rifle bullet, it has such a tremendous velocity that its killing power is great.

I had heard a good deal about these marvelous little weapons when I was in Danang, and many of the Marines had spoken wistfully of the day when Armalites would be part of the armament of every HUS flying out of Danang. Now that day has come.

At 1:30, Col. Linnimeier trundled out to the plane and in a couple of minutes we were on our way.

The crew members of this one-airplane Marine airline, all EM's, wore a unique patch on their flying suits. It showed, with surprising detail, a green grid of rice paddies, and a muddy river flowing down the middle of them; in the background, high, jagged green mountains rose against a gray sky. Superimposed on the middle of this was an accurate representation of their R4D with the characteristic orange nose and tail of government-owned transport aircraft. Around the border of the patch was the legend *Trans-Paddy Airways Soc Trang— Saigon—Viet Nam*. It was a remarkably complete picture of this part of Marine activity in Vietnam, done by expert Vietnamese hand embroiderers, and probably at a bargain rate—embroidery being one of the great bargains of Vietnam.

The No. 1, and only, first pilot of Trans-Paddy Airways was rugged-looking, red-haired Sgt. Ray F. Webb (of Johnson City, Tenn.), and Col. Linnimeier, also a flier, occupied the copilot's chair.

Originally a World War II aircraft, one of the Army's old Douglas C-47 "flivvers of the Air Age," the R4D had been reworked with more powerful engines and an extended fuselage. Now it is quite a hot little airplane.

Tonight, by way of getting in training for the trip, Davis and I went into Danang to the favorite spa of the servicemen, the Forget-Me-Not Bar. There I found a sizable delegation from the Marine establishment already lined up—which was quite OK, since there is no assault mission for tomorrow, or for that matter in the generally known future.

It's easy to see why the Forget-Me-Not Bar is the favorite of the Marines and the MAAG advisers. It is only one of four ginmills lined up opposite the police station compound just off the main street, and it has the same outward dressings as the others: a coarse-gauge wire shield over the front door (standard equipment for bars catering to American servicemen) to deflect possible grenades tossed by VC's, bright neon signs, a garish juke box with rock-and-roll records, and, behind the bar, an array of pretty little Vietnamese bartender girls. But the Forget-Me-Not, according to my Marine friends, is equipped with an especially good grade of Vietnamese pulchritude. Therein lies the difference between Forget-Me-Not and the other bars of Danang.

These Vietnamese bar dolls will serve your drink, talk to you, and hold your hand, all for a small additional fee. If you order the drink from one of the girls, she will charge you double the normal price for it, but will also engage you in picturesque pidgin conversation, take your hand, and ask you to buy her a drink. In the old days, about a year ago, these bar girls were also taxi dancers, but the "morality laws" passed through the intervention of Mme. Ngo Dinh Nhu, the President's sister-in-law, have forbidden the taxi dance as well as other forms of public dancing.

Besides the delicate little Vietnamese bar girls, the Forget-Me-Not has waves of little begging children who come in periodically to get handouts and also maintain nightly vigils outside the grenade-proof door, where they waylay every patron, inbound or outbound.

Some of these moppets are most fetching and winning. The principal performer, who is allowed to remain longer inside the bar than the others, is a tot of three or so whom the boys called "The Twister." Tonight, this tiny drop of humanity was doing the twist expertly whenever he could find a paying audience, and we corralled him and bribed him to tell a story already famous at the Forget-Me-Not, the story of a fight that had happened in the bar earlier this P.M. The combatants were Japanese sailors who had come in as crew of an LST being delivered at Danang and some American servicemen. The little Twister illustrated his story with dramatic gestures, alternately playing the parts of the Americans and the Japanese respectively. According to him, the Japanese were expert with kicks (vehemently described with the sound *Zow*) and the Americans with punches (*Zhaw*).

The Forget-Me-Not was a jumping place full of heavy-beat rock-and-roll music, the roar of conversation, and a few drunken voices saturated with combativeness almost but not quite to the point of combustion. Col. Davis and Razor Blaydes, at one end of the bar, kept a weather eye on the temperature of the Marines present, and seemed ready to move in if an explosion threatened.

The hand-holder assigned to me was Mimi (real name, Diep). I advanced her a donation toward the care of her four-year-old son, left her by a husband who, she said, was a captain in the VNAF, killed before the baby was born. Mimi's figure had begun to show the effect of the diet of Coke she had to consume every night as she drank with the American servicemen, but she seemed to have a good heart, and she filled me in on the dialogue that is supposed to ensue between the American serviceman and his Vietnamese bar girl friend:

Girl: "You big, handsome, patriotic American, come to say my country. I fall in love with you first time I see you. Buy me a drink."

American: "You beautiful Vietnamese girl. I fall in love with you first time I see you. Buy your own drink."

The cops came by a few minutes before 11 to make sure that the closing hour was enforced. Ley-to, the super package of femininity who is part owner and manager of the bar, helped her beauteous team of hand-holders to shoo the miscellaneous crowd of servicemen toward the door. It was fine that the night life of Danang closed up so early, because I expect to be getting up early tomorrow to get ready for the 7:00 A.M. take-off.

Sunday, November 18

Hong Kong, the Paris of our Southeast Asian War! A fabulous city of 3.5 million people, continually strained at the seams with the flood of refugees coming across the border from Communist China; a British colony well ordered by British rule, but still a meeting place of medieval times and the jet age; a beautiful San Francisco type harbor with such a teeming oversupply of cheap Asiatic labor that you can get anything you want in the world at a bargain price. It has grown up considerably since I last saw it seven years ago. I saw new skyscraper hotels and apartment buildings as we cut across the deep blue of the harbor, descended over the bare hills of the islands, and sloped in for a landing on the new 9,000-foot jet runway.

Floating up to us from the direction of Kai Tak Airport came the stench of sewage. When we landed, I found out that there is a relatively new disposal plant somewhere near the airfield. This, with the proper wind, affords a startling greeting to visitors.

Hong Kong is all that I had remembered it to be, and much more. Nowadays it is galvanic with the tremendous influx of tourism, not only from our American forces spread across the Southeast Asia theater of anti-Communist war, but also with waves of regular tourists coming in from Hawaii and Tokyo. Since Hong Kong is the real meeting place of East and West traditions and techniques, there seems no limit to the things you may explore here, on R and R or otherwise.

We checked into the Clover Hotel, one of scores of luxurious, well-serviced hostelries on the mainland side of the Hong Kong Colony. We charged down to the Peninsula Tailor, one of many custom-tailoring shops scattered across the Nathan Road shopping district, and there encountered a legion of other American servicemen having clothing bargains whipped up in 24 hours, to measure. I saw three or four of the passengers from the Marine lift, and one confided to me, "I spent all my money." He must have set some kind of record, because we had been off the plane less than two hours.

There were big plans for this evening. A group of my friends were anxious to go to one of the night spots like the Golden Phoenix, the Bayside, the Mandarin Room or one of the ballrooms such as the Oriental, the Metro, the Blue Sky. The piquant Chinese girls at the ballrooms are both English-speaking and Chinese-speaking, and you may dance with as many of them as you like, at the rate of $4 (U.S.) an hour. Eventually, you may select one girl for the evening. Thus, if you make your selection at 11 P.M., you pay the proprietor $12 for the three hours that remain until closing time, and take her anywhere you like.

The lobby of the Clover Hotel, inconspicuously located on the third floor of a movie theater building, was jumping with Marines, Army, Air Force, and Navy servicemen; tired servicemen on R and R vacations in tthe Paris of Asia. On my way upstairs, I saw the huge, towering Lt. Ed Anderson and another Marine pilot, Lt. Faustin Wirkus, crouched over a telephone in the lobby. The other corners were filled with service types planning lighthearted expeditions for the evening. When I came down after a welcome bath, Anderson, who had been trying for over an hour to make a trans-Pacific call to his wife, was still waiting beside the phone with his buddy.

The evening went as evenings were undoubtedly going for all of the 500 or 600 vacationing Americans who had come in to Hong Kong this week. A bunch of us went first to the Bayview, a "Top of the Mark" type Skyroom on the 11th floor of the Clover hotel building, and found it alive with pleasant Latin American music and dancing. Then we went to the Blue Sky, a taxi-dance emporium, and to a handsome night club called the Golden Phoenix for dinner.

Sometime later in the evening I stopped by the hotel and discovered that Anderson was still trying to get through to his wife.

I also discovered, in the Chinese butterflies we met in the course of the long evening, the same surprising, sharp intelligence that one usually encounters in this, the Master Race of Asia.

The Oriental belles in our little group were Mary, slim, pale, stylish (and undoubtedly tubercular) immigrant from the nearby Portuguese colony of Macao; Annie, a large Shanghai type who had made her escape to Hong Kong recently, a very voluptuous charmer whose voluptuousness by this time was slightly on the downgrade; and Lee, tall, rather angular, also late of Shanghai and another refugee from the so-called "People's Democracy" to the north, with a flashing wit to match Mary's.

The evening was gay, we enjoyed a marvelous dinner, drinks, and several floor shows for the usual Hong Kong discount-house prices (less than half what it would cost in New York, Chicago, or Los Angeles). And I went to bed convinced that, all in all, Hong Kong is a good R and R town.

It would be a pleasant irony if that great liberty port should help give us the strength to do the job of expunging the Virus of Communism in Southeast Asia.

Monday, November 19

This morning we enjoyed another advantage of Hong Kong, especially set up for American military men: the China Fleet Club. Crossing the spectacular Hong Kong Harbor—a vast, sheltered sea space where British and American warships are lost amid freighters from all over the world—was exciting enough to give any landlubber a case of sea fever. We landed at the Star Ferry Pier on Hong Kong Island, and took a new Diesel-powered Mercedes cab (Hong Kong always has the latest word in everything) to the Fleet Club.

This is a five-story building close to the British Navy docks on the island, originally designed as a meeting place for British Navy people. Now, by special arrangement with the American armed forces, it has taken over the large job of making sure that American servicemen aren't gypped in their bargain-hunting among the sharp Hong Kong merchants. There are three stories of showroom space devoted to cameras, jewelry, and women's hand-embroidered sweaters—the kind of merchandise that an Army adviser or a Marine helicopter pilot might be looking for. The only admission requirement is that you must show your ID card or a copy of your orders.

I had an extravagant Chinese lunch with a small Asiatic bundle of energy, called V. C. Kan. Kan, a glib, fast-talking, high-pressure salesman, is a liaison officer employed by the Clover Hotel to make sure that the place gets a good share of American servicemen on Hong Kong R and R.

The restaurant, in the Nathan Road area, was called Han Kung, meaning "Hi Ball." V. C., polite and effective as usual, introduced me to some new items in Cantonese cooking: for instance, snake soup, made from the *hum hok ti*, meaning colored string snake, the *fan chang tao* or rice ladle snake, and the *kwa slui yung*, or banyan tree snake. These three kinds of snakes are chopped up and cooked together in a dish called *seigung*, if the name is of any importance. At any rate, it was delightful to taste, and the bits of meat in it had the savor and texture of chicken. We also had umpty-ump other courses: chicken and mushrooms, sweet and sour pork, *chow fan*, or fried rice with vegetables, pork-filled dumplings, and *tan tak*, custard egg pie. Kan, ever the obliging host, produced some North China delicacies that I mentioned I had enjoyed in Pek-ing and Nanking and Shanghai in the days when China was tottering under the Communist assault, in 1948. Kan whispered to the waiter and soon we had delicious *bao tze*, as good as any I could remember from China itself.

After lunch, I talked briefly to an old friend, Bob Trumbull, the *New York Times* correspondent in Hong Kong. Bob has his hands full serving as a listening post on doings inside China and also superintending *New York Times* coverage of the Vietnamese war and the struggle with the Communists throughout all of Asia.

I asked about the famines I have been hearing about inside China, and he said the reports of starvation seemed to be tapering off, as far as he could find out from the refugees. Most of them come across at Lo Wu, the railroad port of entry into the Hong Kong Colony some 15 miles north of Nathan Road. The refugees are still coming in at the rate of 18,000 a month.

He was very interested in the conduct of the Vietnamese war; he seemed to think it was by far the most important part of our conflict with Communists in this area, but didn't share my optimism about the military operations there. This afternoon, I did some shopping, and despite my vow not to go broke saving money in Hong Kong, as I always had on previous visits, I found myself wading through bargains and money at a breakneck pace, achieving close to the usual rate of expenditure for an American on a two-day pass in this city: about $7 an hour, waking or sleeping. But I have no regrets—Hong Kong bargains really *are* bargains.

Tonight was another delightful R and R evening, starting with a super European-style dinner at Gaddi's, one of the swankiest of the Hong Kong restaurants, and then continuing on to the Oriental Ballroom. This has a large, dimly lit dance floor with tables clustered around it and an orchestra playing ying-yang (Chinese) music as well as cha-cha-cha and twist. Maybe the most interesting feature of the Oriental Ballroom is that when you sit down at table, you are given a kind of menu, which turns out to be a list of names of dance hostesses, each one identified by number. You circle as many as you like, and then, instantly, the girls with those names and numbers appear at your table. You can choose all or nothing at all, although during the period of surveillance, you must pay taxi-dance rental ($4 an hour) for each girl.

Back at the hotel, I found that Ed Anderson had finally made the transoceanic connection with his wife, after many hours of trying and concomitantly resisting the blandishments of Hong Kong.

"Eight dollars for each three minutes," he said, "and we were on about ten minutes. A darn good connection." He laughed. "She was just about paying for my last call from Japan: Ninety-six dollars for nineteen minutes."

Tuesday, November 20

When I got in at 2:20 this morning, I decided to pack and get papers straight. The dutiful bellboy on my floor, apparently looking out for my welfare, said that he had some available females on tap, but I assured him that everything was OK. To bed at 4 A.M.

After less than three hours of sleep—a pretty good record for Hong Kong R and R—I roused myself to prepare for the sad flight back to Danang.

We piled into a bus that would take us to Kai Tak Airport and V.C. Kan, the tiny, high-powered promoter for the hotel, rode along with us.

On the bus, some of the Marines were riding Lt. Robert J. Athans (of Tuckahoe, N.Y.), the new flight surgeon who had been vocal about the fact that he wasn't going to pay for feminine companionship, even in Hong Kong. "Doc," who said that he used to date Anita Louise back in the States, had apparently found an American girl in Hong Kong, and they had spent a pleasant, if conventionally moral, evening together. Little V. C. Kan seemed to feel that his services were called for, and he promised Athans, "We'll have a good girl for you next time."

We took off at one minute after noon, and while most of the passengers quickly settled down to some fast recuperation between Hong Kong and Danang, I wandered around the plane, talking to the Marine and Army people who hadn't conked out completely, and made a quick canvass of their R and R accomplishments.

"Doc" Athans, remarkably clear-eyed and alert after the 48-hour extravaganza, said that he had spent very little during the two-day period, only $35, U.S. He had bought some colored slides of Hong Kong, and "that was about all; I wanted to look around and see what was what, so I could buy more intelligently next time."

More of a spendthrift was the Army captain on board, William Champion (of Huntington Beach, Calif.), a MAAG adviser attached to the engineering section of I Corps HQ, Danang. "I used up $1,000 getting three tape recorders," he said, "two for my friends, one for myself."

Sgt. Russell Bentley (of Brevard, N.C.), who runs the

Marine PX at the Danang camp, also seemed clear-eyed and alert. He said that he had bought a trench coat for his wife, and some clothes for his son, Russell III (both in Washington, D.C.), as well as a shirt and pair of trousers for himself.

Bentley said that he hadn't been too well provided with funds on this trip, because he hadn't known he was going until the day before the take-off from Danang.

"But I enjoyed myself—I saw a lot of things I'd never seen before: this gentleman who's supposed to have had those dreams and built these things." He was talking about the Aw Boon Haw Pagoda. Aw Boon Haw was the king of Tiger Balm, the Asiatic Vick's VapoRub, and "those dreams" referred to the weird collection of sculpture on the island side of the colony: unearthly beasts re-created in plaster in the Aw Boon Haw Pagoda. It was remarkable that, apparently without any help, Bentley had found his way to this monument.

I asked him what he thought about the people of Hong Kong, and he replied, "They were a bit different from what I'd imagined. The way they live in big buildings. I thought they'd have little houses on the side of the hill, and they still do, but most of them live in those big skyscrapers—eight or nine people in a room."

When I asked another Marine, waking up from a doze what he spent most of his money on: "Too much booze. We got a bottle of scotch, the first night, and took it up to the hotel room . . . The thing I liked about the whole trip as much as anything else was the food. Like that sweet and sour pork. You really want more. You can't eat enough of it."

Two boyish Army PFC's, Henry Genile (19, of Brooklyn, N.Y.), and William Obleman (18, of Syracuse, N.Y.), told me how they had struck up an acquaintance with a couple of Spanish girls who turned out to be part of a dance team performing in Hong Kong. "We wanted to meet some round eyes instead of slant eyes," said Genile. "They were the best-looking girls in the place. They told us to meet them at the City Hall—that's a kind of theater in Hong Kong. We went to see that show at the City Hall the first night, and we took the girls home."

I asked Genile what the highlight of the trip was, as far as he was concerned. He said, "One of the highlights of the trip was a hot bath. I sleep in a tent, and after seven months in Vietnam, you miss a bath."

The navigator, Marine PFC George M. Jensen (of Phoenix, Ariz.), was obviously a veteran of many trips to Hong Kong; he had a snapshot of a Chinese girl pinned up over his desk. "She's beautiful," he told me. "Her name's Amy, she works in a bar—where I met her."

Another crew member, S/Sgt Chuck Payne (of Fort Myers, Fla.), thought that "There's no other place like it [Hong Kong]. You see a Chinese guy driving a Mercedes down the street, and the guy with three kids sleeping in the gutter. What a place."

Payne said that he had bought a toy helicopter for his four-year-old son Michael. In toys as in everything else, good buys are to be had in Hong Kong.

"Last time, I went on a buying spree. I spent every damn dime. I got two cashmere sweaters for my wife, Donna . . . you really can get some bargains in things like hand-made sweaters. But I'd tell people going to Hong Kong: '. . . don't buy a thing the first day. Then do your shopping, when you have some idea what the prices are.' "

Payne and S/Sgt D. T. Parry, another crew member, were yearning about a new night-club joint they stumbled on by accident. They got out fast when it turned out to be a bit "far gone."

"It was in a rough section called Sing Sing," said Parry, ". . . and it was weird. It had a lot of seats like train seats, with red and white stripes, and they go down like a bed. There were a lot of young girls around, not dressed for —————, probably refugees. They didn't sell drinks, and there were a lot of Chinese men around. . . . we got out pretty quick."

It was 3:15 when we curved down the coast of China Beach and made our approach to the Danang airfield. We were back at camp.

I looked around for Col. Rathbun and learned that, at last, he had taken an R and R week off and was in Japan. Razor Blaydes, who was acting CO of the squadron in his absence, told me that there is nothing set up for tomorrow except some administrative flights, and "the weather doesn't look too good for any kind of flights." Rain was just beginning to fall, and there were dark clouds billowing up in the east. Soon afterward, it began to rain hard.

Razor said that because of the miserable weather, there haven't been too many missions since I left the Marine camp. But there had been one development: "Instead of coming in for landings in valleys, where the enemy can command us from the high ground, we've been allowed to make some landings on the ridges."

"How did you make out?" I asked him.

"Couple of rounds," he said, to indicate that there was

very slight enemy resistance. Thus, slowly, is progress made in the development of new antiguerrilla tactics.

In view of the bad weather and the diminished chances for missions, I decided to head back south. Fortunately, the R4D is flying down to Saigon tomorrow to pick up some rations, and I can promote a ride with them.

Wednesday, November 21

This morning was one of the gloomiest I've seen, even in a rainy place like Danang. There were clouds right on the deck beside the mountain to the north, and the jungly ridges to the west were completely obscured.

At the mess hall, very few pilots were about, and I discovered that all the birds here were grounded today because something went wrong in the auxiliary servomechanism in an HUS back at Okinawa, and a chopper pilot lost control of his bird. Fortunately, nobody was hurt, but all of the birds had to be checked over.

I found that yesterday "Ciggy" Cignotti left for home, apparently for good. The hard-working, spunky maintenance chief, who has always kept the birds flying no matter how much extra overtime effort is involved, has gone back because of an unexpected misfortune: his wife has had a nervous breakdown. Even Ciggy with seemingly inexhaustible moral strength and a strong religious faith (Catholic), who kept himself in physical shape by making daily jaunts down the taxiway of the airfield, has his vulnerable spot, touched through someone not even in Vietnam.

I got aboard the R4D about 8:40, and 15 minutes later we were heading for Saigon. Red-haired Sgt. Webb, the old dependable, was at the controls of the faithful Trans-Paddy Airways clunker, and with him again, Col. Linnimeier.

I got to the Brink BOQ in Saigon in time for lunch. Checking at the PIO to see about clearances for flights with the Hueys, I found that military affairs have been proceeding at the usual brisk pace in the embattled Delta and elsewhere. In two days there have been two ambushes of American MAAG officers; at Pleiku, a Special Forces sergeant was blown up driving a 2.5-ton truck over a mined area. And of course the Hueys are operating every day. I called Maj. Slavich, who took over the Huey outfit only last week, and asked if I could go out with them on some of their assault missions.

Slavich said cheerfully, "Sure. No problem. We'll see you tomorrow."

D-Zone

Thursday, November 22

I was up at 3:45, getting my gear and nerve together for my first mission with the Hueys. My premission jitters were palpable. I got out to the UTT camp about 5:15, and found Ivan Slavich's tent full of rubberneck types who were also going to make today's mission: a couple of Air Force officers and a double-dome type assigned to "assess the vulnerability of the Hueys," as he put it.

Maj. Slavich is sort of the archetype of the American military man: erect, clean cut, blue-eyed and blond-haired, with a spiky brush cut and decisive manner. He had been both a Marine and a paratrooper before his stint in the Hueys.

Slavich, holding up a map as he gave us a quick briefing, said the staging area for today's operation would be at Song Be. "The LZ is here at the northeast corner," he said, pointing to the map.

"To give you a little background: This is the first time the Vietnamese [government troops] have gone into the D-Zone area. Started day before last when we escorted a Ranger company into an LZ, and there was a parachute assault, a company working with troops in this area.

"The enemy situation: He's everywhere and nowhere." He pointed to the LZ area: "He [the enemy] may have 2.7-inch rockets, and heavy weapons here, but we don't know." He explained the Americans' paucity of intelligence about the enemy: "We are mainly a support agency, so we rely on them [the Vietnamese] for intelligence."

Slavich said today's mission was set up to take one battalion of troops into the LZ with 8,000 pounds of engineering equipment, which was to be used to cross a stream there. "The mission of this element is to establish this crossing site and sweep the area over here.

"There will be 30 H-21's and 10 H-34's [the Vietnamese Army version of the Marine HUS] plus the Hueys. There will be a 30-minute prestrike [T-28 bombing and strafing], and you know the problem there. If you lift your strike early, the VC will come back—we're a little concerned.

"It'll be the second largest helicopter lift. Tuesday's was the largest in history: 42, and the Hueys. Today: 40, and the Hueys.

"After the initial assault of 40 troop-carrying helicopters," Slavich said, "the H-21's will move over to another area to pick up troops who were dropped off on Tuesday." He said that this was the part of the operation he was most concerned about.

"These H-21's making the pickup will be escorted by three HU1A's. And this is where you get hit. When you have a reduced strength of Arvin, then the VC come in and try to police off the area. That's what happened at Tay Ninh." He was referring to a shoot-'em-up episode near the Cambodian border, about a month ago. The VC waited until most of the Arvin forces had been evacuated by the choppers, then pounced.

The two pilots I was to fly with today were Capt. Henry James O'Connor (of Whitewater, Wis.), a platoon leader, and a younger man who was the copilot, Lt. Richard C. Hamil (of Rome, Ga.). Their bird was an HU1A, with rockets and .30-caliber machine guns. (Today Slavich was flying an HU1B, the newest model, which has more power and speed and better machine-gun mounts.)

The HU1A cabin is a long rectangle with the two pilots' seats at the front, and cushions on the floor at the back, with safety belts for four people there. The two crewmen on the aircraft, Sgts. David "Luke" Lucas (of Mascotte, Fla.) and Francis A. "Smitty" Smith (of Bedford, Va.), hurriedly found armor vest and pants for me and showed me where to sit. They were to sit on the outside, with their automatic carbines, and my place was forward of them, my seat on top of a huge box of belted ammunition for the two machine guns mounted on each side, triggered by the pilots. Later on, I knew, probably at the staging area, we would pick up a Vietnamese "observer" who would have the formal function of designating the target, although the gunners and pilots were actually free to open up as soon as there was any VC fire reported or visible.

At 6:04 we lifted off. It was a marvelous sensation to sit in this bubble cockpit, and mosey along at 15 or 20 miles an hour, 30 or 40 feet up, as if we were on a modern magic carpet —very different from flying in the Army H-21 flying bananas or the Marine HUS's. The Huey moved along with the same feeling of weight and solidity that a heavy American car has on a superhighway, and it turned as smoothly as if there were pavement under it. There was very little sound audible except the *pop-pop-pop* of the rotor blades. My legs were bent under me and there was no room for movement. But I felt lucky to be making the ride.

Capt. O'Connor had said I could take Smith's headphones so that I could follow the radio calls "until we get there." Soon I heard O'Connor calling in: "This is Blue Leader. Off with a flight of two." I looked around and saw another HU1A following us as we headed north over Saigon. The lights below were still bright, although the dawn was coming up, but they thinned out as we passed over the northern outskirts of the city and by the time we were over the outlying districts, they had faded to nothing. The electric light system of Vietnam is limited, even in Saigon.

The air space seemed suddenly dead: dawn had not yet broken, there was very little on the radio. O'Connor took advantage of the slack time to point out some of the sights of the route to Hamil, who had flown into Vietnam just two days ago with the first two HU1B's for the UTT outfit.

O'Connor pointed: "See that road up there? That's running north. We'll just follow it.

"This area up to the right is D Zone. That's where they're supposed to be holding out in strength."

Following the dirt road north, we passed over a square of bare earth that seemed to have a triple wall around it, with a grid of regularly arranged houses inside. O'Connor explained to Hamil: "That's a strategic hamlet over there. They're trying to get all the peasants and farmers in one central compound in these hamlets. That way, the VC can't get to them for supplies. They've got a wall around them for protection."

The sun was coming up now in an emerald blaze, and the heat of the day burst upon us. Then, ahead of us, we saw a long landing strip set in the deep jungle: Song Be, the staging area where we would be joining up with the troops and the troop-carrying helicopters. Already, there was a tremendous line of choppers arranged on the field, maybe 25 H-21's and H-34's.

O'Connor, looking down at the clouds of red dust swirling as other choppers landed, said, "It's going to be dusty." Then, on the command channel: "Blue Flight, we will shut down right away when we set down. Plant 'em fast, because of the dust."

At 7:15, we were on the ground, fitting in to the pattern of the largest force of helicopters I had ever seen. Today's fleet would be 47 helicopters, including the Hueys, plus T-28's (fighter-bombers) and L-19's (observation planes). It was exciting to be part of something as new as this: the helicopter war, in one of its largest implementations.

By 7:50 all the troop carriers had arrived and loaded up, and we were off for the run into the LZ. We carried one slightly dyspeptic Vietnamese trooper in our bird. He sat between Lucas and me and spoke no English, but knew enough sign language to grasp Smitty's instructions: "If you get airsick, use your hat."

We heard the flights of H-21's, loaded with troops, as they went down on the deck to begin their low-level, high-speed charge into the LZ:

"Bravo Flight—full pitch, *now!* Charlie Flight—full pitch, *now!* Echo Flight—full pitch, *now!*"

O'Connor called to his Blue Flight, the third platoon of the Hueys: "The approach will be made from the southwest."

We, too, were in full pitch, heading into the sun, with the gunners on either side of me holding their carbines at the ready. As we came up over a row of hills thickly studded with jungly trees, I saw a smear of something rising over a far ridge. It appeared to be mist, but it wasn't: it was smoke. I asked O'Connor about it and he said, "Bomb at 11 o'clock." At that moment I saw an L-19 pulling up over the ridge, and it was clear what the bomb was: a smoke grenade, marking a target for the T-28's, softening up the LZ.

O'Connor had his map unfolded on his lap and was looking for the wide river where the engineers would be doing their bridging operation. I looked out and saw a T-28 pulling up, and the splash of a bomb behind it in a clearing among the solid pompons of trees. We made a circle over a squarish bend of the river and headed back south.

At that moment the first H-21 choppers started coming in to an open field. The ground had raw, tan-colored scars on its face, fresh marks of bombing. The T-28's had done their work well in preparing the LZ just minutes before the choppers came in to land. Now we were circling over the squatting birds at 850 feet. I wondered if there were VC's down there in the trees around the field, or if they had scrammed when the T-28's began their fierce attack.

Time after time, we swung in a wide circle and came back over the bend in the river, each time watching over a new flight of H-21's. But there was no visible firing, and no radio calls reporting antiaircraft fire from the ground.

O'Connor pointed to the north, where a white plume of smoke jutted from a field and spoke to Hamil: "See where the smoke is going off? That's where they'll pick up the troops, later on—the other LZ."

As we continued to orbit over the field I began to wonder about this Huey job of playing watchdog to the troop carriers. If there were any VC down there, then we were marvelous targets. Still, there had been no firing.

At last O'Connor spoke to his platoon: "This is Blue Leader. OK, let's join up and we'll head home."

Once away from the LZ, O'Connor gave the controls to his neophyte copilot. "OK, take it."

We were heading toward a conical hill, and O'Connor instructed Hamil: "Give that big hill a wide berth to the left. They say there are people [Communists] up there."

At 9:02, I saw the red dirt of the Song Be airfield, and within two minutes we were landing. O'Connor instructed his platoon: "Blue Flight, we'll take one hour and fifteen minutes."

A wave of relief passed over me at the successful completion of my first Huey assault mission. It had been very calm and I heard of no gunfire, but I had learned that the hell of this kind of mission was that you could never tell whether everything was going to happen or nothing. Anyhow, now that we were on the ground and there was going to be time out for refueling, it was time to relax.

At the fifth aircraft up the line, where coffee was available, I talked to Slavich. This next part of the operation was evidently heavily weighing on his mind. He said, "That's where we might catch it. The VC might close in. That's the way it was at Tay Ninh, when we got shot up."

While waiting for take-off again, I walked down the line of troop-carrying flying bananas and saw a familiar face. It was WO Bob Kibler of the 93d, looking freshly scrubbed and neat as always, even though he had been out on the mission this morning.

His nerves seemed somewhat on edge, still he said, "I went on that big one two days ago up here, but nothing happened. You never can tell. Yesterday two [of the 93d] birds went out on a medical evac and came back all shot up. Willie Ruf was one of them. They got four or five holes in each airplane." Kibler, the senior pilot of the 93d in terms of flying time—440 hours—here in Vietnam, said ruefully that he had expected to be gone back to the States by now. "But they just say, 'Stand by for replacements'—and the replacements are not coming in."

Instead of heading home, Kibler has been sent out on more assault missions. But at least, he said, his chopper hasn't been hit since I last saw him, on November 14.

"I told my wife not to write after the 10th, because I'd be there. She's on pins and needles. Every hour of every day I expect they'll say, 'The relief is here, pack your bags.' As soon as I get to Saigon, I'll phone her and tell her I'll be there in a couple of days."

Clearly, Kibler is living on nerve until the day he can shove off to join his wife and three kids: a girl, six, and two boys, three and one. "The kids were kind of built up for Dad being there on Turkey Day," he said. "But it's too late for that now." It suddenly occurred to me that today is Thanksgiving.

"When I busted the 400-hour mark," Kibler said, "I thought I'd be out of here in a couple of days. But that's life."

He told me the latest gossip about the 93d: Maj. Paul Ewing, the new CO of the outfit, went out on his first mission the other day, and his was the only bird that got hit. He was out with John Cooney, the senior pilot in terms of over-all helicopter hours, and it was Cooney's last mission.

"There it was. One little man stood up in the middle of a rice paddy and bluep!—he [the plane] got hit. You never know."

I asked Kibler if they got the VC that fired at Ewing. He shook his head negatively. "A T-28 came in and was snooping around for him, but couldn't find him. He was apparently a regular—he was wearing one of those camouflage straw hats.

"Next day Cooney went up to Saigon on orders. His airplane left for the States on Tuesday. He might have made it [home] for Thanksgiving."

Kibler's mind kept snapping back to the matter of a replacement and the possibility of a quick flight back to Jean and his kids. "Dickie Bird Adams is No. 1 on the rotation list," he said. "Lee Hanna is No. 2. I'm No. 3."

Kibler still had some more sweating to do this afternoon, because his chopper was one of those assigned to go in and pick up the force that was to be evacuated—the troop lift Maj. Slavich expected to be the most dangerous of the day. O'Connor's platoon would probably be escorting the H-21's on that job.

On the way back to my Huey, I spotted an Australian officer wearing the crowns and pips of a colonel and a shoulder patch of the Royal Australian Infantry. He was Col. Francis P. Serong, of Melbourne, Australia, and a brief stop to talk to him was very profitable. He was standing near Ivan Slavich's new HU1B.

Col. Serong had spiky, graying hair and the patient manner of the Army veteran, and he was wearing the jungle boots which battlewise soldiers in this area generally wear. It developed that Serong had served in the long British campaign against the Communist insurgents in Malaya, and he had come over here with fellow countrymen in a training unit. I asked him how this war situation compared with that which the British faced for 10 years in Malaya until they finally secured the defeat of the Communists.

"The main factor is that this is an advisory situation, and that was a command situation. That is by far the biggest factor. Second, in Malaya we had a recognizable enemy. Here, you don't. There, it was Chinese—here, the VC look like the Vietnamese."

Col. Serong said that new techniques of helicopter warfare, however, are being worked out here, and that despite the unfavorable differences between Malaya and Vietnam, there is promise in the present tactics.

The colonel was enthusiastic about the HU1B. "It's getting to be something like what a chopper ought to be," he said.

While Serong stood by, admiring the new Huey, I talked to Slavich. He said, "This is the kind of mission we like—when the H-21's don't get fired on.

"You know, we don't fire until we're fired upon. Our sole mission is to protect the [troop-carrying] helicopters, and I'm happy as a clam at high tide if they don't get fired on."

There was still some time before take-off, and Slavich was still on nerve ends, as everyone seemed to be at this point. Again he referred to the Tay Ninh engagement, where the VC gained in boldness as the troops were lifted out until, at the end, the enemy outnumbered the few Arvin that remained.

"We fired about 2,000 rounds each," Slavich said. "We got 50 to 75 VC's, estimated."

He also mentioned the mission of a week ago Monday, when determined enemy fire developed, and Pappy Wright "put a rocket right through the door of the shack."

As long as he was reminiscing about battle engagements, I

asked him about other recent brushes with the VC, and he mentioned the case of CWO Cleatus Heck (of Centrahoma, Okla.). Five weeks ago near My Tho in the Delta, a rocket on Heck's aircraft was hit by VC rifle fire. The rocket sputtered and smoked and threw sparks, but didn't explode, and Heck put the chopper down to a paddy and dunked it in a pool of wet. The other pilot that day with Heck was Capt. Hebert C. Damron (of Hippen, Ark.).

At 11:05, word went down the line of Hueys that we were taking off. We had a new Vietnamese trooper, who also spoke no English, but this fellow seemed to be more highly keyed than the first one. He worried Luke and Smitty more, too. Luke told me that the Vietnamese observers frequently get airsick: The motion of the birds is unfamiliar to them, smooth as it is compared to many other types of choppers. The fact is that many of the Vietnamese have never flown before.

After the H-21's had formed up, we headed north again. It turned out to be an uneventful transfer of troops, and by 1:10 we were back at the staging area. As Capt. O'Connor summarized it, "Another uneventful day"—thus far.

Smitty and Luke tied down the rotor blades and mentioned food: our Thanksgiving dinner. I made my way to the cases of rations that had been cracked open, and extracted some beans with pork and tomato sauce and crackers. Smitty and Luke had similar tin-can lunches, and I noted that one had C-ration labeled *Meat & Noodles*. I asked him: "Is that any good?"

"I don't know," he said. "I don't care for any of this ——
—."

O'Connor and Hamil were talking about today's operation. Hamil's reaction to his first mission? "Not too much to it," he said. "I don't understand this war. I tell you, what you read in the papers and what you hear over here are two different things."

"Neither does anybody [understand it]," said Smitty. When I went on to ask what he had read, Hamil answered, "You read a little something—they get excited about it, usually something bad, then you don't hear anything."

Capt. O'Connor motioned to us to move down the line to a briefing, beside another Huey. While the pilots clustered around him, he started with a topic sentence: "From what I saw, there was no action. Did anyone see anything?" No answer.

"Somebody called there was rifle fire from the right side,"

O'Connor said. "But there was nobody in there—that was Maj. Slavich testing the guns of the HU1B."

"Nobody in there but one scared deer," one wag suggested. O'Connor nodded his head, and went on sternly with a detailed critique of the sloppiness of the positioning of the third platoon in today's flying. After he had raked the pilots over, he summarized: "So today has been quiet. We should be released in one more hour. Crawl into your aircraft and go to sleep." But *he* didn't, he went off to the shade of his airplane to rip energetically into tactics with Hamil.

We waited a long time, until 3:15, before O'Connor finally said: "We can go home." We landed at Tan Son Nhut at 4:35 P.M., the end of a long day.

I went into Slavich's tent with O'Connor while they talked over the day's operations. Slavich said this was the right kind of operation, with no opposition, but was puzzled that there had been so little opposition in the D Zone, which is supposed to be such a stronghold of VC operations.

"There hasn't been a time, when we went down to the Delta, we didn't get shot at," he said.

O'Connor: "Yes, they like to shoot at us going south, not going north. Last mission south, the H-21's got shot at before we were out of the [traffic] pattern."

I could see that Slavich was still tensed up from the responsibility of the day's operations. He talked about Johnnie Lee, the first casualty of the outfit.

"He was out on the line, an HU1A mech. I told him, 'I'm gonna put you in operations,' because we lost our operations sergeant. It would be nonflying duty, and he begged me to let him back on the line.

"He had a wife, and child he'd never seen. He was in his early 20's—his wife was 19 or 20. He was a very quiet fellow. He never got into trouble. We never heard a peep out of him. Well, that's the way it is.

"We're gonna lose people down here, no doubt about it. But it's so different here from Korea. There, you'd lose 40 or 50 people at a time. But down here, you're not supposed to lose people. And it's a problem. You can't play up the casualty business or you'd have a morale problem."

To change the subject, I asked Slavich about the HU1B's that were used for the first time on mission today. "How did they work out, and how about the armament?"

He grinned. "They're a great weapon [the multiple machine-gun mounts]—they go where you point 'em." Slavich said that while we had been out on the missions today, two more HU1B's had arrived and that they would be coming in at a steady rate from now on. Slavich raved further about the new quadruple 7.62-mm. machine-gun mounts, which are power-controlled and can fire over a tremendous field, instead of being rigged to fire only straight ahead, as is the case in the HU1A's.

I borrowed a jeep from Slavich and went back into town tonight, where a sumptuous Thanksgiving Dinner had been laid on at the Brink BOQ, complete with turkey, ham, and all the attendant froufrou. But the Thanksgiving Dinner I had eaten out at the Song Be strip with the Hueys at midday, in the midst of operations in VC territory, seemed a lot more proper Thanksgiving Dinner for Vietnam in November of 1962.

Friday, November 23

I went down to the PI office this morning and found a note from Col. Vann. It was an official report on the operation I had witnessed with the 93d Helicopter Company in Vann's sector, on November 14.

Vann's report confirmed the results we had heard down in My Tho from Col. Cao's troops: 9 KIA's, 15 POW's, 60 suspects—1 small-arms factory, 1 medical depot, 1 radio receiver, and a potpourri of VC weapons, mostly homemade, and "miscellaneous information booths and hiding places destroyed."

It sounded like a pretty impressive score, considering the elusiveness of the enemy, the fact that he was operating in his home ground, and his ability to ditch his weapons and slip into peasant garb when cornered. The operation seemed to indicate that, as Col. Cao had said, "more shoppers" could accelerate the war, and it was largely due to this magical weapon that so many VC's had been caught on this operation.

Another news item gleaned at the PI office today was word from Cmdr. Zornow that there will be a foray of the Vietnamese Junk Fleet, a two-day sweep in search of VC smugglers, a sort of training maneuver in action, beginning tomorrow. The Junk Fleet, a massive project designed to ring the whole coastline of Vietnam with new, small patrol boats, sail- and engine-powered, will be leaving from Saigon for the first time tomorrow. The boats will head down the Saigon River to the southern coast and patrol a strip of the South China Sea, where they join. Zornow said a number of correspondents could go along. I added my name to the list of volunteers, and was told to be on hand at the Navy docks in downtown Saigon at eight o'clock tomorrow.

This morning, I got to see Maj. Gen. Charles F. Timmes, Chief of MAAG in Vietnam, at his headquarters (in an old frame house). He is small, blue-eyed, and baldheaded and wears on his chest the magic sign of a Can-Do Army commander, the curling silver wings of a paratrooper.

The most interesting thing he said about the Vietnam fighting was:

"The most important part is the Delta, and this is where the enemy is located. The hard-core battalions are there, and more than half of the enemy. The [Communist] elite troops are down here. . . . The III Corps Area [the Delta] is where all the casualties have been, practically."

Gen. Timmes said that the successful prosecution of the war will involve spreading American advisers out among the Vietnamese Army units even more than they are now. "We're down to the battalion level now—one officer and two sergeants. But when we get replacements, we will have platoon sergeants down to the company level. The platoon sergeants will go right along with the companies. Last fall, we had only one man per regiment. . . . we'll go down . . . to a squad if necessary."

I asked the general which of the American military jobs in the Vietnam campaign were the most dangerous, and he said the MAAG advisers and the helicopter pilots. He mentioned that in recent months there have been 5 American advisers killed and 16 wounded, and among the helicopter boys, 4 killed and more than 20 wounded. My own count of our war effort in Vietnam showed 68 Americans wounded in action and 27 killed in action to date (we sent our first MAAG representatives down here in 1957). The big increments of casualties began in February-March of this year, when the helicopters came in and started moving Vietnamese troops around in battle assaults. The casualty figures don't include accidental deaths.

This afternoon I stopped in at the Air Force dispensary at Tan Son Nhut to see the latest of the MAAG casualties, a captain who had been twice wounded and seven times ambushed. He is Capt. Derrell J. Savage (of Aberdeen, Idaho), an infantry adviser who has been working in the Delta area.

I found Savage resting uneasily in pajama bottoms on an Army cot in a primitive ward in the dispensary, a mountain of bandage on his left leg. He is lean, graying, and attenuated, as if his nerves have been drawn out to the maximum.

Savage said that his assignment has been to train the Vietnamese SDC in the Can Tho vicinity south of Saigon. He spoke quite patiently about his dangerous job:

"You go out in the company of these units, you expect to have a little contact, particularly if you go with the SDC, because the VC will lock horns with the SDC—they know they're not so heavily armed, maybe not so well trained."

I asked Savage to tell me the story of his previous ambushes. The first one occurred on April 18, "in the Long Toan district. They let about half of the company get through, then they hit us with grenades and small arms. And that's when I got my first one [wound].

"Then, about April 28 or 29, we got involved in another episode with an SDC outfit. It was a kind of meeting engagement. We went down to relieve this outpost, and the VC had it staked out. There were about 200 VC's.

"We were sent in as a reserve force . . . and they [the VC] were strung out for about 1,000 meters, in V-shape.

"I don't know how we got out with so few casualties. We had 6 men killed and 12 wounded—6 killed by VC's jumping out of spider holes they had dug. We estimated we had about 20 or 30 VC's killed."

Then, on May 13, Savage said he had a jeep blown out from under him near Can Tho. "There were four in the jeep, but nobody got hurt. We got out and killed four of them. Or anyhow, we knocked them down."

On this most recent ambush, Savage said he was driving back from a training session with the SDC troops toward his quarters when "a grenade went off ahead. Then the right side of my windshield went out, and I went out.

"I was alone in my jeep, with three other jeeps and a truck in the convoy.

"I remember being knocked off the road. It knocked the wind out of me. I tried to fire with my carbine but it was jammed. I threw a couple of grenades, then I started firing with my .45. I tried to get the carbine working. My NCO in the jeep ahead stopped and started back. I thought I'd hurt my back; I didn't know I'd been hit by a fragment.

"It looked like a grenade fragment that hit in here [he pointed to the back of his leg] and came out here. It didn't hit any bone. It made a hole about the size of a walnut. I think the detonator went through with it."

I asked Savage how he felt about the possibility of being returned to his unit down in the swamps. He has a wife and two daughters back in Idaho and I'm sure that if I'd been he, I would have had some misgivings about going back to the Abominable Delta to risk my neck. He came over to Vietnam in January of this year, and can't expect to be relieved until January next. But he only shrugged.

"I don't mind the shooting so much," he told me, "but I get a little chilly about the mines and booby traps. If you get into shooting, they're bad enough shots so that if you get on the ground you're not in such bad shape. I've moved quite a distance under small-arms fire. You'll have it crackin' at you, but you get used to it."

Savage told about his most recent experience with mines. "Last Wednesday, some of my SDC people were picking through VC area north of Ninh Binh. We got around 15 booby traps. Then we were going through a VC classroom, and a mine went off. It was electrically timed, one of those big 10-kilo jobs. It made a hole big enough to drive a jeep into—and four of my men got blown apart."

I checked with a doctor in the ward to see about the disposition of Savage's case. The doc said he'll probably be sent home, at last.

Junk Fleet

Saturday, November 24

Down at the waterfront park that runs along the side of the Saigon River, I found a press party waiting for the first trip of the Junk Fleet. The meeting place was a gangway leading to the deck of a gray, freshly painted Vietnamese LST, a Vietnamese Navy headquarters ship.

The people of the press whom I saw there were Dave Halberstam, the *New York Times* correspondent, tall, eager, and bespectacled, a Harvard graduate who had also graduated as a war correspondent from the fighting in the Congo; Stan Siegal, a handsome correspondent for Mutual Broadcasting, also very eager but a neophyte in war-corresponding; Michel Renard, a CBS movie cameraman; a Vietnamese movie cameraman who works for CBS as a "stringer"; and with them, a U.S. Navy officer, a lieutenant commander named Louie L. Lindenmayer (of Seattle, Wash.).

Cmdr. Lindenmayer, a sturdy, gray-haired man with the well-worn manner of a sea captain, was wearing shorts and tall socks. A round pin on his shirt identified him as belonging to the Vietnamese Junk Force: a junk superimposed on a brown background. He identified himself as senior Junk Force adviser, and when we asked about the mission we were going on today, he said rather vaguely, "The general purpose is for sailing down the river. These boys have manned their junks. It's a training cruise."

That didn't sound very dynamic or exciting, but when we inquired further, we were told that we would be, in effect, on patrol. Some of the swampy Delta country along the Saigon

River was in dispute with the VC. We would also make a patrol along the coast into the South China Sea and probably stop at Vang Tau, which in the old days of French domination used to be called Cap St. Jacques. Warming to his job, Lindenmayer told us a little more about the mission of the Junk Fleet: "The main objective is to deprive the VC of infiltration along the coast—that basically is it."

Siegal wanted much more exact information: "What are their tactics? Do they just pounce on some guy, or is it a regular surveillance?"

Poor Lindenmayer, who had just arrived here two weeks ago and had been on this new Navy job for only five days, answered noncommittally, "They watch everything—all the boats."

Lindenmayer led the way across the deck of the Vietnamese LST to the far rail, where, looking over the gunwale, we saw a wooden sailboat—apparently new, for her planking looked unsoiled and even unscrubbed as yet—and were told that this was to be one of our boats for the trip. We climbed down to the deck of this sturdy-looking sea cruiser, about 50 feet long, and found that it *was* new.

On board was a Vietnamese crew in commando-type berets, and olive green American-type fatigues. It was the same kind of uniform that American and Vietnamese troops wear in the field on land operations, strangely out of place on a boat. But Cmdr. Lindenmayer said that these men are all experienced in junk operations and have served as junk sailors in civilian life.

I saw another type of trooper on board: men in blue uniforms and steel helmets, who are the Viet Hy, fighting commandos, or Junk Marines. They will be used for boarding and amphibious operations with the Junk Fleet.

At 8:50, we shoved off from the lee of the towering LST, under the power of our (American-made) gasoline engine, turned upstream, and made our way east toward the mass of ships anchored in the Vietnamese Navy Yard. Another junk, equally new, appeared from the opposite shore and joined us in our slow peregrination upstream. On board I noticed a heavier concentration of Viet Hy troops.

Cmdr. Lindenmayer told us some astounding statistics about this fleet: that it already consists of 250 junks and that this number will be at least doubled in the next few years. It will be a powerful screen to cut off the resupply of arms by sea to the embattled VC anywhere along the 900-mile coastline of Vietnam.

We chugged up the river for 10 or 12 minutes, joined by other boats like ours as we went. Soon we had three other command junks, six motor boats, and five 40-foot motor-sailers with the junk rig. We turned and headed downstream at 10 or 12 knots, our boat leading the procession.

On the stern deck, I watched the troops loading their M-1's. The sun was bright and hot, and some of the troops shed their jackets. Cmdr. Lindenmayer pointed out to me the tat-tooed words *Sat Cong* on their torsos, above their hearts.

"All of our junkmen have that tattooed on their chests. It means 'Kill the Communists,' and it's part of joining the Junk Force—it's required." I remarked that it was pretty definite and irrevocable evidence of anti-Communist sympathies, a pretty drastic guarantee of loyalty. Lindenmayer smiled. "But it *is* required," he said. "A Vietnamese requirement."

When the southern city limits of Saigon were behind us and the wild green marshland was sliding by on both sides of the placid river, a command was issued in Vietnamese. It was evidently an order to keep a sharp lookout on the banks, for there was a clicking of bolts as rifles and carbines were primed for action. So was the .50-caliber machine gun on a tripod mount on our bow. But the 40-mile trip to the sea was une-ventful.

I learned in talking to Lindenmayer that he had been a chief petty officer in the Navy during World War II. Most recently he had been aboard a fleet tug out of Pearl Harbor.

When I asked him how he liked the blandishments of Saigon, he said very agreeably, "I'm pretty well nailed down. I've got a good-lookin' wife, and I'm here on business."

He added, "It'll be very interesting and a lot of satisfaction to see the show [the Junk Fleet] get on the road." He thought there were advantages to using the Fleet as a way to stop the smuggling of arms and supplies and ammunition to the VC from North Vietnam and China. "The main advantage is they're not particularly conspicuous. . . . They're also able to ease in along the coast."

He was enthusiastic, too, about the low cost of the junks. In his short time here he had been to the largest boat-building yard where the junks are being fabricated, at the seaport called Phan Thiet. There, he said, the product is a 40-foot motor-sailer, and they are being brought in for about $6,500 each—engine included—a good bargain for the U.S. The overall cost of the fleet will be about a million dollars: not very much if you consider that you would get only three HUS's or HU1A's for that much money, or perhaps one jet fighter plane.

I watched the crewmen breaking out their lunch: loaves of French bread, which they kneaded into balls of dough and downed with cans of cherry pop. The Vietnamese seem to be as fond of soda pop as we are of beer, wine, and booze.

When we hit the heave of the ocean at the mouth of the river, the sky clouded, and rain began to fall. We crouched in the low cabin, which was filled with the stench of oil; the boat pitched and heaved as we headed east into a heavy sea. None of our crew of 10 or 12, however, seemed to feel any queasiness in the stomach.

We rocked and rolled across the strip of open ocean south of the river, slowing because the seas were heavy, and eventually came to a bare brown promontory: Vang Tau. We hove to opposite a harbor and a downtown section of weathered concrete houses, French style, and a muddy beach with headlands of rock at one end.

Now began the maneuver phase of our strip: A group of 18 or 20 Viet Hy boys in bathing suits dived overboard and swam toward the shore. Cmdr. Lindenmayer became very secretive about the significance of all this, but very evidently it was some kind of rehearsal for a frogman assault on a port held by the VC.

Halberstam, Siegal, Renard, and I went ashore and checked into the small (formerly French) hotel for the night. It is irrationally filthy. We were told by the U.S. Navy advisers here that tomorrow morning the junks will hoist their sails and practice maneuvering in formation. Ho-hum. The only hope of any excitement is that we may be called in to help with some land action in the Delta as we chug back up the Saigon River tomorrow. Apparently, we're not going to do any searching for smugglers on this trip.

Sunday, November 25

This morning we took the troops aboard the junks and hoisted the sails, which are an intriguing purplish color, and did some firing with the .30-caliber and .50-caliber machine guns—but only at a red-flag target floating at sea.

On the way up the Saigon River (it took us nearly seven hours from Vang Tau), we had a radio contact warning of an alert, and when we stopped at an outpost that had a dock and bamboo fences around it, it seemed that we might be involved in a chase of some VC who had been spotted sneaking around the outpost. But by the time we docked and got the dope, the target had disappeared.

When we got back to the Saigon dock at 10:15 tonight, we heard that we had missed a good-sized story: An outpost had been attacked last night up in I Corps Area to the far north, near a place called Phuoc Chau. It seems that a battalion of VC troops made the attack during the small hours of the morning. The Arvin garrison had support from .105- and .155-mm. howitzers, and the approaches to the outpost were ranged and numbered. So when the VC began their attack, the artillery began to fire, and so did the garrison. The VC made a head-on attack and were caught flat-footed: There were 108 confirmed KIA's. Also, our people captured some .57-mm. recoil-less rifles, a good supply of machine guns, submachine guns, and rifles, and a large stock of grenades. It had been a resounding victory for the Arvins.

Monday, November 26

This morning I tried to promote a ride up to Phuoc Chau but, as sometimes happens, nothing in the transportation line was working out. The Army aviation section wasn't running anything up there and I couldn't get orders for the Air Force flight in time to catch this morning's take-off—anyhow, the flight was turned back by the weather. I asked for orders to Danang so that I can catch the Air Force Mule Train (C-123) as soon as possible and get a look at the Phuoc Chau scene.

At the PI office, that center of late bulletins on all our military activity, I learned that the VC made an attack this morning on another outpost, Tra Vinh, about six kilometers west of Saigon. Here, as distinguished from the engagement of Phuoc Chau, we took a beating. Galfund was trying to get the dope, but hadn't secured it yet. All he had been able to find out was that it was a very light engagement, compared to Phuoc Chau, and that a MAAG adviser was wounded.

The PI people passed me one bit of stimulating news today: Maj. Gen. Reuben Tucker, an old paratroop buddy who was in charge of the MAAG in Laos and was run out by the Geneva truce committee, will be in Saigon tomorrow. I must try to see him. It might be a good chance to get the straight dope on Laos, since there are few men better qualified to know what really happened in that area, and none I know who are as forthright as Tucker. Once I wrote about Tucker that when he came into a room, he was like a landing boat sending out bow waves of energy. He's been that direct and dynamic since I've known him.

Tuesday, November 27

I had my orders for the Mule Train flight to Danang this morning, but the weather north of here is still impossible, and the flights canceled out.

This afternoon, I managed to intercept Gen. Tucker as he was coming through from Thailand. The old blond-mustached fighter is as indomitable as ever and, if anything, more, rather than less, blunt. He still has the same outthrust chest and drill master's voice, and apparently his fondness for fighting hasn't forsaken him either, though he seemed a little nonplused about his recent puzzling encounter with a nationality who, he said, are not interested in fighting. I knew that Tucker had gone into Laos last spring with a MAAG of more than 250 men. The mission was to train the Laotians to fight against the Communists and, perhaps more important, to persuade them that it was worth while to fight.

I had heard about his pink-sheet (top-secret) communications to CINCPAC on the noncombativeness of the Laotians, memorializing the way they would disappear after he had arranged them nicely in battle formation. When the Geneva negotiations brought about a cease-fire in Laos last summer, the U.S. MAAG, under Gen. Tucker, was ordered out—and so, officially at least, was the enemy, the Viet Minh MAAG from North Vietnam and China. In Tucker's language, "We were run out October 6." With a cease-fire technically in effect and the fighting officially supposed to be ended, the military security that enveloped our participation in the Laotian struggle was ended and I could hear Tucker's version.

"With all that firepower, they'd [the Laotians] shoot at the clouds," he said, as if it were the most heinous crime imaginable to waste firepower—and perhaps, if your country is going down the drain under a Communist onslaught, it is.

"Those people—they're not interested in fightin'—only eatin', sleepin', and fornicatin'. And if you look around [in a fight], they might not even be there. I used to think they were the worst Goddamn cowards in the world. But it's in their philosophy. They're just not mad at anybody or . . . anything."

I knew Tucker would give me a straight answer, so I asked him why we couldn't get the Laotians to fight for their freedom when the Viet Minh (VM) apparently were succeeding in persuading them to risk their necks for the Communist point of view.

Tucker said, "The Viet Minh put one or two Viet Minh in

each squad and they'll say to a guy: 'OK, Corn Pone, you go down the center and we'll come around here and meet you at the end, and somebody'll be shooting at you. But if you come back, I'll shoot you.'

"They [the Viet Minh] were the sparkplugs. The Laotians think that the Viet Minh are nine feet tall. They're real professionals. In Laos, all you have to do is fire three rounds and yell 'Viet Minh,' and they'll scatter like a covey of quail."

Tucker said that the Geneva truce arrangements could be reduced to a simple useless proposition: "They agreed to agree to do something." But he said the status of Laos as of the moment is that the Reds "have three-quarters of the country. They can take it any time they want."

He said that his own MAAG was handicapped by the fact that the advisers were not supposed to stay with Laotian units during battle engagement, although "we had a few good actions where we encouraged them pretty close." Tucker said that he felt, as Gen. Timmes did, that American advisers should be spread out with the units in the field, and that if the Laotian fighting opened up again and the Reds were determined to finish the job, we should be more aggressive. "If they [the Reds] pull the cork out of the bottle, we should lead the way and let them [our Laotian allies] go along with us."

That was the kind of fighting talk I expected from Tucker, who, although he's over 50 and has had a little heart trouble, still makes parachute jumps and believes in personal leadership. He's made more than 200 jumps, and has set such a dramatic example to his five sons that two of them have already been jumping. Bruce was a paratrooper in Germany, and Jeff, 19, a junior at Citadel Military Academy, is a sky-diver.

I knew Tucker during World War II, when he was CO of 504th Parachute Infantry, and I went through a couple of actions with him and his 'troopers near a town called Altavilla in Italy, where all the officers in his headquarters company were killed or wounded. Tucker and his boys got on the objective, which the 36th Division, a much larger unit, had tried unsuccessfully to do. But the 504th eventually was driven out too, when overwhelmed by a superior force of German infantry, artillery, and tanks. Later, I saw Tucker in Korea, where he was a general on the United Nations' Staff at Seoul. I knew that he must have been happy to head up the American MAAG in Laos, because it was a field command with tremendous responsibilities and, most important, it was basically a fighting job—and there is no denying the fundamental fact that Tucker likes to fight. He is one of the breed of fighters, and more honor to them when they are oriented to fight for self-determination and freedom against the forces of dictatorship.

I asked how he would capsule our war situation in Southeast Asia and he replied, "Where's the silver lining? There isn't any—unless it's here." He said that in Vietnam, we have the great new advantage of the helicopters and the tremendous American firepower—if the kinks of our whole new panoply of helicopter war can be worked out.

At the Brink mess hall I talked to a colonel who was just back from Danang and had the latest scoop about Phuoc Chau, Alexander R. "Bud" Bolling, Jr. (of Carlisle, Pa.), son of an Army general. Bolling said that the enemy casualty figures had checked out at 124 VC confirmed killed (bodies counted), at a cost of only about a dozen wounded on our side, only three of those seriously injured.

Bolling said that the Phuoc Chau victory was of national significance in the Vietnam war, and that "well-coordinated intelligence did the work," meaning that we had a tip-off that the attack was coming, and were ready.

"The attack by the VC was of regimental strength, and everything went off beautifully. First, a flare was fired after a VC stumbled over a tripwire. Our artillery had the concentrations numbered and let 'em have it. Also, there was a lot more small-arms fire than people here thought. One Vietnamese [government] machine gunner had 40 dead in front of his position. The VC were routed and could have been chopped up all the way, but the weather was right on the ground, so helicopter operations were hampered." But 124 dead VC was a handsome score.

Wednesday, November 28

I was up at five o'clock today to catch the C-123 to Danang. Took enough gear in my rucksack for a couple of weeks' living in the field. My plan was to get to Phuoc Chau, talk to the young American who was the MAAG adviser there, Capt. Graham Vernon (32, of Tallahassee, Fla.), and the Vietnamese machine gunner who had killed the 40 VC, and take a look at the captured weapons: Czech-made machine guns, Chinese grenades, and .57-mm. recoil-less fieldpieces.

But the Phuoc Chau jaunt wasn't to be. There was a solid front of clouds over everything north of Nhatrang and we couldn't even get into Ban Methuot. We flew for an hour with clouds on all sides and were back again at Tan Son Nhut at 11:40. This afternoon, I managed a military connection by phone to Capt. Vernon, who had come in to I Corps HQ at Danang. It was a bad phone connection—as what military connection isn't?—but I was lucky to make any contact at all.

Vernon said that he had been sent in to the Phuoc Chau outpost, manned by about 100 Arvin troops, about a month ago. Things had been relatively quiet until that attack early Sunday morning. The only episodes until then had been some small-arms fire, some sniper rounds thrown into the camp at night.

About the attack: "I was sleeping in a hut, and I woke up when I heard our own firing. The VC had hit that tripwire about 3:20 A.M. We got the artillery right in. It was .105-mm. stuff, firing from 8 kilometers [5 miles] away. We brought that artillery in to within 40 meters of our perimeter.

"There was a lot of firing and an awful lot of confusion. It was my first action, and it seemed like the Fort Benning demonstrations, like the night firing—the tracers and all that. It was the same butterfly feeling as before a ball game [he played lacrosse in college]. I was firing with my carbine and my .45. I was awfully anxious that the attack would fail, because I didn't know the way to get out of there."

When I asked him if he had killed any of the VC, he said he didn't know, in the confusion of that night action.

He told me that the VC assault was supposed to be a "coordinated attack from a semicircle, but they attacked in echelon—their coordination went wrong. The artillery really chopped them up."

Vernon, I learned, has a famous military antecedent awarded the Congressional Medal of Honor in 1879. He was William Vernon, who won his distinction in the Yellow River campaign against the Indians in Montana. Capt. Vernon's father was also a military man, a lieutenant colonel.

By now it is practically too late to get a firsthand look at Phuoc Chau. Tomorrow, I'll go out to the UTT base at Tan Son Nhut to do some more flying with the Hueys. Slavich has given me permission to fly on as many assault missions as I like, provided my presence doesn't interfere with operations.

D-Zone

Thursday, November 29

Up at 3:30 and out to the UTT camp in time for breakfast. I was assigned to an HU1B flown by Capt. Damron and Lt. Billy Sprague (of Chandler, Okla.). Sprague came into Vietnam only a few days ago—in fact, he flew one of the new HU1B's in, and he's an expert in the marvelous HU1B multiple-machine-gun mount.

I found the Damron-Sprague chopper down on the line, and it was a treat to get aboard such a handsome, brand-new aircraft. These birds have quite a different configuration from the HU1A's, and are much less "improvised"—they have come from the factory with all sorts of handsome equipment built in, instead of having bits and pieces added by mechanics after delivery out here.

The cabin is the same rectangular shape, but the seats for the gunners, behind the chairs of pilot and copilot, are back to back and nicely padded in leatherette. They even have headrests. There is also a bench-type seat at the back, and much more leg room than in the 1A configuration.

Billy Sprague, whose father is a Pontiac dealer back home, spoke about the extra speed these birds have, perhaps 20 miles an hour more than the HU1A's, and he summed it up like a true son of General Motors: "These are the Cadillacs of the skies."

But the greatest improvement is in the armament: those four 7.62-machine guns, mounted two to a side just above the landing skids on each side of the cabin, marked by two curving silver ammo belts that connect them with big ammunition

225

boxes in the back of the cabin. Billy Sprague was very proud of the guns, and showed me how they could be moved left, right, and up and down with Cadillac smoothness through a gunsight grip operated from the left-hand pilot's seat. "Those are wonderful guns," he said. "You can hit a barrel at a thousand yards." Back in the States, Billy had been an instructor in the art of gunnery with this rig.

The pilots told me that they would pick up a briefing at Lai Khe, the staging area. We knew only that the general LZ area was going to be the D Zone, the same VC stronghold area north of Saigon where I had made my first missions with the Hueys.

We lifted off at 6:39, after the crew chief, Sp/6 Joseph Reed (of Philadelphia, Pa.), made some last-minute preparations involving the guns.

As we droned northward, the venerable crew chief dozed, with a rubber plug in his ear. Probably he had been up late last night working on this new HU1B and was dead tired. The gunners and crew chiefs in the Huey outfit really live heroic lives, flying on missions by day and staying up at night to maintain their birds. There are enough pilots so that there can be some relief in assigning assault missions; but all of the gunners must do double duty as mechanics.

At 7:07 we were circling to land at Lai Khe, where a fleet of H-21's, L-19's and T-28's were already lined up. Sprague and Damron were still raving about their new craft.

Sprague: "We can cruise at 120 knots with no sweat.

Damron: "A much nicer plane. This thing flies so nice, I hate to turn loose of it. It's so smooth, sometimes you think you're flying a fixed-wing."

While the rest of the Hueys were landing, an HU1A came in beside us, and the two pilots wandered over to talk to us: CWO Joseph Kirkpatrick (of Memphis, Tenn.), and Cleatus Heck. They told us that they had been here at Lai Khe two days ago, just after the VC had made an attack on the place, overrun the airstrip, and "shot hell out of the town."

Heck and Kirkpatrick had hauled two military advisers, Cols. Porter and Blazzard, up from Saigon to look at the damage, and they had taken two wounded back with them.

Kirkpatrick said, "They [the Arvin] didn't have control of the place yet. We made two or three passes before we could get in. They [the VC] came in this way—right across the runway. They attacked that blockhouse over there and burned a couple of houses.

"It's miraculous how the VC can evacuate their wounded.

They've got a wave that come in on an assault and take care of casualties. Right here, they [the defending forces] found a pool of blood and a great deal of hair, in one place where the [VC] medics must have worked."

Heck said, "In places like this where the VC wins, they [defending forces] don't find a damn thing. They even police up the brass [empty cartridges]."

I inquired a little further about this raid, and it developed that the VC raiding party had made their attack in three successive waves, the way I'm told they frequently do. First, an assault wave breaks the perimeter of the outpost under attack. A second, thrusting wave goes through the assault wave, capturing arms where possible and pushing farther into the outpost. The third wave is a clean-up group, which takes care of casualties and evacuates them (and leaves propaganda leaflets). Not bad for people working with small numbers and home-made arms and ammunition.

While Heck and Kirkpatrick were talking, a line of trucks loaded with Vietnamese troops came up and stopped across the runway from us. H-21's were still coming in, and the troops, climbing out of the trucks, began to move across the runway to the long line of choppers. Like the last air-phibious assault I had seen here in the D Zone, this attack was going to be a mammoth demonstration of tremendous military power. I hoped it would have a larger net effect. The results of that last D-Zone effort had been about zero.

Further down the line of Hueys, Capt. Gerald H. Hanson (of Monmouth, Me.), the platoon leader, spread out a military map on the ground and was about to brief the Huey pilots: "There are six flights [of H-21 troop carriers]—two lifts. The prestrike [bombing and strafing by T-28's] is at 0755 to 0810. We'll crank it up at 0800." He pointed to the map. "We'll take off and make a turn to the right and go right in—about 11 minutes."

It was a quick briefing. "Any questions?" Hanson asked.

"No friendly troops in the LZ?" someone asked.

"No," said Hanson. "No intelligence about it [enemy opposition]." He laughed. "You never see the guy until after he's firing at you anyhow."

He turned to the Vietnamese interpreter who had come up for the briefing. "Their job is to point out the VC," Hanson said, fulfilling the legal obligation of the moment.

He is much like Slavich in appearance and manner: blue-eyed, blondish, with very close-cropped hair and good military bearing.

227

I climbed aboard the Sprague-Damron HU1B and took a seat on the canvas-covered shelf at the back of the cabin. Our Vietnamese trooper and Joe Reed took the back-to-back gunners' chairs in the middle of the cabin. Sitting in the rear with me was the other American gunner, Sgt. Irving Tate (of Moultonboro, N.H.).

We lifted on schedule and were in maximum pitch almost from the start. The H-21's charged almost immediately into their final run to the LZ and we were right on top of them. In one of the fields below I saw three or four of the mountainous gray water buffaloes the Vietnamese farmers use as domestic animals, with black-clad figures on their backs. Tate swung his automatic carbine to cover them, anticipating the call that came on the interphone from Sprague, "You got those people covered over on this side?" At that moment the bullocks stampeded, charging across the field, riders and all. Those particular VC peasants were probably not very dangerous at that moment, because they were holding on for dear life.

Now we had almost reached the LZ. A fleet of broken-back H-21's were squatting in the field, their rotors spinning as the troops poured out.

Then came trouble. Somewhere away from the plane, and below, I heard a single detonation, the sound audible above the roar of our rotor and engine. Was it VC? "Blue Three secured fire from our side. Keep your eyes open for someone running here." It was Sprague's voice, the words chopped off as we swooped down the length of the LZ and pulled up sharply, turning at maximum speed, on our ear almost like a straight-wing aircraft. We streaked back over the other side and saw an HU1A making an approach from the other direction. We turned and came in behind him, and saw the rockets streaking from underneath his rotor, the protruding white tails plummeting into the trees at the end of the LZ. Almost in the same second came the yellow flash of the rocket explosions.

Orbiting again, we heard the calls of some of the H-21's, making their approaches to the LZ: the voices of the pilots were hiked up with tension now that firing had started.

"OK, roll out and hold what you got." That was the control airplane, one of the L-19's with one of the H-21 outfits directing his aircraft.

"Charlie Leader, you're about two miles out on your final." That would be the third flight of one of the H-21 outfits coming in to make a landing.

We swept over a row of rubber trees, curving back south to cover the H-21's that were about to make their landing.

"This is Bravo Five. We received fire about three miles south of the LZ."

"Which side did you receive fire from?"

"The right."

Damron noted that we must be in that vicinity now. "We're close to that area. Want to check it out?"

"Roger." Sprague was looking at a folded map. "It's probably right up there, wouldn't you say?" He was pointing toward an area of thickly studded trees, and about that moment I heard a single loud report: possibly VC fire.

The others heard it too. Damron said, "Looks like around to the left. Let's make a pass." With that, he kicked the Huey up on its ear, and we dived straight in toward a stretch of the jungle and skidded along just above the treetops. Billy Sprague bent over the mirror of his gunsight. But there was no sound of firing. We pulled up steeply and turned back.

Someone in the Hueys was trying to reach us: "Blue Three, you see anything?"

"Negative. We're coming to the LZ now."

The L-19 was trying to reach the fifth plane in the second flight of H-21's: "Control to Bravo Five, was that automatic fire?"

"Negative. It was heavy antiaircraft—not automatic."

Then the control aircraft talked to us: "Blue Flight from Control, have you made a pass on the area indicated by Bravo Five?"

Damron was answering: "Yes, sir, no fire yet."

Billy Sprague opined, "Well, it's too bad we didn't see some of those ————."

Damron was still messing around with the map. He pointed to it again and spoke to Sprague: "This should be the area." Again, I heard a single blast coming from somewhere down below—it sounded almost like a shotgun, quite loud. It must have been the same heavy-caliber anti-aircraft that Bravo Five had called in about. And apparently it was, for at that moment we heard a call: "Blue Leader received fire from that farmhouse." Sprague heard the firing, the call, and saw the farmhouse. "Let's go over there and get 'em."

Damron gave action to the suggestion, and we dived straight for the farmhouse at one edge of the LZ. Suddenly I jumped sharply. A fusillade of sound was tumbling from the left, an unbelievable waterfall of firing breaking over there, and in that second I realized that it was our own guns, triggered by Sprague. The muzzles were depressed to hit into that treeline, the muzzle blast was practically in our ears as we sat in the back of the cabin.

The ripping sound of firing continued, unbearably long. The tracers, curving red balls, were hitting into the line of trees as Sprague, bending over his gunsight, traversed his guns and trained his muzzles down. We swept over the treeline and the farmhouse. Many hundred rounds of 7.62 swept through that area, each muzzle a firehose spraying steel.

Damron pulled us up and we made a sharp turn at the far end of the LZ, coming back over the field but at a higher altitude now. Sprague was exulting: "Put 'em right in that treeline. Boy, you can really put 'em in."

At 8:52 we heard a call from Hanson, leading our flight of Hueys: "OK, Blue Two. Let's head for home." This meant that the torrents of fire we had poured into the treeline and other VC areas had had their desired effect. The LZ was secure enough so that the H-21's could come in and land their troops without being shot at. Once more, the Hueys had done their job well.

As we were turning homeward, a word of thanks came from the control airplane: "This is Control. Blue Two, thank you very much for your assistance." And Blue Leader, acknowledging: "Rrroger."

Over Lai Khe, Hanson passed on instructions: "Blue Flight, don't shut down. We'll have to go back and arm if we have any more operations."

As we came down for a landing, I asked Tate if he had seen any signs of life back there at the LZ—any people moving where he was firing with his carbine.

He said no, "just they were firing in there. We were going too fast to see anything." That had been my own reaction to the attack.

While Reed and Tate were securing the rotor blades, I asked Sprague what he had seen on the ground, when he was firing his long blast with the four machine guns. "The rocket ship marked the target for us," he said. "I raked the treeline. Did you see the tracers?" I said I certainly had, his shooting had been very sharp.

Our plane had shut down and the fuel truck was slowly heading in our direction, but the HU1A's seemed to be getting ready to take off again.

Damron explained that the HU1B's had no rocket mounts as yet, so we could rearm right here—all we needed was machine-gun ammo. But: "The others are going to have to go back [to Tan Son Nhut] and rearm, and come back, if there's another lift. They fired all their rockets. We'll stay here and wait."

Damron told me we had fired 1,000 rounds on our pass at that treeline. While we were waiting, I asked him about his wild and woolly history since he came in with the first detachment of Huey people six weeks ago. He said that he has made between 50 and 75 assault missions since then. "We seem to be getting less resistance now," he said. "Maybe we've got 'em persuaded."

Damron said that the aircraft he had been flying in, before he shifted over into this 1B, had been a magnet for VC hits. "That aircraft had ten hits," he said. "One time we got four hits on one mission. That was the time we got hit in the rockets, when I was with Mr. Heck. That round set the rockets on fire, and they kept on burning. Heck and I took the bird into a paddy, and the crew chief [Spec/5 Emory Gilley, of Samson, Ala.] tried to put out the rockets with an extinguisher. After he worked on the fire with a fire extinguisher, it started again, and he got out on the landing gear and put the fire out with water, from his hat." (Gilley has been put in for the D.F.C.)

Damron told me a little about his family. He has two adopted kids in Okinawa, a boy and a girl. "It was very hard to do this—it took us four years to complete the task. It was very hard to convince people that we could adopt children. There was a lot of resistance to it because, being in the Army, we have no fixed home."

Billy Sprague, our copilot and expert gunner, has an even more numerous family: four children, who are back in Oklahoma with his wife Maryann. His folks and Maryann's live in the same town, only two blocks apart.

The two pilots were still being very vocal about their liking for the new HU1B. Damron, talking about its speed: "You can move flank to flank, and back to front, with no trouble at all."

Sprague said, "It's like getting out of a model A and getting into a Caddy." And he added, "Oh man, that thing's smooth."

While we were talking, I noticed that three choppers from the 93d were parked on the other side of the runway. I went over to see them and found CWO John Walsh, the pilot with whom I had flown on a mission out of Soctrang. Walsh, who had been flying on our troop lift today, was still full of excitement about the firing we had encountered over the LZ. "That guy [the VC] sounded as if he was right in the cockpit with us. He must have had a hell of a heavy weapon."

But Walsh had another item uppermost in his mind: the fact that he is high on the list for replacement and that he is really riding on the ragged edge of his nerve, waiting for his DEROS (Date of Return Overseas). This term has become the password among military people on duty in Vietnam, as "Points" was in World War II. Walsh, with 350 hours of combat assault time here in Vietnam, is naturally anxious to get to his DEROS, although he actually has considerably less combat time over here than CWO Kibler, of the same outfit, who is up to 454 hours of combat support time now. Walsh said that although he has fewer hours, he is probably on a hotter seat than Kibler, since he hopes to be the first to be relieved. (He has a wife in Fort Devens, Mass., and two children there, two boys, aged five and three.)

"There are only about ten of us left from that original group, down at the 93d," Walsh said. "It's getting pretty hairy. I'm about ready to call it quits."

A distinctive heavy thumping sound suddenly became more audible in the southern sky, and we saw a line of our HU1A's coming back with a new load of rockets. We were all still on stand-by, but there was still no word about any further action for this afternoon.

I found Pappy Heck's HU1A, the one that had been so frequently shot up. The red-haired hillbilly was standing by patiently, but Gilley wasn't about. The gunner on Heck's plane today was 23-year-old PFC John Dickerson (of Mapleton, Utah). I had heard from the other gunners that he is the hottest shot of the bunch. I asked him about this morning's action and he was explicit about a couple of kills he had made. "I fired 120 rounds at the time," he said.

"I fired 10 rounds at one [VC]. He fell down, and he was still layin' in the area when we left. The other rounds were at that building where we wanted to keep their heads down—where we fired the rockets. That second guy, he was at the LZ [the building at the edge of the LZ]. I'd say I got two today. One had a rifle. The other, I don't know whether he had anything or not. They were in those two different places."

I asked Dickerson how he felt about this kind of battle episode, and he said, "You don't have time to get scared while it's actually goin' on. Goin' into it afterwards, you can."

Dickerson, who has very sharp light blue eyes and a blond mustache, looks like a true son of the Western plains, which in fact he is. His father, Cecil Dickerson, is a rancher, as well as being general foreman of a Union Pacific railroad yard.

I asked young Dickerson how he accounted for his marksmanship, and he said, "I live on a ranch in Utah, and I used to shoot rabbits from horseback." His father calls him "the best shot in the Army," and his mother, too, is proud. "My mother is a little worried about me, but she says, 'If you gotta do it, you gotta do it. You volunteered to go to Vietnam, you can't back out, you gotta go ahead.'"

Apparently Dickerson, like Capt. Graham Vernon of Phuoc Chau, can brag of antecedents who were distinguished in the American Indian wars. Dickerson had a great-grandfather named John who chalked up an illustrious record fighting against the Ute Indians.

Dickerson figures he has 15 kills to his credit by now. Flying as gunner the day Heck and Damron caught the VC bullet in their rockets, he distinguished himself with some expert shooting against the VC's who were potting at them. "I got two of them that I'm sure of, that day," he said. "Maybe four."

But the best bit of sharpshooting he did was three weeks ago, when the Hueys were receiving some fire from a bunch of trees, and it developed that the VC snipers were sitting up in the trees with their rifles. "I knocked one right out of the trees," said Dickerson proudly.

He has had his share of narrow escapes. "I guess my closest shave was when a round missed me by about 25 inches," he said. "It missed the fuel tank by an inch and a half —and it was a tracer [meaning that but for an inch and a half, the plane probably would have caught fire]. It was an automatic weapon. It must have been to get three hits so close together. One passed underneath the ship and got the rocket tube, and the other one hit the rocket."

I asked Dickerson if he had any trade secrets to account for his excellence in gunnery, aside from his zealous physical program (he had been active in wrestling and boxing, back in Utah, and had fought in the Golden Gloves at 155 pounds). Here was his advice to would-be sharp-shooters: "You have to be quick, flying at 90 knots. You have to use a lot of Kentucky windage. You have to see where you're hitting on the ground and then work up to the target."

I asked him if he had seen very many VC's with weapons, and what the weapons were, what the VC's look like. He answered, "They usually wear black clothes, some in black shorts. Every time I've seen 'em, you can see the type of weapons. When we get down low, you can hear them [the bullets] go by. They crack."

Since there was still no word about further missions this afternoon and there was time, I hunted out the second-ranking gunner among the Huey crewmen, an older man named Jim Stonaker (33, of Griffin, Ga.). Sp/5 Stonaker is a graying veteran of 12 years in the Army. He served 14 months in Korea during the hostilities there, was wounded twice, and won a Silver Star for gallant conduct with the 21st Medical Company, attached to the 14th Infantry. He claims nine or ten kills now in Vietnam, "most of them in the Can Tho area." He got four of those VC's in one day, down in the Mekong Delta area. "One fired out of a tree at the 21's, and I got him when he got out of the tree. The other three got into a sampan, and I got them in the sampan. That was the first day I had fired the M-14. I test-fired it that morning." Stonaker, like Dickerson, has spent a lot of time hunting; in his case, foxes, squirrels, and deer in Georgia.

And like Dickerson, he has suffered through his share of narrow shooting scrapes. On the day Johnnie Lee was killed, Stonaker's bird took a round through the star insignia on the ship, and the bullet lodged in the bulkhead. A piece of shrapnel from that round nicked Stonaker's helmet. (It was in that engagement that Capt. Steine, one of the pilots of Stonaker's aircraft, got hit in the armor vest.)

Like Dickerson, Stonaker has become celebrated among the UTT boys, and like Dickerson, he was glad to pass on hints about the conduct of his trade. He puts a lot of stock in the use of the visor which is a part of a gunner's helmet. "If you use the visor in your helmet—it's colored and it'll pick up a flash if anybody's shootin' at you—it'll help you to get a bead." When I asked Stonaker about his reactions to the business of gunning VC's down, he said, "The main thing is you're studying too much, keeping your guns in operation, and making sure you don't miss anything. If you've got a good pilot, you don't worry too much."

About today's action, he commented, "We fired a couple of times into the trees. And we went back and made a pass on the trees—the Hueys were doing good gunnery. I seen one [VC] stretched out on the ground when we left. The machine guns got him on the first pass. I think it was Mr. Heck that got him."

I asked CWO Heck about his sensations on that celebrated mission when his Huey had been hit in the rocket and he had taken the smoking bird down to the rice paddies to extinguish the blaze.

He smiled broadly. "I don't know what happened—I was too scared to look back. I could hear it, that was enough." While I was talking to Heck, a jeep rolled down the line of Hueys, tooting his horn. Hanson, the platoon leader, interpreted the signal: "We can go home." The time was 12:48. Joe Reed, who came here a week ago with a couple of HU1B's, interpolated, "Well, one mission done, ninety-nine to go." This had been the crew chief's first action.

As we got ready to take off, Hanson was hurrying to finish his after-action notes. He said the mission today had been successful, the suppressive fire of the Hueys had cut down VC resistance—although it took four VC's killed to do it.

Hanson, who came from a family "poor as church mice," in his words, evidently does a lot of thinking about the killing involved in this war, and now he spoke about it:

"What we're trying to get across to the VC is that if they fire at the helicopters, they'll get killed. We won't fire unless they fire first. And it's working. At first, we got shot at a lot. And we raised a lot of hell. Nowadays, you might get some guy standing up in a field taking a shot at you, but not so much any more."

Hanson, who married a Japanese girl from Fukuoka eight years ago, has two children: Debbie, who is seven, and Rae, a boy aged two, "named after an old colonel who was really outstanding, Rae Smith, at Fort Benning."

The thought of the women and children being killed and injured in this war, as they are in any war, sets Hanson's nerves on edge. "We don't want to shoot. We don't want to kill people. Every time I get near a village, I get nervous, because there are women and children there.

"It's thrilling to shoot rockets into a house where you've had some [enemy] fire. But sometimes if you talk to a MAAG adviser afterward and he says a woman had her arms blown off and her children were blown apart—that's all, it's too much.

"When you get back to the hard facts, we're on a test, testing the armed helicopters. War is hell, and people get hurt. No two ways about that. But we have to use our heads."

Capt. Hanson, who will be 30 next July, said he came in when he was 17 years old. He started as an enlisted man and, like many other Army men I have talked to here, he was sorry to miss the Korean hostilities. He said that now he is planning on retiring after 20 years of service. "I can't give up now—only seven and a half years to go—the pickin's are too slow up in Maine." By pickings I'm sure he meant the chances of civilian employment in Maine.

The over-all shape of the shooting today, Hanson said, quoting his notebook, was that in the first area where we fired, our rockets hit into a group of VC's, and there were three kills. Then "the crew chief of No. 5 [Dickerson] saw a VC firing and got one here."

Judged by the standard Hanson had laid down: that the mission of the Hueys was to persuade the VC's not to fire at the troop-carrying helicopters, and to make them aware that if they did fire, they would be killed—today's mission was a success.

Ten minutes later, when we were all airborne, I noticed that huge mountains of gray clouds were building up in the southern skies. When we landed at Tan Son Nhut, we learned that a typhoon, supposed to be bringing 125-mile-an-hour winds, was approaching from the east, across the Pacific.

"We'll have to strike all our tents," Slavich said. "If the typhoon hits, everything will be scattered everywhere; and it'll probably take out all the tents, if we don't strike 'em."

Preparations for the storm were going on at fever pitch, as Slavich and his executive officer Capt. Gene Burress (of Peoria, Ill.) scrambled about madly, trying to arrange lodgings for the UTT company under hurricane-proof roofs: the hangars of the airport and the hotels in town.

At last, word came from Weather Central that the typhoon won't be hitting until tomorrow, at the earliest, so I have had a calm evening making notes from the action reports of the Hueys, in Slavich's tent, where the records are kept. It has been a peaceful evening, marred only by Slavich's venturesome puppy dog, a German Shepherd named Princess, who is certainly not long on discipline. If Slavich is a formidable, well-trained military man and insists on good military behavior among his troops, he allows the opposite kind of conduct in Princess, upon whom he lavishes disproportionate affection and forgiveness.

"I told my wife I'd better have something to occupy me beside work," he said speaking of Princess. And taking care of that little nosy, adventurous, and uneasy beast seemed a full-time occupation. Besides working her over with a flea comb, flea spray, and deodorant spray and making sure she was well fed, Slavich had the problem of disposing of a small nuisance Princess parenthetically deposited on the tent floor. It seems she isn't completely housebroken either.

Friday, November 30

There was a low overcast and a high wind this morning, the coldest day I have ever seen in Vietnam—good pretyphoon weather.

While waiting for further developments in the typhoon situation, I worked over the afteraction reports of the Hueys and discussed some of them with Slavich.

"It's tough duty here for some people," he said in summary, knowing full well that he was foremost of the "some people" he mentioned. "But we have an important idea to prove."

Slavich, who studied history at the University of San Francisco and wrote a thesis on the Tong wars in that city, seems to be well oriented in the propaganda content of the new kind of war we are fighting here in Vietnam, and all over the world. "We certainly need a stronger propaganda arm, a better psychological warfare development," he said. Like Hanson, he has been thinking a good deal about the application of our tremendous firepower in the Vietnamese war, and the harm it can do when misapplied. "All your firepower is no good if you kill women and children," he said. "A MAAG adviser told me after a VNAF machine-gunning of a village that a woman was running around with a dead baby, yelling that Americans are bad. It'll be a long time before we can do any good in that village."

Slavich pointed to the afteraction report of one recent mission as exemplary of the things he was talking about. It was mission No. 29 in the Huey battle record, on November 23. The Hueys were supporting an air-phibious assault staged by the 33d Helicopter Company, an H-21 outfit, which was working in an area north of Saigon called Thu Da Mot. In this case, according to the afteraction report:

"A/Cs [Hueys] Number 2 (Stone-Wadlack-Pounders-Dike) and Number 3 (Ebrom-Wood-Carter-Leathers) saw ten VC, some carrying weapons. No firing and A/C didn't fire because women and children there. . . . Final lift to evacuate troops, fire rec'd—three VC (estimated) doing the firing and area surrounding their general location was thoroughly saturated with machine gun and rifle fire and it is estimated that three VC were killed."

This was just the kind of intelligent behavior among the Hueys that Slavich was talking about. The Huey crews saw the

VC's actually carrying weapons, but didn't fire on them because of the women and children. But when some of the enemy troopers opened fire on the H-21's, the Hueys "thoroughly saturated" the area—and I could understand, having seen it happen, just how thoroughly that saturation was carried out. As Hanson said before, we want the VC to know that if they fire on the troop-carrying helicopters, they will be killed.

At 11:07, the phone rang and Slavich had a report from Weather Central about the approach of the typhoon. In the midst of feverish preparation to strike the camp, Slavich was going mad. "God, of all things to have happen," he moaned. "It'll be a mess. It *is* a mess."

I decided that the best thing I could do in view of the fact that there would be no flying for a bit, was to pack up my gear again, and shove off for Saigon. I got to the downtown section and checked into the old and tired Continental Palace Hotel, a good enough port in a storm or typhoon.

The Swamps
of Soctrang

Saturday, December 1

Lucy, the typhoon that was so threatening, seems to have pooped out. There were heavy rains all day long, and the sky was filled with gray clouds, but by dinnertime even the slight winds had died and the rain had stopped. It developed, as usually seems to be the case with predicted typhoons, that Lucy had changed her mind about running right through the middle of the city, and moved about 50 miles south of Saigon.

I took advantage of the miserable weather—most everyone seemed to have found a secure place to wait out the hurricane in relative comfort—and used the time to go over the casualty reports I coud assemble from the Saigon headquarters. I wanted to get some idea of the total number of casualties we Americans have suffered here in Vietnam, and it seems that today is a good day to tabulate it, since as of today, the total number is an even 90—27 killed in action, the remainder wounded. Of these, the largest number have been American MAAG advisers, with helicopter pilots and crewmen running neck and neck. Next, in order of numbers, follow the U.S. Air Force pilots and crewmen and the Special Forces.

After poring over the casualty reports—so much of a writer's life is blasted clerical work!—I decided I had better make some plans for picking up with the war action as soon as possible.

I checked with Al Galfund and he counseled me to return

to the Hueys as soon as possible, because they will be involved in whatever big operations will be coming up in the next few days or weeks. I called Ivan Slavich and found out that the Huey people will be moving into a new screened-in living area and probably won't be going back into operation until next Monday or Tuesday. So I'll stay here, not sorry to be sentenced to a couple of days of inactivity in Saigon, which, despite the recent morality laws, still has plenty of diversions.

Sunday, December 2

I've enjoyed my couple of days and nights in Saigon, which isn't too bad a city, although it is nowhere near comparable to Hong Kong today, and certainly not comparable to what Saigon used to be in the old days of French domination, when it was one of the wildest cities in the world. When you come to it from a tent, as I did—I suppose such things are relative—it's luxurious.

Saigon is small-townish and restricted and most of the streets and the street life seem terribly foul. The climate is usually suffocating, though at the moment we've been in a cool spell. Last night it was down to 70.

Seeing the plethora of cars here, most of them new, I am reminded that, like the thousands of motor scooters buzzing around, they couldn't have been bought without heavy American subsidy, because the Vietnamese currency is next to worthless in the international money market.

The women of Saigon are lovelier than ever in their *au dai* (pronounced "ow zai") costumes. The *au dai*—consisting of a tight, figure-hugging tunic with long sleeves and a long skirt slit up on both sides to the hip, worn over billowing silk pajama pants—is probably the most flattering costume invented for Asian women. (*Au dai* means simply "long costume" and is distinctively Vietnamese.) It isn't so effective for American women—in fact, I've heard of several cases where the wives of American stationed in Vietnam have tried the *au dai* and found that bulges on hips, thighs, and waistlines tend to be exaggerated rather than concealed by it.

But for the Vietnamese women, who are slight, delicate, and almost never fat, it seems perfect: a diaphanous, fluttery, intensely graceful costume making them into sleek will-o'-the-wisps. And the *au dai* also has the effect of minimizing the figure defects of the Vietnamese: The billowing trousers conceal bowlegs, and if the Vietnamese belle is slightly lacking in the bosom department, you would never know it from seeing her in her skin-tight tunic top: The makers of undergarments with sponge rubber pads are reputed to do a tremendous business in Vietnam, and the store windows up and down the main shopping streets of Saigon offer testimony to this effect.

The Vietnamese women stick to their classic costume, and you see very few of them on the streets in Western dress. As many of the Americans have told me, the women of Vietnam give the effect of being quite beautiful and extremely stylish—at least in the sophisticated environment of Tu Do, Saigon's main street. And to see them streaming along, living signatures of silk and satin, graceful even on bicycles or sitting behind Vietnamese braves on scooter bikes, is one of the most pleasing visions hereabouts.

All up and down Tu Do, and in fact scattered across the town, are hand-holding bars, with names like "Josephine," "Sporting" or "Capitol" or "Tu Do." All bars have heavy screening at the front to keep out grenades; large, bright, and splashy neon signs proclaiming their names in English script; and inside, following the American fashion, dim lights and tall stools where you can take your ease with the bar girl you pick out/or up. The routine is that you buy the girl a drink—tea or soda pop—for 80 piasters (about $1.10) and you pay 80 P's for your own drink. You can get by for less if you sit at one of the tables and chairs ranged near the bar, which are tended by a waiter instead of a Vietnamese dolly in *au dai* costume.

In general, prices here in Saigon seem to be about what they were when I was last here. The Continental Palace, where I am staying now, costs about $10 a day, including meals. That doesn't sound so bad, unless you consider that it is an old wreck, in the tradition of chandelier-type hotels of about 1900, with red damask decor and worn red carpets, cold water for washing, and a beat-up restaurant and bar. The Caravelle is only three years old, and it could be called a hotel without distorting the meaning of the word, although the prices are furious. The Majestic, a high concrete block by the Saigon River, is the other major hotel in town and has some air-conditioned rooms. But it is old, cramped, improvised, and uneasy—as if part of it had stopped in the French days of 1935, and the rest of it was at a loss to figure out what had happened since.

Tonight, at the Brink Terrace, I sat in on a correspondents' bull session. Included were Dave Halberstam, Roy Essoyan of the AP, Peter Arnett of the UPI, and Mert Perry. In general, the griping and the humor in this war news center didn't seem too different from such patterns of the past.

Most of the beefing was about Mme. Nhu, because in a recent radio interview with Stan Siegal (who calls himself Stan Lawrence on the air) she had said that the American press are worse than Communists, they are "intoxicated with Communism," and they are always writing stories favorable to the Communists! In that interview she cited the supposed fact that the *New York Times* didn't run a story about the recent Arvin victory at Phuoc Chau. Halberstam said he resented that, because the *Times* had run a long story on that engagement. And he added that the Vietnamese are new to the idea that the press should be free and not controlled by the government. We were all stung by the reference made by Mme. Nhu (who seems to make a specialty of putting her foot in her mouth) to the "crazy freedoms" of the Americans.

The conversation turned to François Sully, the former *Newsweek* correspondent who now has a Nieman Fellowship at Harvard, and to Jim Robinson, the NBC correspondent thrown out by the Vietnamese, who is now in Hong Kong trying to get back into Vietnam.

"He could get back in by the Ho Chi-minh Trail," one wiseacre suggested, referring to the supposed network of trails from the Laotian border into the mountains of Vietnam, by means of which reinforcements and supplies are brought in from North Vietnam and Communist China.

" 'Port of entry Kontum'—they could stamp that on his passport," said the helpful wiseacre. It was the same old good-natured beefing of the press corps that I had heard for many years while covering wars, but this time it was in the new idiom: The complaints are directed toward a *foreign* (and sovereign) government, not good old Uncle Sugar.

Monday, December 3

Today was an inactive one, spent in the most tedious of a writer's jobs: documentary research into military reports. But I did arrange action for tomorrow, and possibly for the next week. The Hueys, now recovered from the hurricane alert, are launching a five-day operation in the swamps of Soctrang. Slavich says I can go with them.

Tuesday, December 4

I found the UTT company already installed in the new quarters at the airfield. Now, instead of wall tents thrown up over concrete slabs, their quarters are buildings, with roofs and walls composed of screens.

There was still considerable bustle as the officers and enlisted men moved their belongings into the new lines of houses, but Slavich told me the Huey boys are ready to go into action immediately.

During the typhoon scare, most of the officers were quartered in the Five Oceans BOQ, a ramshackle hotel in Cholon, and the EM's were housed in a maintenance building at the airfield where a fleet of M-114 personnel carriers (tracked vehicles used for carrying troops into battle assaults) had been kept.

At the same time, new reinforcements of pilots, crewmen, and new HU1B's have been coming in from the States. The UTT is growing rapidly.

Slavich told me that the wheels of action had already started to roll for today. "We're moving 6 aircraft, 11 officers and 18 enlisted men to Soctrang. We'll be there with the 93d . . . there'll be five days of operations down there. That's about all the details we have so far. Except—Capt. Hanson will be officer in charge. We had to combine the second and third platoons to come up with six aircraft. They're leaving at 12:30."

I got permission to go along with the flight, and as I was getting my gear together, Joel Steino came in. Burress said that Steino is now acting leader of the 1st Platoon, and it became apparent that his sense of humor hasn't yet forsaken him. He protested that since that bullet hit him in the armor vest, he is very skittish about action—I knew he was overstating the case for a gag effect—"now, every time they call fire, I put at least 500 feet between me and them [the VC]."

Hanson came in for his orders from Burress and Slavich and I asked him if he had any further details about the operation in Soctrang.

"I figure it's not the VC they're after this time so much as the caches of weapons," he said. "There are some .50-calibers they want to get."

I mentioned that I had heard that the VC had recovered eight 50-caliber machine guns from a B-26 crash down in the Delta in the last week. And that if they have secured those weapons with decent mounts, they could be murder for any helicopters, with their 7,000-yard range.

Hanson said, "Yeah, I hope we can get them before they——" He left it unfinished, but anyone associated with the helicopters would know that with enough well-placed

.50-calibers, ground troops could shoot helicopters out of the sky any moment.

While we were waiting for further word on the take-off, I asked Hanson about the .50's we were going to try to knock out down in the south. He said, "There are two spotted at one place and three at another—they could be the guns from the B-26, but I don't know."

He added with some inevitable dread, "We couldn't take much of that stuff [the .50s]. If we have to take it, I'd rather take it in close, because farther out, they [the bullets] might be on end [tumbling, therefore, having a tearing or ripping effect]. They'd take the whole tail off."

But the main item on our five-day operation was going to be a series of air-phibious attacks against the VC concentrations spanning out from the Can Tho and My Tho zones, where the greatest VC forces are gathered and hence the greatest battle activity has been going on.

Bob Hanna, Slavich's driver, gave me a ride down to the flight line. He was already primed for the Soctrang missions: "They should be good. I think I'll be able to come down with the old man [Slavich] tomorrow. Should be a good one."

Hanson sent me to aircraft No. 881, with two pilots whom I had seen before on D-Zone operations, CWO Joe Kirkpatrick and Capt. Earnest Wood (of Milledgeville, Ga.). The crewmen were Pvt. Donald MacNevin (of College Point, Queens, N.Y.) and PFC Edward L. Stewart (of Quincy, Mass.).

We arrived at the Soctrang airfield at 1:25, about an hour after take-off, and were met by Capts. Chuck Benedict and Don Toth, who had come down to the flight line principally to see off a group of pilots and enlisted men who were about to shove off for home. The moment of DEROS at last. Blond, athletic-looking CWO Kibler, as immaculate as ever, but now clutching a beer can in his hand, was absolutely joyous, and he had evidently been celebrating since yesterday, when his relief had showed up.

"Hello, world," he trumpeted. "In less than a week I'm gonna be on Broadway. I'll either be at a show or back at the hotel room with my wife—or both."

Kibler outlined his activity since he got the word yesterday. "All night we've been playing Christmas carols—we went to bed at 3 A.M. Tonight, Saigon! Tomorrow, New York.

"Until then, I'll be sweating out every take-off and landing. Doc [the medical officer was also going back] has

244

sleeping pills and 'up' pills. First you take the sleeping pills, and then when you get there you take the 'up' pills.

"I'm not touchin' the ground, and I haven't even hit full pitch," Kibler summarized. "I'll *never* fly another H-21— because there's none of 'em in the States; they're all out here, and I *ain't* comin' back here."

As he spoke, a procession of those broken-back birds appeared on the northern horizon. They were choppers from either the 33d or the 57th, both of which outfits are going to assist with the five-day operation, since the 93d, as usual, doesn't have enough birds available for a major operation.

I went over to the O Club with Kibler, Dickie Bird Adams, and Capt. Delahanty and WO Hanna, all of whom were leaving today.

Kibler told me that he had been carrying an American flag in his cockpit—"I'm damn tired of flyin' without any colors"—and on the flag he had lettered the legend: *50 hours combat support—top this*. Still clutching his beer can, he said he was going to play "Jingle Bells" just one more time to celebrate, but the electricity as usual, was off.

Shortly afterward, an Army Caribou came in and taxied up to the operations hut—the DEROS boys' transport to Saigon had arrived. Kibler, Adams, Hanna, Delahanty, and eight enlisted men made their way out to the aircraft. They were feeling no pain.

Climbing aboard, still immaculate and wearing his full array of fruit salad on his chest, like the good military man he is, Kibler had one last word. He sighed: "I've never been so nervous in all my ———— life. I hope they've got the world's most experienced two-engine pilot in this ———— aircraft."

When the plane was gone, Toth, Benedict, and Ewing filled me in on what had been going on with the 93d since I left. Chuck Benedict and Lew Stone (another very much embattled veteran of the 93d) told me the most recent event was getting shot up on a resupply mission down to Father Hoa's mission. (Father Hoa, a Catholic priest, maintains a famed encampment of militia in one of the Delta lands to the south of Soctrang.) Ewing gave me a concise account of the episode: "Some yokel in a field with a length of pipe and a hunk o' lead [homemade gun and bullet] opens up on us as we were passing over. It went through the engine—and I didn't even know it until later.

"But we're gonna go back into Father Hoa's territory

245

now. There's a big VC training area down there and they're supposed to have some of those .50-caliber machine guns down there, near the VC training area."

At 6:35 P.M., we had the official word on tomorrow's mission from the matter-of-fact Chuck Benedict. Standing on a chair wearing rubber go-ahead slippers, wrinkled green pants, and a T-shirt, he indicated a swampy area with a pointer: "It'll be the 21st Division we'll be hauling—they're generally air-minded—30 loads, 10 men [per load].

"We have three objectives tomorrow: They'll be labeled A, B, and C.

"Starting from Camau, objective A is on the right, here. The second flight of 10 elements will come in after the first, initial lift is completed. We'll go back to Camau to refuel. Then we'll go to third objective—it's over on the coast.

"Objectives A and B are VC villages. Objective C is a supply and breakdown point." He indicated a point in extreme southwestern Vietnam on the Gulf of Siam. "Apparently supplies are coming in by sea here. . . . We'd like to have the yak on the radio restricted to emergency or fire . . . I'll be Mail Call Control . . . use your chalk [sequence] number and your flight when calling your fire. Just say, 'Bravo Four' or whatever it is and Big Brother [T-28 fighter support] will know where you're at. . . . Big Brother will be with us so if you see fire, try and spot it."

Benedict propped some crudely made drawings up on the mapboard, showing the details of the objectives where the troops would be landed. "This objective lays generally east and west. Mangrove swamps all around. . . . The first two or three ships come in, I recommend you cock your guns a little. But if there are a lot of hooches [native huts or houses] over here, I want the Hueys to watch the hooches."

Those huts might be full of VC activity, and Benedict wanted the orbiting Hueys to keep an especially sharp eye on them.

Objective B was apparently also a swampy mangrove area, possibly with native huts spread through it. Benedict reported that on his reconnaissance, "I couldn't tell with binoculars how deep it [the water] is, so the first aircraft in, if it's over their [the Vietnamese troops] —————— head, you'll have to make a command decision. . . . It looks like an old Louisiana swamp."

Before he turned the podium over to Capt. Leach, who would give us the intelligence briefing, Benedict had a word of caution on casualties: "In the event anyone has anyone injured, get on your 38.9 [radio frequency], so you can come out with your casualty to Camau—that's where your doctor is."

Leach gave the G-2 briefing: "There are .50-caliber machine guns in the Camau area. That's about all that's known about them." Perhaps these were the stray large-caliber antiaircraft weapons Slavich and Burress had been talking about.

It was easy to see from this briefing how much the old broken-back H-21 troop carriers relied on these Huey people to keep VC fire down during the course of landing assaults. I sensed this responsiblity in Hanson, Wadlack and Hamil, sitting next to me as they strained to hear every word.

After the briefing, Gerry Hanson indicated to his Huey boys that he would now give a small extra briefing for them. Since the Hueys will have to start earlier to be on hand at Camau for the start of the action, and will have to refuel before the troop-carrying birds take off, Hanson had some special instructions: "Get up at 5 o'clock. Breakfast at 5:30. We'll be on the line at 6:10. Take-off at 6:20.

"You know what the LZ's are. If you get a casualty, it's best to come back. Call Suzy, that's Division CP at 38.9. Switch to 38.9, say: 'Rascal Relay. This is Flint Leader. We have a casualty aboard—we're on our way.' "

Then there was a word about the way in which the enemy will be engaged: "It's an enemy area. Just because they're out there, you can't assume they're VC. But if he's holdin' a rifle, *zapp!* If he doesn't smoke Salem, let him have it."

After the Huey subbriefing, I asked Dick Wadlack (of Wilkes-Barre, Pa.) if I could buy him a drink at the O Club. He said, "No thanks, I don't drink before a mission. I think I'll take a look at the movie." In the maintenance hangar of the 93d, benches had been drawn up and preparations were being made for the showing of an old flick, *David and Goliath.*

As I walked over to the O Club with Don Toth, I noticed that the green bugs were with us again.

Wednesday, December 5

Despite a liberal wetting-down of my bunk with DDT spray, enough bugs got through the mesh of the net to make sleeping difficult during the night hours. I turned and tossed, hearing the raucous chatter of the O Club and the singing. The nerves of the three troop-carrying helicopter outfits scheduled to make the assault mission today were stretched thin.

"Our little green friends are everywhere," said one half-awake shaver as I approached the washbasins this morning.

As we headed for breakfast at the mess hall, Don Toth said, "The Hueys are doing very well—a lot better than the T-28's. The Air Force wants to get in the act. They're assigning five T-28's and a C-47 flare ship for this mission."

It is a fact that the Hueys and the T-28's are competing for the job of protecting the troop-carrying helicopters. Both are trying very hard, but of course, as Slavich pointed out earlier, the Hueys can get right down there on the ground with the H-21's and hover and shoot up any VC who are making trouble. This takes guts—and I am reminded at that moment that this is our mission for today and the next four days to come.

No. 883, the helicopter I was assigned to today, was an HU1B, with Dick Wadlack and Dick Hamil as pilots. Today we had only one gunner, Sp/5 Bobby L. Roberts (of Melba, Idaho). Bobby was making his 56th mission this morning, and the way assault missions added up in the UTT outfit, he might very well bring the total up to 60 before the day was over.

I knew that Hamil is a relative newcomer in Vietnam: Today would be his fourth assault mission. I was going to be riding behind him and watching him fire the multiple machine-gun mount, if any firing was to be done. I asked him if he had fired at an enemy before, and he said, "No. But I fired at the range."

When we came swooping into the first LZ, I saw one house burning, and our gunner, Roberts, explained that the T-28's were having a prestrike.

We flew circles over the LZ as the green clad Arvin troops spread out from the H-21's. There were no men, women, or children visible in this first sweep into VC territory.

On the second drop, the troops were put down near a canal village. The dark specks of soldiers looked like the green bugs of last night, fanning out across the wet field, moving fast. They must have been running toward the village.

One of the village houses had been set afire by the prestrike, perhaps indicating that there had been some VC fire from that particular area.

As we circled the muddy canal, with the thatch houses lined up along it, and the barns and sheds spread out over the emerald-green paddies nearby, Wadlack tapped Hamil, who was bending over the gunsight, to keep an especially sharp eye on the houses we were passing over. I watched Hamil turning his gunsight, holding a bead on each house as we swept over it. I could see no people moving there.

When we got back to Camau, I asked Hamil if he had heard any firing or seen any activity.

"I saw some people trying to get under the trees or anything they could get under," he said. "I saw one old papa-san in that village, leaning against the wall like he thought he was hit. But no shooting."

VC fire seemed to have been conspicuously absent. I checked down the line of the H-21's, and one of the pilots, Lt. John Henderson (of Franklin, N.C.), said he got one round, but it was fired while he was still at 1,200 feet. "I heard it, but it didn't hit anything. It was before we went down."

In the line of Hueys waiting for fuel, I spoke to Sprague, who was still flying with Hanson today. "I saw a guy diving like a ————— bullfrog," Sprague said. "But no gun."

Apparently the only action on the two lifts was some shooting by Sp/6 Edwin Bellow (of Melrose, Ill.), an H-21 gunner on the aircraft piloted by CWO Gary Wilkerson (of Reno, Nev.), taking some Arvin troops to the first LZ.

Bellow told his story: "We were coming into the landing area, and this guy was on the edge of the trees. He started running into the woods, and my BARman [the BARman in the Vietnamese squad aboard the plane] fired at him too. He was down when we lifted off."

At 9.53, we Hueys were airborne again, thumping along above and behind the H-21's bearing their third load of troops.

The 10 choppers in our brood, making their usual low-contour approach, had an interminably long run, almost to the Gulf of Siam. The LZ was a huge salt-water lake that had a stubby black beard of mangroves as well as a liberal spattering of tree trunks. It seemed impossible that the H-21's would land troops here, but they did—right in the middle of a huge mangrove growth.

On our way back to Camau, we picked up another load of eight choppers heading for still another assault landing, and escorted them to a seacoast town where, like the last bunch, they were put down in mangrove puddles. There was still no firing.

It was time to fuel again and go on stand-by for further troop lifts, so I sought out the senior American adviser on today's operations to see if I could get some word on what had happened.

He was tall, lean Col. Daniel Boone Porter (of Belton,

Tex.) who looks for all the world like Gen. Bradley of World War II fame: respectful, gray-haired, with a dry voice and a courteous manner. He said there were no results yet of the action. "I saw some people running like bastards, that was about all."

Another MAAG adviser, Maj. James Butler (of Redlands, Calif.), said he heard that one VC had been captured in the last lift. It didn't sound like much of a bag, but then this is a godforsaken neighborhood, and the purpose apparently is mainly to try to intercept some of the smuggled goods being brought into this area quite regularly by the VC. According to the stories, this is a shrimp-fishing area, and the VC smugglers pick up cargoes of dried shrimp, take them out, trade them for whisky, trade the whisky for arms, and bring the arms back to the VC's of the area.

While we were on stand-by, we grabbed a bit of Rations Combat, Individual, the kind filed in circular tin cans, and after a hot wait in the shade of the fuselages, we at last had word of another mission. We were to escort two H-21's down to the Gulf of Siam area, where we had dropped the last load, and pick up some troops stuck in a seacoast town.

This, too, turned out to be an uneventful excursion. We circled over the *café au lait* shoreline interminably, while the H-21's seemed to hesitate about landing in the shallow water off the beach. We could see the troops wading around in the sea water, and felt relieved when, at last, the two choppers put down in the tide flats, and picked up the stranded troops. Later on we heard that the pilots had suffered from vertigo, flying so low over that muddy tide-flat water, so that they didn't know sea from sky and had difficulty landing. Their bearings were off, they landed in the wrong place, and they had to wait while the troops waded a quarter of a mile through the shallow water.

It was 5:55 when we finally touched down at Soctrang, bone-tired from a 12-hour day of missions and stand-by, which would count for the Huey crews as four assault missions. The helicopter force of 22 H-21's, 7 Hueys, and 2 L-19's had all settled at the airfield and were securing for the night. I suggested to Hamil and Wadlack that the Huey crews were going to have a pretty steady diet of flying, maybe even all day every day, since they would have to be up whenever any of the H-21's flew. Wadlack said, "I'd rather fly than sit around here." And I agreed with him.

There was a mass trooping to the O Club, for after the long hours in the heat and the hazard of paddy country and mangrove swamp, some sort of libation seemed to be called for.

At the bar, where every cubic foot of standing space seemed to be occupied, I asked Paul Ewing what reports he had heard thus far about today's actions.

"The Arvins got six VC's just beyond the Alpha LZ," he said. "Today they [the Arvins] were after materials, especially in Zone Charlie [that would be the smuggling area on the coast of the Gulf of Siam]. Tomorrow, they're after people."

At the briefing after chow, Chuck Benedict repeated that tomorrow's mission will be devoted to the pursuit of VC troops. He mentioned that today the Arvin troops had located one VC quartermaster depot near the third LZ and set it afire.

He remarked that the terrain on today's missions, particularly at the third LZ, was especially moist. "Some of the MAAG advisers got surprised. They were over their ass in water."

He indicated the LZ's for tomorrow's assault missions and skipped through the briefing: "Breakfast 5:45 . . . 6:55 crankup. Take-off first flight 7:10. It'll put us in [to Camau] a few minutes before eight. The troops'll be ready. The Hueys will leave [here] early—give 'em time to get refueled. . . . Call signs remain the same." He indicated an area on the map with a pointer. "Objective A is on the south side of this little town. The second objective is two clicks below the first objective, and five clicks to the west.

"The VC villages: like the villages today. I think this'll actually be duck soup tomorrow."

I glanced at Capt. Falls, who was standing next to me, to see his reaction to that prediction.

"That's bad," Falls said, *sotto voce*. "When they say it'll be easy, there'll be trouble—that's the tradition."

I went by Don Toth's sack and saw him stretched out blissfully, a pair of pilot's earphones on his head. He hadn't even bothered to fix the mosquito bar around him to keep off the bugs—it was that pleasant an evening. I knew what was going on with the earphones: Toth had bought a Sony tape recorder in Japan or Okinawa, and was enjoying some of his favorite music. He saw me looking at him inquisitively, and explained: "Frank Sinatra. It's Stereophonic with these earphones—it surrounds you." Even Soctrang can have pleasurable moments with the right equipment.

The traffic at the O Club was still thick. I know from experience that it will thin out as the series of assaults progresses and the men grow more tired and more anxious to save what nervous energy they have for the next day's effort. But now the five-day campaign against the VC is new, and the joint was jumping.

At the bar, I fell in with Lt. Lew Stone. He had been copilot with Maj. James Gray, the first CO of the 93d here in Vietnam, and he had been wounded in an action up near Danang, when a Communist .57-mm fieldpiece blasted out the side of their H-21.

Stone, a sturdy, olive-skinned, moody man who doesn't talk very much, has stood up remarkably well under the strain of being shot up a number of times. (Maj. Gray was eventually invalided home and Chuck Benedict had been acting CO until Paul Ewing came in to take over.) But he has continued to make flying missions at a steady pace. His comment on the nervous impact of being shot down amid such amounts of blood and gore was simple: "It took me three or four missions to get over it." I'm sure that was a large understatement, even from such a taciturn man of action as Lew Stone.

Thursday, December 6

The "Vietnamese Curse" (which is perhaps more truly identifiable as the curse of any tropical region) struck me hard during the small hours of this morning. With the aid of one of the miracle drugs, a locally celebrated antibiotic called Polymagma, the onslaught of the disease was halted, and I was able to get up in reasonable health at 4:30 A.M.

Lugging armor vest and pants, after breakfast I made my way to Gerry Hanson's Huey, No. 878, on the far side of the runway.

Hansons' copilot was Lt. Billy Sprague, and I was certainly glad for that, because the Oklahoman's marksmanship with the 7.62 multiple-mount is sensational.

The gunner-crew chief today was Sgt. Alfred Compton (of Lynchburg, Va.), a huge 28-year-old Korean war veteran with an awe-inspiring walrus mustache.

As the greenish light of dawn trickled down the line of rickety H-21's and waspish Hueys, rotors and engines were starting up.

At 6:35, the Hueys lifted off, and thumped off over the translucent green floor.

At Camau, we settled down to wait for the refueling truck and the arrival of the H-21's of the three helicopter companies flying today, the 93d, 33d, and 57th. Across the field, the steel-helmeted, green-uniformed troops were being isolated into plane loads.

Pappy Heck, flying an HU1A, ambled over to pass the time of day with Hanson and crew while preparations were going ahead. The jug-eared hillbilly pilot was always ebullient, full of fight and fun. I asked him if he had gone around to the hangar to see the movie last night. Pappy said he hadn't, and gave me a concise reason why not: "It was one of these English jobs about all them women got pregnant with that monster —nuclear physics and all that junk." I could understand his distaste without further details.

By eight o'clock all the H-21's were on the landing strip and loaded with troops. In our HU1B, we had taken aboard a little Arvin soldier who was technically supposed to OK our targets. A slight impediment to this arrangement was the fact that he didn't speak one word of English, not even "hello," and we returned the favor in Vietnamese.

At 8:02, we lifted from the tall grass beside the runway at Camau and climbed up to about 300 feet, where we waited for a group of five anvil-shaped H-21's to fall into loose formation below us. Then we all headed for the LZ.

Billy Sprague immediately began to wheel his gunsight grip nervously from side to side, and Compton, clutching his automatic carbine, moved over to my side of the back of the cabin, the right, secured himself with a long safety belt, and started a sharp vigil on all signs of life passing underneath our landing skids. Our little Vietnamese soldier, who was apparently making his first flight, was too awe-struck by the marvel of it all to do anything but wonder.

We began to circle as the H-21's squatted down like constipated birds in the combination meadow-riceland. Sprague, his eye glued to his remote-control gunsight, kept his muzzles trained on the line of thatch-roof houses that rimmed the meadowland.

We had made the complete circle around the nearby town and some of the birds were already lifting, having discharged their troops, when we heard the first gunfire—the savage ripping sound of machine guns, ours, theirs, or both.

I surmised that one of our H-21's was firing after being fired at while the troops were unloading.

As we turned at the far end of the field, I heard another long burst of machine-gun fire, this time a slow, individual popping of guns, which sounded like larger-caliber weapons.

There weren't enough phone jacks in our aircraft, so I

couldn't listen to the calls, but I figured that we would swing back and make a pass at the place where the firing had originated. And that was what we did.

Turning to the right, we came streaking along the edge of the canal. Billy Sprague squeezed his triggers and our own machine-gun fire burst in on our ears with the usual shattering impact. The house that I saw rising up out of the green marsh ahead of us was our target. The orange balls of the tracers were bouncing into the ground around it, up into the trees beyond, then truing up, centering, raking right through the house.

The rattling burst from Sprague's guns went on right to the end of our long run. But before we had reversed our direction, I was aware of a Huey charging in behind us, a 1A, and it was firing at the same house. Two people in white shirts were running in the line of fire, toward the house. The HUIB's machine guns were popping, more slowly than our 7.62's, and at the same time, furry white streaks charged from the Huey into the house and the greenery around it: rockets, and I heard them: *chunngg!* But the running VC's had disappeared into the grass.

We came out over a wide muddy river. I could see something burning farther upriver—an innocent little screen of smoke weaving up from the green. But to be prominent at this distance, it must have been a considerable fire: Perhaps the Arvins had found another ammunition cache.

I saw another group of five choppers beyond the river, moving in the opposite direction. Evidently our assignment was to convoy them into another LZ. This assault was a short one. The H-21's lifted over one final barrier of palms and plunked down into shimmering green rice paddy. There were no signs of life as we circled over the nearby canal town, while one by one, the flying bananas lifted off, having deposited their troops in the muck. I had heard no gunnery, and neither had Hanson, Sprague, nor Compton.

In a few minutes we were back in the tall green grass at the edge of the Camau runway. A HU1A charged in, stopped, swung into a fast turn, and sat down next to it. It seemed barely a moment before Capt. Robert T. Dunnuck (of Kansas City, Mo.) was over to talk to Hanson, who was still sitting in his pilot's chair.

Dunnuck was still floating on a wave of excitement: "I got a rocket right through that ———— house. That ———— village was crawlin' with VC."

Hanson nodded and Dunnuck charged off toward the

next Huey that was landing. I asked Hanson to reconstruct what had happened down there, he being the cool type who could manage it. "We got automatic fire from that village. He [Dunnuck] went back and caught a mess of 'em in there. He blew the ——————— out of 'em."

Sprague and Compton ambled around our bird to check it for damage but evidently we had suffered none.

Dunnuck and his two crewmen were busily reloading the rocket tubes. He apparently had fired seven rockets.

We saw the crewman of Kirkpatrick's bird also at work replenishing rockets—apparently another HU1A had fired seven rockets into the VC strongpoint in that last village.

We, too, rearmed and at 8:54 lifted off again. It seemed only a few minutes before our fat, fluttering wards were down on the deck, moving practically on top of the rice plants and then settling down in the slime and mud of the LZ.

Looking down, I saw the leading choppers canting up, tails high, fresh off the ground and gaining speed, and in the same moment I heard a long rattle of machine-gun fire, at least two guns together—the interlocking rounds making the texture of sound thick and heavy.

We circled around the edge of the LZ as the last H-21 birds lifted, and again came the rattle of guns. We turned and came in for a pass, streaking toward the gray shapes of houses and the slick, muddy canal with flowerlike palm trees arched over it. But Billy Sprague wasn't firing this time, neither was Compton, although his automatic carbine was perched at the ready. Perhaps there were no visible targets—I could see none. But behind us an HU1A fired its rockets as we curved away from the river bank.

Hanson, recovering from the turn, turned back in pursuit of the flying bananas that were already heading north. Sprague, bothered by something, tapped Hanson on the shoulder and was talking to him on the interphone. Plainly, he wanted to go back to the embattled town, but Hanson was shaking his head negatively.

Evidently he felt his responsibility was to convoy the H-21's until they were safely out of the area, and never mind continuing the fight back at the village. Presumably that fight was being handled by the Arvins whom the choppers had landed in the LZ.

But before we got too far, Hanson evidently had a call from another group of choppers going in to another assault, our fourth for the day. We swung in a wide, easy circle to come up behind them, obviously to take them into their LZ, a parquetry of green next to a town.

Again there was firing, the ragged, ripping sound of automatic weapons—probably ours, because the volume of the sound was so heavy.

Our Arvin liaison started yelling something in Vietnamese and pointing, drumming on Sprague's shoulder; Sprague, meanwhile, not to be distracted from his gunsight.

We circled twice over the town, the Vietnamese still talking and pointing. At last Sprague squinted in the direction of the pointing but evidently saw nothing, and his expression grew more dyspeptic as he looked. Neither Compton nor I could see anything either.

This time we stayed with the birds all the way to Camau, and at 9:32 we were down again. And this time we shut down —obviously we had to refuel.

I asked Billy why he hadn't fired when the HU1A let loose with the rockets. ". . . because one of the H-21's was right on top of them," he explained. "I was afraid I might hit some of the Arvin troops, and our ass'd be mud." But he had seen four VC's just beyond that squatting chopper and hoped that the Arvins took care of them.

The morning had evidently been a very busy one for the other Hueys, and for the H-21's as well. While we waited for gas, I stopped by to see Bob Dunnuck, who was still excited: "You saw that second guy running. I zapped him."

Dunnuck said that Dickerson, the sharp-eyed gunner who is so famous for his kills in this outfit, had evidently spotted the enemy fire coming from that locale. Dunnuck fired his rockets into the house.

Dickerson, light-eyed and blond-mustached, gave us his usual cool summary of what had happened:

"Somebody reported firing that first time. I saw a man standing in the doorway and a flame coming out of his gun. We cut loose and they took off, they were running toward the water. I got 'em as they were running.

"The second time, just before we got to the village, I saw three VC's firing from the door of a hooch. It was almost a steady flame comin' out, and I could hear the bullets goin' past the ship. I emptied a whole clip at 'em.

"On the last one, I saw four of 'em firing. I zapped one of 'em."

Dickerson said that he had fired 80 rounds altogether with his M-14 on this morning's assault missions. And so his probable score of kills of VC by this time was 22.

Billy Sprague told us how he shot up the house where the VC were gathered. "I put 1,000 rounds into that damn house. I'm satisfied there were some good kills there. When I laced that canal, I was tryin' to get into that draw on the right where they were calling some firing. All together, I fired 1,500 rounds."

Billy also wanted to show me something wild and woolly which he had noticed after yesterday's mission. There was a bullet hole in our fuselage, a rent in the metal skin perhaps an inch and a half long, probably caused by a spent or ricocheting round. It could have hit us any time yesterday. It had struck the fuselage about a foot behind the rear seat of the cockpit, but we couldn't find the bullet. It probably went out the open door on my side.

I went over to the Huey of CWO Kirkpatrick and the other pilot, Lt. Donald Farnham (of Wilmington, Mass.), and got their hairy story. Jim Stonaker, runner-up to Dickerson as the best sharpshooter, and the other gunner, Sgt. Henry B. Downs (of Atlanta, Ga.), got one or two VC's to add to their tallies.

Stonaker said, "Most all of the people I was firin' on this morning was in houses. In the next-to-the-last one, that house right on the point."

Lt. Farnham had also done good shooting against VC's firing from houses this morning. "This one fellow was standing in the door with an automatic weapon. He started to duck—maybe he saw the machine gun. I followed him right into the hooch. Maybe fired 200 or 300 rounds—and 7 rockets."

Still, the day of operations seemed to be a long way from finished. We were on stand-by. We cracked out the C-rations at about 10:15, and now, getting somewhat savvy, I snagged the chicken and peas *pièce de résistance*, which wasn't bad—it had a minimum of cold grease.

After a 10-minute lunch, I heard the report that we had another assault mission. The three HU1B's flying would be convoying an Eagle flight, a mobile reserve of about 50 troops, to try to box off a concentration of VC's. We cranked up at 10:35 and three minutes later were following the four ugly ducklings southward.

Very shortly they were squatting in a collection of small rice paddies near some gray thatch sheds, and the troops were splashing into the paddy water. There was always one of us Hueys sweeping down the flanks of the LZ, ready to fire.

It seemed that we were going to follow these H-21's back to Camau, but instead, we made a gentle curve around to the east, and started orbiting, this time over a paddy area to the right of the LZ. We had lost sight of the troops completely, but there must have been some radio contact between Hanson and people on the ground, because we seemed to be stuck over that area interminably. My nerves were strung out, waiting for the sound of Billy Sprague's firing each time we passed over a certain gray shed, but nothing happened.

Suddenly our orbiting took on a weird pattern. Twice we charged directly toward that shack in the middle of the field —and 125 knots seems a bloody great speed when you're at 25 feet altitude, practically tripping over rice plants.

Each charge at the shack (where incidentally there were no visible signs of life) was accompanied by all the steps of a firing pass—except the firing.

We were sashaying all over that field, but I noticed that on the last two passes in the direction of the shack, we came very close to a small island of palm trees stuck out in the middle of the paddy field. I felt there must be some significance to this, especially since our little Vietnamese liaison officer, a lieutenant with two pips on his shoulders, kept gesticulating and pointing—full of incomprehensible Vietnamese ideas.

Sprague and Hanson seemed to have little use for the advice of the Arvin lieutenant. But Hanson was spending a lot of time and energy on the radio, his Adam's apple rising and falling; and I would have taken a bet he was talking to an American on the ground—probably the MAAG adviser in charge of the Eagle flight we had just convoyed into the rice paddy.

And that was correct. Imperceptibly, in our various passes across the rice paddy area, we had worked our way toward the original LZ where we had delivered the Eagle flight. Now, looking down from atop a treeline, I saw the green-clad soldiers, perhaps 30 visible in three or four rice paddies and, near us, a larger, green-clad, and helmeted figure—an American, it appeared. He was waist-deep in the water, striding fast, and as we closed in on him, I saw his face upturned toward us, the broad white grin showing: the MAAG adviser. He carried a PRC-10 radio pack with whip aerial on his back, and even at this moment, he seemed to be talking into the telephone-type receiver—evidently in conversation with Hanson.

We hovered a moment above him, then eased down onto the water, our heavy steel landing bars just touching the surface, the rotor holding us above it so that we didn't sink in: an expert job of pilotage by Hanson.

Evidently the MAAG adviser had been instructed to get

aboard, for he hauled himself onto the tubular landing struts, thence into our cabin, trailing a local river of water. Hanson instructed Compton to pass his flight helmet (with built-in mike) to the adviser, and they had a quick two-minute conversation while we rocked across the paddy, 12 feet up. We sat down again while the adviser vaulted into the water, then we faded up into the sky above him. I recognized him from a previous amphibious operation with the 93d. He was MAAG adviser for the Eagle Force, Capt. Richard Jones. Hanson had been trying to orient him and his Vietnamese troopers toward a group of VC's hiding in the island of palm trees in the middle of the paddy—the spot we had dived on several times during our recent maneuvering. Still in a great rush, Hanson lifted the Huey over a couple of treelines, and I spotted the clump of palms again. We lunged at it, but this time we turned sharply and came back over what appeared to be a heap of uniform clothing—a dark green or black suit of some kind, although at that distance it was difficult to tell whether it was inhabited or not. There could have been two or more VC's in that wet lump of cloth. Near it, I could see strewn papers, as if someone had dumped a filing cabinet into the middle of the rice paddy.

Playing his bubble mount like a baby carriage, Hanson flew us straight down to the pile of rubbish, our rotor blast ruffling the water so that it was hard to tell exactly what we were looking at, and we sat there, perhaps 10 feet up, looking down at the green clothing, which now appeared to be discarded uniforms of some sort.

We moved away, turned abruptly, swept back, hovered over it, moved away in another direction, and came back once more to hover right over the pile of clothing, spots of water splashing up our windshield from our rotor blast. As Hanson held the chopper in that position, he gave me the first indication of what was going on: "Did you see them?"

I shook my head. I had seen no signs of life, only the apparently untenanted uniform. "Is it a dead VC?" I asked.

"No—he was alive," Hanson said. "Three of 'em, four of 'em."

Now, we saw four H-21's skimming across the paddy toward us—evidently the Eagle flight troops of Capt. Jones, being brought over to pinch the VC's we had been watching. But, with the maddening and absolute illogic usual in a war situation, the H-21's abruptly sat down three or four paddies away from where we were. The troops piled out of those birds with great dispatch, but in the wrong field. Our little Vietnamese lieutenant, seeing the error of their ways, was screaming at the top of his lungs, apparently unaware that his voice wouldn't carry over the roar of our engine and rotor.

The bunch of troopers who had plunged into the paddy closest to us were climbing over a tree-lined divider between fields, and seemed to be moving in our direction—but with the muddy bottom of the lakelike terrain underfoot, it would take some time for them to reach our neighborhood.

The first of the Arvin troops finally reached the spot. Astonished, I saw two of the steel-helmeted troopers dragging something from the water. It was something black, it pulled itself together and stood up—a man, with the rifle muzzle of one of the two Arvins pressed in his back. In that second, it seemed the Arvin trooper had flipped some kind of wire or cloth around the arms of the VC and wrenched them up behind him.

We scooted over toward the VC and his captors. Hanson put on the aerial brakes, and while Compton covered the group with his carbine, Hanson brought the HU1B expertly down so that the landing skids touched the surface of the water. Now I could see what Hanson had in mind: We were going to haul this prisoner aboard and take him back to Camau.

Under Hanson's expert guidance, our chopper moved sideways toward the two Arvins and their prisoner. One of the troopers was prodding the trussed-up VC in the middle of the back with the barrel of his M-1, and the other Vietnamese trooper was feeling around in the deep water, searching for a firearm the VC had probably ditched. (I later found out that the enemy had an American M-1, which the Arvins recovered.)

We slid up next to him, and the big-mustached Compton and I grabbed the wringing-wet VC and flipped him onto the steel floor of our Huey. In a second, we were lifting and canting away from the paddy, and turning toward the north and Camau.

The VC, obviously new to the American kind of levitation, and probably to any kind of airplane transportation, pulled himself as far away as he could from the open door. And while streams of water poured from his black clothing, I had a good look at the enemy.

He was lean, stringy, and small. He had a leathery peasant face, was of good military age, 24 or 25, and right now, thoroughly scared. He was panting, gasping for air, shaking his head. His slant eyes gleamed with fright; if he had been a round-eye, his gaze probably would have been rolling.

He wore a black long-sleeved jacket and black trousers, and his feet were bare.

Compton, keeping the muzzle of his carbine pressed firmly against the man's fourth vertebra with one hand, frisked his upper body with the other. No further sign of arms. He then fished out a sturdy webbing safety strap and cinched the captive's upper body in a tight safety loop. After that, the crew chief kept the carbine muzzle firmly in contact with the enemy's back.

Sitting on the floor next to the VC, I watched him carefully while I scribbled notes in my diary book. I didn't like the way he moved his legs, edging them bit by bit away from the door and toward me. I could see his eyes locked in my direction, fixed on every move I was making. I couldn't see how he could raise any trouble, but in previous war situations I had been a few times outsmarted by prisoners, and didn't want any repetitions.

As I made my notes, our Arvin liaison officer was prominently disposed to do nothing. He simply sat in the gunner's chair at the center of the cabin and stared. He had been doing that ever since we hauled the VC aboard. Perhaps he had been a little too shocked by the whole thing to lend a hand and might have favored simpler treatment like drilling the VC through the forehead.

The trip back to Camau seemed marvelously short. Apparently Hanson had sent word by radio that we were bringing back a prisoner, and a crowd of Arvins were standing by to take custody of the foe. The moment Hanson shut down our engine, an Arvin lieutenant, with two enlisted men behind him, was ready at our door, carbine in his hand. Compton unhooked the cargo strap and prodded the prisoner, his arms still tied behind him by the original cloth, into the none-too-gentle care of the Arvins. The VC's snarling expression showed that he didn't take an optimistic view of this development. Billy Sprague kept a ready hand on the huge nickel-plated revolver in a long holster on his hip, but the VC attempted no break. He was still panting and baring his teeth as they hauled him away.

Sprague had this eye witness account of the capture: "This guy was layin' so low in the water than when he exhaled, he was blowin' bubbles." He had one other bit of intelligence to contribute: "The VC had an M-1—that Arvin sergeant got it on the ground."

We were on stand-by again, and already three of four of the H-21's were starting up, their rotors spinning. "They'll be going down to pick up the troops and the captain," Hanson said. "And we'll probably go with 'em."

Before we could take off Lt. Don Farnham came running breathlessly up to our chopper. He hauled out a heavy metal object and showed it to us: a cast-iron hand grenade.

"The Arvins took it from that VC you brought back," he shouted, blast and noise of our rotor making conversation a little difficult. I could only surmise that our captive had hidden the lethal object behind his knee with rubber bands, as they are wont to do. There were a couple of rubber bands stretched around the grenade as Farnham held it in his hand.

At that moment, Hanson shut down his engine, and I decided to ask Farnham if I could recover the grenade. After all, as a war souvenir, it had some very personal value.

I caught up with Farnham a hundred yards or so down the line and quickly won the grenade away from him. It was a satisfactorily heavy piece of cast iron with smooth cylindrical sides and a worn detonator pin and clasp on top. The detonator clasp and cotter pin were shaded with rust, but the grenade was by no means handmade. The cast-iron barrel was machine-turned, and at the throat, it carried the numbers "5-62" and a Chinese character, possibly indicating that it was of Chinese Communist origin and had been made in May of this year. I wrapped it carefully in a handkerchief before I dashed back to the Huey, all the time very much aware that weapons captured from the VC are notoriously unsafe. But at least the pin of the weapon, the part that movie war heroes are supposed to pull out with their teeth, was still in place at the top, and I could hear no ticking apparatus to indicate that the grenade might be booby-trapped with a time mechanism. Furthermore, the VC owner had apparently been lying in the water with it for half an hour before we picked him up, and it had been attached to him for 20 minutes while we brought him back, so presumably it was not too great a risk to carry it.

By the time I got back to the Huey, Hanson was ready to take off again, so I said nothing about the hand grenade for the moment.

At the next LZ, someone fired a white smoke bomb to guide us, and we headed for it. Hanson in our 1B was leading the way, but the H-21's, persisting in error, landed in the wrong field again. We circled while they loaded up the troops, there was no hitch, and we soon touched down again at Camau.

This time we did shut down and go on stand-by. The time was 1:02, and thus far today we had made five regular assault missions and two Eagle assault missions, according to Hanson's count.

I talked to Compton confidentially about the hand grenade, he being a genial and imperturbable sort, and we devised a method whereby we could insulate the hand grenade with an extra armor vest, in case something unforseen should develop and it should blow on our way back to Soctrang. We got it back to Soctrang without trouble. We were ready to quit for the day but were still on stand-by.

Compton, I discovered, was no stranger to shot and shell. He had been a BARman with Fox Company, 2d Battalion, 179th Infantry Regiment, 45th Infantry Division, in Korea, until April of 1953, when on Hearbreak Ridge he fell under Chinese mortar fire with a fractured jaw, broken nose, and head wound.

Since then, he has shown some of the Woman's World virtues. He married and fathered two daughters, Shiryle, eight, and Carolyn, six. They are on Okinawa now, with his wife Betty.

He came from a broken home, he was reared by his mother, his parents divorced, his father remarried. Compton's mother is a secretary at the Lynchburg (Va.) General Hospital. Like many another of the picked servicemen of Vietnam, Compton has been in the Army more than 10 years. He joined at 17 in December of 1951, and he's a career soldier.

I met Chuck Benedict near the day room and asked him about today's net results.

"We [the 93d] had one casualty: the crew chief on Mr. Donahoo's aircraft. Name is Eller, PFC Eiler.

"They were en route to the LZ, and some joker in the paddy had at 'em, with an automatic weapon. A round hit the door, and shrapnel hit Eiler in the face—close to the eye, but didn't hurt his eye.

"He got [i.e., killed] the VC and told the pilot he was OK. They went in and delivered the troops."

Later I found Eiler, a mild, pleasant youth of 19, in the operations shack. He is now wearing a pink mottling of mercurochrome on his face where the fragments hit him.

"We were comin' into the area," Eiler said, " 'bout 15 seconds from touch-down, and a VC jumped out to the front and the left side.

"He was in the house, only about 20 yards away. I think he had a single-fire weapon. The bullet hit on the right side of the doorframe and hit one of the Arvin troopers right along the ear, and I got hit in the face by fragments.

"The Vietnamese that got hit in the ear was so God-damn mad, he just jumped out—about 15 feet up, right into the paddy.

"I had all tracers in my carbine, and I shot about 27 rounds at the VC. I shot into the house, and I seen him divin' into the house. Then a Huey came in and blew the house down. [That would be Lt. Dunnuck, whose sharpshooting with the rocket knocked out the rest of the VC snipers.]

"My eye was hurtin' more than anything, I had about three pieces of shrapnel in the face. The pilot wanted to know if I was hit, and I told him, 'I'm OK, sir, go ahead.'

"He couldn't hear me because of the vibration. But he had another ship standing by—he had passed on the word to them —in case anything happened. But he wanted to get the troops in—and we did."

Eiler passed on rapidly to something close to his heart: "It was my last flight, and I'm goin' home. My relief came and took over yesterday, and about 30 of us of the original bunch —our reliefs are here, but we're waiting. Maybe we'll get the chance to get home for Christmas. I'm hopin' we can, because I missed last Christmas [at home] and the one before."

Like Dickerson and Stonaker, the ace gunners of the Hueys, Eiler was a hunter in his home terrain too. He has a .32 Special lever action and a .22, and has done considerable hunting with bow and arrow.

There was a briefing again tonight in the operations building, and Chuck Benedict presided as usual, this time wearing a clean T-shirt and shorts. His audience of 38 to 40 pilots—mostly warrant officers with years of flying behind them—were also garbed in the lightest of clothes.

"OK," Benedict began. "Rehash on today's mission. No results again, yet. We had what appeared to be [enemy] fire in every landing area . . . no one injured, with the exception of one crew chief [Eiler]."

He rushed on, his bulldog jaw protruded. "Tomorrow we have five objective areas." As before, he went over his own reconnaissance of the LZ's. "On the second objective," he said, "we may land on the beach—if the beach isn't too bad."

Somebody called out, "I've been down there and it's pretty bad." Benedict smiled. "They all are, except Cap St. Jacques." The pilots laughed, because the French in their colonial days had set that beach up as a miniature Southeast Asian Riviera.

The audience grew tense as Benedict progressed to the next objective: "This is the suspected .50-caliber area." A groan of apprehension rose from the pilots, most of whom had been forewarned about the presence of these VC weapons in the Delta area.

When Benedict, pointing to the map, added that ".50-calibers are reputed to be to the north of this area. So we'll stay away—over here," there was a small sigh of relief.

He went through the radio call letters, the load the H-21's would be carrying (again, a battalion, about 400 Arvin troops), the procedures for casualties, for Huey operations, etc.

Finishing, he said, "It promises to be real interesting tomorrow. Same as today—but no sweat." I wished that I could share Benedict's determined optimism: Certainly today had been a considerable sweat.

Friday, December 7

We started in the early morning darkness, as usual, taking off at 6:30 and landed at Camau—which is getting to be home away from home—at 7:15. Then we started the day's assault missions, which are getting to be almost routine: the 12-hour days, the interminable series of landings in VC paddies, the VC gunfire, and the emphatic American response. The whole, after several days of hideous hurrying and frequent nerve-snapping tension, tends to blur into a uniform color: marsh green.

Compared to yesterday, this morning's operations were quite tame. On our first landing, I heard one popping burst of gunfire from the H-21's as they were coming in for a landing. But there was no audible VC fire, and Billy Sprague didn't touch his trigger.

On the ground at Camau after the fourth troop lift, Hanson said, "Not a round—that's the way I like 'em. I saw some [VC's] down there, scurryin'—but no shootin'."

Pappy Heck had his usual pictursque phrase for what had happened: "They were all running out of those willows. They were some kind of breaking the four-minute mile."

Big-jawed Wadlack came up to Hanson and asked plaintively, "Can I fire next time? They were running out of the willows with weapons." Hanson smiled and said nothing, knowing as we all do, the rule that we are to fire only when fired on, technically at least.

Pappy's witticism on that subject: "The VC are cleared to fire, only sometimes they won't."

Heck said one thing had given him "the itchiest trigger finger I ever had" this morning. He saw a VC flag, with the

265

yellow star, only about a mile from the LZ. "But what can you do if they won't shoot?" he lamented.

The Hueys have stricter rules of engagement than the troop-carrying H-21's, which are sometimes allowed to stretch a point, especially if they see a peasant carrying a rifle or other firearm. It was one of the H-21 gunners attached to the 93d whom I had heard firing this morning at the first LZ, under just such circumstances. He was PFC Kenneth B. Eaves (20, of Quincy, Mass.).

"I saw this guy running for some cover," said the towheaded Eaves. "I think he was tryin' to get in the water. He was heading right for the water lilies.

"He had something in his hand—it could have been a gun. We've been told if you see anything suspicious, let 'em have it. He was acting suspicious, especially when he dived for the water. I fired about 25 rounds at him. When you're firing, you have to lead your rounds in—I didn't see him fall but I saw the tracers and the splashes."

Eaves is another serviceman with a background of military accomplishment in his family history. His father, Errol S. Eaves, was a lieutenant colonel with the 26th Infantry in World War II.

Kenneth has had about 45 assault missions since he started flying as a gunner in early October, and plenty of action. Soon after he started flying in that capacity, his H-21 was lifting some troops into a village, and in the briefing the Americans had been told that the village was solidly held by the VC. "There were about three of them in a boat, making haste. I fired into the boat and knocked 'em into the water."

Twice Eaves had been in a chopper that was fired at. "One time, someone was firing an automatic rifle at us—there were water splashes about 15 feet ahead of us. That time we were operating out of Can Tho.

"And one other time, when we were trying to bring back some pieces of that B-26 that crashed, the VC's hit our lead ship. Kibler was the pilot of that lead ship. We heard the slight crack in our ears and Kibler's ship got hit. It seemed to come from a hooch in a flat area there."

The tall, slim, mild-looking Eaves seemed full of fight. He said that he will try to get back into action after he is sent back at the end of his tour of duty here in Vietnam. He wants to come out again, with the Special Forces. "I plan to make application to the Special Forces School when I get back."

I asked him what his father thought of his resolution to be

such an active fighting man. "My father said it has to be done —he did it in World War II."

Capt. Hanson told me that "We still have one more Eagle flight. They're checking the results of a strike that went in this morning." While we were waiting, I saw Capt. Jones, the Eagle flight adviser whom we had picked up in the paddy yesterday. Now he was going by in a jeep. He said he would probably be going out with the Eagle flights tomorrow. When I asked him if I could go along with him and do some paddy splashing, he said yes. "Meet me or Capt. Tuten at 7:45 at the pavilion." He pointed to an open-sided shed at one corner of the landing strip.

I didn't get to go on today's last Eagle flight of the day: I was bumped by a general who had come down from Saigon to take the back seat of Hanson's HU1B.

I hitched a ride back to Soctrang with an H-21 being relieved for the day. The pilots were two warrant officers, Carl R. Flippen (of Beaumont, Tex.) and Frank Donahoo (of Amarillo, Tex.).

While we were waiting at Camau and when we got on the ground at Soctrang, I had a chance to talk again to Eiler. After having been splattered in the face by the splash of a bullet yesterday, he had come back for "just one more" mission today.

He told me about some of his close ones during his tour of duty with the 93d. "I had one come right by my ear, when we were at Danang. One by my ear and one by my foot.

"That first mission here was really something. We were going after a big supply dump, and were getting shot at by all the villagers all the way in. A lot of Arvins [the troops they were carrying] were getting shot. The Arvin battalion commander got hit in the arm, and he almost bled to death. . . .

"You can't forget the sound of bullets. One hits the ship, you think it's going to fall apart. A lot of guys think if the blades pop in a turn, it's a bullet. But if one hits, you always get a sound you can always tell: *whop!*"

I asked Eiler what his plans were when he got back to the States. He said he hadn't quite decided yet whether he would "reopt," but he added, "if I do, it'll be for OCS [Officer Candidate School] and Flight School. I've had a lot of old-timers tell me that's the thing to do."

His eyes were bright as he told me about "the new Chinook" (the new Vertol double-rotor helicopter, which has jet power and much more speed). "I've wanted that thing since it first came out. I want to become a flight engineer on it, if I can."

Eiler added that he has persuaded his mother that he should stay in the service and chalk up his 20 years. "She likes the idea of 20 years in the Army, and I can retire. But if she knew any of this ———————— was goin' on, she wouldn't like it."

At the O Club, washing away some of the day's grit, I asked Billy Sprague how the Eagle flight had gone.

Billy said: "You missed the action. The Eagle had a lot of opposition. More than they could handle."

One of the H-21 pilots told me the story of the general who had displaced me on the Huey. The general had gone mad trying to prevent the American helicopter crewmen from firing. The yarn was all over the camp of the 93d by this time.

"They got to the area with the Eagle, and they were fired on. But the general didn't want them to fire. Hanson took them over to another place, and damn if they didn't get fired on there too."

This time Hanson's gunner (that would be Compton) reacted too fast to be contravened, and opened fire. My H-21 informant told me: "Hanson's gunner got seven of 'em on a dike and zapped 'em. . . . They went back with the H-21's to pick up the Eagle, and they were engaged again—and this time the general really went mad. Somebody called for an air strike to support the choppers, and the T-28's came in and dropped napalm. They burned out the town, and a gunner worked over some houses. The general was yelling, 'Who ordered the napalm?' " The pilot looked flabbergasted: "I guess I'm not old enough to understand this war."

Later on, at the shower, I saw Wadlack, who had been flying in one of the birds escorting those Eagle flights. He, too, was puzzled by the turn of events in that paddy. "On that last Eagle there were three Hueys, and we all got fired at. But the general was yelling: 'You're firing at civilians.'

"That's the way it was when Johnnie Lee was killed. They were civilians, they were running to get guns so they could zap us. Like today when they were running. Today we let 'em run and get their guns, tomorrow they'll shoot us down."

After chow, there was another briefing, again conducted by Benedict in the operations room. But this time, since I was expecting to go in on the ground, the whole proposition seemed quite different.

Don Toth, my good friend and an officer whom I respect immensely, has begged, borrowed, or stolen an extra .45 automatic in a shoulder holster for me, for tomorrow's splashing. A VC with murder on his mind isn't going to ask questions before he shoots. It's much wiser to shoot first. I mentioned this with thanks to Don Toth. He said, "Yeah, sometimes you have to do unto others as they would do unto you, but do it first."

Tonight, crawling into my sack, I am full of sinister imaginings about tomorrow's job. I guess that is the way it is usually when you are going into something dangerous and new, and strange.

Saturday, December 8

I flew down to Camau on No. 149, with Don Toth and CWO Carlton Nysewander (of Pasadena, Calif.).

Mechanically, I made notes of the names of the crew chief and gunner, PFC Duncan Carter (of Fayetteville, N.C.) and Sp/5 Payton Runan (of Benton, Ark.), just as if I were going to be with that crew all day. And I soon returned to macabre imaginings of what was going to happen on the ground when I plunged into the muck with the Arvins of the Eagle flight. It was a good thing that I had some practical worries to be occupied with: like ways to keep my camera and exposure meter out of the water, and procedures to keep my musette bag and notes dry.

At the Camau strip, I didn't have to go to the pavilion to find Capt. Jones. He was making himself heard, it seemed, all along the dusty runway. Garbed in jungle boots, well-worn greens, a camouflaged-netted steel helmet, and the same PRC-10 radio with whip antenna I had seen on his back before, and still smiling the same white, tight, energetic smile, he was making tracks up and down the line of the four choppers that would be carrying the Eagle flight. He was the soul of energy —yelling directions to the Eagle flight soldiers to get aboard the choppers and whirling his finger toward our pilots, ordering them to crank up and get airborne.

The terrible roar and clatter of preparations for an airmobile operation broke over us suddenly, the fortissimo noise a symphony of the new kind of war—a cascade of roaring, thumping, shouting, windblast, and dust—as we climbed aboard the helicopters.

Jones vaulted into the troop compartment of our chopper and in a firm voice demanded, "I want earphones." And he got them pronto from the crew chief. As we lifted off, Jones was at the back of the cabin, with the crew chief's helmet on, the whip antenna scratching the top of the cabin. His involvement at the moment: intense interphone conversation with the pilots about where the Eagle flight was to be landed.

Jones turned to give me a fast briefing on the run we were making. He pointed to a spot on a plastic-covered map. I had heard about Jones that he was "a real hairy adviser" (in the sense of being eager and dynamic) and the role fitted him quite naturally. He didn't even bother to engage me on interphone conversation, but shouted loud enough so I could hear above the roar of the chopper: "Father Hoa's troops are on *this* side, and we'll be on *this* side." He stuffed the map under his arm and went up to the pilot's compartment for a quick consultation, explaining to me en route, "Much confusion."

While Jones was going over some vital points with Toth and WO Nysewander, I seemed to have attracted the attention of the little Vietnamese soldier next to me. This South Asian warrior smiled at me with a mouthful of gold teeth (and a powerful garlic breath) and seemed very seriously interested in my identification bracelet, my unusual canteen, the .45 automatic I had borrowed from Don Toth, and the size of my rubber-soled shoes—which also amused and amazed the other soldiers no end.

These seemed to be able, alert troops, with battle-worn gear and good arms and steel helmets, and a sureness that apparently came from many helicopter operations. This was fitting for an elite striking force used on sudden raids and flanking attacks against the VC's.

In much too short a time the chopper was settling into a patch of tall marsh grass and we were rushing out the door.

In a matter of seconds, my feet were on the edge of the metal floor with the watery field only inches beyond. Then I jumped into yielding grass and muck, the wave of wet swallowing my legs. The water was above my knees, hip-deep on the little Vietnamese. With every step I made the mud sucked at my feet, and each step was a resounding *plummp* as I struggled to wrench my leg loose for the next forward movement.

We were in a breathless hurry, and running hard—if you can call our movements through ankle-deep mud and crotch-deep water "running." My movement was a series of rapid and agonized wrenches: plummp, plummp, plummp. My legs grew lead-heavy, and we were still moving fast. I wondered how long the athletic condition of the Vietnamese soldiers would hold up under this kind of test—and how long mine would.

But mainly there was the worry of the unknown—the

threat of suddenly erupting VC fire as we headed for a tall green jungle of reeds perhaps 10 feet high.

The surprising thing about the mud bottom was that it was hard to keep your footing on it. You would think it would anchor you, but when you tried to move, you seemed to teeter and lurch, because it was so uneven. I fell down twice, the second time more disastrously than the first: I tumbled forward up to the armpits, struggling to save my camera and light meter, in my musette bag, from catastrophe.

At last we reached the tall reeds, which had a solid black underfooting of mud, far drier than the marsh-grass terrain but still adhesive and octopuslike in its grip. Jones, fiddling with his radio, took time to advise me: "If you start to sink in, move the other leg quick so you won't get stuck."

In a moment I could test the advice. We came through the reeds to a canal, about 12 feet across. It seemed of indeterminate depth. The only thing to do was follow the example of the Arvins, who jumped in and started to wade across it without delay. I got stuck twice in that muck-bottom ditch, but managed to wrench my immobilized leg loose by swinging the other one wide. At the far side of the canal the water was waist-deep on me. Somehow, the Vietnamese were scampering across it and climbing up the muddy bank beyond, nimble as monkeys.

Jones was standing on the bank, slick with mocha-colored mud to the waist. He seemed a prominent landmark amid that vivid greenery, tall, blond, and angular, with a brilliant red scarf at his throat. But there was yet no firing.

"This is Nutcracker," Jones was saying into his radio receiver. "Could you let me have a vector to my objective?"

While waiting for an answer, Jones talked to Sgt. Dat, the young interpreter-sergeant. Dat was predictably tiny and light in weight, but he was individualized by a quick smile. Jones was trying to get him to convey something to Lt. Van, the Vietnamese commander of the Eagle flight.

Van kept a prudent distance and independence of the American adviser. He was tall for a Vietnamese—maybe five-foot-eight—trim, athletic, even handsome in the Asiatic sense of having well-chiseled features and an athletic-looking body.

Jones said earnestly to Dat, "Tell Capt. Van we have airplane come and tell us if we are on the objective or if we must go on."

Lt. Van hesitated, his face as noncommittal and unsmiling as before, while Capt. Jones listened to some pertinent message

271

through his telephone-type radio receiver. And he told Dat, for transmission to Van, "We are on the objective." As Dat translated, the Vietnamese commander's face grew more agitated, and almost immediately a colloquy followed, there on the canal bank, while the rest of the soldiers were wading across.

Jones contended that we should go to the nearby village and search some houses. Van's contention was that we should go back the way we had come.

Jones asked why. While Lt. Van was talking ahead at a great clip, Jones asked Dat many times, "What did he say, what did he say?"

Van saw Jones' anxiety to know what was being said, and explained again, with obvious testiness.

The little interpreter unfolded a map and explained briefly: "VC this way. We go in this direction, we find VC." The interpreter tapped on the map with a finger.

Jones pursued the subject vigorously. "How far—seven-eight kilometers?" Lt. Van went into a long diatribe.

Jones was asking: "Well, what does he want to do—go on or get picked up by the helicopters?"

Lt. Van seemed to hedge a little. We could go on a little way into the village, then be picked up by the choppers. By now, our 50-man force had all assembled on this bank of the canal, and ahead of us dikes with pathways on top led toward some houses. There was actually some dry ground in this little stretch.

I noticed that we had a German shepherd tracking dog with us, cared for by a steel-helmeted Vietnamese, and Van allowed the trainer, a cadaverous, dyspeptic man, to move along with him as he headed for the houses.

Jones, meanwhile, was trying to contact the helicopter flight to have them come in and make the pickup. He had evidently been sold on Van's idea of being taken the six or seven kilometers toward the VC.

There was no life in the gray, weather-beaten farm buildings scattered along the little stretch of level ground. We had pulled a blank here.

We walked on past the houses and plunged into a rice paddy. We were sloshing again, our feet slipping, the mud sucking them with every step, but the net depth of the water seemed to be generally lower—somewhere between knee- and hip-deep—and the footing somehow a lot steadier.

Jones was watching for the H-21's and his alertness paid off. He spotted the flying bananas way off, long before I did, and neatly extracted a mirror from his pocket and began signaling. "These *are* good," he said of the mirror, with the enthusiasm of a connoisseur.

The pickup operation went along very well. The choppers came in only about 100 feet from where we were waiting, and we waded desperately toward them, struggling determinedly head-on into the rotor gale.

How many times I had seen that same circuit of motions and efforts from the other end of the operation. Now I was on the uncomfortable end. Those choppers, blasting air and water into your face, and a target for any VC snipers in the general area, looked like Home Sweet Home from the depths of a paddy. We hauled ourselves aboard, very happy to fall, wet and muddy, onto the corrugations of that metal floor and lean against the relative comfort of the tubular fuselage.

As I understood it, we were to be airlifted a few kilometers closer to the VC—or where Lt. Van was convinced the VC should be. But we didn't pursue the project. Jones and Van engaged in a warmish discussion over a map while in the plane, with Sgt. Dat in the middle as usual. It was decided eventually not to go to the new location, because there was going to be another mission later today, and this might interfere. Once we were on the ground at Camau, Jones told me, "It's too far. The VC will slip away. They'll have time."

The H-21's had all returned from their morning missions, it seemed, and there was much consternation among the chopper jockeys: Nine birds were out of action, all of a sudden —thanks to a series of weird accidents. Two of them had gone down in the first LZ, not from enemy fire but in simple crack-ups. One of the cracked-up aircraft was from the 33d, and the other from the 93d. The one from the 93d was flown by company CO Ewing, making his first assault mission. With his characteristic luck in being shot at and otherwise vexed, Ewing had received another bad shake.

A third chopper had rammed one of the crashing birds and damaged its belly sheet metal. Three others had overspeeded (blown out their old, tired engines by pulling too much manifold pressure). Then, in a strange, unrelated accident at Camau, a Beaver (Army light plane) had drifted on landing, sliced into and damaged the rotors of three parked H-21's, and after frantically wheeling around to avoid hitting other aircraft or parked jeeps, had piled into the swamp. No-body hurt—but plenty of planes knocked out in a streak of bad fortune.

There had been no enemy opposition reported. Yet sometimes crack-ups seem to stir up more commotion among pilots than enemy opposition. Just by chance, the CO of the 45th Transport Battalion (the over-all supervising agency of Army helicopter operations in Vietnam), Lt. Col. Robert Hoffman (of Portsmouth, Ohio), had flown down from Saigon this morning. He was much concerned at the moment, because it looked as if the two H-21's that had cracked up in the LZ would have to be destroyed to prevent their falling into the hands of the VC.

Col. Hoffman was still amazed by the accident: "I was in there watching 'em turn over. It seems to be the condition of the landing area."

We ate a luncheon of C-ration at Camau, and I had a chance to talk to the interpreter, Sgt. Dat, about Capt. Jones. Dat called him "Catajone" and said he much admired this American fighting man. "He very serious man. He only man in division do not like to talk about girl. Maybe he have wife that he love very much." I had already learned that Jones does have a wife of whom he is much enamored, the former Helga Hartt of Hamburg, Germany. They have two sons.

At this juncture, Jones came by with the other MAAG battalion adviser, Capt. Jeff Tuten (of De Land, Fla.).

Jones told me about the plan for further missions today, pointing to a map. "There are two Eagles, one a long one— Capt. Tuten will take it. We'll take the other, which is to go to this area, circle twice and not to land unless we see massed VC boats or ground firing."

Tuten told me *sotto voce*: "He'll probably go in, all right. He's hairy enough." Tuten also told me I should be sure to check for leeches since I had been splashing around in the swamps this morning. Plunging around in a paddy, you are very apt to pick them up and they can silently and apparently painlessly suck a good deal of your life's blood away. "We had a lot of leeches this morning, a lot of my people," Tuten said. He had taken out the second Eagle flight this morning. "You'd better take a good look." My sneakers and socks were grimy with mud and made sloshing noises with every step. I made a mental note to check them as soon as I could sit somewhere.

As I moved toward our chopper with Jones, I had a moment to ask him about the hazards endured hereabouts. He said coolly: "The closest I ever came to being killed was when I cracked up in a helicopter last month." Regarding the progress of the Vietnamese anti-Communist war, he said, "The only thing about this war is that you can't get two people to agree on anything."

We took off a few minutes later with his Eagle flight: four H-21's and about 50 troops. The flight in to our objective seemed short. I used the time to check my mud-grimed feet, shoes, and socks for leeches (found none), and carefully went over my camera and light meter to see how badly they had been damaged by this morning's immersion in mud and wet.

Then, without any apparent hesitation, we were landing in a paddy. We troops plunged into the muck, stumbled to a canal about 25 feet wide, and waded through that. Crossing the canal, I held my musette bag, .45, and camera equipment over my head and climbed out with the others on a long and surprisingly dry rice field, with regular furrows of land down the whole length, each hump about three feet from the next, with a mud puddle in between. Beyond this, among some trees, we could see houses—but no people.

As we started down the furrows of this dried-up rice field, where the stubs of the plants of the previous growing still stood, we seemed to be moving at an accelerated pace. The leaders were running, hopping nimbly from one rice furrow to the next. I was having enough trouble with the mere business of leaping (and always landing with a squish in ankle-deep mud), but I didn't want to be left behind in this hostile territory, so I, too, thudded along at a run. So we went, a ragged skirmish line spread across a hundred yards of stubbly rice paddy, Dat and I almost at the tail end. And then I heard a sudden spasm of small-arms fire breaking out ahead.

Now we could see more of the houses along the canal, and I surmised the firing was coming from that direction. At any rate, our men were running faster now, our pace became more frantic.

In the storm of the firing, I thought I could make out the heavy, slow tones of a BAR and the sharper crackling of a tommy gun. There were also some single shots, which I took to be VC fire, since the Communists are more apt to have primitive, nonautomatic weapons.

Up ahead, some of our troopers must have stopped to fire —it's difficult to shoot a machine gun while on the run, despite what happens in the movies. I tried to see what was going on ahead, but with the heavy mud, the leaping, the sweating and breathlessness, the general discombobulation of trying to run with all my gear, and the general outbreak of firing, I wasn't registering much.

Dat had cut off to the right of the series of rice hillocks and was running down a ditch which at least had the virtue of being altogether under water, so you didn't have to concentrate on leaping from one furrow to the next. I tried the ditch and found it was as slow and mucky around the ankles as the furrowed field. I went back to the furrows, thumping after the small, helmeted, green-clad infantrymen now bunching near a canal at the far end of the field. There I could see a bamboo bridge leading across to the line of gray thatch houses.

Nobody was venturing across that bridge yet, but after one more quick flurry of what sounded like the ripping pace of an automatic carbine, suddenly there was no more gunfire.

I caught up with Jones, now soaked from head to toe with mud and sweat, who somehow managed, as usual, to look as if he were cussing without actually doing so. Perhaps it's because he smiles a lot, and in the midst of struggle and misery, that tight smile becomes a grimace. Just beyond him, heading toward a clump of foliage, was Lt. Van. He is as handsome in his Vietnamese way as Jones is in the Western fashion, and he wore the same drawn, determined look. Like Jones, he was wet from helmet to toes with mud, sweat, and paddy water.

Some of our troopers must have got across the canal by some other bridge—it was too wide and deep to wade—and I could hear a new burst of small-arms fire breaking from the direction of the houses.

Capt. Jones was talking into the receiver of his radio again and looking back toward the rice paddy we had landed in 15 minutes ago. I heard the crackling of machine-gun fire back there, several heavy, overflowing spasms of it: one, two, three, Hueys were zooming—and a white mushroom cloud of rocket explosion where some of those projectiles must have hit. We felt the shock of those rocket impacts, and then the sound, slower to travel, as they hit: *Chunngg! Chunngg!*

Another Huey swept in behind us and we heard a whipping windstorm of machine-gun fire: evidently the fire of an HU1B—the sounds of the 7.62 multiple-mounts are faster and slicker than the old-fashioned .30's in the 1A's.

Van and Jones were both looking back anxiously now, and their concern was punctuated by another earth-shaking rocket impact and chuunnging sound as a projectile hit and sent out a smashing cloud of debris and smoke, the puff of white smeared by something flying, perhaps bits of a house.

Van's attention was snapped ahead, toward the village, as firing broke the air in several levels of intensity at once: BAR's, carbines, and the random punctuation of single shots scattered all over the auditory map—comets of sound.

Jones was saying in a determined voice, for the benefit of

Dat, to be passed on to Van, "I have a report [from the helicopters] of a lot of people behind, back there."

Another dispute seemed to be in the making; Van seemed to understand more English than he admitted to. With a grimness and determination to match Jones', he spilled out a string of Vietnamese and gesticulated toward the firing ahead, on the other side of the canal. Plainly, he wanted to go ahead, to the village, and Jones wanted to go back.

"Say VC in village," Dat translated, pointing ahead toward the canal town. The Hueys that had been strafing and rocketing the supposed VC concentrations seemed to have evaporated from the sky. This lent some credence to Lt. Van's urging, especially since at that moment another splattering sound of automatic weapons broke from the direction of the houses. But it did sound as if most of the firing was by rapid-paced, deep-toned American weapons.

Some of our troopers had crossed the main bridge over the canal by this time, and Van and Jones were following. I went after them. We had just reached the other side when another blast of small arms rang out in a field of tall, tawny grass between the bridge and the nearest house. I saw three helmeted Arvins running in that field, and beyond the nearest one, the shape of a man in brown rising from the grass with his hands up. He looked frightened to death, pale and unsteady; but he was of the correct age to be a VC trooper and he wasn't making any mistakes. He held his arms well up as he moved gingerly toward the three riflemen. He was well aware that his life was in the balance and at the slightest sound or movement, he would be rubbed out with the squeezing of a trigger.

That was written in his face—but guerrillas in this VC town weren't taking any chances. From a far corner of the same field, as if on a signal, another human shape began to emerge: a straggly haired woman in wrinkled black peasant-sharkskin. And then, one by one, an assortment of children, who materialized like eighth notes behind her from the brown grass.

The Arvin troops were covering the brown-clad peasant and his supposed brood—all of whom carried out the illusion that they were harmless rice farmers and family people surprised in their innocence by government troops. But firing had been coming from this field, and beside the bridge stood a white sign, hand-lettered, on a bamboo pole. I surmised it was a VC sign, and Dat confirmed this by translating: " 'All the people must fight against My Diem and must fight against the invasion by My Diem.' " It wasn't difficult to understand how

VC propagandists, in this area where VC organizers were the rule rather than the exception, could make it seem that this "American Diem" who came from someplace far off, was actually invading this territory. As for the device of planting a brood of children and a likely Vietnamese mama-san in the same field with a gunner or two—that was probably a clever bit of dissembling too.

Our troopers were moving into town now, and I admired the way they worked. They kept a security screen out on both sides of the river, with well-spread riflemen scanning the fields for any further VC hostility.

And on the right side, where the first peasant had been scared up a minute or two ago, they rooted out another likely VC of military age, but of course (by now) unarmed. He wore a surly grimace on his round face, and kept his arms well up in the air, but it seemed a safe bet that he wasn't going to be doing much talking or cooperating. A couple of Arvins prodded him along with their rifles, and as they did, I saw a curious thing happen.

This peasant had been wearing a black coat and trousers (and was barefoot), but now, as he was pushed along by the troopers, he slipped out of his black jacket and threw it to one side. Strangely enough, he was wearing a white jacket underneath it—as if there would be any logic in this kind of double costume in the hot Delta country.

It seemed evident that he was ridding himself of the identifying uniform of the VC. I had noticed before on Huey strikes that the peasants who want to identify themselves as "goodies" wear white jackets (like the hero of a Western movie). Here was a living example of the way a peasant could change his color to suit the need of the moment. One minute, a black-clad VC squatting in a field and blasting away with a homemade popgun, the next minute a surly peasant in a white jacket, identifying himself as a harmless farmer.

In fairness to these supposedly "harmless farmers," it should be pointed out that thus far in our penetration of this village, no rifles or other firearms had yet been unearthed. But there wasn't much time to comb the bushes for evidence. Our patrol had their hands full looking out for any sudden hostile move in the hooches of the village.

On the right, the point of our column had scared up two more likely VC types. One of these two, a husky youth, did exactly what the last captive had done: As he walked ahead of prodding Arvins who menaced him with M-1's, he skillfully shed his black coat and displayed a white jacket.

This likely type had been snatched from a hooch where an old man now stood in the door. Van asked the old one, who had a scraggly beard like Ho Chi-minh, while Dat translated for Capt. Jones: "Did the VC come through here?"—which seemed a stupid enough question in view of the sign that Dat had just translated for me.

The old man answered shortly, in rapid words that sounded like a snarl, and were translated by Dat: "He say he doesn't know."

I noticed that the Vietnamese animal trainer I had seen on this morning's Eagle flight, complete with his shaggy-coated dog, was moving along the right bank of the canal. The dog, still wet from swimming canals and paddling through paddies, was sniffing along the edges of a hooch, but the building didn't yield any likely suspects.

At this end of the town, the Arvin troops seemed to be relaxing their security precautions a little. In the few minutes we had been in the main part of the town, the peasants had shown some friendliness. One Arvin soldier munched on a large piece of beancake given him by a villager, and Jones, apparently keeping a weather eye out for anything like looting, asked the soldier if he had paid for the delicacy. Through the offices of Sgt. Dat, the soldier answered yes, for the price of "two P's" which would be about three cents.

Another bearded oldster ceremoniously pressed a green coconut, chopped and trimmed for drinking, upon Jones. Jones paid him a five-piaster note. However, the captain seemed a little bit dubious about actually taking a swig of the liquid from the decapitated nut. Those things can be explosive to the insides of an American unused to native bacilli.

At the far end of the main canal in the town, another VC sign proclaimed a propaganda message. Dat translated for me: "It means 'Finish the Revolution.'" The VC line is that the revolution against the French colonial masters and their supposed American successors won't be finished until Diem and the Americans are thrown out and a Communist state set up. Further proof of VC hostility in this neighborhood: Just beyond the main canal, on this west end of town, a couple of rice fields had been fortified with rotor bumpers—lines of bamboo poles, 10 or 12 feet long, stuck in the rice furrows to foul up the rotors of landing helicopters.

By this time, Van and Jones were on the verge of another disagreement: Where was the helicopter pickup to be? Presumably, the mission had been completed, the town swept of VC's and a bag of four suspected VC troopers on hand for transport back to Arvin headquarters and questioning. The rice field next to the area fortified by rotor bumpers was clear, and Jones urged that the H-21's be brought in there.

Lt. Van, still looking intense and anxious, indicated the wild stretch of marshland beyond this paddy and said, "VC out there." His solution was to go back through the town and head toward the rice paddy we had originally landed in.

This infuriated Jones, who was in the midst of trying to radio the control aircraft for the H-21's. He said to Dat, for translation to Lt. Van, "Either we get choppers now or they go back. They're unable to stay long enough to pick us up on other side of town. Shall we stay overnight?"

He was hitting on a sensitive point, because Lt. Van, like most of his troops, had no overnight gear, only his map case and carbine. Seeing Jones and Van exchanging fierce looks, the troopers rapidly sensed what was afoot. Jones stomped off toward the field he had designated as a likely pickup zone, mumbling, "I'd stake my career on it." Eight or ten of the Arvins hesitated, then followed him.

Van, his face a storm cloud, stood facing the other way, while most of the troops, spread along both sides of a deep drainage ditch near the field Jones had chosen, remained indecisive. It was clear that, after several hours of splashing around in the muck and firing and being scared to death, most of them shared my feeling of wanting to be picked up. But they didn't know which leader to turn to.

Out in the paddy, Jones talked into the receiver of his PRC-10 and looked up toward a section of sky. I watched the green marshland beyond the paddy very carefully, half believing that it was filled with VC, as Lt. Van had indicated.

At this juncture, a little L-19, the control aircraft for the H-21's, appeared and swooped down over Jones, pulled up sharply, and came back to make another pass. Several times, evidently while Jones talked to the pilot, the L-19 dived down and made low sweeps over the field, and once I heard the sharp crack of a rifle coming from somewhere in the green marsh to the west: VC fire, for we had no troopers over there.

I jumped across the drainage ditch at the edge of Jones' rice field—incidentally landing with a catastrophic splash six inches short of the far bank and ending up with my chest in the mud. As I reached Jones, he was extracting a cardboard container from his pack and preparing the metallic object in it: a smoke bomb. I asked him if he had heard that shot fired in the marsh to the west, and he said no. He was not about to give up his plan for the pickup at this point in the proceeding—that was clear.

Lt. Van's opposition seemed to be weakening by this time, and he began to splash over toward Jones. With almost visible relief, the troopers followed him. And Jones spoke a good word for the Vietnamese commander: "At least he's eager, he wants to fight," he said to me. "You have to give him that."

By now Jones had rigged his smoke bomb and with a pop, it arced and made a red smudge in the air above the paddy, a smear so bright that it looked like a chalk mark.

At that moment, we saw four awkward whirlygigs churning in toward us from the southwest at low altitude. As the familiar heavy thumping noise assailed us, Jones shouted to me: "The choppers are coming in two by two."

The lead chopper touched down in the windy lake of the paddy, and a group of 10 or 11 helmeted Arvins waded toward it, following an imperious pointing gesture by Jones.

It was a tense moment, made hideous by the pressing awareness that these choppers offered us our only chance of escape today and the possibility that there might be VC's ready to pounce on the last few of us from the next field as our numbers diminished.

As the second chopper came in, Jones pointed at me, and the group of Arvins around me. A group of about 14 Arvins and I started toward the squatting H-21, fighting against the rotor blast, which whipped water into our faces.

One of the group was the trainer who had ushered the police dog through the town on a leash. Now he struggled heroically, elbowing his way among the other Arvin troopers, to get to the door. But the dog was not cooperative, he strained in the opposite direction. The trainer and I and the dog reached the rear doorway of the H-21 at the same moment. The man gave a tremendous heave and slung himself and the dog onto the slippery floor in one stunning leap, powered, apparently, by sheer nerve and adrenalin.

The rotors and engine roared, the bird was lifting, and I flung myself after the other muddy troopers, sliding across the floor to the opposite bulkhead. The bird seemed to be stalled at an altitude of about one foot. While the engine screeched, we edged haltingly forward 10 or 12 feet, still barely maintaining our altitude, and then slowly slipped back into the paddy. Without hesitation, the crew chief shoved one, two, three, Vietnamese over the lip of the steel doorway into the paddy. The engines roared again, we hovered and at last seemed to

281

gain two or three feet. Then the pilot kicked the tail up, and we were moving forward at an accelerating rate and slowly gaining altitude. Ahead of us, at the end of this expanse of paddy, I saw a treeline looming tall—and we were roaring along at a height of about 12 feet. At last, from someplace, the pilot discovered a source of power, and we scraped over the top of a tall palm and banked away from the paddy.

Back at the Soctrang base an hour later, I tried to get some sort of official run-down on today's results in terms of VC's killed and captured, some military assessment of the results of our efforts against the enemy. But all military attention at Soctrang seemed to be centered upon the number of accidents that had disfigured our helicopter effort today. It seems now that we are going to be short nine helicopters for tomorrow's missions and will have to borrow some more aircraft from another helicopter outfit, possibly the 33d.

Tonight, Chuck Benedict conducted the briefing wearing field greens, both shirt and pants, and field boots—probably in deference to the CO of the 45th Transportation Battalion who was on hand to check up on today's rather costly operation. I heard very little about the ground operation of the Arvins today—such as Jones' Eagle flight, which had filled up so much of my life today with dread and discomfort.

"I'd like to start off with a rehash of the mission today," Benedict said. "The trouble today was a combination of circumstances: the mud. You think the water is solid, but there's mud. You're tense, I'm tense. There could be rotor bumpers, dikes. We can't do low-level reconnaissance for you —because we don't want to tip it [the air-phibious assault] off. We have to be especially cautious."

Benedict moved on to the ground operation, but in a summary way. "Contact was made. Even R. A. Jones had some contact.

"The landing around the lake—this caused the VC to move south. We had quite a lot of fire, especially in the third objective. Any questions?"

Several of the pilots made reports on enemy opposition to their choppers. Capt. Bert Leach said, "We killed one [VC] on the left, and one on the right."

Benedict continued: "The over-all operation has been lengthened one day. Tomorrow's operation will be out of Camau. The next day's out of Rock Jaw (Rack Gia)."

He went on to say that tomorrow there will be an effort to surprise a VC headquarters believed to be in a certain area, which he pointed out on the map. "Our signal people with special super-duper direction-finder equipment have located some radio stations. This means a headquarters. If they are operating tomorrow, we'll go after them."

Concluding the briefing, Benedict said, "We had a bad day today. But we can go on from yesterday." Then acknowledging the superior rank from headquarters, he introduced Col. Hoffman, who also spoke about the accidents that had marred the day's proceedings.

"I want you to know that I'm on your side," he said. "And as Capt. Benedict says, you can go on from yesterday."

Later, at the shower, I carefully checked through my clothes for leeches: none found. I threw away my socks, which after this one day's ground operations, were blackened with mud and torn into rags. Fortunately, the baby-sans who clean the barracks buildings can usually be persuaded to do laundry, so I can recover my sweat-stained, mud-slicked field outfit. The camera gear and lenses seemed to have survived the day without damage, unbelievable as that might seem. In the midst of the paddy splashing, I had concluded that only underwater cameras of the type used by frogmen would come through this kind of experience without being completely ruined.

I cleaned and oiled the .45 I had borrowed from Don Toth, sopped up the water drops on the moving parts. The shoulder holster was thoroughly saturated.

I sought out Capt. Hanson and asked if I could rejoin the Hueys for tomorrow's assault missions. He said yes. It was nice to have a handy excuse, like being out of green field clothing, for not going out with the foot troops tomorrow.

Sunday, December 9

I hadn't realized yesterday that Americans had suffered some casualties in our accident-ridden series of assault operations. Yesterday, in accordance with the temper of the day, the injuries were accidental or attritional. A crew chief on Maj. Ewing's H-21 got a broken thumb and bruises on one leg as he was bounced around when Ewing's chopper hit the dike and cracked up. And one of the gunners on the Hueys had a similarly strange accident. As he was firing downward with his carbine, the bullet bounced off one of the .30-caliber guns mounted outboard of the fuselage, and ricocheted back to stick in his foot. Altogether, it seemed that for both the H-21's and the Hueys, yesterday was best forgotten.

Down at the staging area, Camau, I found Capt. Jones and he said he had heard no official run-down on yesterday's operations as yet. It seems that down here in the swamps, as up in the northern mountains, after-action reports of Vietnamese results are slow to reach the Americans concerned.

While the Hueys were being refueled, I asked Jones about the complimentary things his interpreter, Sgt. Dat, had said about him. Jones smiled that same tight grin I had seen on his face in action, and as he usually seemed to do, he came right to the heart of the matter: "I've been here eight months, but I haven't been on R and R yet. If I went on R and R, it might be the last nail."

By way of background he told me how he happened to meet Helga in Germany. Like many another picked officer here in Vietnam, Jones had been through parachute and Ranger training, marks of the hell-for-leather, hard-as-nails military professional. He had been sent to Germany in 1957, and met Helga on a leave in Munich. She had gone there for a meeting of a gymnasts' club—apparently she was as much of a devotee of physical fitness as Jones.

I asked Jones how he felt about this Vietnamese war. His answer: "You have to feel that it's a personal problem—that if they [the Vietnamese] go under, *we* go under."

As far as the toughness of the fighting in Vietnam is concerned, he said, "Life here is about number 10 [about the bottom, on the Japanese scale of value, which many servicemen use]. But at least it's not cold and you don't have to climb hills." Of course, he was referring to the fighting down here. There are plenty of hills to be climbed up north.

I asked him about the food, and how he manages to fit in with the Vietnamese pattern of meals—a problem that troubles many of the Americans. "I usually take a can of chili along and mix it with rice," Jones told me. "And these villages, they've usually got chickens and eggs."

The tall, gray-eyed warrior said there is one part of the duty down here that is hard to take: "It's going through a village after a napalm strike." I knew what he meant. Part of the job of an infantry adviser is to make reports on Air Force bombing raids, and that means napalm: that searing, incendiary jelly which burns flesh and keeps on burning, and which sometimes is dropped by the fast-moving straight-wing planes on the wrong targets, sometimes with pitiful results among women and children. Even if they are VC's, as Capt. Hanson said before, it's not very pretty. "I'd rather do most anything than be sent down to check the results of a napalm strike in a village," Jones said.

The current season isn't very good for hunting out VC

guerrillas in the Delta, he told me. "This is an interim time. You can't see 'em on the ground. The crops are at their height. But in about four months it'll all be brown stubble. You can see 'em a long way off. And in the monsoon [rainy] season they leave a trail of mud in the water and you can follow them."

But even in this off season, Jones seemed to be endlessly eager to do his job. At that moment he was on stand-by, or I wouldn't have been able to get him to talk this much.

Jones' father is a retired route foreman for a dairy company in Oakland. Dick said that his parents in Berkeley follow the Vietnamese battle news pretty closely, and that they are always worried when they read about a MAAG adviser being hurt or killed, since the military authorities don't usually allow the name of the officer to be mentioned until some time later.

This morning, it developed that Jones' Eagle flight was going to remain on stand-by while we Hueys and the H-21's had a chance at action, taking a battalion of Arvins into a village where they were supposed to find the VC headquarters and the radio station that we had located with high-powered monitor apparatus. The station was on the air today—we were after it. We would land troops in a nearby village.

The fat-bellied H-21's, now pregnant with troops, were off at 8:35, and we followed one minute later. Today was to be a large effort, and our air armada was escorted as well by the sleek, fast-moving T-28's, which were weaving in figure 8's diagonally across our flight path. Today, they would be on emergency call only, and we Hueys would have the job of watching for VC opposition.

A few seconds before 0900, as the choppers settled in, we Hueys went beyond the LZ and flew down a broad canal the color of watery mud. By the time we were over the middle of the LZ, some of the H-21's were beginning to take off. There must have been a report of gunfire by radio, because Hanson suddenly flung our Huey into a low-level pass over the canal town beyond the LZ. We came in close enough to see several sampans drawn up on the bank and three others floating in the canal. In the rush of the pass, I couldn't make out any people in them. But there must have been some, because in a few seconds I heard the always-surprising blast of our machine guns. I saw the tracers striking into the water, and splashes along the edge of the canal, among the sampans.

I looked back to see what the other two Hueys would be doing, especially since they were 1A's, equipped with rockets.

(Our 1B's haven't yet been altered to carry the rocket projectiles.) I glimpsed the rocket streaks from the first of the HU1A's, heard the *chunngg*, the hoarse diapason chord we know so well.

We followed the empty H-21's north for a few miles, then cut off again to pick up a southbound group. Not a shot was fired by the H-21's, on the second assault; and not a soul visible in the houses ranged along the canal.

We made three more assault missions this A.M., including escorting Jones' Eagle flight in to a raid that was supposed to catch some VC's off guard. But they were too smart for us. I saw Jones after we brought the Eagle Force back and asked him what he got: "Nothin'—not a soul."

We went on stand-by for 90 minutes, but the Vietnamese high command in this area apparently weren't as enterprising in their use of helicopters as Col. Cao and his American adviser Col. Vann had been during our Can Tho operation.

While we waited, I saw Stonaker, the No. 2 gunner of the Hueys, and asked him how his score of VC's was coming along. "I got two more to my credit yesterday and one today."

Now I was able to get Stonaker's view of the firing we had seen the Hueys doing yesterday, when they shot up the village behind our Eagle people on the ground. "We's escortin' the Eagle flight. One [VC] started to shoot at us. Three more runnin' for sampans. As we went by, a guy with a BAR opened up on us. I got him down. Later on, a guy was comin' out of a house as we strafed, and when he thowed up to shoot us, I shot 'im. It looked like a Thompson [tommy gun] he had."

He said that he had been in the Huey behind us at the first LZ this morning, when Billy Sprague shot up the people in the sampans. Stonaker, who had been flying with Wadlack and Farnham, told me that Farnham had fired the rockets we saw hitting into the houses. And Stonaker had gotten his VC for today in the following fashion: "On the first lift, when we flushed all of 'em out of the trees—there was five or six in the group. He [one VC] started firin'. One broke and ran for the water, I shot 'im and he fell.

"A bunch of 'em went into that house. We fired into two houses. Mr. Farnham [his pilot] fired into the house with rockets."

One of the H-21's had been hit by ground fire today, but the bullet didn't hit anything vital, and the bird, No. 10 in our first LZ formation, got back safely. I found out about it from one of the pilots, CWO Jess Leonard (of Wichita, Kan.). "We got hit on the left door, it hit an access door, and it made a hole in the skin, and hit the side of the oil cooler. It made a good-sized hole. It was when we were just lifting off, and we were about 20 to 50 feet up. The crew chief claims he shot the VC. The crew chief was Sp/6 Jim Beck, from some place in Florida."

While we were waiting for the word to go home, I talked to Hanson about the shooting Billy Sprague had done today, and on the previous missions I had flown with him.

"Billy is right on," he said. "He was an instructor on these guns, and he really gloms right on to a target." He had glommed very well when I saw him shooting.

Sprague filled in some of the chinks about his life: "I was with the 45th Division in Korea in 1952, on the spring offensive. That was a real enemy—and that was a rough war. We had nothin' up there—tents. This war isn't so bad."

Billy said philosophically that "if you don't have education, you have to get experience—like this war." It is a practical way to look at his involvement in Vietnam. He lacks formal education, and as a first lieutenant he has a meager salary to pay for the upbringing of his four children, two girls aged 13 and 7, and two boys aged 9 and 5. I had seen Billy doing his job as a gunner and pilot with endless energy and daring, I had seen his rough-cut face peering over his 7.62 gunsight in quite a few dangerous situations—and I knew that he was prepared to risk his neck for the career he had chosen. And if his personal obligations included four children, that probably was one more reason for his doing such a good job against the VC's in the hope of recognition and advancement.

Now Billy told me about his parents back in Oklahoma. "My folks are country folks. There is nothin' but oil and cattle out there—the ground won't raise nothin' anyhow. My father's a Pontiac dealer. He won a trip to Las Vegas last year—a sales contest. I was hopin' that I'd make the trip, but——. He had a heart attack couple of years ago. He liked to have another when he saw all those bare-breasted women over there." I hoped Billy will be able to get back to Chandler and his wife Maryann, the four children, and his parents in November of 1963, when he gets his DEROS and heads for the States. I hope they'll all be able to go to Las Vegas together and that the senior Sprague can again take the same pleasant risk.

We were back at Soctrang before 2:30 this afternoon, and for once, there was time for the dust-grimed and weary crews to take showers, get some sun and clean clothes, and perhaps a drink, before dinner.

We are nearing the end of our series of missions and the

pilots and crewmen are wearing a little thin. Therefore, when Benedict briefed us for tomorrow's operation and said, "Tomorrow's going to be rather a light day," there was a palpable sigh of relief.

About today's operation, he said, "Recapitulation on the day's mission: Those drops we made were all successful. And only one aircraft hit today." No word about the VC radio station yet.

Benedict said that tomorrow's mission will be up in the northern and western section of the Delta area, known as Rack Gia. He went through the usual routine about radio calls, casualties, refueling, and the description of the LZ's. But the big feature in tomorrow's mission will be that "the VIP's are going to come along at the tail end." Benedict wasn't clear exactly who the VIP is, but he'll be a U.S. Senator, and he'll be coming down from Saigon. (It was Senator Henry M. Jackson of Washington.) "The Senator says he's going to get his feet into a rice paddy," Benedict told us.

Monday, December 10

Today was the last day of operations in this six-day series of assault missions, but there was no letup in our headlong pace until we got back to Soctrang at 3:50 P.M. We had made six assault missions, the first beginning at 8:20 A.M.

Today's shooting episodes involved more sampans than usual, since our LZ's were scatttered around the big rivers in the vicinity of Rack Gia. The gunners claimed eight VC's, and both Pappy Heck and Capt. Bob Webster fired rockets, and Billy Sprague, in whose bird I was flying, fired about 30 rounds near the second LZ.

Lt. Don Farnham gave us a circumstantial report: "I saw at least 10 troops coming out of the huts on the first LZ. They were setting up defensive positions. I called the leader, he called Tiger [the T-28's], and they called to tell him the [Arvin] troops were pinned down there. [In other words, the ground troops had run into opposition in that particular area.]

"At the second LZ, I saw a shipload of troops running up the bank, getting into a sampan. I didn't see the troops until we were going—about to leave the area."

Dickerson, No. 1 gunner among the Huey crewmen, claimed two more kills, but only tentatively. "I saw flashes about a mile out of the first LZ, where somebody had reported fire. And we got some fire from a sampan outside a hooch. I let loose as we pulled out of the LZ. There were two sampans together, and two guys fell or jumped into the water."

I checked with Maj. Ewing to find out what concrete results in terms of VC killed the Arvin had reported thus far. He said they had listed 30 killed, confirmed (i.e., the bodies were there).

One concrete result of today's operations was the capture and destruction of a small-arms factory that made both guns and ammunition. That neat job was done by an Eagle flight, which we in Hanson's Huey were lucky enough to accompany. We escorted four H-21's into a complex of rice fields that were surrounded by swampy wilderness, and later, when we convoyed the H-21's back to pick up the troops, we saw thin clouds of white smoke rising from a line of hooches at one end of the complex: some VC supplies being burned. But there was no audible shooting or visible enemy engagement.

I talked to Maj. Jim Butler, the American adviser who went with that Eagle flight, and he said that the arms manufacturing materials were hidden under what appeared to be brush piles. In the brush, Butler's people found the raw materials, principally hunks of sulphur, and also some documents and maps indicating this might have been a VC command post, apparently of battalion strength. But the VC's had scrammed before the Arvins and their American adviser reached the place.

It was an active day, and I had heard a good deal of VC fire at the second LZ. You can be reasonably sure, when you hear popping single shots, that it's coming from unfriendly hands on the deck.

The big feature of today's operation was the advent of high-powered VIP's on the scene. We were all curious as to whether or not Senator Jackson, who had pledged that he wanted to get his feet wet in an LZ, had his wish.

Apparently this had been achieved, but not before one of the advisers (whose name I must censor, of course, for reasons of military security) had made a few indiscreet radio transmissions on the subject.

The adviser, thinking he was on the intercom channel, broadcast on the command channel: "I hope the VIP gets his feet wet."

Chuck Benedict heard that transmission and he warned the adviser on the command channel: "You better get back on the intercom."

And the adviser moved his foot even more solidly into his mouth: "Oops—disregard that last transmission." (The

Senator was upset by all this, I heard later, and asked, "Who sent that transmission?" His pilot, Capt. Hanson, rose loyally to the defense of the Army. "I think it was the Air Force, sir," he said.)

I had to change from one Huey to another to make room for the Senator and his party. I saw the VIP squad walking down the landing strip at Rack Gia, very important-looking. Besides the Senator, who was wearing field greens like the others, there were a two-star general and five or six chicken colonels and lieutenant colonels.

Then a light colonel, much nerved up and harassed, came running up to Hanson's HU1B. He was upset about the fact that, as he said, "Senator Jackson has been on the ground for a long time, and I don't know what to do with him."

He was fishing around for Hanson to volunteer to carry the Senator on his HU1B, but Hanson eluded that. "Better put them in an L-20, where they can observe. . . . I have to have five aircraft for the mission." However, Hanson could see what was going to happen, and suggested to me that I'd better "get on another bird," and the colonel, by this time counting on a Huey ride for the Senator and his party, advised Hanson: "You better not fire."

Hanson (determinedly): "I'm going to have to fire, sir. I have to lead my men."

The Senator and his party, including the two-star general, did make the flight with Hanson's Huey, and were put down in a rice paddy. As Hanson told about it later on, the Senator acquitted himself nobly.

"I explained the rules of engagement to him," Hanson said, "and he [the Senator] said, 'I wish they'd fire so we could fire.'"

Furthermore, Hanson said the Senator had the kind of ruggedness we should expect in our leaders. Despite a bad case of the Vietnam Virus, he insisted on being put down in the paddy. When he got back into the aircraft—he was wet to the waist and pale. But he heard a radio transmission about 25 VC in the Condor (second Eagle flight) area and said he wanted to go down there. But the full-of-fight Senator missed out on seeing any shooting. Things were quiet among the Hueys, and Hanson didn't have to fire.

Tonight, the helicopter base at Soctrang was really rocking. In honor of the end of the six-day operation, there were steaks, and drinks on the house before dinner.

The O Club sounded like a real blast. The hoarse, celebrant voices were singing their favorite hymn, "Him, Him,

———— Him" and milder ballads like "Clementine" and the "Missouri Waltz." I walked down the main street of the camp to the enlisted men's bar, a screened tent strung with Christmas tree lights in celebration of the advent of the season. Like the O Club, the bar was braced at least two deep with drinkers, the celebrants singing the same songs, the same highly favored Army words were ringing out in uncoordinated conversations. I talked to a young crewman in a T-shirt who was coming out with a can of beer, and he explained, as if in praise of his high morality in staying clear of the club: "I don't ———— with the club, I get my beer and go."

In both the EM Club and the O Club, the basic thread of conversation, aside from the favorite four-letter words, was today's conflict with the VC. At the O Club, I heard Chuck Benedict and Bob Webster talking about the large numbers of physically fit men of military age who appeared all over this objective. Obviously they were VC's, but since they were usually without arms they weren't legit targets. Benedict told about a group of men in two large canoes, all able-looking military types. "I called Blueboy [Air Force] and an Arvin observer went down to look at 'em, and decided they were friendlies." In another place today, the T-28's decided the people in question were VC's, and shot hell out of some sampans, but no bodies were recovered.

Webster said he saw a group of men running, and "a woman ran out to give one man a package, he stopped to get it, and she ran back to the hooch, and he went on. Probably it was lunch."

I asked Capt. John Falls about the quality of the men assigned here to the Vietnam campaign. I knew that Falls was a Korean war veteran like many of the Army officers, and I wondered how he thought Americans here compared with those in Korea. He said, "In the Korean war there were a lot of people who missed World War II and wanted to get in. Now they're veterans—professionals—doing the job because it has to be done."

That's the way it seems to me: These people, Army advisers, helicopter pilots, Marines, Air Force, all seem vastly skilled and dedicated. They say The Best Go West, meaning Vietnam, and in my experience to date, this is certainly true.

But my experience is far from complete. I must get to Saigon and make arrangements to head north and see some action with the Special Forces boys, who are campaigning against the VC in a very different kind of environment. I shouldn't have any problem getting to Saigon because all of the choppers from the 33d, the 57th, and the Huey outfit are going up tomorrow.

Tuesday, December 11

I missed my flight to Saigon this morning, because I decided that while I was down here, I should try to get to Father Hoa's celebrated military camp. Father Hoa is one of a handful of Catholic prelates in this country who have organized their own militia to fight against the Communists. President Diem, being a stanch Catholic, has arranged for arms and ammunition and supplies for these religious organizers in their holy war against the Vietnamese Reds.

I was told at the day room that there might be a resupply mission going down to Father Hoa's swampy stronghold to deliver some of these vital items, so I gambled on the chance that the chopper flight would come through. Unfortunately, it didn't.

I called through to the PIO in Saigon, to set up a jaunt up to the mountain country around Pleiku and Kontum where the Special Forces operate most prominently. Allan Galfund, who has been my helpmate in arranging several of these jaunts before, told me he didn't think there'd be any problelm, once I got to Saigon.

Waiting around for the advent of a flight down to Father Hoa's, I stopped by to ask Maj. Ewing if he had any further word about our six-day campaign against the VC's. He said the latest advices indicated that there were about 40 VC's killed in the operation, "less than they hoped, in view of the large numbers of people in there."

There was one other item I wanted to check with him: the radio station we were supposed to have sought out with an airphibious landing two days ago.

"They didn't get it. The closest we came to it was that the Air Force reported a radio in a sampan. They brought fire to bear, but the results were undetermined."

Ewing, like many of the pilots of the 93d, is a mustang, meaning that he rose from the ranks to officer status. He was an EM in the 521st Airborne during World War II, was in the southern France invasion and in the Battle of the Bulge. He got out of the service after the war and went into the restaurant business in Blacketsville, Wis., but it didn't work very well, and "I missed the service." He got back in the service in 1949, in time for the Berlin Airlift, and was sent to Germany.

"My wife and I decided that the future wasn't too secure,

but since she couldn't have children, we'd better adopt two German kids. The future for them would be better than staying in Germany."

Maj. Ewing spoke humbly about the great fulfillment these children—David, 11; Pamela, almost 9—bring to him and his wife. "Without them, there wouldn't be too much to live for. The big thing is to bring them up so they can do their part in society. Without them, my wife and I wouldn't need very much." It seemed strange that a man with such traditional home-building virtues should be here in the heart of the Vietnamese war, getting shot at by VC and leading one of the few embattled U.S. Army outfits in the world today.

At the mess hall, I sat with two new pilots who arrived yesterday to join the 93d. They were both young and bright-eyed and had the fashionable skin haircuts. They were CWO Jim Steelman (of Salem, Mo.) and CWO Jim Bell (of East Moline, Ill.). I asked them how they liked living at Bugville.

Steelman said temperately, "We're living a lot better than some people here"—which was certainly a mild reaction and one that showed a rapid understanding of the low standard of living among the Vietnamese.

Bell said that they haven't been bothered by the bugs—I should add that the green and black bugs have been conspicuous by their absence for the last two nights—and the mosquitoes are not troublesome. Bell said, "At the 57th, where we stayed in Vietnam first, the mosquitoes were fierce. They'd carry you off if you weren't looking."

That joke about being carried off by the mosquitoes has been alive among the military at least as far back as Guadalcanal, where I remember hearing about the two mosquitoes buzzing around outside an antibug canopy and one saying to the other: "I'll pick up the net and you drag him out." And the other replying: "No, don't do that, if we do, the big fellas'll take him away from us."

Steelman said that after his indoctrination with the "big fellows" of the 57th, he had used his bug bomb a little too zealously on his first night here at Soctrang. "When I sprayed the canopy, it was so strong inside that I had to go outdoors."

Another incidental note on camp life in the Delta and its discomfort: Walking into the barracks building, I saw WO Leon Currie sitting in his room with his leg in a pail. He had just come back from the Army 8th Station Hospital in Nhatrang with a leg swollen to balloon size.

"I thought I had something special," he said. "But everybody has it. It's only a fungus infection."

After waiting for word of a resupply flight to Father Hoa's camp and hearing none, I was alerted by Don Toth to the fact that one of the militant Fathers of the Delta area, Father Phuoc, was here at the Soctrang camp at the moment, with an American adviser, Maj. Edward Betts (of Carbondale, Ill.). Betts had the job of getting the fighting Father some transportation to Saigon. It developed that Father Phuoc's military supplies are being cut off by a recalcitrant province chief, and he is going to appeal to the highest government authorities, to President Diem if possible, to intercede and give him the strength he needs to survive in a strongly VC area.

I saw the good Father, a handsome, earnest man with grizzled hair and a philosophical mien, standing with the adviser beside the operations shack.

The black-robed priest told me in French that he and his militia control the southern tip of an island in the mouth of one of the Mekong branches. There are 26,000 Vietnamese on this island complex, but "only 900 are under our control. The rest are VC-controlled."

Father Phuoc said that he has one SDC company and two Civil Guard platoons as his fighting force, and that the province chief was going to take away one of his Civil Guard companies. Maj. Betts explained the significance of this: "If he can't get troops, he won't go back. They [the VC] would grab him."

Betts told about the difficulties of reaching Father Phuoc's outpost on Gung Island, in Long Sien Province. He said the only way to get there is by chopper. "To go by boat is suicide. One boat effort was ambushed. . . . They always put up the VC flags when we go in there."

I left Maj. Betts trying to arrange for Father Phuoc's flight to Saigon, but before leaving the area, I got a small fill-in about Betts. Baldheaded, light-eyed, and warlike, with a knife scabbard sewn in the back of one of his combat boots, Betts seems a good, earnest adviser-type—but it wouldn't be too hard to imagine him as the middle-aged manager of a business in the States, which he might have been if fate had turned things differently for him.

I asked him how his wife stood up under the long separation involved in his year's duty in Vietnam, especially such hazardous duty as his.

"We're not overly patriotic," he said, "but we decided we should have our share of the separation everybody has to have." This seemed, in fact, a very patriotic adjustment to our nation's continuing state of war with the Communists.

The afternoon wore on without any sounds of helicopters taking off. For one day at least, the place was peaceful.

I went into the town of Soctrang with Don Toth. Despite the fact that I had spent a total of about 10 days at the Soctrang base on two visits and had made many assault missions with helicopters from the base, it was my first view of the town from ground level—probably more than most of the hundreds of pilots and crewmen who fly out of this base ever see.

One reason is that the town, or parts of it, are periodically off limits—when there is a hand-grenade or shooting episode, for instance.

The town itself is built around two muddy rivers, the heart of the downtown section being located between the two streams. The main street is like Danang: a series of flystands selling furniture, cloth, sheet music, books, and food—and some of the businesses boast signs with English lettering, for the benefit of the wealthy Americans.

Beyond the second river, in an area which is off limits to American troops at night, there are two monuments to different character traits in the Americans. One is a Catholic orphanage, which has been principally supported by the pilots and crewmen of the 93d and the other helicopter outfits that work with them. Very close by, just beyond the graveyard of the Catholic church, is a squarish, forbidding two-story house of Victorian architecture, with closed shutters and a spiked fence around it. Don identified it as "The Graveyard," most famous bordello of the area, patronized by Vietnamese troopers (and occasionally by Americans).

The Graveyard seems a living recreation of the bordello which Hemingway describes so vividly in *Farewell to Arms*, on the Italian scene. The genus bordello, Southeast Asian style, appears to be as much in the French provincial idiom as in the Italian form.

Don told me how much the 93d had contributed to the support of the orphanage in terms of clothing and furnishings. He also told me a story about one of the Negro helicopter crewmen of the 93d who was a devotee of the delights of The Graveyard.

Don said that Maj. Ewing finally spoke to the Don Juan and urged him to mend his ways, not for moral reasons, but because he might be caught by the VC's some night.

The colored boy wasn't at all dismayed by this possibility. According to Don, his answer was a simple one: "They can't hit what they can't see."

We drove in Toth's jeep through the sun-baked rice town between the two chocolate-colored streams and then around the Soctrang helicopter base. I was surprised to see that every bus passing the airfield on the highway was being stopped and searched and every individual checked, as might happen at an international airfield customs station. It would be too easy otherwise for an innocent-looking Vietnamese peasant to toss a grenade onto one of the 93d's choppers.

Beyond the triple rows of barbed wire that mark the main gate of the base. Toth pointed out to me still another strange feature of the Soctrang base: the brightly colored concrete building where the room-girls live. "We call it Capehart or Wherry housing," he said, with obvious ironic reference to the relatively luxurious living quarters on military bases in the United States.

"A lot of those baby-sans are widows of Vietnamese soldiers killed in action," Don told me. So far, we have lost fewer than 150 killed and wounded; whereas the Vietnamese have suffered more than 11,000 killed and wounded, about one-third of them killed, in what is essentially as much our war as Vietnam's during the past year.

I was glad to hear that preference, even for the hard jobs of room cleaning, laundry, and camp maintenance, is given to the Vietnamese widows. In this part of the world, where overpopulation combines with national poverty to keep the people on the edge of starvation, jobs with the American military establishment are in great demand. Even the lowliest employment, such as that of a washerwoman, who would ordinarily earn a dollar a day or less, is in demand. The good-natured Americans can always be counted on to pay a little more than the minimum wage.

Tonight, I glimpsed a *sub-rosa* phase of camp life at the helicopter base at Soctrang—a phase you might not be aware of if your experience at the 93d consisted wholly of going out on missions. With the new medical officer of the 93d, a pleasant California captain named Jim Hall, I went to town to watch a necessary and wise bit of preventive medicine in action. Whether the town of Soctrang is off or on limits to the personnel of the 93d, there remains the matter of preparedness for the times when it will be open, however briefly. Concretely, this means that the bar girls in the four places of entertainment available to servicemen must be watched and given medical treatment to keep down the spread of unlovely diseases among officers and men.

With Hall, I went around to the Paradise Bar, the

Bungalow Restaurant near the main bridge, and the small hotel between the two rivers where some of the MAAG enlisted men live.

The net results of the night's operations were that three girls, two working in the Paradise and one at the Bungalow, were fortified with penicillin shots. Both places were decrepit, dingy, and straight out of Charles Adams.

A by-product of our trip was the story gleaned from a Vietnamese *femme fatale* who is manager and part owner of the Paradise. Helen, aged about 32, is typical of the Vietnamese businesswoman types who are so frequently high-powered entrepreneurs and earn satisfactory capitalistic incomes related in one way or another to the presence of American servicemen in Vietnam.

Helen came from Hanoi, in what is now Communist North Vietnam, in 1955. She was one of the more than a million North Vietnamese refugees who fled to the relative freedom of the south.

She was married to a wealthy Vietnamese who worked for Shell Oil, and when the Communists won out and set up their new government, she fled in a 60-foot speedboat, one of the three large motorboats her husband had left her when he died during the Communist war. She made her escape with her nine-year-old son, carrying a small fortune in piasters, her late husband's life savings.

She and her boat were picked up by a French steamship, which charged her 27,000 piasters (about $2,000 at the then-current rates); eventually she ended up in a villa at Nhatrang, the principal French seashore resort in Indochina.

"We lived very well on the money," she told me. "But it didn't last very long.

"I lived with a sergeant—he worked for Ordnance—for four months. He had a wife in America and finally he went back home. But he writes every day, and says he will come back to Vietnam and pick me up. He made up his insurance to me, and he says he is going to be divorced."

Now, Helen says, her first ambition is to accumulate enough loot to send her son, now 16, to Paris to study at the Sorbonne. Next in order of priority is to marry the Ordnance sergeant, if he really sheds his wife.

The only place of entertainment we didn't visit this night was The Graveyard, and I regretted that, since it should be a picturesque place, to say the least. But even in the places that were reachable tonight, Doc Hall worked hard and skillfully to save the officers and men of the 93d a lot of grief, whatever the twists and turns of morality involved, and whether or not the Soctrang bars are on limits.

Coming back through the checkpoints of the airfield on a bright moonlight night, Hall was telling me how much he admired the courage and devotion of the pilots and crewmen of the 93d. "It beats me how they can keep on doing this day after day, sticking their necks out and taking those big chances. But somehow they do. It just beats me." I told him I felt as much admiration for the helicopter people and advisers, the Special Forces and Navy men, and the American Air Force pilots, as he does.

The Special Forces and Strategic Hamlets

Today was only a day of getting somewhere so as to get somewhere else, where something would be happening. Fortunately, the first place I had to go was Saigon, and now I could see it from the point of view of the servicemen coming out of the swampy Delta battlefield for a leave. And it was glittering and seductive. With its neon signs, its bars attended by hand-holding waitresses, and its restaurants where you could get something more than C rations or the hopelessly massacred mess-hall fare that Army cooks turn out, it seemed a genuine neon-embossed fleshpot.

This morning, I left Soctrang at 9:30 on a northbound Army Caribou, along with nine officers and men heading for several days of leave in "The Ville," as the chopper boys call Saigon.

One of the enlisted men was PFC Jim Harper (of Dalton, Ala.), the crew chief who broke his thumb in the crash of an H-21 at the LZ three days ago. He has his left hand in a cast now. Also in the group was gunner Edwin Bellow, whom I had talked to a couple of days ago about some gunnery exploits against the VC. Also boarding the plane at the last minute were CWO Fitts and Capt. Toth. All were obviously prepared for a few days of rest and recreation, or rape and riot, depending upon the individual taste, in Saigon.

I asked Bellow and Harper what they are going to be

299

doing in Saigon, a stupid enough question, and I got an answer in accordance: "Business," said Bellow. "Three-four days of business."

During the afternoon hours I managed to arrange for my trip up to Pleiku, the headquarters town for II Corps. It is in the middle part of Vietnam, up in the rolling, high country (with large patches of jungle) inhabited mostly by mountain aborigines, still known by the French name of "montagnards." Here the American Special Forces are busy organizing and training the montagnards in self-defense forces. Through Air Force contacts, I am set up now to fly on tomorrow morning's C-123.

Tonight I ran into Don Toth, Charlie Fitts, and another 93d pilot, John Walsh, as they were taking their ease at the sidewalk café on the outer edge of the Continental Palace Hotel. I persuaded them to come to the Atterbae Restaurant, a worth-while relic of the days of French empire, and then to the Capital Bar, a hand-holding institution, where behind heavy-gauge anti-grenade screens, you can trade pidgin inanities with Vietnamese charmers and even, perhaps, make arrangements to pursue your friendship after hours. You can engineer laws against dancing, but masculine instincts can't be legislated out of existence. At least, that is the theory upon which the night life of Saigon, like the night life of Hong Kong, Singapore, and Bangkok, is predicated.

Thursday, December 13

I was up at 5:45 to get to Tan Son Nhut in time to pick up the ride with the Pleiku-bound C-123. The trip was uneventful, although probably most anything would have seemed uneventful after the recent workout with the Hueys and the paddy splashers.

The loadmaster, T/Sgt Herbert W. McElvoy (35, of Pascagoula, Miss.), said we were carrying 600 pounds of mail and 3,900 pounds of other cargo. A spot check showed that that cargo included mostly food, radio parts, and also some incongruous club supplies like pool tables.

Sgt. McElvoy, who looked as if he had put in plenty of years of service in the Air Force, got a far-off mistiness in his eye as he told me about his four children back home. Returning to the sharper realities of the present, he related that he has been here only about a month and during that time has flown 45 hours in the C-123's and made one combat support mission.

We were sweeping in now to a landing on a long black carpet of runway flung out on the bare brown plateau, Capt. Berube's hand steady on the controls, as befits a veteran pilot, aged 30, with three children. But we swung suddenly into a sharp dive and a very steep, high-speed landing, wherein Berube threw his turbo-prop engines into a violent propeller reversal in a final show of the potentialities of the C-123. "Boy," he said proudly, "that was a typical assault landing."

I bummed a ride with a pickup truck heading for Corps HQ and found the imposing, fortresslike concrete structure on top of a low brown hill. In this bare pastureland, the building commanded the surrounding terrain like a chateau or citadel. Indeed, at the gateway through the surrounding barriers of barbed wire, the HQ was labeled, in Vietnamese, *Thanh Collo,* which the driver told me means "Citadel." I think part of the name at least has that meaning, though the dictionary gives *Thanh-tri* as the Vietnamese equivalent.

The black-top road leading to the Citadel skirted Pleiku, and among the trees of the town we could see the inevitable concrete houses of the French era, now occupied by the Vietnamese. We also passed several trudging montagnards: two of them with Malayo-Polynesian caste of features and physique and dark brown skins, both stripped to the waist, with some sort of fragmentary loincloth around their middles and wicker baskets filled with rice on their backs. This was the classic montagnard figure I remembered from my previous trips to Vietnam.

We also passed one woman with identical garb: a loincloth of rags and a wicker basket with straps across her shoulders, her breasts bare. These mountain people, like the others I had seen, were larger, darker, and less Asiatic-looking (their eyes were rounder) than the lowland Vietnamese, who are basically a provincial Chinese people.

At the Citadel, I was dumped off at the transient quarters, another series of concrete buildings, and was startled to see the care lavished on the gardens of these living quarters. All sorts of blossoms bloomed, the hedges were trimmed, every garden seemed to be well tended and groomed. I could surmise why this tidy landscape existed: I had already heard of Colonel Wilbur Wilson, the American who commanded the MAAG troops at II Corps Area HQ. The colonel is better known in Army circles as "Coal Bin Willie," since he has such a passion for tidiness. At a stateside Army post, he once ordered that the coal bins be whitewashed. I had been told that Coal Bin was very zealous about keeping his gardens around the living quarters in good shape, and that he is quick to mete out punishment to those who disfigure the over-all pictorial effect.

I fell in with a paratroop major who is entrusted with public relations (among other duties) at II Corps. Maj. George A. Peters (of Galveston, Tex.) is a real Geronimo sort with lots of airborne experience and a veteran of 82d and 11th Airborne Division service in World War II and Korea. This rugged, rough-faced, and jump-happy officer said that he had "been on operations and convoys in all the war areas in Vietnam, in L-19's and H-21's, and in the Hueys and Otters, but have never been shot at. There must be someone up there looking out for me."

Peters guided me to the II Corps HQ offices and introduced me to the operations officer on Col. Wilson's staff, Maj. Lloyd Picou (of Houma, La.).

With his map to illustrate, Maj. Picou told me how the fighting in this area differs from that in the Delta.

"Wherever we kill four or five VC's, we figure we're doing well. We don't have the concentrations that they have down south.

"Here we figure that we keep them [the VC] more fragmented even than the First Corps [in the far north]. The areas where the Arvin has to go to are mostly jungle or swampy areas." This latter would make sense, because the guerrillas wouldn't have much chance for survival roaming across bare, mountainous cow country like this, unless they picked localities that are more closed in, more confined. It immediately sprang to mind that campaigning up here in the plateau country must be just as distasteful as in the swamps of the south or the mountain jungles of the north.

I asked Picou, a deep-voiced French-Amercan of serious mien, if I could go out with one of the military operations. He glanced dubiously at my sneakers, saying, "they're no protection against bamboo stakes [VC foot traps]." He added ominously, "There are an average of three Arvins a week with foot wounds from bamboo stakes.

"The best procedure is to see what has developed by tonight—then we can see where you could go. We all meet in the [O Club] bar, there's very little to do in this town, so everyone goes to the bar. We can talk it over there." (I already knew that Col. Wilson enforces a 4-P.M. curfew in the town for Americans under his command.)

Maj. Picou said there shouldn't be any problem finding some ground-pounding mission for me to accompany. "Patrols are going on constantly. Our aim is to have two-thirds of our operational forces actively engaged in operations, the other third in R and R.

"The majority of our operations are small-sized, company or less. We have a series of battalion operations planned. We want to get into new areas, so that there will be no area where the VC can say: 'This is a safe area.' "

He pointed to a map of Vietnam: "Up until October 1, Arvin forces controlled nothing in this province. I don't know how much we control today. But all of the white areas—meaning food areas—are under Arvin control today. That means the rice-growing areas: 75 to 80 per cent—are under Arvin control. This is the important area."

Tonight, at the mess hall, which was not too different from Stateside headquarters messes, I met Lt. Col. Myron Murley (of San Francisco, Calif.), the executive officer of this detachment and acting CO in the absence of Col. Wilson, who is at the moment on leave.

Col. Murley, another former paratrooper, took me to a situation map in Col. Wilson's war room, and pointed out what he called "the three basic concepts" of the campaign here. The first of those concepts, he said: "To interdict the frontier." The frontier here at II Corps is the juncture of the Laotian and Cambodian borders with Vietnam, a very popular supply route by which the communists from North Vietnam and China can send in arms, ammunition, and other war materials. Second on Murley's list: "To secure the road nets," and here he explained that many of the roads in this Corps Area have been opened up just in the last year. Before that, they were subject to ambush and were generally insecure. But air patrols and an abundance of well-armed convoy troops have changed this picture. And thirdly: "To deny the VC supply points." The colonel said that the VC still have some "secret base areas," which are more or less secure, where they can amass supplies and circulate more or less freely, and that there must be denied the enemy—or, in more concrete terms, the VC must be driven out of such areas.

It was a good, quick over-all briefing on objectives in this vast area, comprising more than a third of Vietnam. I told Peters afterward that I really wanted to get out with some of the Special Forces, which have the job of accomplishing these objectives at the lowest level.

Friday, December 14

This morning Maj. Peters said he would take me by the Special Forces HQ in Pleiku so that I could find out which might be the most active sector.

First, however, we drove to an assemblage of tents spread out at one edge of an old landing strip: the camp of the 81st Transportation Company, a new H-21 troop-carrier outfit.

Scattered along the flanks of the strip were the same sway-backed flying bananas I had seen in such profusion in the Soctrang operations.

The acting CO of the outfit, Capt. Paul F. Anderson (of Roebling, N.J.), told me that the 81st went operational here in Vietnam only two months ago and that there have been no aircraft hit and no casualties yet.

Anderson said the new outfit's hairiest mission so far was the rescue of the Arvin 20th Special Battalion, when they were trying to cross a river called the Yali. "A flash flood messed up their crossing, which was at night. Our outfit left out of here about 11 o'clock [P.M.]. A VNAF flare ship, a C-47, located the area and illuminated it for us. But a ground fog moved in, so we were unable to get in.

"We went back to Kontum and came out again at first light. We pulled out 37 people from logs or out of the water. And a later lift got 23 or so more. The total was 60 or 70—19 or so of the others were drowned.

"It was tough to try to navigate at night, and so close to the Laotian [border]. So the pucker factor [nervous strain on vital organs] and the wear on seat cushions were high."

Capt. Anderson also told us about the most successful operation the outfit has pulled in this area, aside from saving the lives of the Arvins caught by the flash flood.

It was in a VC area about 15 miles due east. "We got good results down there. It was on October 16, we ran 400 people in. I think there were 69 [VC] killed. They [the Arvins] got 30 tons of rice. They broke up a VC training camp and burned six months' food supply for them. They got a VC battalion commander and psy-warfare [propaganda] chief. Down south [in the Delta area] they're more engaged in everyday assaults. The area up here's so damned large, and the VC work in small groups. They hit a village, get some rice, and fade into the jungle." Anderson said that his outfit had a job supplying the Special Forces in this area and that he'd be glad to give me a ride out to whatever bases I wanted to visit.

Maj. Peters then took me over to the Special Forces HQ, also atop a bare brown hill, and introduced me to the acting CO, Capt. M. H. Jenkins (of Sullivan, Ind.). Jenkins told me about the seven outposts spread out in this Corps Area. His headquarters camp here at Pleiku is what is called a B detachment: six officers and 23 enlisted men. The smaller groups, scattered across the seven bases and the area, are smaller, called A detachments.

Jenkins, an alert, personable officer, said that the Special Forces detachments have been less than two months in this area, but they have already done a good job of "sanitizing the border." They have the mission of training and arming the montagnards so that they will be able to defend themselves against marauding VC's, who generally come looking for supplies, with propaganda experts (psy-warfare types) to justify their actions and lecture the villagers on the "fight for liberation."

Maj. Peters told me that a small, helicopter-borne raiding party might be scheduled for tomorrow or the next day, if he could secure the necessary Arvin troops. He gave me a small fill-in about the advantages of smaller-sized raiding parties:

"If you go in with a battalion-sized effort, there's so much to move that the VC get the word and shove off. But the small units can move faster, the VC won't be so apt to fade away. . . . I'm convinced that the platoon-strength patrols are about the best, thirty men, maybe three choppers."

That sounded to me like a fairly small force to be darting into the middle of a VC area where larger enemy forces might be lurking, but I couldn't back out at this point! Perhaps fortunately for me, the mission was canceled later in the day because, as Peters told me, "the Corps commander says he can't spare the platoons. We'd need two platoons for an overlapping day and night operation."

When I asked Peters if I might get transportation to one of the Special Forces bases and possibly make a patrol with them, he told me that a couple of other correspondents might be coming in tomorrow— Dave Halberstam, and Ken Armstrong of a Cleveland (Ohio) television and radio station. Peters would try to lay on a chopper to take us around to some of the Special Forces bases, so I could make up my mind which would be the best story. I said that would be just fine.

VIETNAM DIARY

Saturday, December 15

We three rubbernecks—Halberstam, Armstrong, and I—took off this morning in an H-21 of the 81st Helicopter Company bound for Plei Yit, one of the outstanding Special Forces bases of the area, according to Peters. The flight was a resupply mission to Plei Yit and Plei Mrong.

Before we took off, Maj. Peters gave us a small briefing about the raids the VC have been making on the villages. These raids, Peters said, are a measure of the VC's desperation. He said he would be looking sharp for fires as we flew today; the VC's have burned 10 or 12 villages in the last few weeks. "The VC have good intelligence. They know the Special Forces program is getting results. They want to intimidate the villagers."

He also pointed out that the Arvins in this Corps Area have constructed 86 new villages for the montagnards under the strategic hamlet program, and have relocated about 30,000 of the mountain tribesmen.

"In November, they [the VC] started this series of burnings," he said. "Once in a while they come in and propagandize the village when they burn it," Pete said. "The line is 'Resist the Diem aggression—don't work with Americans—they will fence in your village. The Vietnamese government doesn't have any strength. We are the ones with strength—we'll burn the village.'

"The problem is that two-thirds of the population are montagnards . . . they don't know about democracy, except that people hurt them or help them.

"The VC are very effective in their propaganda. The main propaganda theme is that once South Vietnam is liberated [from the Americans and Ngo Dinh Diem], they will set up an autonomous republic, separate from the rest of Vietnam."

Most of the way to Plei Yit, Pete watched for any trail of smoke that would signal such a village burning. But none appeared on the face of the brown, rolling countryside, where smooth hills slipped underneath us like sleeping brown animals. I could see occasional patches of close-studded tall trees, the same kind I had seen in the north. This sort of jungly patch, I supposed, would be the terrain where the VC's would hide out.

We swept into a clearing edged by some trees, with a montagnard village on the far side: a collection of neat, thatch-roof stilt-houses in rows, with a deep ditch around them, and a

DECEMBER

line of bamboo stakes set up in a kind of barbed-wire barrier.

We landed there, amid twirling clouds of red dust, and were met by crowds of montagnard troopers in green American field uniforms and a group of American Special Forces advisers, looking lean and fit in their fatigues, jungle boots, and green berets. The troopers, although larger than the lowland Vietnamese, still appeared to be midgets next to the tall Americans.

One of the group was a sturdy, blond-mustached captain named Stanley Hyrowski (of Youngstown, Ohio). He led us along a dirt road and into a cleared area, where in sandbagged outpost positions, montagnard troops were preparing to fire rifle grenades. It was only a practice maneuver, designed to familiarize the little mountain men with American weapons, but as Hyrowski said, "Pretty soon they'll have real targets.

"We're building command teams," he said. "The teams will go out and seek out the Viet Cong. We teach them submachine gun, carbine, hand grenades. We try to stress offensive actions."

After the small group had finished firing their rifle grenades into the far end of the maneuver field, I talked to one of their coaches in this art, Sp/5 Norris H. Hammond (of Florence, Ala.).

"I'm very pleased with 'em, considering they've never worked with anything but crossbows. The submachine gun is probably their best weapon. It's light and doesn't require much aiming . . . Of course, my main job is to see that they don't kill each other."

Hammond said that the instruction went very well today, and just this morning, 300 montagnards had a chance to fire the rifle grenades.

The other Special Forces man immediately connected with this phase of weapons indoctrination was a redheaded, curly-mustached veteran, SFC Alex Vizena (33, of Gary, Ind.).

The thing that impressed both Hammond and Vizena most strongly was the poverty of these mountain people. Vizena, whose father is an ironworker and who himself has worked in steel mills and presumably knows about hard living, said: "These people have absolutely nothing. I've written to my home parish, St. Francis Xavier, in East Gary, Ind., to get clothes for these people. They just don't have any clothes. They've got rags."

Vizena feels a great affection for the montagnards. "These are happy-go-lucky people. They remind me of stories I've heard of the American nation. They're simple people and they will share anything with you. They get the biggest thrill out of giving an American a cigarette."

Vizena's work is of the most rugged sort: training montagnards to fight and leading them in attacks. He, too, wears paratroop wings. He was in Europe for three years with the 11th Airborne—and there, incidentally, he met and married his wife, the former Lotte Rasch of Copenhagen, Denmark. They have two children, both girls. The oldest is two, and the youngest, Vizena said, is eight days old.

Hammond, aged 24, was a radio announcer for four and a half years at KDA, Nashville, Tenn. Naturally, he has the gift of gab and has picked up some of the local montagnard languages: Sedang and Jarai. Right this moment, summoning the next group of trainees in for their bit of rifle grenade firing, he bawled out to one of his candidates who was straying in the wrong direction: "Oi Dyick." I asked him what that meant, and he said with a laugh: "It only means 'man.'"

With Capt. Hyrowski, we three correspondents went over to the Special Forces camp, a collection of thatch huts, with a long mess table perched outdoors. Hyrowski offered us a bottle of beer—it's pleasant to think that such minor luxuries can sometimes be provided for these picked American troops in the midst of a dangerous job.

Over the beer, it developed that Capt. Hyrowski had been in the 11th Armored Division, and a PFC in the 63d Armored Infantry Battalion in World War II. He certainly doesn't look old enough for that.

Also at the table was Sgt. George M. Clark (of Denver, Colo.), who now was hanging his head low after suffering a recurrence of malaria, which he had originally contracted in Korea in 1951-52, when he was an infantryman with the 2d Division.

As we walked down to the clearing to get aboard the chopper, I asked Maj. Peters which of these Special Forces bases he regarded as the most dangerous, which most exposed to potential attack. He said Plei Mrong, our next stop.

A large crowd of mountain soldiers were on hand to welcome us when we arrived at Plei Mrong. Here, as everywhere, the distinctive thrumming sounds of helicopters are the best automatic crowd assemblers. People are drawn from miles around as if by magnets, when the characteristic drumbeat is heard.

In the crowd were the two commanders of this A detachment at Plei Mrong: Capt. William R. Grace (29, of Arlington, Va.), slim, concentrated, thoughtful, and his second-in-command, Lt. Paul Leary (26, of Abilene, Tex.), an animated Celt.

Grace took us over to the mess hall for lunch, a thatch hut which, like the Plei Yit encampment, offered such desirable items as beer and canned whole milk from California, served by a devoted little montagnard cook.

Besides these things, there were dehydrated potatoes, beef, and baked bread. The long mess table, with 13 places for Special Forces officers and enlisted men, also presented reminders of the surroundings in which these people have to function. There were bottles of Chloroquin and Primoquin, malaria depressants, and several bottles of remedies for the Vietnamese curse: Intromycin and Polymagma.

From the mess shack or any one of the six longhouses made of thatch—barracks for the montagnard troops—you can see a forested mountain bastion rising to the west, three or four miles away. Grace and Peters explained that this is a "secret base" area for the Communists, a VC stronghold. The Special Forces people were taciturn about it, but later Peters explained to me that one of the big objectives of training montagnard troops here is to sweep that area and keep it clear of VC. This, Peters said, is one good reason why the duty at Plei Mrong is considered dangerous: "It's just surrounded by VC, that's all."

Grace said they are training montagnards to be a strike force, as Peters indicated, so that they can make sweeps through this VC territory and secure it for the Vietnamese government. "We took the loincloths from the montagnards six weeks ago and gave 'em a gun," Grace said. "We have 70 Banakei, 120 Jarai, and 60 Sedang down from Kontum." It sounded like a good diverse selection of the different tribes.

As they were talking a young, hard-looking sergeant, Joseph Vaccero (25, of Fort Lauderdale, Fla.), came in to the mess shack and demanded a beer. He looked as if he needed it, he was drawn and sweaty, and it developed that he was just returning from a patrol, which had taken him and a platoon of montagnard strike-force trainees on a sweep through VC territory, for three and one half hours. But on today's sweep, Vaccero said, they hadn't found very much in the way of VC sign. "We found an amimal trap and went in further beyond it," he said. "I went in there about 150 meters—and somebody had been layin' down there. But no people . . . and we didn't run into any bamboo stakes."

The group of Special Forces men who had now gathered

at the mess table told me about their first experiences with foot traps and sharpened bamboo spikes in this area. "We had trouble with foot stakes at first, five or six people got. stuck," Leary said. The first wound from the spikes was suffered by the detachment's medical man, Sg. Donald Wolford (of Williamson, W. Va.). Husky Sgt. Wolford was there to detail it: "Those bamboo spikes were stuck in the ground about six inches apart. I was wearing jungle boots, and the spike came in at the top of my foot, went in about an inch."

Leary explained that there is a belt of these *punjis* still standing about 100 yards from there, originally sown by the VC—he would take us over and show us that field of homemade booby traps. He said he would also show us the foot traps. Like those I saw up in I Corps Area, these are holes in the ground camouflaged with matting and greenery on top and set with *punjis*, which are supposed to have been contaminated by some local poison, frequently as simple a poison as human waste.

The choppers that had brought us here had to leave for Kontum and Pleiku. The other rubbernecks shoved off with the choppers but Maj. Peters and I stayed a little longer. I asked Leary and Grace to show me the VC *punjis* and foot traps.

In a large field at the outer end of the Plei Mrong maneuver ground there are thousands of these sharpened spikes set in the ground at all kinds of crazy angles. You had to walk through them as if on eggs, and I saw how you could easily stick yourself in such a setup, especially if you stopped to talk to someone, or backed up, or moved any direction unexpectedly, as you might if you were surprised.

Leary and Grace (both of them, incidentally, sons of Army officers) showed me some VC foot traps as well: hundreds of them scattered over the area, most of them deliberately caved in to disarm them. My guides showed me one clever wrinkle: Besides the vertical *punjis* in the bottom of these holes, there were some in the sides, angled downward, so that if you stepped into the hole and tried to pull your foot out, there'd be a fish-hook effect.

A chopper had just come in, and as Grace, Leary, and I walked over to the parade ground that serves as a chopper landing field, Grace filled me in on some of the casualties suffered by his Plei Mrong detachment. Aside from the injuries inflicted by *punjis*, there was recently an episode with a mine that blew up a truck, injuring a Sp/5 named Billie G. Fell (of Haleyville, Ala.). He said that Billie is still in the hospital as a result of that mine detonation. And of course, many montagnards—fortunately, no Americans—have been hit by sniper fire from outside the camp at night.

I discovered that Grace was a West Point graduate, Class of 1954. I asked if he was No. 1 in his class, and he replied wryly, "I nearly was No. 1 in the Class of 1955."

I noticed that the Plei Mrong complex includes two villages inhabited by montagnards, not just one. They are close together and protected by a bamboo barrier and a dry ditch, which will be filled eventually with bamboo fences.

Under a tree between the two villages, we passed a group of montagnard men and women drinking their native rice beer. I asked Grace if they were celebrating something, and he said no. "They just like the stuff."

That rice booze, Leary told me, can be dynamite. He said he had recently sat in one one of their social affairs and drunk the rice wine, and "I'm so saturated with Polymagma that it isn't helping any more. You have to shift over to something else if you get too much Polymagma or Intromycin or paregoric."

Maj. Peters and I climbed aboard the H-21 with a group of Arvin troops going into Pleiku. I suggested to Grace that I come back to Plei Mrong as soon as I could get my gear from Pleiku. Grace advised that if I had an air mattress, I would do well to bring it.

We flew back to Pleiku on a bird piloted by WO's William R. Beatty (of Seattle, Wash.) and Charles E. Holloway (of Orlando, Fla.), of the 81st Transportation Company (Pleiku). Holloway, a brand-new arrival in Vietnam, is being broken into the job. He holds some kind of family record among the pilots: five children.

Back in Pleiku, I stopped with Maj. Peters at his liaison office with the Vietnamese Army HQ in town. Pete was anxious to point out that perhaps I should take a look at one other outpost in this area before going back to Plei Mrong and the patrol activity there. Illustrating with a map, he suggested I might do well to go down to visit the MAAG advisers at Phu Ban province (south of Pleiku), which has been an active zone for Arvin clear-and-hold operations in this area. He said that in this neighborhood, nearly 15,000 montagnards have been resettled in strategic villages.

Peters introduced me to another officer on his staff, Capt. Richard O. Edwards (of Rome, N.Y.). Blond, mild-looking Capt. Edwards, who incidentally is married and has two children, ages nine and ten, has been here nine months, and has made "six or seven" [Arvin] operations from four hours to ten days. Like many of the advisers, Edwards was a Korean war veteran, and among other military accomplishments on that troubled scene, he spent 33 days on Pork Chop Hill during the fighting of 1953. At that time, he was badly wounded in the head, and was unconscious for five days.

Pete began to look somewhat strained and uneasy around the gills, and suggested that we head back up toward the Citadel and the living quarters. He told me as we drove that he had picked up amoebic dysentery in Korea, and that he recently had been under treatment for it. "It was getting worse instead of better," he said. "I found out that the montagnard boy was bringing me unpurified water."

Between the hazards of foot traps and drippy tummy, it would seem that there are enough dangers to occupy an American's time here without having to wage a shot-and-shell war with the VC as well.

Sunday, December 16

Today I flew down to Phu Ban in one of the 81st L-19's, and had a quick look at one of the celebrated clear-and-hold operations up here in the plateau country.

My pilot to Phu Ban was Capt. Floyd J. Tiemann (of Lincoln, Kan.). Capt. Tiemann has been in Vietnam just one week, but he flies with the sure grip of a veteran. He has about 1,000 hours in choppers, 2,000 in straight-wings. On the interphone he told me that his wife and child are in St. Paul, Minn. "We expect a new one [child] about Christmas," he said.

The huge, sprawling operation at Phu Ban seemed to be difficult to get a grip on, but I did see some of the new strategic hamlets being built, and some of the Americans involved. I also managed to see some of the VC propaganda material captured by the Arvins in their latest clear-and-hold effort hereabouts.

The Americans had their tent camp beside one of the tributaries of the Ia Ayun River, which runs down through the center of this area. The sector adviser, Maj. Clement Will (of San Antonio, Tex.), told me there was a temporary lull in current clear-and-hold operations here, but, he said the troops have been successful recently.

"Thursday, our troops hit about a squad of VC. The VC pushed in more than usual, and the troops killed one of them [the VC].

"We found documents, medicine, propaganda, a Chinese

switchboard and handset radio, and .60-mm.- and .57-mm. recoil-less ammo. . . . It might have been a province CP."

Lt. Charles Kleebauer (of San Francisco, Calif.), an infantry adviser assigned to the 1st Battalion of the 41st (Arvin) Regiment, said:

"The idea is to get 'em [the montagnards] out of the hills, where the VC's have control, and resettle them along the road. This road eventually will be open to Tuy Hoa. The point is to get them out of the woods."

Maj. Will showed me some of the propaganda, which was illuminating, to say the least.

Than Qui Hoat, a Vietnamese interpreter, dressed in khaki-colored civilian clothes and dark glasses, read to me from a pile of magazines and maps and VC credentials. All of it followed the propaganda line of Communists across the world. It spoke of the people's "self-ownership" and the "breaking of the Yankee-Diem axis." The only joker, in Vietnam as elsewhere in the world, is that they don't mean to give "self-ownership." They certainly haven't in North Vietnam and Communist China.

One propaganda magazine, a series of mimeographed typewritten sheets stapled together, included a cartoon. The drawing showed an American hand stretching out over a strategic hamlet, and it was captioned: *Outspreading of guerrilla warfare in Area D* (the D Zone).

Near the cartoon, a vitriolic article announced: "America proclaims that they are friends of our people. But they come as owners and directors. They say that they are allies but indeed they are masters, they think that they are civilizers, proud of the white race, and [they] look at our people with despising eyes.

"How angry we are! The anger which bursts into our hearts makes us feel that we are drunk. We cannot stay in inaction. We cannot suffer their attitude any longer."

Some of the stuff was quite out of date, and with the usual attitude of the Communists that it doesn't matter when news is released (the important item is the propaganda impact), another "magazine" was dated 1961. It was apparently still being circulated as current propaganda. It said, according to Than: "If you have a chance to pass the D Region in 1961, you will certainly be impressed with the wide spreading of guerrilla warfare. In that summer, the revolution progressed in six villages, and now more than three districts have won self-ownership and are trying to defend themselves and break the Yankee-Diem axis."

This was practically a carbon copy, with names changed, of what I had seen in China during the Communist revolution there, and in Malaya, and in Korea.

In the file of captured documents, there were passes and safe-conducts for VC's on sick leave or carrying military supplies down the Ho Chi-minh Trail:

This is a witnessing paper that the group of porters of village _____ and district _____ for _____ quantity _____ duty _____ time _____ from _____ to _____ and date.

Another pass, a safe-conduct for a VC guerrilla sick or wounded, read:

I recommend Comrade _____ in _____ group being sick, to stay at _____ now has recovered to go back to his duty. Date and station chief _____.

In this tent camp I met an American civilian, a lean, pale, and vigorous chap named Carl Young (of Dunkirk, Ind.), who is entrusted by USOM with the job of helping to settle the montagnards in their new strategic hamlets. He said there are two such villages being built here by the side of the river and near the through road that we are trying to clear as far as the coast. The villages are called Bom M'Rok and Bom Ambla, and have, respectively, 1,000 and 1,400 inhabitants. The montagnard population, Young said, is growing by leaps and bounds as the mountain people voluntarily come in to escape the VC areas of influence.

Lt. Kleebauer said that in this area there were 6,865 montagnards on September 1, and now, as of December 21, there are 14,606. Sometimes the montagnards are shooed along by Vietnamese troops making clear-and-hold operations, but many times they come in under their own power.

Maj. Will told about a group of 369 montagnards who crossed the river in the last two weeks, swimming their cattle with them. They are being settled in one of the new strategic hamlets that Young is helping to set up.

Will agreed to show me one of the new villages, but before we went over there, I talked to a couple of the elder sergeant types at the camp, who had been here since the early days of American operations in the area. One of them, S/Sgt William P. Bennett (32, of Iowa City, Iowa), an administrative sergeant wearing shorts, has been here for nine months, and he remembers the first insecure days. "When we first came here we couldn't go to the Robal River to get a bath. You had to go to the Song Be. You would get [sniper] fire from the other side of the Robal. But now it's pretty well secured, right here, anyhow."

Maj. Will, Carl Young, and the local Vietnamese chief, Maj. Chi (a lowland type), took me out to the nearest village, still very much under construction. I saw the usual collection of wooden frame bungalows on stilts, some with thatch roofs already attached. Strangely enough, the embryo village was quiet, the men all gone. The reason, Maj. Chi said, stemmed from the fact that the rice crops have to be harvested. Sunday has no special significance to the pagan montagnards.

Maj. Will, Young, and I walked through the village and saw a few of the women folk sitting in their platform houses with their children, weaving a hand-loomed cloth of black, with purple patterns worked in—a distinctive design effect that I had seen in the mountain tribes of Formosa, and among some of the Malayo-Polynesian peoples of Indonesia.

It was interesting to see a *new* montagnard village, because every other one I have seen on previous trips has been encrusted with smoke and grime. The people here looked as impoverished as ever, as we walked around giving the kids candy from some USOM kit bags we had brought along.

Despite their newness, the houses conformed to the classic montagnard pattern: principal Items inside were sacks of rice and maize, and open cooking fires with no vent in the thatched roof above to let the smoke out. And in these new houses there were always huge, dusty pottery jars, the jugs for rice wine or beer which are the original and only measuring sticks of montagnard wealth, such as it is.

In their new condition, it was easy to see the splendid handwork that went into the houses: the ingenious weaving of bamboo and thatch and the clever carving of logs. Like the thatch houses of the Pacific islands, these were fastened together without nails.

The dusky-skinned kids climbing to their bare-breasted mothers were as unhealthy as you might expect in such a primeval culture. Many of them had distended bellies (worms and undernourishment), the eyes of some were puffed and reddened (trachoma), and many of the mothers had rampant skin infections.

Young said helplessly, "If we only had a doctor! Not one doctor in this area! Isn't it awful? We have the money for doctors and medicine all allocated. But no doctors."

315

I had heard the dreadful medical statistics of Vietnam: 700 doctors for the whole country, and of these, about 300 have been absorbed by Diem's 200,000-man army. That means only 400 for the whole country of 14.8 million. And the montagnards up in the remote hills are the worst off of all.

Young 'said that, so far, only one doctor had come through this area, a Dr. Vorogopolis, a USOM public health official. "He could spot their diseases as if they had a label on their chests: He'd call out 'trachoma' or 'worms' or 'VD.' But there just aren't any more doctors."

My guides dropped me off at the landing strip, where a chopper was coming in to transfer some troops to Pleiku. Maj. Chi, a good average lowland Vietnamese (the lowlanders are frequently disliked by the montagnards), filled me in about the over-all problem of this province, which he said is 5,000 square kilometers with a population of 63,000 (only 3,000 of these are Vietnamese). "Of the 60,000 montagnards," he said, "34,000 are now under Vietnamese control."

Maj. Will added: "In the short time since I came here— that was in July—the program really got under way. Since September especially, when they organized the new Phu Ban province. In the first days, you couldn't use the road, now you can. Since September, they [the Vietnamese government] have brought in 3,000 people and 500 head of cattle."

I flew back to Pleiku as the sun was going down, in an H-21 with Capt. Thomas R. Messick (of Roanoke, Va.) and CWO Barney Tomlinson (of Wellington, Utah). That cold and forbidding Citadel, perched on the high, dark hill, really looked like home. The large truck driver who gave me a ride back from the airstrip, Sp/4 Joe Monia (of Lorain, Ohio), confessed that he had the same feeling of being at home up here in the plateau country of II Corps, and in this war. "This is the war of my generation," Monia effused. "Some people have World War I and some have World War II. This is mine."

Offhand, I would say that Monia has a legitimate claim. He has been in Vietnam for eight months, and has already once been ambushed by the VC when he was attached to the MAAG at Saigon. Back there in June, he and the Vietnamese convoy taking a payroll to a Vietnamese Army base were jumped by VC's, and drove them off with casualties on both sides.

"I opened up on a couple of the little bastards," Monia said. "I hope I caught a couple of them. I wasn't scared until afterward—when I thought about it."

Later tonight, I checked with Peters to see if I'm cleared

to get a ride over to the Special Forces detachment at Plei Mrong, and go with them on patrol. Pete said yes.

Monday, December 17

I flew into the Plei Mrong base with two H-21's from the 81st, hitching a ride with a resupply mission. At the mess shack, I saw all the familiar faces, and some new to me. The crewmen and pilots from the 81st choppers came in to get coffee because one of their birds had broken down. One of the crew chiefs, Sp/5 Mervyn Thompson (of Taft, Tenn.), asked the Special Forces people about the montagnard trooper whom the 81st had evacuated last Friday. He had been on patrol and had got hit in the back by a bullet—which of course didn't make me feel too jovial about my upcoming ground-pounding mission.

Sgt. Joe Vaccero told us about the plan he had been making for ambushing some VC's tonight.

"I've been over the ground twice," he said, "and I think we can get something.

"I'll take 45 men. I may be the only American, or I might take Woelfel [SFC Lou Woelfel, of Brooklyn, N.Y.], if Billie Fell, the other medic, gets back to camp."

I asked Vaccero how he sets up this kind of night ambush and he said, "You just get into position, and you try to stay awake—sit, stand, or stay awake somehow. We're going to pull it off between the rice paddies in the woods. It's thick woods between the rice paddies."

Vaccero asked if I wanted to go out on his ambush for tonight, and I told him I was figuring on a patrol this afternoon, if there was one, and probably wouldn't have the energy to go out on an ambush tonight as well.

Vaccero said he had to shove off: "A montagnard kid fell off a jeep and I have to give him first aid."

Before Vaccero left, I got a quick fill-in on his background. He was born in Trenton, N.J., grew up in Hopewell, and now lives in Fort Lauderdale, where his father is a pusher (foreman) for South Florida Steel. He has a younger brother, Jim, 23, who is now in the 82d Airborne Division at Fort Bragg.

I asked Vaccero if he has a wife, and he responded: "I'm not married. I need a wife like I need a hole in the head. In this business, that's all I need . . ."

I went over to the headquarters building with Lt. Paul Leary to check up on the patrol schedule for this afternoon.

Inside the thatch building, some of the troopers were setting up two-by-four timbers as dividers. Leary patiently watched one montagnard trying to nail some boards together, and at last interceded and took the job himself.

"Charlie Brown," he said good-naturedly to the little trooper, "you're real smart. We're going to give you a Ph.D. right here. You'll be the only montagnard around these parts with a Ph.D."

While we were waiting for word on the patrol Lt. Leary dug up some snapshots for me showing the construction of the camp, some firing on the rifle range, and a picture of one dead VC being held up by Leary and the "old man" of the detachment, Sgt. First Class Marvin Compton (aged 36), of Ashville, N.C. Compton is a squarish, baldheaded trooper who looks rugged enough to have been through every turn and periphrasis in the Army manual and out of it. He came in at that moment while Leary was showing me the picture of the dead VC.

In the picture Compton was holding up the VC's head, and now he explained: "The reason I was turning my head away was, I was about to throw up."

Leary said that this particular VC was picked up in a night ambush, and they wanted to capture a VC alive for purposes of intelligence. "But somebody opened up—we don't know who, and killed him." He added: "The main reason Compton was about to throw up was that the VC had a powerful smell. He defecated all over himself when he was shot, then he started to stink and bleed when they brought him in here. I almost threw up too."

At about noon, Sgt. Antonio Duarte (33, of Richmond, Calif.) came in to tell us that a patrol was going out at two o'clock, with PFC Michael Boyd (23, of Wilmington, N.C.) and Sgt. George Hoagland, III (of Tucson, Ariz.) leading.

Duarte explained: "The purpose of them goin' is to see if they can locate any of the VC hideouts or caches. It'll be north-northeast.

"The VC secret base is to the west. [I remembered seeing that heavily wooded bastion as it was pointed out by Capt. Grace.] But there are red areas all around here. Matter of fact, we consider this entire area as a red area."

Duarte, swarthy and husky, explained why he wasn't going with us: "We went on patrols every day last week, and two nights, that's why I'm restin' now."

In the longhouse that serves as a barracks for the American Special Forces people at Plei Mrong, I borrowed a short-barreled .38-caliber revolver from SFC Marvin Compton (36, of Asheville, N.C.), whose bunk was across the room from mine, and also put some steel innersoles inside my sneakers, to afford a little protection against the *punjis*. These innersoles, which are thin and appear to be made out of fabric, like the kind you get in the five and ten, are standard equipment for patrols in this area.

With PFC Boyd, a handsome young man with thin nose and prominent blue eyes, I went out to the quadrangle between the Special Forces sleeping quarters and mess hall, and there met the other American leader of the patrol: Sgt. Hoagland. Hoagland, heavier and older than Boyd, was already sizing up the strike-force soldiers lined up in the bright, hot sun of the quadrangle.

Boyd, looking tall, lean, and blond in his camouflaged tiger suit and jungle boots—and very intent—picked out his squad for the patrol from the raw material of some 60 men standing at attention.

As the troops were assembling in a separate group for the patrol, the radio operator, a mite who must have weighed 65 pounds as against his PRC-10 radio's 25, showed up with bare feet. Boyd was patient, and said to the interpreter, "Tell him to get shoes and hurry back."

Then he addressed the squad, via interpreter: "Does every man in this squad have a basic load of ammunition?" Apparently the answer was affirmative: nods through the ranks.

We shoved off a couple of minutes later. Boyd, all business and decisiveness, told me he will be about third or fourth in the line, and Hoagland will be at the tail end of the patrol. I decided to go along with Boyd.

We walked toward the northwest gate of the camp, out past the many layers of barbed wire. We filed through the narrow opening of the gate, then fanned out in skirmish formation along the wagon trail, past several caved-in foot traps and a few bamboo *punjis* that hadn't been flattened. The wide trail soon gave way to a narrower path, and then we cut away from the footway, and Boyd explained to me in a whisper: "We won't get any VC unless we get away from the big paths."

The blond warrior called the little radio operator, whose already too-large clothes seemed to be expanding over his tiny frame as he struggled with his load. Then the American leader spoke into the radio: "Control Control, this is Day-Go. Control Control, this is Day-Go. I read you loud and clear.

How you me?" He got an affirmative answer from Control, the radio station at Plei Mrong headquarters.

As we moved on into open woods, with just a fringe of underbrush, Boyd signaled to the troops behind him to spread out wide for good security.

Then we progressed into a jungle of brambly, tangled trees and thick underbrush, following what was really only a series of animal trails, as fragmentary as they come. Sometimes we breasted our way through thick vines, following some mostly imaginary trail vestige; sometimes we went on all fours through paths that could have been made by animals or crawling men. And sometimes I was convinced there was absolutely no trail, for we were picking our way through brambles, bamboo, and other blind undergrowth.

Boyd evidently had gone over the map with great care. He probably had even been over a good deal of this terrain on foot and had some specific locations in mind that he wanted to check. If our present course was any indication, those areas would be just about uninhabitable.

The little troopers worked in admirable quiet, a major sign of good training and discipline. Now, when through the tangles of vegetation I could see the thatched buildings of a settlement, Boyd seemed especially stern about imposing absolute quiet. In a very faint whisper he told me, "This is an unfriendly village. We're going north beyond the village. We won't go through it. I don't want them to pass the word that we're coming."

We skinned around the village in the ragged edge of the woods, and on the far side found ourselves on a slope leading down into a rice paddy.

At the foot of the slope ran a stream, overgrown with heavy reed grass. We sloshed through it, and I was reminded of the paddy-splashing in the Delta area: the same specific sickness of being drenched in your clothes and of the mud sucking at your shoes as you stepped.

We crossed the edge of the paddy, trying to walk along the dikes between the fields and slipping much too often into the knee-deep rice-lakes, because the dikes were muddy and indistinct.

Then, just as we were about to leave the paddy and go up a steep bank on the far side, we saw three brown, boyish figures suddenly emerge from the far side of the field. They were splashing as frantically as frightened water buffalo. In fact, they were running just as hard as they could run toward the sloping hill ahead of them. We watched their brown bodies moving, the splashing of their running; in a second, they disappeared into the reed grass, then ran up the slope and into the woods.

Nobody had fired a shot. The inaction was understandable, because these could have been neighborhood boys, simply frightened by the advent of our patrol. But Boyd was worried. "They'll probably run off and tell the VC."

We went up a steep red-earth slope beyond the rice paddy, using the notches carved in the earth by the natives. As we reached the top, a single file of montagnard women were disappearing on a diagonal course toward the woods, but they weren't running. They were moving with impressive ease, considering that they carried the usual round wicker baskets on their backs. They seemed anxious to make it clear that they were merely hurrying (only VC's run).

We plunged through a dense thicket, crossed a narrow stream, our feet sploshing into deep red mud, and then scrambled up another densely tangled bank, where much of our progress had to be on hands and knees or in a low crouch, because the trails were very low, and must have been made by small animals. It was one of the thickest jungles I had ever tried to go through, but by following the animal trails, we were able to move. The process was a little difficult for me because of the camera equipment dangling from my neck: Camera and light meter seemed to have a perverse talent for tangling with briers and reeds and vines.

But I was glad to have all my encumbering gear with me, especially the .38 I had borrowed from Sgt. Compton. In this kind of jungle, a first cousin to the jungles of Guadalcanal, New Georgia, and Bougainville, you could come face to face with an ememy without a moment's notice.

The traveling was hot as well as rough. I was drenched in sweat from hat to shoes, besides being thoroughly lacerated on face, hands, and wrists by thorns, sharp leaves, and whipping branches. This was like running a hurdle race in a garbage dump, and I was continually out of wind.

It seemed to take us a quarter of an hour to traverse a hundred feet of this kind of terrain, but Boyd, Hoagland, and their little mountain troops never let up. They charged ahead with apparently undiminished vigor.

Then, on the lower reaches of the densely forested bank we were climbing, I saw Boyd crouching silently in a tangle, as if he had decided to stop and philosophize. Through the mottled jungle, I could see that he held a green-colored grenade in his hand, and he was listening intently to something specific, not philosophizing. He motioned to the troopers to move away along the thick, tangled hill, and he told me in a very soft whisper, "I'm going to put one down."

He motioned to me to back off, but I still didn't understand what he was up to. I saw him pull the pin of his grenade and was still preparing for the moment when he would throw it. But he didn't—he dropped it somewhere nearby and moved away, rapidly.

There was a metallic thud with strange, dull echoes, and I began to understand what was happening. He had found a VC hiding place, apparently a cave, and had thrown a grenade into it. Boyd motioned me to follow, and I came up to the cave mouth. Amid the green foliage, I saw an earth-hole opening about three feet across, and now a thread of blue smoke eddied from it.

"Two beds in there," he said, and I thought he was saying "two deads in there." I shone a flashlight into the cave, but it was still cloudy with smoke. I couldn't see anything in there at all.

Boyd was explaining: "Those kids brought the word, and they [the VC] took off. There's nobody in there."

We crept up the bank, literally on our hands and knees, because the thick undergrowth seemed to begin at a height of about one foot. Boyd was moving up the slope to my right with the leading members of the patrol. The soldiers were like bunnies. Somehow they seemed to be able to move at twice the speed I could make, and faster, too, than Boyd.

Hoagland was investigating the cave that Boyd had dropped the grenade into. I surmised that Hoagland, who was one of the explosives and demolitions experts of the detachment, was going to use his science to blast in the wall of the hideout.

Signs of commotion and whispering were coming from the right, so I battered my way up through the underbrush on all fours, and found that the blond American and his first sergeant had discovered two more caves, side by side. These, judging from the size of the entrances, were larger than the first one.

"There's rice in these dugouts, and two beds—maybe more," Boyd whispered. "My squad leader says these caves are connected with the other one."

I asked about the VC's, and he said, "There may be some people in there." He smiled slowly. "I don't want to go in there and find out." He would leave that job to a massive demolition charge, which Hoagland would lay.

With all the creeping on this thickly jungled hillside, I had lost my light meter somewhere. I looked at my lens and saw that it was covered with mud, and the lens cover that was supposed to protect it from such damage had disappeared.

Boyd and I squatted in a thicket near the double cave, waiting while Hoagland presumably readied an explosive charge in the thick jungle at the bottom of the hill, where the first cave was. Boyd scrambled around in the bushes and found my exposure meter and lens cover. He seemed as much at home in jungle thickets as most of us would be in our living rooms.

While we were waiting for Hoagland to set off his charge, Boyd told me, "We almost had a couple. The Sections Chief said that was an unfriendly village, and the kids ran up and passed the word when I passed through that field." He used the first person as if whatever happened to the patrol was thoroughly his fault.

Boyd sent his point men up to the top of the slope to see if there were any more visible caves, and he called over the little ragamuffin radioman and spoke into the phone type receiver while the radioman stood beside me. "Control Control. This is Day-Go. Can you read me? Control, this is Day-Go. We found a VC cave, possibly 300 meters northeast of Kya Ya. We are destroying the cave." But there was no answer from Plei Mrong. Apparently the batteries of the set had gone dead.

Hoagland's charge had not yet gone off. "The fuse is lit," Boyd said, but we waited interminable minutes and nothing happened. At last, the explosion, the sky smudged with flying debris, the clatter of bits of earth and branches falling back into the jungle.

I tried to stow my camera equipment to minimize damage from this thick, impossible terrain while Boyd went down the slope to look at the cave. He came back up with Hoagland, who told me, "I blew in the top, but I couldn't get the wall in." I looked at my watch: four o'clock.

We hauled ourselves up to the top of the slope, then worked along a trail in tall green elephant grass. Hoagland went back to blow in the other two caves connected with the lower one, and Boyd told me, "There must be more caves along here, but we've got to be heading back." Right now he was using his military compass to get a head on home.

With the caves destroyed, we started heading generally south (the sun was on our right), stopping occasionally while Boyd or some of the troopers went off at a crouch into the surrounding bushes to explore animal-type trails. Boyd marked the compass bearings of these possible VC trails on his map for future reference.

We hurried along the narrow trail through the swamps, and finally emerged on a wider path that looked familiar. Then, at last, we were moving among broken foot traps and *punji* fields, which also looked familiar. I knew we were still in VC territory—although this part had evidently been traversed by montagnards or American Special Forces men as witnessed by the broken foot traps. I had my .38 out, because the wall of thick jungle vegetation was close to our trail, and a VC could jump out at any moment with no warning. But none came.

It was 5:10 when I saw the periphery of our outpost: a deep wall of barbed wire, decorated with gleaming beer cans to make it visible. Just outside the barrier, Boyd pulled the magazine from his carbine and waved it, signaling to the patrol to unload their weapons. A clicking and clatter of bolts and magazines followed. The patrol was over.

When the troops were dismissed, Boyd, Hoagland, and I dragged our wet, sopping shoes up the hill to the mess shack, and Boyd had a can of beer. Capt. Grace was at the table, back from his trip to Pleiku today, and Boyd told him, "We almost got a couple." That seemed like vast understatement for our agonizing struggle with the mud, briers, paddies, streams, vines, and hills. We were still sopping wet to the knees with mud and paddy water and soaked with sweat from there up. I remembered the philosophizing of one of the MAAG advisers back in the Delta country: "It's always got to be wet in war. If it was in the middle of the Sahara Desert, it'd be wet."

Fortunately, the Special Forces boys had rigged a primitive oil-drum shower near the barracks, and we were able to scrape off some of the mud. It was cold in the shower as the sun went down and the night cold of the plateau descended, but altogether it was a worth-while experience. Especially since I had a double Charley horse.

At dinner, Sgt. Billie Fell, the Alabama boy who had been blown up by the mine aboard a truck, was back from five days in the 8th Station Hospital at Nhatrang and two days of R and R in Saigon. Billie, a baby-faced youth, was wearing a clean T-shirt marked FELL. He talked about his R and R in The Ville:

"I spent $150 in Saigon, and I got a tiger claw, 11 shirts, a shirt for my boy [son], a ring [girl-type for his daughter], two pairs of pants, and two pictures."

Billie was mysterious about the pictures, but he told how he had visited the Capitol Bar, a familiar landmark to Americans in Vietnam. Some of the boys asked about a certain hand-holding hostess they knew in the Capitol: a girl named Helen. "Old Satchelmouth," some of the boys called her, referring to her loose-jawed appearance. And Billie told us how Helen also knew Boyd.

"She said she remembered Boyd drank beer, cried for three hours, and passed out. She said, 'He's sick.' "

Boyd said, "I passed out all right," but he denied the allegation that he had been sick.

Joe Vaccero said he was in the jeep behind Fell the day of the mine explosion. "I was about 300 meters behind.

"We thought Billie had internal injuries because he was spitting blood, but it was only because he cut his lip."

After dinner, while Vaccero and Compton prepared for their two ambush expeditions for tonight, a bunch of the boys sat around the radio room at the end of the barracks. Baldheaded, wedge-shaped Compton, the "old man" of the detachment, came through the radio room looking like a mountain with his load of gear, which included field jacket, pistol, canteen, medical kit, and blanket folded over his harness. He said, explaining the blanket, "It gets damn cold out there in those ambushes, about four o'clock in the morning." And he added generally, "You can't sleep and leave it to the montagnards. You just take pep pills and stay awake."

Compton shoved off with Vaccero to get their ambushes going at two different locales, and the Special Forces boys fell into a bull session in the radio room, by the light of a kerosene lamp brought by SFC William Bowles (of Fort Lauderdale, Fla.), who would be running the radio tonight.

The talk drifted, the way it often does, to the subject of R and R. The comparative delights of Saigon, Hong Kong, and Bangkok were discussed. Hong Kong won hands down.

Then Wolford, the strident-voiced medic, went after a subject that was apparently one of his favorites: If the men of this detachment could pool their resources, they could buy Benquet, a Philippine gold-mine security and the cheapest stock on the New York Exchange at $1\frac{1}{8}$, and make a fortune. Failing that, they could make self-inflating air mattresses for the recruits in basic training. "They're too tired to blow up their own air mattresses," Wolford said.

Before I hit the sack, Grace showed me the bunker that I should go to in case of a VC penetration during the night. When I went to the sack, Wolford was still talking about whether or not they could make a fortune investing in Benquet.

They had a can of half-popped popcorn to help while away the time, and a pile of old *Stars and Stripes*, which supplied the raw material for the bull session.

Tuesday, December 18

I was awake at 5:30 this morning and heard Compton's ambush patrol coming in. The metallic sounds of weapons and military gear were clanking as the men climbed the slope to the camp quadrangle. Then I heard Compton cussing in a loud, firm voice. Apparently the ambush patrol was drawn up on the slope while he lectured them:

"You'll never catch a ——————— VC. I say no. I say you're stupid. Now, I want you to cough, cough, God-damn it. Cough: A-Hey! A-Hey!" He mimicked loudly the sounds of hacking and throat clearing.

And he resumed his harangue: "Come on, cough! What's the matter? Can't you cough? You've been coughin' all night!"

He wasn't getting the reaction he wanted, evidently: Only a few nervous throat-clearings followed his sardonic instructions. So, apparently in the interests of discipline, he started the group on physical training: "Now, jump-jump-jump." I heard him jumping and the clanking as the montagnards followed his example, in full battle gear.

I went over to the quadrangle where I could see the figures of the troopers in the predawn light doing jumps and arm movements, their equipage rattling. After about five minutes of jumping, Compton went after them again. "Cough now, spit, and cough. A-Hey! A-Hey!" There were a few dismal coughs and hacks in polite response.

I went into the mess shack and Compton came to talk to Grace. Compton said: "I set up three ambushes, but nobody would have come by—they [the montagnards] were like a herd of elephants—they coughed and hacked and farted all the time."

Grace said calmly, "They'll pick up, like this last bunch." This sage advice seemed to pacify Compton, and he went off to bed.

I sat over a cup of coffee with Grace and discovered that his father, an Army colonel in World War II, had been wounded twice during that struggle, once at Anzio and once in the Vosges Mountains of northeastern France. The war left the elder Grace hard of hearing, but he was able to go on with his career of teaching until recently, when the war residual got worse and his hearing diminished.

Grace said that his father is a great teacher. "I never really understood math until my father told me some of the history of it and made it mean something."

Grace told me that his wife is in Berkeley, Calif., with her family. "I met her while I was studying Korean at the Army Language School in Monterey. She was a history major at Stanford, and I met her on a blind date."

At breakfast, I had a chance to ask Boyd and Hoagland: "Why are we here, what's it for?"

Boyd said simply: "To keep the Communists from taking over Vietnam."

George Hoagland answered more generally: "To hold back the Communists. It'll be a long job and it'll cost a lot of money."

After breakfast, I loaded my gear on a truck, loaded with troops, which Woelfel was to drive into Pleiku this morning. Duarte was driving the jeep that will be leading our convoy.

The dirt road was very rough, and we rattled around very loosely in the truck. The bumps were bad enough in the front seat, but it was worse for the troops braced on the wooden benches in the back. The morning was bright and clear, with blue sky. The air was bracing as we trundled through a string of villages. To the west, we could see the lump of mountain which is the VC secret base. If we could see them, certainly they had us under observation all the time.

About half an hour's run from the camp, we came to a paved black-top road, about one and a half lanes wide, and from there on it was relatively smooth sailing right into the Special Forces B detachment headquarters in Pleiku. This had been my first road convoy in Vietnam, but it was completely uneventful—even though part of the road wound through an area supposedly replete with VC's and the first part of it was under direct enemy observation. This was the same section on which Billie Fell had been blown up with his truckload of soldiers by a VC mine. That's the way war goes: 99 per cent perspiration, 1 per cent sheer terror.

At the Special Forces headquarters in Pleiku, I talked over the patrol I had seen, and the work of the Special Forces troops in this area, with a somewhat elevated Special Forces officer who didn't want to be quoted by name. But he said something quite different and interesting about the conduct of the war here: "This business of killing VC—you could keep it up till hell freezes over. That's for the birds. What we need is the thing that Magsaysay had [in the Philippines]—the hand of friendship. Give 'em churches and schools."

We had a bull session on the subject, since it seems to me that we Americans have to offer more than the hand of friendship, and churches and schools. We also have to extend great military strength, so that the Vietnamese can meet the Communist threat with the kind of language the Reds understand: force, mounted by free nations interested in the spread of self-government and self-determination.

I found my way up to the Citadel and talked to Maj. Peters about going out with one of his platoon-size patrols from Pleiku: one of those fast-moving helicopter raiding parties of small size which are becoming the fashion in antiguerrilla warfare in Vietnam.

Peters said he was still stymied by the Corps commander. Then, a check with Col. Max King (of Kansas City, Mo.), senior AAF adviser for the Corps Area, established the fact that I'd need further permissions from the Vietnamese government headquarters in Saigon before I could make T-28 flights with the birds operating out of Pleiku.

I decided, however, that what I want is to get back to my helicopter friends in the battle-ridden swamps of the Delta, or up in the north.

So, with little visible action coming up in this area and a trip to Saigon indicated to get my *permisos,* I twisted my own arm, succumbed to the lure of Saigon, and promoted a ride back there this very afternoon.

The ride down to The Ville by C-123 Mule Train was as uncomfortable and noisy as ever, but this time, with my sneakers, greens, and hat thoroughly beat up, and face and hands scratched and gouged by the jungle and stray *punjis,* I seemed to be in better temperamental uniform for this kind of travel.

Tonight, walking along the Tu Do, I was surprised to encounter Sgt. Duarte taking his ease at a sidewalk café, drinking a glass of Bireley's Orange pop. He had zipped down from Plei Mrong on one of the Special Forces "spook" planes, an unmarked, unaccountable, and unscheduled aircraft. It developed that he is in town to take a preliminary test for OCS tomorrow morning. I wished him good luck and bought him another Bireley's to celebrate, knowing that something stronger would be inconsiderate. He wants to be in full possession of his faculties for tomorrow's ordeal.

Christmas, a Battle, a Free Election

At the PI office, I found out there are no large-scale operations going on at the moment to involve my helicopter friends in either the swamps of Soctrang or the mountainous Danang vicinity. Nor are the Huey's involved in contemporaneous operations.

I discovered that, during the last couple of days, a couple of MAAG people had been hit by snipers: one a lieutenant, the other a sergeant but there had been no large air-phibious attacks. The main thing that seems to be happening is a reshuffling of Corps Area boundaries, which has slowed most everything to a walk. It seems that a new Corps Area is being created out of the oversized II Corps, where I have just been spending time.

The main effect of the redefinition of Corps Areas—principally, the creation of a IV corps, which will comprise the whole Delta area—is that much of the Vietnamese and American personnel will be moved around. The fair-haired boy in the Vietnamese military establishment, Col. Cao, will be boosted to the rank of general, for instance, and made the CO of the entire Delta area. And the former senior American adviser in Pleiku, at 88 Corps HQ, Col. "Coal Bin Willie" Wilson will be shifted to the new III Corps, running from Ban Methuot down to Saigon. Anyhow, there seems to be much *pilikia* as commands are redefined, and a temporary hiatus as people are

329

moved around in the new command setup. Add to this the coming of the Christmas season—Christmas trees and decorations are out in all the American messes—and you can see that things are going slowly indeed in Saigon these days.

I took advantage of the slack time to check through some permissions I need. From the Vietnamese DGI (Department of Government Information), I picked up an official certificate I needed to fly with the VNAF. This was done rapidly, largely because the Vietnamese in charge spoke a colloquial American.

By nightfall I was on a trail of a group of AAF people with whom I had not previously come into contact—the "Dirty Thirty," a group of adviser-pilots who have high seniority in Vietnam duty. Originally 30 AAF pilots—now there are many times more than that—came over as advisers to help the Vietnamese fly their old C-47 (DC-3) fleet in miscellaneous assault operations: dropping propaganda leaflets on the VC, flying psy-warfare experts to talk to the enemy by loudspeaker, dropping supplies by parachute from the air, and, principally, flying over embattled outposts and dropping magnesium flares so as to illuminate the enemy. They are part of the VNAF, but get American pay. Like firemen, the Dirty Thirty are on 24-hour alert, and respond with lightning speed to VC attacks.

Tonight, I was able to make my first mission with the Dirty Thirty out of Tan Son Nhut. I went out to the airfield with Mike Renard, the CBS cameraman who made the Junk Fleet trip with me. Tall and bespectacled, Mike has a name among correspondents for taking crazy chances in pursuit of a story. There wasn't any need for special quantities of intestinal fortitude tonight. There was eventually, however, an emergency call to drop flares on an Arvin outpost in An Giang Province, on the Cambodian border.

The flare mission started out of an office—and emergency living quarters—at Tan Son Nhut, labeled in English script: DIRTY THIRTY. Inside the office, we found a suite of American furniture, American filing cabinets, and three Americans, two in gray flying suits and one in green pants and T-shirt. They sprawled over the PX-type furniture of rattan with synthetic leather cushions, all looking very large and pink by comparison with the Vietnamese Air Force pilots in the adjacent lounge. The Americans, all captains, were Jack Ford (of Minneapolis, Minn.), Ron McCoy (of Elkton, Va.), and Ty Lewis (of Cutbank, Mont.). Mike and I spent about a half-hour, waiting around with the three Dirty Thirty pilots, in the air-conditioned office, before the emergency call came through.

Capt. Ford, a big, handsome man of light Anglo-Saxon coloring, had been on duty since 5 P.M. today and would be on stand-by until 5 P.M. tomorrow. He was to be the first of the three to go out on any calls that came in.

Ford and the others told us about some of the narrow escapes they have had in flying over VC territory. They were proud of the Vietnamese motto they carried on their red baseball caps, their distinguishing uniform: *Bam Melam,* which the pilots told us proudly, indicates the sexual power of a goat. Ford said, "When a top-echelon type comes to inspect us, we never know whether to tell them what the motto means or not."

The pilots told me about the Dirty Thirty captain who has been put in for the D.F.C. for getting his C-47 back to Saigon after it was badly shot up by VC in the course of a psy-warfare mission.

Ford told me: "Capt. Kleinheinz—his first name was Ernest and I think he came from Michigan—was one of the first to get hit. It was in May of 1962. He came back with one engine feathered, and an oil line hit in the other engine. But somehow he kept it running. When he got it back, it was blowing oil all over the place."

Ford said that five or six of the Dirty Thirty aircraft have been hit by VC fire, and one man killed in a crash on July 16. And shooting episodes happen almost every day. Lewis gave us an example: "A few days ago near Ban Methuot I saw three VC's on a ridge, and right about then, I heard *brrddt* [their machine-gun fire]. It was right on the ridge above the place where we were dropping supplies. But no [bullet] holes."

Capt. Ford said, "We're part of the Vietnamese Air Force, but fortunately we're on American pay and allowances. My wife pays $180 a month rent, more than a VNAF captain gets in monthly pay." He grinned. "I try to steer away from that subject, talking with the Vietnamese."

Ford was just saying that on a stand-by like this evening's, "sometimes you drop flares and sometimes you don't," when a slim, smiling Vietnamese lieutenant came bursting into the room. He was "Charlie" Chan, an Americanized type who said nothing to us except, "Quickly, quickly"—knowing the rest would be understood: We had a mission.

Ford jammed his feet into boondocker shoes, without stopping to lace them all the way, and we rushed out and followed Chan aboard one of their old Vietnamese C-47's. Inside the dimly lit cabin, we found a crew of five Vietnamese squatting among a row of black cardboard flare containers, each about four feet long, which filled up the floor space. There were 28 of them. Mike and I took our places on a couple of the cafeteria-tray-type seats (1943 model) that ran along the sides of the cabin.

We took off quickly, flew 75 miles west to the Cambodian border, and milled around in the sky pitching out flares over a canal, which gleamed dully in the pale green light.

We saw the flying lights of two T-28's as they came in and strafed and bombed.

There was a lot of bustling of dark forms up and down the corridor between our cockpit and cabin, and agitated conversations on the radio with the T-28 pilots. Jack Ford and Charlie Chan split the job of flying the bird while we made endless orbits over the area.

Each time an alarm bell rang, the little men in the dark cabin wrestled the fat black flare tubes to the open door on the left side of the cabin. Each flare started as a green point of light with a trail of smoke behind it, and as it came closer to the ground, a pale image of a bare field or the glitter of a canal materialized. I missed the actual firing passes of the T-28's, but soon there were five fires burning down there, apparently kindled by bombs.

At 12:55 our crewmen were bundling up the flare containers, and two of the little men, having finished their work, were wrestling goodnaturedly. Soldiers—the same all over the world.

It was 1:13 when we landed at Tan Son Nhut and taxied in past a line of gray C-47's like ours.

Leaving the ship, Ford noted that "We fired 24 [flare tubes]." Walking in with him, I got a fill-in on what had happened: "I was talking to the fighters [by radio] and Chan was talking to the JOC [Joint Operations Center] in Vietnamese. It was a three-way conversation. The VC were already on their way out when we arrived. The fighters [T-28's] took about 10 minutes to catch up.

"There wasn't any arrow tonight. [The outposts are equipped with electrically lit arrows to indicate the direction of the VC attack.] We dropped [flares] on the outpost and they asked us to make the strike to the south of the canal."

I asked him about visible results, as far as he could spot them. "You never know what you've got," he said. "It wasn't too showy tonight. Sometimes, with napalm, there's some fireworks."

Ford drove us to the Tan Son Nhut gate in his jeep, and I asked him how many flying hours he chalks up in a month. "I get about 40 or 50 hours a month," he answered. "I've got about 20 combat support mission, like tonight." He smiled and added: "I wouldn't trade jobs with any captain."

Rolling back to Saigon in a taxi, I thought, what a strange war this is, where a young American officer can live in an air-conditioned billet in Saigon—in Ford's case, an Air Force hotel called the Five Oceans—and go on these night forays to the scene of an attack, dropping flares to light up guerrilla war, getting shot at while droning around in the shadows of his own light for an hour or so during a fighter attack, and coming back again in the morning to his comfortable billet and a reasonable facsimile of American food.

I got back to my own room—I am staying now in the house belonging to John Mecklin, chief of the U.S. Information Service (USIS) in Vietnam—and spent the next hour or two making notes and trying to work out a program for future action in Vietnam. I've been here nearly two and a half months now, and it is probably time to go. I feel beat up enough, but with Christmas coming up in a few days, it seems chicken to leave. Right now it seems best that I should stay long enough to spend Christmas with some of the friends I have become so attached to here. And it seems a shame to leave when many more air-phibious assaults—even bigger than those I have seen, and perhaps critically important—will certainly be coming up after this temporary lull in operations.

I also am aware that I feel a curious attachment to this war and the Americans in it: a strange disinclination to go back to the peacetime world at home which somehow seems less important and certainly less exciting. As Joe Monia said at Pleiku, this is an important war. I might not be able to claim it for my own generation, as Joe does, but I can't deny that it's important to me, as maybe it should be to more of us.

Friday, December 21

Today I wasted two hours trying to get an identity card demanded by the PX authorities. And other bits of red tape went agley. My arrangements to make a flight with a T-28 on a strafing and bombing mission out of Tan Son Nhut fell apart, at the last minute.

Later in the day, I went over to Cholon, the Chinese part of Saigon, to look up some of my new-found friends in the Dirty Thirty and have dinner in the Five Oceans. I found Capt. Ford, and had a chance to pursue some of the threads we had explored in the midst of our flare-dropping mission last night.

Ford told me that he had gone into the Army in 1945 at age 19, before World War II ended. But he was too late to participate in those hostilities. He married in 1945 and between wars he and his wife lived in Minneapolis, where he worked as an advertising copywriter. Then he was recalled as a member of the Reserve to duty with the 21st Troop Carrier Command, and at that time flew in what was then called Indochina out of Haiphong and Hanoi, now part of Communist North Vietnam. So he is, in effect, no stranger to this general area.

I asked him how his wife and two children like his present duty in Vietnam.

She hates every minute of it," he said. "If she had her way, I'd be a junior copywriter rather than a senior captain."

I asked Ford about the meaning of the Vietnam campaign, in his opinion, and he answered articulately: "My rationale is pretty standard. This is the point where we chose to draw the line. I agree that the line had to be drawn here. I didn't have any hand in choosing it, but if they chose this one, more power to them." That seemed a cool, patriotic, and unimpassioned analysis.

Over dinner, I also talked to Capt. John Phipps (of Montgomery, Ala.), another of the Dirty Thirty, and asked him about the future of the group: Will the Vietnamese eventually be able to fly their own C-47's without American help?

"When the VNAF get enough C-47 drivers," said Phipps, "these fellas can go home."

I said, "Of course, they came originally as advisers."

Phipps said with a laugh: "Yes, they came to advise the No. 2 flap."

"And answer the telephone," said Ford.

Monday, December 24

I finally managed to get a ride up to Danang so that I could see my Marine, Air Force, and Army buddies up in the north for Christmas.

Before I left Saigon, I saw some MAAG adviser friends going home, not quite in time for Christmas. Two of them were Capts. Scofield and Starboard, who had been through so many hellfires down in the Delta. Scofield, who has a good sense of humor, said that he had gained 30 pounds since he came out of the Delta and fell into relatively tame duty in Saigon. I said no, that after a very severe Vietnamese diet down there in the swamps, he needed the weight.

He said, "No, it wasn't so bad. Just a diet of *nuoc mam*, rice, and dysentery bugs."

Col. Daniel Boone Porter, the senior Army adviser in the Delta area, had also got his relief and was free to go home. Porter, a World War II veteran with 30 years of Army service behind him, has the vigor and enthusiasm of a teen-ager for things military. He seemed to be leaving this military effort behind with some regret.

"I was seven when we went into World War I," he told me, "and like most people of that time, I had no trouble feeling patriotic. I didn't have to be told to wear a uniform, I loved it. I got gold-plated goose bumps when a band played."

Even now, Porter seems to have that same eagerness. I asked him how many chopper missions he had been on, and he said modestly that he didn't know. "Something over 100. For a while, I was on every one of them. I kept track until I went over 500 hours flying time."

I got up to Danang via the Mule Train Special, in time for the beginning of the Christmas celebration. It was probably not much different from celebrations all across Vietnam—the sentries were out here too but I saw many friends, and one especially who should be mentioned in this kind of a diary.

It was after dinner tonight at the Marine camp. Roaming around, visiting the various parties, I at last came to the sergeants' party at a bar they had set up in one corner of their barracks, now labeled HOLIDAY INN and especially decorated with Christmas trimmings as well as the usual assortment of *Playboy*-type art.

Col. Rathbun came in, looking at once as drawn and durable as always, and they waited for him to make a speech. There was a respectful silence, and then he said: "I just want to say that you are the best bunch that ever got together at any one place."

There were cheers, and they sang "For He's a Jolly Good Fellow" with fervor. I waited for that resounding Anglo-Saxon response to the song I had heard in the 93d—inferring good-naturedly that it was all baloney. I could feel the sergeants hesitating for a moment as to whether or not to add the "————————" but they didn't. Their respect for Rathbun won through.

At the same party I saw Lt. Eric Coady, the tall, husky All-American boy with whom I had flown on some assault missions. I remembered his telling me about his father's war record in the 11th Marines and the Solomons, and how much he respected the elder Coady for coming successfully through the misery and danger of World War II as a fighting man.

Now, Eric, like most of the Marines in sight on this Christmas Eve, was feeling no pain. His drinking had put him only moderately out of joint, but it apparently gave him the impetus to ask me something that had been on his mind for some time. He approached me and asked if I would give him a copy of *Guadalcanal Diary*. I said I had no copy with me, but did have a copy of another of my books, *John F. Kennedy and PT-109*, in my bag over at the barracks. If he would come over later on, I would inscribe it for him.

When he showed up at the room, I had written in the book and had it ready for him, and I was reading the small newspaper put out by the Marine unit called *The Ridge Runner*—after "Rathbun's Ridge Runners."

The paper was a Christmas edition, and on the front page there were Christmas messages from Maj. Gen. Leek, the Marine commander, and Vice Adm. Moorer, commander of the Seventh Fleet, assigned to the Southeast Asia area.

When Eric came into the room, he picked up *The Ridge Runner* and began to read aloud the messages from these two commanders. Both were concerned with the importance of the American war effort in Vietnam, the sacrifices involved, and the separation of our servicemen from their loved ones in the Christmas season. The phraseology was conventional, not to say corny, but Coady read them very carefully. "Excuse my drunken reading," he apologized.

"What did you think of those messages?" I asked him, thinking that in his lubricated condition I would get an extremely frank answer.

"I thought they were fine—just fine," he said. And then he added, without prompting and right off the top of his head: "You know, my wife and I don't have any children—hopefully, we will have. But that's in the future. I'm thinking about the people who are alive now, like my father. If I should have to give my life here so they could have freedom—well, I know it would only be one drop in the bucket, but it takes a lot of drops to do something, so it would be all right with me." I thanked him, knowing that he meant it. Obviously, he had thought about it a good deal.

Tuesday, December 25

Christmas Day was bright and sunny, a novelty in Danang at this season. I was down at the flight line at 6:30, waiting for today's helicopter business, which—bless the Marines—will go on as usual, Christmas or not.

I noted that the briefing room had been reorganized and systemized somewhat since my last visit here. Maj. Bob Rick, who was to lead the first group of four birds taking off today, told his pilots that the mission will be a transfer of troops from one base to another, a relatively routine job. He said, "I'll find out at Tam Qui where we're going to take the troops. I'll pass the word somehow. I don't want to be the only one who knows where we're going—in case anything should happen to my bird."

The armor-vested pilots trooped out at 8:08, and I stayed behind, because Lt. Joe Baranowski, the OOD, told me there would be a later flight out to "Shotgun Alley," the "shoot-'em-up" area around the outpost of Ashau, to deliver some hot chow and a Christmas cake to the Americans stationed there.

Two birds made the flight to Ashau and several intermediate stops. We delivered everything as scheduled and, as far as we know, didn't get shot at. I shared the belly compartment with Cpl. Mike Shrouf, another Marine who like Eric Coady has a high sense of responsibility. Shrouf's father was also a military man, and he died on Formosa, with the American MAAG.

Back at the camp, there were Christmas services this afternoon conducted by Cardinal Spellman, who had arrived in Vietnam for a whirlwind tour of the American bases. The old man seemed unsteady on his feet, but he stayed around to bless everyone who wanted it, and I heard from his retainers that he had shown this same dedication to duty in all of his stops here.

On the military grapevine I heard bad news about the 81st Transportation Company, the new H-21 outfit I had flown with, out of Pleiku. On an air-phibious assault, they had suffered their first casualty, a pilot killed by a bullet in the head. It was Charlie Holloway, a new pilot (with five children) who was on his first assault mission. I had once flown with Holloway from Plei Mrong to Pleiku. I made a mental note to get down to Saigon at least, and possibly all the way to Pleiku, with Ralph Davis, who'll be flying the R4D that way tomorrow.

Tonight, at his barracks room, I saw Bob Rick conked out

337

for the night inside his mosquito bar, reading a paperback Whodunit. A good general's-aide type (he had recently *been* a general's aide) Rick is always clean-cut, military, well disciplined, and alert. After the day's mission of moving Vietnamese troops around, his flight of four birds had also been assigned the job of an emergency medical evacuation: flying a dead Arvin battle casualty back to Danang—grisly enough duty for Christmas Day.

I asked Rick about the title of the pocketbook he was reading.

He said, "I don't know, I just picked it up." But I looked at the cover and I saw that it had an ironical title: *These Lonely, These Dead*, by Robert Colby.

"You've had a helluva Christmas Day," I said.

"It passed the time," he said noncommittally.

Wednesday, December 26

The afternoon was wearing out when I finally reached Pleiku and found my way to the 81st company, to get the story on CWO Holloway and his recent death in action.

I checked in with Maj. George Washington Aldrich, Jr., the CO of the company. A capable and experienced veteran of infantry action in the Korean war, Aldrich had been out on this recent mission when the outfit got shot up. He gave me a clear, calm account of what had happened.

"It was a joint mission with the 8th [Helicopter Company, flying out of Quinhon]. They had 15 [H-21's], and we furnished 15. We got down there with 14—so it was 29 [troop-carrying helicopters] all together.

"There were six different LZ's, and there was no prestrike in the LZ's—not much more than a map reconnaissance." Aldrich made note of that fact without editorial comment, but I gathered as I talked to him later in the evening, that one reason his birds had been so badly shot up was that there had been no softening-up attack. Here again was the question of whether the troop-carrying helicopters should come in to a hostile LZ without any preparation and take it by surprise— and risk being shot up in the process—or follow on the heels of a preliminary bombardment by some fighter aircraft, T-28's or Hueys.

"We went on the first lift. We operated [staged] out of Tuy Hoa. We went up to 2,000 [feet] until 10 or 12 miles north of Tuy Hoa, then to treetop level.

"An L-19 marked the LZ with red smoke, and he [the L-

19] said there was ground fire in the area.

"Holloway was flying in ship F8, the eighth ship on our flight, with Gressang [CWO Daniel Gressang of La Pintada, Panama].

"As soon as we got into the area, about 300 yards from touch-down, there was a tremendous volume of [VC] ground fire. Our aircraft machine guns started firing.

"The first three aircraft didn't get hit. It was the fourth, eighth and tenth. And three of the aircraft from the 8th [Helicopter Company] got hit.

"Holloway's ship got hit in the forward rotor housing, one went past Gressang's left ear, and one hit Holloway through the forehead; Five rounds came through the door, and three of them hit the fuel cell [tank], and two exited.

"Gressang got Holloway back to Tuy Hoa and put him onto a medical evac helicopter. He died about 35 minutes after he was hit."

I asked Aldrich if I could see Gressang and get his account of the episode, and the CO said yes but warned, "He is still upset."

It was much later in the evening, in the tent that serves the 81st as an O Club, that I found Gressang.

Aldrich had told me that he had kept Gressang flying steadily after the assault mission on which Holloway was killed, to keep the pilot's nerve up. Aldrich told me that the death had been "very messy. The blood was running out of the plane into the blister. They couldn't get Holloway's foot out of the cockpit. Also, there was a big hole in his head."

But Gressang's nerves were extended even farther than I had expected. He looked at me blankly and answered my questions mechanically, with the shortest replies, as if he were functioning only as a machine. He summarized the mission in the shortest way: "We dropped the troops off and took off and got hit."

"How high were you?"

"About 50 feet off."

"What did you hear of the firing?"

"It was all automatic. But you couldn't tell which was which."

There were long pauses between question and response, and I knew I was rubbing on Gressang's nerves and didn't want to aggravate him. At this point, he seemed sick to death of the whole subject and wanted to finish the interview with a minimum of talk.

"What was the terrain like?" I asked, hoping I might

move him to talk a little more with an unimportant question.

"Heavily wooded. Short trees. Heavy brush in between."

Another mild question: "What radio calls did you make?"

"I made radio calls." This time he went on a little more: "I called in twice to have the medics standing by."

I asked if he remembered the moment when Holloway was hit. What did he think about Holloway's wound?

He fixed me with a blank stare: "I thought he was dead."

I didn't want to prolong the agony with Gressang. But later on I had a clue to the reason for his being so distracted. Capt. John Baird (of North Attleboro, Mass.), who was flying in the second ship behind Holloway and Gressang, told me, "Gressang was always squeamish about such things as blood. And this was a bad one."

Thursday, December 27

This morning I had a chance to see two of the aircraft that had been shot up a couple of days ago. Capt. Donald Coggins (of Beaumont, Tex.) pointed out the yellow spots of primer paint on the two birds, one of them being the helicopter in which Holloway had been flying.

"The one that hit Holloway came in over the top of the console [instrument panel]. The other one, that missed Gressang by an inch or two, cut halfway through the gunner's safety belt [the gunner was Sp/4 Arthur M. Whitmore, of Norfolk, Va.]."

The crew chief I talked to, Sp/5 Robert E. Lewis (of Tacoma, Wash.), indicated the position by the rear door where the crew chief of Holloway's plane, Sp/6 James Mooney (of Jefferson, Iowa), had been standing. "He was the fortunate one," said Lewis. "He was bracketed." He indicated bullet holes on both sides of Mooney's position. I made a mental note to search out Whitmore and Mooney later in the day.

Tonight, after a relatively uneventful day visiting the Special Forces outposts at Dak To and Dak Pek, and watching Special Forces medics giving medical aid to the montagnards —mostly cases of worms and VD and other infections—I found Mooney and Whitmore in the sergeant's tent-club.

Whitmore, a veteran of 10 years of Army service, and the Korean war, gave me a fighting man's calm account of what had happened the day Holloway was killed.

"I saw some people firing as we were coming in, and I started firing into the trees. Something jerked me back—that was when the bullet must have hit the safety belt.

"Mr. Gressang talked to me, he asked me to get Holloway's feet off the controls. They were rubbery, and I didn't know he was hurt. . . .

"He [Gressang] told me to get back and help Mooney with stopping up the holes in the fuel cell. When we got back and put him [CWO Holloway] on a litter, we thought he was dead. But he must have been in shock. He died pretty soon after."

Sgt. Mooney explained about the holes in the fuel tank, caused by VC bullets. "I used my glove to plug up the hole in the fuel cell. And I put a bandage on Holloway's head."

Mooney seemed more generally depressed than the veteran Whitmore, and not very communicative.

In fact, the traces of the death seemed to linger on in the sergeants' club. Such is the impact of a first death, especially strong when casualties, as in this war, are few and far between among the Americans.

Some of the men at the bar seemed to be determined to get drunk tonight, and one baldheaded sergeant particularly glommed on to my ear to beef about the fatal action near Tuy Hoa. As far as I could disentangle it, his complaint seemed to be that the 81st had been shot up needlessly, because it was flung into the LZ without preliminary fire cover. Most of what he said, however, revolved around a few Anglo-Saxon expletives: "This Goddamn war is all ————. It's a ———— war."

Less irrational, much calmer, was a senior sergeant named Danny Ferroni (of Brockton, Mass.), who had been a crew chief on Capt. Coggins' ship as it got shot up coming into the LZ behind Holloway. One of the Arvin troops on that ship had been hit by the VC gunfire as it came in for landing. Five bullets went through the fuselage.

Danny told me how he was wounded three times during World War II when he served with the Marines, once on Bloody Ridge on Guadalcanal, once at Tarawa, and once bayoneted in the right leg at Saipan. He shifted to the Army in 1948 and served a stint in the Korean war, this time without being wounded.

Now he told me about the passage of arms at the LZ where Holloway was killed. Ferroni had responded quickly, as a good military man should, although that engagement was the first time he had been fired at on this bit of duty in Vietnam.

"I saw two of them in black clothes, with short trousers, coming out of the foliage. We were in a turn, at about 40-50 feet, and I could see their machine guns. They were firing. I fired three bursts at 'em, and they dropped right there." Ferroni was speaking like a military man whose business is soldiering, with a good background of experience in combat behind him. And he wasn't taking an opportunity to get drunk about it. Only enjoying a relaxing beer or two. One of the interesting things about this war is that the Americans fighting it have all shades and gradations of experience. Most of them, fortunately, are of the experienced, battle-hardened, professional soldier type.

Friday, December 28

This morning, I arranged a flight with a T-28 mission to napalm, rocket, and strafe some VC positions. While waiting for final word about this, I talked to Maj. Aldrich about his company's fund-raising efforts in behalf of WO Holloway's wife, Grace, and family. The company had collected $385 for the family and Aldrich said the widow would have $10,000 in GI insurance, and just over $400 a month in widow's payment, including Social Security. He had carefully figured it out: $254.10 a month in social security, and $1601 a month in service-connected death payments.

When I walked over to the headquarters tent to get picked up for the T-28 ride, the same baldheaded sergeant whom I had seen in such a disjointed condition last night, loudly and rather incoherently complaining about the war, sidled up to me and mumbled ashamedly: "On m' ass last night—just pass it over. We all . . ." He left it unfinished but I knew what he meant, and said sure, I understood.

The napalming mission was a neck-snapper. Before the flight began, Col. King introduced me to the two VNAF pilots, Lts. Si and Tham. Both were thoroughly eager-beaver types, Americanized, influenced by the aggressive example of senior adviser Lt. Col. Max King. And they flung their little T-28's around with a vengeance.

I rode with Lt. Si. Col. King was to have flown a third bird in our formation, but his T-28 washed out at the last minute with a mechanical malfunction. A jovial, blue-eyed tall son of the corn who was a B-17 and fighter pilot in World War II, King normally flies the T-28 missions "just about every other day." He told me that he makes the missions with his boys mainly for the sake of morale. "I want the pilots in this outfit to have a high morale, and everything that it takes to make a high morale. I want them to have uniform devices, like scarves and jungle hats, and star patches with tigers in them, everything they need to make them feel they mustn't let the outfit down. And it's the same with having American advisers around. They try harder if the American adviser is along."

When Lts. Si, Tham and I took off with our highly explosive loads, I was just as glad that Col. King didn't come along: His presence might have inspired the two Vietnamese hotshots to even more violent maneuvering in the course of dumping ordnance on the VC.

At any rate, we had a full load of rockets, .50-caliber machine gun ammo, and 500 pounds of napalm each.

We took off at 10:07, sizzling in the clear heat of the canopy while trapped by the usual mountain of gear, and headed north over what appeared to be scattered farms beyond Pleiku. Abruptly we climbed over a steep green ridge, more than 5,000 feet high. Then we were diving in a breathless pass toward high-ribbed mountains covered with almost solid jungle.

We made nine neck-snapping passes into two separate collections of huts designated as VC villages. It was, as Col. King had said, a solidly VC area: "An interdiction target: No friendlies."

We whirled at maximum speed around the green-ribbed mountains for a good 15 minutes, while the guns stuttered or the rockets arced—two passes during which there was no sound, only the sharp pull-up, and behind us, the boiling orange flames of napalm devouring the groups of houses. The steepest pass was a machine-gunning dive into a jungly mountainside marked as a VC strongpoint. Lt. Si seemed to have momentarily forgotten his wife and three children in Nhatrang he held our nose down until far beyond what seemed the last moment. When he finally hauled back and skimmed us over the ridge top, there was a very unpleasant "graying-out" effect whereby our vision grew suddenly black, and our body parts seemed to be weighted with outriggers.

We saw no signs of antiaircraft on all these passes, and the raid was a success: Si and Tham filled out the report of 20 structures burned in enemy territory. After the aerial gymnastics—upside-down peel-offs, wing-overs, violent pull-ups—I was still teetering on the edge of nausea. Si, who seemed a mild man when not obliged to be a tiger at the controls of a T-28, asked me solicitously (with gestures) if I was sick. I was glad to be able to say no, even if it wasn't completely true.

I went to the local Air Force headquarters at the II Corps Citadel while the Vietnamese T-28 pilots filed their reports. Col. King, having effected a repair of his own T-28 so that it would be workable this afternoon, was saying to Capt. Glen Hellenga (of Alderwood Manor, Wash.), the reconnaissance duty officer, "Now we've got to get some more targets for this afternoon." He would be going this time. Later in the afternoon, I hitched a ride into Saigon with a Special Forces "Sneaky Pete" aircraft, a C-47 heading for The Ville just in time for the beginning of the New Year's Eve holiday.

Saturday, December 29

This morning I got into the PI office (fortunately, they don't shut down on Saturdays and Sundays like some of the bureaucratic sort in Saigon) and got Allan Galfund going on the job of promoting a ride for me up to the only American military hospital in Vietnam, the 8th Station, in Nhatrang. I had decided it would be a good place to spend New Year's Eve. It seemed to me that, of all places in Vietnam, this would be the spot to be on such an occasion: the place where the wounded and sick of our mammoth war effort against the Communists in Vietnam are taken care of and given hope and health again.

Calling on some of his friends in Army aviation, Galfund was able to set up a flight to Nhatrang tomorrow with marvelous dispatch. It will be an Otter, carrying Special Forces people, with room for one more.

This much accomplished, I set about making some other vital preparations. It was the wrong time of the week to pursue the subject, with a weekend coming up, but it occurred to me that I should also go after an issue that should be a large part of any story about our war in Vietnam: free elections. I asked John Mecklin of USIS for help in finding a strategic hamlet, or any other part of this country, where free elections are being held.

In the final analysis, elections are the final test of the validity of our war effort. If a country can elect its own government all of the blood and dying of a civil war are going to be worth while: If not, it's in vain. And the final fallacy of the Communist promises always boil down to this: The people under communism don't have the right to elect their own government.

Even if I can't arrange it today, I must pursue the objective of witnessing an election before I leave this country.

Mecklin said he thought that it was a good idea, that the Diem government is trying to encourage free elections, sometimes to an unbelievable degree.

Sunday, December 30

The Otter I boarded for Nhatrang carried four Special Forces men—three officers and a sergeant—heading farther up into the country. I thanked God that the Special Forces, at least, operate out of Saigon on Sundays—and so do many of the Army aviation units.

Also on duty this morning was the hard-working dispatcher whom I had seen at all sorts of odd hours working at the Army facility in Tan Son Nhut, Sgt. Cyril Manning (of Harlingen, Tex.). Manning is the kind of hard-rock, patient, endlessly devoted career Army man of which model we could use many thousands more. He's about to reach his 20-year mark, and "I'll retire and it won't be bad. I think I'll go to New Orleans—a good town."

The ranking passenger on our flight to Nhatrang was a huge slab of a man, Maj. Vincent Lang (of Mount Angel, Ore.). Redheaded, with a skin haircut, a neck like a courthouse column, and shoulders like a water buffalo, Lang had been a heavyweight champion boxer in the Army in the Panama area in World War II. He still looks capable of fighting his way out of a cage of wildcats.

Lang is an archetype of the Special Forces man: he is physically prepossessing and formidable, alert and experienced, and I'd estimate he could take care of himself and his men in any imaginable circumstances. With red eyebrows and body hair, and bright blue eyes, and a body so fighting-fit, he must look like an horrendous apparition from the north to the tiny Vietnamese.

Now he's heading for Nhatrang to open up a new branch of the rapidly expanding Special Forces complement in Vietnam. He will head up the B detachment in that area.

Lang told me that he "fought at 190, and now I'm 210. My wife says I'm growing up." Lang says he has six children already, and he thinks she's pregnant again. He slapped his bald head in desperation: "I say seven is my lucky number."

Shortly after 10, we swept over the long, arching bay of Nhatrang and landed next to the array of tents and hooches which are the 8th Station Hospital. I said good-by to my Special Forces friends and checked into a tent along the main company street of the camp, a strip of sand.

Wandering around the camp, I found that there are two main wards full of patients—but at the moment, only one battlefield casualty. He is Lt. David Ganly, 25 (of Saddle River, N.J.). Two other war-wounded were evacuated to the Philippines yesterday.

I found Ganly sitting beside a bed in Ward II, wearing pajama bottoms and a loose network of bandages on his upper torso. A MAAG adviser working out of Quang Ngai, he had been shot through the body by a sniper two weeks ago, and was finishing his 13th day in the hospital, and hoping to go back to duty in a couple of days.

Lt. Ganly is dark-eyed, serious, short, but husky. His father is a partner in the New York accounting firm of Richards, Ganly, Fries and Pruesch. There's something Ivy Leaguish about Ganly, even in baggy Army medical pajama pants—something about his polite self-possession, his diction, his choice of words. He went to Mt. Herman School, in Massachusetts, then on to Yale (Class of 1959), where he majored in architecture. Talking to him, you feel that he grew up in a privileged environment. He rowed for four years in Yale, most of the time in the critical position of Bow Oar. He has been in Vietnam for nine months, and this recent bullet was his first wound.

Ganly said that he had been driving from Quang Ngai to Ban Ly in a jeep on the day he was hit.

"It was a branch road off Route 1, a dirt road with trap rock pounded down. In my opinion, the area was reasonably secure.

"The strange thing was that I didn't see anything or hear anything. It was a funny sensation—it felt like the chop of a hand. My first thought was that I hit the steering wheel. I [had] turned sideways, trying to tune my radio, and thought I might have bumped against the wheel. I was trying to reach the regimental senior adviser [Maj. Paul F. Braim] because I was supposed to be there at 2, and it was 2:10.

"I realized I couldn't have hit the steering wheel, then I looked at the area [his ribs] and saw a hole in my shirt. I looked out to the side, and didn't see anything out there, but I fired a couple of shots out there just for the hell of it. Then I speeded up and finally drove on to the regiment. I had called in to the regiment and asked for an ambulance, but the message was garbled. An Arvin medic put some foot powder on it [the wound] and that was it. But Maj. Braim called in and got some choppers in and they took me to Quang Ngai."

The wound was caused by a rifle bullet, which hit Ganly

in one side and came out the other. Miraculously, it missed all the vital organs, although the surgeons felt at first that it must have damaged the peritoneum. A subsequent exploratory operation showed that no lasting harm was done, though it "burned the peritoneum." From the very beginning, apparently, he had been able to walk around, although "I was a little stiff."

I talked to some of the nurses and found out about the three battlefield casualties recently evacuated to the Philippines from here. One of the latest to leave was a Special Forces sergeant, Don M. Jones (of Presque Isle, Me.), who was with some montagnard troops out in the back country near Ban Methuot when he was hit. With a shattered arm, Jones had to walk a long way across country, and then was carried by truck, before eventually being flown out via helicopter. He will have to have a new graft of bone and elaborate repair to the nerve structure of his upper arm. The nurses told me his comment when he looked at his X rays: "It looks like a broken light bulb."

One of the nurses, redheaded Capt. Betty Rogers (of Windber, Pa.), took me on a guided tour of the hospital. The illnesses are what you might expect among servicemen here: gastroenteritis, hernia, a broken arm, an infected appendix on the verge of being operated upon, and a mysterious intestinal ailment (Vietnam is full of them) suffered by a sergeant to the point of death.

The surprising thing was the number of Vietnamese cases in this hospital. There were two Vietnamese soldiers, both battle casualties who had suffered broken arms and legs and were undergoing courses of surgery. Their limbs originally had been badly set by native practitioners—which, it seems, is more the rule than the exception in medically underprivileged Vietnam. The Vietnamese cases are admitted only through the intercession of some interested American—perhaps a Special Forces sergeant or lieutenant.

Also, there were two montagnard children, including one boy whom the GI's called Woody Woodpecker, because of a recalcitrant topknot in his hair. Woody was hit by a stray rifle bullet, which broke a leg, and he was not tended for 11 days. But he had the good fortune to be brought in by an American Special Forces officer. He's been operated upon twice already, and further operations are in store for him before he'll be able to walk again.

There's another unusual Vietnamese case in the hospital, a four-day-old baby, born with a congenital hernia. Two days ago the baby was operated upon, and he will probably be discharged to his parents tomorrow.

I met the head orthopedics man for the hospital, Dr. (Maj.) Spencer Walton (of Buffalo, Wyo.), and asked him about some of his fracture cases. Maj. Walton said the lack of medical attention for fractures here is painful, but an inevitable result of the shortage of medical talent and facilities in the country.

He told of a visit to a vastly overcrowded Vietnamese hospital in the Quang Ngai vicinity at which "I saw nine major fractures in one area [hospital area]. They had been one, two, or three weeks without attention.

"One woman had a gunshot wound and a shortened femur as a result. She had already united the fracture in bad position. It would have taken a course of operations to fix it: middle of the thigh, bent like this [he made a Z shape]."

"What did you do about the nine major fractures?" I asked him.

"I operated on 'em that day," he said simply.

Capt. Betty Rogers took me over to meet the head nurse, Maj. Louise Bitter (of Houghton, Wis.), and I learned a little about both of them. Tall, erect, bright, and decisive, Capt. Rogers has been a nurse for 12 years, 8 in the Army—2 in Germany. She came from a coal-mining district in Pennsylvania, her father was a coal foreman.

Maj. Bitter has been 20 years a nurse, 18 years in the Army, a veteran of service in World War II, on the island of Tinian in the Marianas. She looks younger than her years, although she walks as if she had the medical weight of 13,000 American servicemen in Vietnam on her shoulders—which in fact she does.

The head nurse lives in a bamboo hut by herself but, like the other nurses, has to share the shower with the males of the officer detachment. When the girls want to take a shower, they pull a flag up to the peak of the shower building.

At Maj. Bitter's hooch, now decorated with paper Christmas wreaths and a tree complete with tinsel and lights, I had a drink while listening to some lush Jackie Gleason tapes on her Sony recorder, a very elaborate gadget from Japan. I talked to Olga Drobek, an orthopedic nurse, and I asked her what she misses most in Vietnam.

"Privacy," she said. "Here you live in a goldfish bowl, with mostly open-sided hutches. Everybody knows everything you do.

"That's why I like to go to Saigon or Bangkok and have a

348

room of my own. And I like the white tablecloths and the stemmed glasses, and shining plates instead of partitioned [mess] trays, and having your own flush toilet."

I went back to my tent, which is a long way from white tablecloths and stemmed glasses and flush toilets, and got ready for sleep in my mosquito bar. My tent mate is the dentist, Dr. Murray Lieberman (of Brooklyn, N.Y.). The other two people supposed to be in the tent are on leave at the moment.

Before I went to bed, I sought out the head of the hospital, Maj. Paul Hartenstein, the acting CO (born in Austria, family in Lawton, Okla.). Hartenstein said the most amazing thing about the American casualties coming through this hospital is that "they want to go back to their outfits. I think if they're once wounded they should be evacuated—once is enough in this war—but almost to a man they don't want to get out, they want to get back to duty. Lt. Ganly got mad at me because I wanted to send him back to the States."

I asked what, in his opinion, is the motivation behind this urge to get back to duty. "My guess," he said, "is that they want to get back to their friends and do work that counts—but also, frankly, this is the only shooting war we have, so it's a very good thing careerwise, and most of the men are career men."

Hartenstein, a small, bald, suntanned man wearing shorts, spun some yarns about the battle injuries which are continually funneling through the 8th Hospital. One of the strangest was a helicopter company pilot who was shot in the rear end while on a helicopter mission. The bullet came up into the man's intestines and hit his kidney. Dr. Hartenstein patched him together but, as he said, felt the kidney-repair job would have to be done in the States, where better facilities were available. Then came the strange development. "Some doctor feeling around up there sure enough found a cancer of the kidney, which probably otherwise would have killed him [the helicopter pilot]."

Dr. Hartenstein said there have been all kinds of rumors coming back to Vietnam about this helicopter driver: "Rumors to the effect that he died, and that he lost his leg, that it was amputated because the sciatic nerve was affected, but the true story is he's all right. In a way, he's lucky he was hit."

Monday, December 31

Most of the available spare time around this hospital detachment was spent today in preparing for tonight's year-end blast. Hospital business went on nearly as usual. The tiny five-day-old was turned over to his father, a plump, bespectacled Vietnamese. The nurse on duty, Lt. Ida Callan (of Gerard, Ohio), handed the infant over to the parent with the advice, "Take care of him." The proud papa shoved off with the child, Ngo Thai Tho.

The sergeant who is sick with a mysterious bug, possibly amoebic dysentery, grew sicker today, despite the fact that they removed some of his intestine in the upper right quadrant.

I spent part of the day helping Ganly and a wardmate, Special Forces SFC Frank Robinson (of Wally Station, Ga.), make plans to snag a bottle of booze for tonight's celebration. Neither has an injured stomach, so no harm can be done.

Tonight, while parties were being held in five or six different areas of the 8th Station Hospital, Ganly and Robinson removed to one lighted corner of Ward II—the rest of the ward was darkened—and celebrated over a bottle of gin.

Ganly mentioned his superior officer in the MAAG at Quang Ngai, Maj. Lewis Robinson, who was drilled in the foot while flying on a reconnaissance flight aboard an L-19. The round came up through the floor and took out a piece of the major's Achilles tendon. They had to send him back to the States for extensive surgery and treatment.

Sgt. Robinson, a little more thoroughly oiled this evening than the decorous Ganly, was beefing about some of the aspects of the Vietnam campaign. "They'll never get me in another Army Peace Corps again," he said.

I asked Ganly how he would size up this campaign. He had said that he will "probably wind up in international trade or the State Department," and for this reason and his experience with the MAAG, he seemed well qualified to answer the question about our Vietnam venture.

"We've got to hang onto this piece of real estate, from several points of view. But I think some of the ways of spending money could be improved." This seemed a diplomatic enough view for a future foreign servant of the U.S.

I went by the mess hall, which was still lit, with a group of GI's in T-shirts still sitting around and conducting a baloney session, before the New Year should arrive. I listened in to one of the conversations. One husky boy was saying, "We brought him in dead as a mackerel, and there was only a line in the [*Stars and Stripes*] newspaper. We're gettin' killed and hurt in this war, and we're only 'advisers': —————." Another GI sage, similarly lubricated for the evening, added: "We got people gettin' shot at, but Americans can't do anything here: The French and the Vietnamese, they can do something, but not Americans."

Another, more good-humored: "They say nothin's too good for our servicemen—so give 'em nothin'."

A mammoth cook in T-shirt and white apron was off on another subject. "I say Vietnam is the best. I tried to extend, but they wouldn't let me do it. This is the only place you can get pleasure for a dollar—maybe less. Maybe you can get a girl on the beach for 50 P's [70 cents]."

The same kind of loose-jointed, roaring symposium was being conducted to the tune of much beer at the hospital enlisted men's club. I went on from there to the Cockpit Club, a former French villa now refurbished by Army aviators into a social center and decorated for this season with Christmas tree lights, bread loaves, chocolate cookies in tinfoil, and unshelled shrimp in a pile. At the bar a Vietnamese couple and a big American warrant officer served drinks.

At the Cockpit Club a score of people, helicopter ambulance company pilots, pilots of the new Army attack plane, the Mohawk (now under trial in Vietnam), some stray H-21 pilots—always there are H-21 pilots, anywhere in Vietnam —a few nurses and doctors—all were pouring libations and getting ready for Old Lang Syne.

Despite Mme. Nhu's ban on dancing, two couples twisted to the music of the record player, and we all tried the limbo to the appropriate music, skinning underneath a broom handle.

Suddenly the music was shut off, two of the Mohawk pilots sang their war song to the tune of "Glory, Glory, Hallelujah":

"The T-28's go flying at 7,000 feet and they
     never see a God-damn thing,
Glory, Glory what a helluva way to fly . . .
The L-19's fly at 2,000 feet and they
     never do a God-damn thing,
The Mohawks go flying at 150 feet and they
     do every God-damn thing,
Glory, Glory what a helluva way to fly. . . ."

They finished and some local adherent of the H-21's broke out with a chorus of his own emendation:

"The H-21's go flying, and they fly at 50 feet and
     they see every God-damn thing."

I tended to agree with him, but in the society of the Mohawk pilots, he was given a round razzing.

With midnight coming up, one of the pilots began a count-down: "Five—four—three—two—one—New Year's!" The lights went out momentarily while the girls got kissed, and then there was a quick restoration of current, and a short session of the limbo and the twist.

I got a jeep ride back to the tent camp of the 8th Station Hospital, with Lt. Don Naylor, a pilot of the 57th Medical Detachment. A light rain was falling, and the Vietnamese Virus took the moment to strike me. Doubled up with cramps, I dispatched purple Polymagma pills to the rescue, and recovered enough to take a quick look around the camp before retiring. The lights were out in Ward II, even the light that Robinson and Ganly had improvised at the rear end, and I surmised they had seen the year in, then retired. The noise of some celebration was still coming from the direction of the sergeants' bar at the other end of the camp. In No. I ward, where the critical cases are kept, the lights were still on at one end of the building, and a girl was screaming: the little montagnard girl whom they call "Bright Eyes," who had been operated on today for a tumor.

Another bit of business for tonight: Spec/5 Robert Lupu (of Ferndale, Mich.) was resting comfortably in Ward I after losing his appendix. The operation had been performed at 11 o'clock. I walked on back to my tent in the rain thinking that New Year's Eve is always somehow anti-climactic: It's too late to do anything about the opportunities you've missed last year, and too early to be optimistic about the year upcoming. But I am sure of one thing: Whatever may develop in our global struggle with Communism, there's plenty of fight left in Americans. My stay in the Vietnamese war has convinced me of that, and I am cheered by the realization.

Tuesday, January 1, 1963

The C-123 that carried me back to Saigon this morning made a loop up north first and landed at Quinhon, the base of operations for the 8th Helicopter Company, one of the first H-21 outfits to come into Vietnam and the first to suffer fatalities in action. We stopped very briefly, but I noticed that the company has put up a functional monument to two of their first men killed in action. The two large hangars at the airfield are emblazoned with the names (CWO) *Joseph A. Goldberg* and (Sp/5) *James E. Lane*. The 8th has had its ups and downs since those first fatalities, but now it is settling into a well-greased utility and has comfortable native-style bamboo hooches in what is probably the best-looking helicopter camp in the country.

On our flight down to Saigon, I talked (by interphone) with one of the pilots, Lt. Frank Renaldi (of Chicago, Ill.). He said his outfit is planning to go home on February 28, and he is exceedingly glad about that, because "my wife is expecting her first baby on April 10." And he added, as if apologizing for his anxiety to get home: "I don't think this situation [the Vietnamese war] is strong enough to warrant a man being away from his wife when his first child is born. It's such an emotional situation for the woman, when the first baby comes." I said I agreed with him and certainly didn't think he should apologize for wanting to go home, especially when his unit is going home anyhow. I said he should relax and enjoy life. He said he would.

Wednesday, January 2

This morning at 7:45, with an undoubted lack of wisdom, I approached John Mecklin's door upstairs with a view to finding out if any progress had been made with my project of witnessing an election.

I knocked. "Who is it?"

"Tregaskis."

"Come in."

Going in, I said, "I didn't want to disturb you too early."

"You managed it." The upshot of this inauspicious beginning was not bad, Mecklin suggested that I should see an official in the Vietnamese VGI, Dung Duc Khoi.

I called up Khoi, and since he is an Americanized type who speaks colloquial English and understands the American anxiety to do things quickly, I made an appointment to have lunch with him and talk over the project. We met and he made constructive suggestions about the way in which I could see an election in a strategic hamlet. He agreed that it was a good idea, and he said he would help me to set it up.

A quick, decisive man and a thoroughgoing Vietnamese intellectual, Khoi was very forthright about Americans and their involvement in the war here. He said:

"Americans—the Civil Service type—are much too cautious. They try much too hard to be canny. They are more

Oriental, you might say, than the Orientals. The American virtues, like honesty, even to the point of table-banging, are more apt to win friends and get results than caution. Most American civil servants are cautious because they want to preserve their careers."

Khoi mentioned the American Special Forces as having the same kind of dedication to a cause that the Communists have.

He told me how as a Viet Minh recruit at the age of 16, during World War II, he was sent to paint a sign on a wall saying: *Down with the Japs*. The Japanese were then occupying what is now Vietnam, and Khoi said he felt it was an honor to be asked to risk his neck in an act of such outward defiance of the enemy who occupied the country. He said, "the Viet Cong make their pitch on the grounds of independence—that is their main selling point. In general, the Americans are losing this war because they are too self-seeking and too indecisive."

I said that he knew and I know that the Communist promises of independence are a travesty and a fraud, and that to be convinced of this, all you have to do is read the easily obtainable textbooks of Leninism, which lay down the principles of every Communist revolution across the world, promising a Dictatorship of the Proletariat (actually the Dictatorship of the Communist party, a small minority), which is the antithesis of free government.

I told him about some of my friends in the helicopters, the Special Forces, the MAAG adviser teams, the Air Force pilots, and the way in which they are boldly sticking their necks out almost every day, taking mortal chances and making decisions that could cost them their lives or crippling injuries, for the sake of a duty they felt, a sense of obligation, to our nation.

Khoi nodded tolerantly, and said that there were Americans whom he respected immensely—including the American secretary in the Embassy whom he expects to marry shortly.

Checking at the PI office later, I found that something of great importance had happened, and was still happening, down in the Delta area near Tam Hiep. Allan Galfund was just finishing a telephone conversation with Maj. Slavich of the Hueys, and conveyed to me that "five birds are shot down near Tam Hiep. Four H-21's and one Huey. There are four casualties: two serious, one may have died."

As the telephone reports continued to come in, the casualty figures were revised upward: three Americans killed, and seven wounded. I got on the track of a ride to the area tomorrow, through Air Force contacts.

Thursday, January 3

I missed out on a good chance to go down to Tam Hiep this morning with a Huey sent down by Maj. Slavich, to help evacuate the American bodies.

I pursued the possibility of another ride with Maj. Bob Mauser, the Air Force PIO. He said that an L-28, a little liaison plane with the ability to take off and land in short fields, would be leaving Tan Son Nhut this morning, and might be going down to the Delta area.

"How soon can you get out here?" Mauser asked. He was calling from Air Division HQ at the airport. "Right way," I said.

When I reached the Air Force operations office at Tan Son Nhut and saw the little, wide-winged helioplane taxiing up, I realized I would be the only passenger. The other press correspondents whom Mauser had talked to about making the flight hadn't shown up. It developed that the L-28 was a "rubberneck plane," with no specific mission, and since I was to be the only passenger, I could fly around as I wished—of course, subject to the exigencies of air traffic and the conduct of the war. A very lucky break.

Climbing into the gray, sporty-looking little plane, I asked the pilot, Capt. John Downing (of Fort Walton Beach, Fla.), if he could fly me down to Tam Hiep, and maybe also Soctrang.

Capt. Downing called through to the Joint Operations Center command and asked if we could make the landings at those two spots, and the request was approved. Furthermore, he said, "We'll fly over the area, and we can see what's on the radio." He meant that if the fight was still going on, we could be clued in through listening to the radio calls.

We lifted off a few minutes later, and were heading south over the ricelands.

The day was clear, with silvery mounds of clouds. We flew over the familiar Tam Hiep landing strip raised above the swamp. I could see a line of H-21's parked there, and a smudge of troops and the metal shapes of trucks and jeeps next to the light green lagoon.

At about that moment, on the radio, I heard a voice in English: "This is Bluebird—there's a spook on your right wing." Then there came a spate of excited Vietnamese voices.

I asked Downing if he thought those were the voices of T-28 pilots making a strike somewhere near here. He said:

"I think it's up in the other area—up near the Cambodian

border, where there's another action going on. There was a paratroop drop up there yesterday." He pointed to his map, indicating the terrain around Tay Ninh. "It's a four-day operation up there—it's still going on."

We went beyond Tam Hiep for about 10 miles, and Downing swung the aircraft into a gentle curve. We circled a vast green paddy area, which looked like any other sectional patchquilt of paddy, and then I saw two downed H-21's, close together, with an assemblage of overlapping vehicle tracks marked in the greenery. Some kind of tanklike vehicle had scratched a series of straight lines across the paddy, some of them leading up near the two H-21's. About a mile from the two H-21's sat another of the flying bananas. And spread over the quadrant of green were limp globs of parachutes. There must have been a sizable paratroop drop in connection with the action.

We flew over the pair of H-21's, and from them, out to the single one.

I heard a radio call, very clearly: "We have two American dead aboard—can we make arrangements?" I wondered if that was a chopper coming into Tam Hiep, but Downing thought it was an aircraft taking the American dead into Flight Control at Saigon.

We circled the area one more time at a lower altitude and Downing pointed toward the two choppers. "You see that other chopper in the field? It's wrecked." I noticed now a lump of metal wreckage, which appeared to be a different fundamental shape from the two H-21's. The H-21's appeared undamaged from the air; the other pile of wreckage looked like a small section of an auto junkyard. That would probably be the remains of the Huey that had been shot down.

I asked Downing if he could make a pass over the downed birds so that I could see what had happened and make some pictures. There were two white T-28's orbiting the field, apparently looking for VC's, and we dodged in as they completed a pass.

This time, rocketing in at maximum speed, we swooped down on the green deck and I could see the two H-21's clearly now and the pile of wreckage nearby. There was no sign of life around the planes, and I knew the spooky feeling that comes over you when you're in an area of action. When you see no one moving, you'd better beware, especially in this guerrilla war, because the chances are you're near the front.

Downing pulled up sharply at the end of our pass and turned, and as we did, I could see a column of smoke rising from a river near the wrecks: Possibly ground action was under way there. At the same time I saw an H-21, her flower-like rotors turning, flying low above the area of the crash.

Capt. Downing was excited. Quite on his own, he swung our bird around again, streaked in a dive at more than the helioplane's prescribed maximum of 170 knots, and swept down over the splashed H-21's one more time. I made some close pictures of the birds as we zoomed. I was more than ever convinced that this was still a hostile area: quiet and empty as Main Street at 3 A.M., Monday morning. Yet, there was no audible shooting.

Downing turned our bird back toward Tam Hiep, and shortly afterward, at 10:47, we touched down beside the string of parked H-21's. A group of Hueys were parked together at the far end of the strip.

I walked along the runway and saw the tall, spare figure of Col. Daniel Boone Porter, the senior MAAG adviser. I had thought he was on his way back to the States, but here he was, still on duty and close to the heart of the action.

"How's it going?" I asked him.

"Things went wrong this time," he said and added, "This was more like what you and I were used to in the old days."

I walked over to one of the parked H-21's; it was from the 57th Helicopter Company. I talked to the pilots, Capt. William S. Gardner (of Waynesboro, Miss.), and CWO Roy C. Adams (of Amarillo, Tex.). Adams had the distraught look of someone looking upon violent death for the first time in war. "We've been picking up medical evacs and bodies," he said very quietly. "There were 13 bodies, Arvins, and two Americans—crew chiefs."

Capt. Gardner said he hadn't been flying on yesterday's operations—it seemed as if today's doings were more than enough. Both pilots seemed pale and shaken.

I asked if the LZ area was secure by this time. Adams said, "It's supposed to be. But as far as I know, it never was." That was enigmatic enough, but clear indication of plenty of death and destruction still around to upset men's cerebrospinal systems.

The crew chief, PFC Royce Lawson (of Wise, Va.), was more circumstantial about it. "They're still shooting around there," he said. "Two birds picked up holes this morning."

Farther down the line, I found my friend Capt. Don Toth of the 93d. Don told me the most important bit of intelligence about the battle that I had yet heard: "It's over, except for the sniping," he said. As maintenance officer of the company, he had his hands full with plans to recover the downed choppers from the LZ. He took a moment, though, to tell me what had happened to the 93d in this strange battle. It had started when Lt. Lew Stone, the durable 93d pilot who had been the first of the outfit to be shot down, months ago, was shot down in the LZ. "He let his troops out, but had got hit in the transmission and couldn't get enough power to take off. He called for the next chalk to come in, and Flippen and Nysewander both came in and they got shot down. The crew chief who was killed [Sp/4 Donald Braman, of Radcliffe, Ky.] was on Nyse-wander's plane. Then two other birds went in to help, Fitts and Jim Bell in an H-21, and then a Huey went in, also trying to help. The Huey got flipped over when it got hit."

I found out later that the pilots of the Huey were CWO Dick Wadlack and Lt. James E. Stone. The gunner on that ship was a Negro, Sgt. William L. Deal (of Mays Landing, N.J.), killed almost immediately by a VC bullet.

One of the H-21's downed in the LZ had already been repaired and flown back, thanks to the good offices of Toth and his salvage crew.

Another H-21 had just come clattering in, with huge smears of oil on his fuselage—the second of the 93d flying bananas to be recovered from today's operations. With the second bird came Capt. Karl Streever (of Stanwood, Wash.). Like Toth, Streever was soaked with mud up to his thighs from plunging around in the paddy on the repair detail.

I looked at Nysewander's chopper, the one in which Donald Braman had been killed. The fuselage was ripped open like a beer can: five visible holes, one big enough to get your hand into. There were bullet holes around the forward door where the gunner had been standing, and a hole near the bubble where Nysewander had been sitting and took a bad arm wound.

Two more H-21's were coming in: evidently medical evac planes, for a couple of ambulances with large red crosses bounced out to the landing strip to meet them.

The H-21 stopped, and a crowd of Vietnamese soldiers rolled a kind of ramp up to its wide rear door. Then the procession of wounded began. The stretchers were brought out, the prostrate men with fresh pink-colored bandages—bandages across chests, wads of bandage on arms or legs, eyes covered with the bandage—the wretched cordwood of wounded men, their faces frozen with shock. That is, except for one with a dark fragment of blanket spread over his face and an especially inert form: these lonely, these dead.

358

Besides the helicopter casualties, we had lost a MAAG adviser, killed: Capt. Kenneth N. Good (of Ewa Beach, Hawaii) under VC fire with his Arvin troops.

I still hadn't been filled in on the way the ground operation had progressed in this area. All I had heard was what had happened to the helicopters—but the heavy load of Arvin wounded and dead was a reminder that the American casualties, as usual, were relatively slight, compared to the Vietnamese.

I found my way to the headquarters tent, where Gen. Cao (wearing two bright new silver stars on each shoulder, sign of his new promotion to Corps commander) was standing talking to Col. Vann, our senior adviser for this particular (7th) division.

As I came up, the general hurried off, but I managed to ask him: "Are there more wounded to be brought out?"

Cao, still hurrying away, said, "Talk to my divisional commander." He certainly didn't want to talk about the engagement: his first campaign of the New Year. A long way from being a resounding victory.

I talked to Vann, however. The blond, dynamic adviser, now ridden and haggard, said bluntly that the fight had been a defeat for the Arvin forces. "I'd estimate we have over 100 casualties," he said. "And about 35 killed." Then Col. Vann, too, hurried off, his face much less composed than Gen. Cao's.

Don Toth was getting ready to fly into the LZ to recover, if possible, the two H-21's and the wreckage of the Huey still there. I asked him if I could ride in to get a slightly closer look at the birds, and the scene. He said certainly.

On our way to the chopper, Toth pointed out the H-21 in which he had made his first flight into the LZ this morning. There were two large holes in the tail and the rear part of the fuselage. "That's how I know the snipers were still at it this morning," said Toth.

I flew in with Toth to the paddy, but came back almost immediately to Tam Hiep. The area seemed calm and quiet, although Don told me he still considered it technically under fire. I left Toth and his salvage crew wading in the muck.

Back at Tam Hiep, I tried to pick up as many bits and pieces of the story as I could from the helicopter pilots and crewmen. Most of them who had flown into the LZ yesterday were still haunted by the specter of sudden death and injury. One of the crew chiefs, Sp/5 Charles Rowland (of Junction City, Kan.), said "We were evacuating 'em until 9:30 last night. I never saw so many damn dead Vietnamese in my life. They were three deep all the way to the door."

I heard that durable Lew Stone, who had been wounded in the back and an arm by bullet fragments at the LZ, had recovered well enough to join the 93d again at Soctrang. I prevailed on Capt. Downing, the helioplane pilot, to fly me over to Soctrang in search of Stone. By the time we found him, the afternoon was wearing out, but his story was certainly a key to the whole of this military action at Ap Bac (which seems to be the name of the settlement nearest the paddy fields where it was fought).

Calm, thoughtful, deliberate as ever, Stone did not seem at all spooked like many of the H-21 boys I had talked to earlier who were way out on the periphery of the action compared to Stone. But they were also a long way from him in battle experience.

Stone said that, strangely enough, on the night before the mission, he had been awarded his Purple Heart for the wound he had got on August 30, when he was shot down with Maj. Gray.

Stone said that the early engagement at Danang had been a bad one, and birds he had been flying had been shot up five times after that, but the Ap Bac battle was "about the worst engagement I was ever in." As Stone unfolded the story, I realized several salient facts about Ap Bac:

It had been a mammoth effort of combined coordinated arms mounted by the Arvin forces. There had been more than two regiments of troops of various kinds—regular Army forces, SDC (Militia), paratroopers, armored infantry in Armored Personnel Carriers (APC's), some troops being brought in by landing boat via the rivers, heavy forces of artillery, three American helicopter companies, and a large assembly of Air Force, American and Vietnamese, in T-28's, B-26's, and troop-carrying C-47's.

Yet with all this vast force, the VC fought stubbornly and well, and after inflicting heavy casualties on the Arvin forces, they pulled out during the first night.

Stone said that the day's operations began calmly. "We made three lifts. They were uneventful. But inbound on this [fourth] lift, everybody called enemy fire. We were the latest to pick up fire. My aircraft was hit about that time: They shot out my fore and aft control.

"I brought it in backward. When the troops were out, I tried to get it out of there. But my engine quit. It had taken a round.

"I called for Chalk 6 [the helicopter behind him].

"He [Nysewander] landed and we got aboard the aircraft immediately. But his gunner got hit right away, and I took over his gun. We started gettin' hit real bad. We all got out except the gunner—he was hit bad. Nysewander was wounded, a bad one in the arm.

"We got down into the paddy on our backs, in that —— —— mud. Flippen [copilot of one of the rescuing aircraft] and I crawled back to the bird, trying to help the gunner. The VC were really raking that aircraft. Flippen and I got shrapnel in our arms and hands.

"We saw the Huey come in and get shot down. We pulled out the pilot, the gunner, and the crew chief. [When he was talking about the crew chief, he meant the Vietnamese observer, an Arvin soldier.]

"From then on, we got pinned down behind this dike, on our backs in the mud. From 10:20 till 17:40, with no food, no ————. But there was plenty of water! We lay on our face or on our back. Fire was flying around in every direction. Finally we got back into the ship and got the machine gun out. Then they [the VC] really pinned us down.

"Several of the Arvin troops were with us in the paddy. They would raise up and get hurt. There were a lot of wounded when they got us out of there.

"It wasn't too bad till they [the VC] started firing mortars. We thought the war was over—but they only fired three.

"There were all those APC's [designed to carry troops under fire], but they wouldn't come up to us. They'd come up a little way and then they'd pull back. They'd try to come out one at a time and get shot up, then they'd pull back.

"Finally the American adviser with the APC's, Capt. Shelton, got to them and convinced them to come up and pick us up. He told us he'd had to talk 'em into it.

"Before we left, the B-26's came in and worked the woods over. The earth really shook. And they worked it over with artillery too. They were laying on real artillery before we left."

I asked Stone what would be the lesson of the Ap Bac battle, where we could mount such a large coordinated effort and take such casualties from the enemy, inflicting so few in return. (The rumor was that only three VC bodies had been found in the mud fortifications where they had their strongpoint.)

Stone thought about it carefully. "We had a lot of armor, boats, artillery—and we [the helicopters] parked 'em [put down the troops] right into the best place. But we seemed to have come right into the middle of a horseshoe of fortifications, and we were receiving fire from three sides. I heard the VC had mud trenches all the way around. It was just one of those bad breaks for us."

Capt. Downing was anxious to start back for Saigon before nightfall, but I wanted to talk a few minutes more to Stone, the kind of devoted military man we should have more of if we are to win the global struggle.

Like many of our career military men, Stone married a foreign girl while on duty abroad. His wife, Anne, is from Germany. They were married in October, 1953, when he was in the Army Ordnance School in Eschweg. Anne is now in Alexandria, Va. (A tragic sequel: On January 11, Stone was killed in a helicopter crash. Charlie Fitts died with him, and so did my friend Don Toth.)

Capt. Downing put our little L-28 down at Tan Son Nhut before the sun went down, and there was still time to catch up with the PIO and find out what had happened on other fronts of the Vietnamese war today. It developed that our side had suffered one more defeat last night, up at the Special Forces base in Plei Mrong, where I had made the patrol with Boyd and Hoagland and met some other good type Americans.

The story about Plei Mrong was that Capt. Grace had taken out a reconnaissance in force, setting out to sweep the VC secret base area. But as soon as the Grace strike force was safely away from Plei Mrong, the VC moved in, overran the camp, and left something like 80 casualties behind them, about half of them killed. The report was that two of the American sergeants were wounded, but there wasn't any dope yet on their names. (I found out later that one of the wounded Americans was Billie Fell, the indomitable youth who had skipped the hospital and returned to Plei Mrong after being blown up in a truck by a VC road mine. This time, Billie was hurt in the groin by a flying bit of debris. He was sent back to the 8th Station Hospital in Nhatrang.)

The Year-at-War for Arvins and Americans in Vietnam seems to be starting off with an overshadowing of bad luck. But, as Stone said, that's the way it is in war: you can't win 'em all.

Friday, January 4

This morning I had word via the Vietnamese Department of Information (Khoi and company) that I will be able to see a popular election in a strategic hamlet tomorrow. The senior officer in the American military headquarters in Saigon, civil affairs section, a Col. John L. Beebe (of Augusta, Ga.), is going to visit the hamlet as an observer, and he and I will go together. We'll start early tomorrow morning.

There's been a big flap today about the press coverage of the Battle of Ap Bac. Some of the news stories of that defeat for our side have charged that all sorts of mistakes were made by the Arvin high command in the conduct of the campaign. Probably there were many mistakes—there always are in a battle.

One of the younger and brasher correspondents wrote an excited, emotional story about the fact that during the Ap Bac engagement the Arvin artillery killed three of their own troops and wounded 11 by mistake. I talked to Galfund about it and reminded him of the old artilleryman's slogan: the V-sign, given with two fingers, to indicate that in an artillery barrage, 2 per cent of our own troops will be hit by shorts. That doesn't mean that artillery couldn't always be better, but people get hurt in a war, like it or not.

I'm afraid the critical news dispatches about Ap Bac will do a lot of harm in the U.S. Ap Bac was a defeat for us, yet it really was very little except the Phuoc Chau victory in reverse. At Phuoc Chau, as noted earlier, we beat up the VC and left 127 enemy dead, at a very small cost to us in casualties. At Ap Bac, the VC apparently a very well-disciplined and well-dug-in outfit did it to our side—but not quite as badly. That's the way war goes, a bloody business any way you look at it.

Saturday, January 5

I met Col. Beebe at the MACV headquarters this A.M. We started out for the strategic hamlet with Beebe's interpreter, Lum, and a station-wagon jeep (Willys) and a driver lent by the Vietnamese Information Department.

Col. Beebe seemed large, prepossessing, and unruffled; a big-shouldered man with a distinguished mane of gray hair. He wore a slack suit, and dark glasses, studiedly unmilitary. He explained to me: "I am unofficially here [for the election]. I took the morning off for it. We want to make sure that they know how this is, that we are unofficially here. The Vietnamese are understandably concerned about any interference with their government. They've had a history of conquest by many outside powers—many Americans fail to recognize this."

I said I realized this. But our high military officials are

always telling me that G-5, the civil affairs section, is the most important of all the military branches in the mission to Vietnam. Yet, I said, every time it comes to an involvement with political affairs in Vietnam, our people shy away.

Col. Beebe smiled tolerantly, as if several books could be written on that subject. I pursued the matter of today's election and asked for a rundown on the place and issues involved, and so forth.

Beebe told me that it is a strategic hamlet election in the capital province of Gia Dinh, which includes Saigon. He said that he understood that a committee is to be elected to run the affairs of the strategic hamlet, about 12 miles out of Saigon.

He spoke more generally as we whipped along the good black-top road heading beyond the city limit. "My favorite saying about this war is: 'We're here to win people, and not just mountaintops.'" Which was certainly general enough. And he went on: "They [the Vietnamese] don't want to be Chinese, French, and they're darn sure they don't want to be American: They want to be Vietnamese."

Our driver swung us into the porte-cochere of another of those concrete French houses, which now sported the orange and red banner of Vietnam at a flagstaff. It was the headquarters of the Gia Dinh province chief, and we met the assistant chief, a small, earnest Vietnamese captain named Vo Van Hai. Hai explained that the province chief, Maj. Xich, was out on a military operation today; therefore he, Hai, would accompany us to the strategic hamlet in question.

Capt. Hai told us that there are 293 strategic hamlets in this province, and there have been elections in 124 of them by this time. Capt. Hai told us (Lum interpreting) that these elections, like today's, have been conducted to choose governing boards for the hamlets. Today's election, he said, was to choose a committee, a chief and three assistant chiefs, or "president and vice-presidents." I also learned the name of the hamlet: Thanh-Loc.

As we started out again in our jeep wagon, Beebe explained to me: "They're starting out with voting at the hamlet level. Then they'll go up to the village level, then the district, then the province. There are 40 provinces."

We rolled off the black-top onto a dirt road and started across rice fields, while the captain explained to us that this area was cleared of VC only a few months ago. He tried explaining in English: "Sometimes we met a VC—who hide maybe 200 meters away, and they shot. They are cleared for five months."

We bounced through a succession of fields, following our dirt track, and came to a small town with a few shops and flystands. We stopped in front of a dirt-floored concrete house, and there met the village chief, a substantial Vietnamese, middle-aged, in a wrinkled gray business suit, and shirt and necktie. We were introduced to him—his name is Nguyen van Dai—and we went over with him to the improvised electoral hall, another bare concrete government building with a dirt floor. Near it was a sentry tower, with an armed guard on duty, watching for VC activity around the periphery of the hamlet.

Outside this building, I could see a mob of about 100 people, and directly in front of the building, when we pulled up, a squad of blue-uniformed Republican Youth were standing at attention.

The blue-clad guard presented arms while Col. Beebe, Capt. Hai, Village Chief Nguyen van Dai and I went into the precinct hall.

Inside, the building was rigged with bare wooden benches, the first one set aside for the American visitors and their hosts, the rest filled with townspeople waiting politely for us.

A young, handsome Vietnamese master of ceremonies began to speak, apparently welcoming the visitors to the election and explaining the by-laws.

Lum explained to us what was going on: "Two months ago, the hamlet had a temporary committee, appointed by the district chief. Now they will select a real committee—they will establish the relationship between the committee and the people."

That sounded fine enough, and when I checked it through further with Lum, the process seemed to have a democratic basis. Up at the front of the room was a blackboard, which listed something like 300 registered voters in this village of around 700 total population. The suffrage, said Lum, is open to men and women of 18 and over.

"The first meeting was held two weeks ago," Lum said, "to pick out the candidates. They had their second meeting a week ago.

"There are two tablets—how do you call them?" He was referring to the two slates competing for the three jobs in the hamlet committee, and the chief or president. The ballots showed four each, and each of the two slates had distinctive marking for the benefit of those unable to read. The ticket headed by Nguyen van Ngoc was identified by a crude mimeographed drawing of a sugar-cane plant. The other slate, headed by Nguyen van Thanh, was marked with a picture of a hoe. All the voters had to do was to vote for the sugar-cane or the hoe party. Before the balloting, there would be a chance for the heads of the two slates to talk to the voters and make their campaign promises à la America, and then the vote would be cast, by secret ballot.

At the front of the room, I could see the appurtenances of a secret election: a voting booth, made private by a crude cloth drape; a ballot box painted orange with red stripes; and a couple of desks where election officials checked off the voters as they came through to cast their ballots. Capt. Hai explained that there are two padlocks on the ballot box, and the keys for these two locks are entrusted to the leaders of the sugar-cane and the hoe parties.

Then the two panels, the prospective leaders and committeemen, came up before the voters, and stood, while the candidate for the office of leader made his presentation. The first leader, Ngoc (pronounced "Ow-k"), stepped forward to make his speech. He was a man of about 28, with a rough peasant face and, when he opened his mouth, a gap in his front teeth.

Lum interpreted as Ngoc spoke earnestly: "He called on the people to elect him. He said he has done many works for the hamlet and he will bring security to the hamlet."

The second candidate, an older man (Thanh), whose face showed the weathering effects of farming in the rice paddies, stepped forward to make his pitch. His speech was short, and Lum interpreted: "He says he has done many things for the hamlet, and he will bring security and prosperity and happiness."

The two panels sat down and two citizens stood up in order to defend the two panels. The second of these, wearing a white Western-style shirt, seemed absolutely terrified as he spoke into the microphone. He touched it rigidly, his hand shaking, and when the speakers boomed with a trace of feedback, he was so frightened it seemed he would run away. Our Western inventions like elections and public-address systems were almost too much for him.

Then there was a short question-and-answer session, like a New England or Swiss town-meeting format, and the questions, as well as I could follow them, dealt mostly with "the farmers' bill," which apparently is the empowering legislation for the strategic hamlet program. A woman asked if arms would be provided for the townspeople according to the farmer's bill, and "if they have trouble" (Lum's interpretation), will they be protected? Both candidates answered her: In an emergency, the district chief will protect them. I suppose the basic issue of security for the farmers depends on a strong central government, but apparently plenty of reliance is also put on the local chiefs to supply arms and organization.

The citizens who had led the discussion filed out, and the election began, the voters stepping up one by one into the booth, coming out with a marked, folded ballot, which was ceremoniously dropped into the wooden ballot box. I went outside with Beebe and, with the village chief's permission, talked to a couple of voters, saying that I wanted to pick them out at random as they came away from the ballot box. My first interviewee was a 66-year-old woman. Tiny, shriveled, and toothless, she nevertheless spoke with enthusiasm and frankness. Lum translated: "She said she likes the sugar-cane candidates and voted for them."

I asked her why she favored them. "They are very capable men," Lum rendered, "and they are young. The other group are older. She selected the younger men, as they are more eager."

I singled out another voter, a farmer named Ng Uyen Van Sung. A man of 54, he was wearing the ordinary peasant garb of black pants and jacket, and his head was shaven. He grows potatoes and sugar cane, and has three grandchildren. He didn't tell me how he voted, but was proud of the fact that he had already voted twice before in national elections: once to choose a delegate to the National Assembly (in 1959) and again to elect President Diem, in 1960.

I asked him how he learned to vote. He said (Lum's translation): "He doesn't read very well but in today's election, he can choose between the sugar cane or the spade."

The national elections also involved slates identified by pictures, and as in today's election, the candidates made campaign speeches. At the polls, the contest between candidates was close. However, in the presidential election of April 30, 1960, Diem's opponent was apparently a patsy, and he received very few votes.

Beebe and I went back into the election room while the votes were being counted; a mark was made on the blackboard each time a vote was called: *"Ong Will Yung Ow-k"* (a vote for Ngoc) or *"Ong Will Yung Than"* (a vote for Thanh). The final tally was 180 for the sugar-cane party and 48 for the hoe party. There were cheers and clapping and Col. Beebe was called upon by the young chairman, Tran van Thanh, to make a speech.

Beebe said, "We appreciate the opportunity to come here

and see your election." Hard-working interpreter Lum translated sentence by sentence into Vietnamese.

"We realize that the election has been delayed a little because we have been here. We of America appreciate the value of elections. We have fought and died and our fathers have fought and died, just as you have fought and died, so that we can have the same privileges of elections.

"I noted that those who were defeated applauded when the results were announced. Those who were elected truly represent all the people. It is a great honor for them to have been considered by members of your hamlet for these very important jobs. When our country was in the same stage of development, it was called a land of opportunity. I see Vietnam also is a great land of opportunity.

"It was only because you asked us to come that we came. It looked to be a very fine election. Thank you very much."

The election over, Beebe and I started off with Capt. Hai and the village chief. As we moved toward the car, the blue-uniformed Republican platoon snapped to attention and the voters stood rigidly. As we moved into the car, they gave three well-coached cheers: "Hello! Hello! Hello!"

On the way back to Saigon, Capt. Hai was telling me: "We are developing the country. Have much development still to do." And he added a candid note: "This is most difficult kind of election—because [people in this hamlet] never live under VC." The inference was clear: Peasants who had lived under VC government wanted no more of it. They would reach out eagerly for free government. Those who had not lived under a Communist regime were harder to convince.

Beebe told me about his wife, Lucille, who is back in Georgia waiting for his return after his 15-month tour. "She's a good soldier," he said. "But like any other wife, she's gettin' awfully anxious for me to go home."

He drifted back to a favorite subject: the war. "There's a big job to be done here. The people are looking at two armies, the VC and Arvin. If they're satisfied the Arvin is their Army, the war's over. The VC depend on the people—so do the Arvin."

The colonel said that he is planning to leave for home on the 26th of this month, and then after leave, he'll "go to Fort Gordon [S.C.] and start training people for this kind of work all over the world. Our country has just realized the job that the soldiers can do for the civilians. We've been very successful with our military jobs so far. But influencing by noncoercive means, believe me, that's a still-to-be-developed skill. In every case, you're operating in sovereign nations, where you don't want the people to think you're trying to coerce them."

The big, courtly Southerner said that he has two more years of service before retirement. He had a long career in the Army in World War II as a company commander and assistant G-3 of the 20th Armored Division. After the war, he was in NATO at Fontainebleau, France, and then went to Fort Gordon as assistant commandant of the Civil Affairs School. I asked him if he won't be missing the work he does in the civil affairs section when he retires. He said, "Yes, it's two years before I retire, but I have a feeling I'll stay in the fight somehow."

Back at the Brink mess, I talked to a couple of my newspaper friends, and told them proudly about my excursion to an election in a strategic hamlet. They made impolite remarks to the effect that the Vietnamese government had set up a convincing election for me and Beebe, but I countered by citing some of the facts that couldn't have been rehearsed. It's easy to sneer at a tiny, poor, former colonial nation trying to win its way to self-government and independence: but I for one would give Diem and his government plenty of credit for trying and for somehow convincing the government soldiers to risk their necks for our side. They take heavy casualties every day, every week, in this bloody civil war; every month the Vietnamese Armed Forces suffer about 1,000 casualties, about one-third of these killed in action. By contrast, our total battle casualties in the year during which we have been making a maximum effort here, have been less than 200 killed and wounded. I told my friends that Diem's government might not be as perfect a democracy as the U.S.A., but it is one hell of a lot better than the People's Republic of North Vietnam or Communist China, and the Arvin soldiers and fliers generally seem willing to back up this proposition with their lives.

Sunday, January 6

There were still some tag ends to be pursued on the Ap Bac battle story. Estimates of VC casualties now range as high as 50. We had more than 100 killed and wounded, of these 40 killed. As usual, the VC evacuation and medical teams apparently carried off many of the wounded—several bloody field operation sites were discovered—but in all, a total of nine bodies recovered. The VC troops managed to fade into the civilian population, as usual.

Through my Army aviation friends, I got a ride down to

the Delta this morning, on the trail of Col. Vann. I flew in to Tam Hiep and found him at his headquarters, still occupied with getting the last wreckage of the shot-down helicopters out of the Ap Bac LZ. Vann had been on the griddle for two days, being questioned by the high American brass on the subject of the Ap Bac engagement. He moved nervously, he seemed to have lost weight, and his blue eyes were bloodshot. He ripped, as usual, to the heart of the matter with a vigor that disregarded connective tissue:

"They [the brass] want to know, why did I change the fourth LZ? It was not changed. It was chosen because of the tactical needs of the time.

"They asked, 'Why did you land them so close to the enemy?' [My answer is:] I'm delighted when I get a chance to get at the enemy.

"Everybody is trying to jump to conclusions about what this proves and doesn't prove. The loss of at least the additional helicopters was [because of] an admirable and questionable policy of landing and evacuating the downed crews. This has been a point of issue before. Every helicopter lift that goes in, I have an adviser with. It would be easy for the helicopter crew to climb out and take cover. It's not so bad for them to be on the ground. The advisers are [on the ground]."

Col. Vann, still roaring mad, went on to say that the Ap Bac operation bogged down because of all the downed helicopters. He said he felt that the whole question of sending in choppers to pick up the crews of helicopters shot down in a LZ should be reviewed. However, he backed off a little. He said that the Ap Bac situation was special: "It [the use of helicopters to rescue chopper crews] was justifiable, because there were badly wounded Americans."

I asked him about the conduct of the infantry engagement by the Arvin troops in the battle.

"There were three main criticisms," he said. "First, the failure of South Force to move in. [That was an SDC militia force, which would not advance.]

"Second, failure of the APC's to move. Third, the parachute force. They were dropped on the wrong side of the river. It was a decision that I opposed. They [the Vietnamese high command] wanted to reinforce defeat rather than ensure victory. I believe they meant to leave the flank open so that the VC could escape that night—which they [the VC] did."

That was tough talk from a dynamic, hard-hitting adviser with a long string of successes in coaching the Arvin to his credit. Now, he was the irate, defeated adviser who had been running through oceans of trouble with superior brass. There will be a lot more oceans for him as public sentiment is aroused by this latest defeat in our new kind of war. A few American casualties can set off chains of congressional investigations—as if, somehow, Congress could legislate the bleeding out of our war with the Communists.

In the course of orbiting around several of the Delta bases today, I ran across the tracks of Col. Porter again. He was still out in the field (at Can Tho), still on the trail of the lessons to be learned from Ap Bac—and apparently not at all eager to hurry home for his new peacetime duty in the States. He said, "We still have a weakness—a failure to completely seal off an enemy. I believe that by moving troops in by helicopter, on foot, by boat, or by 113 [the Armored Personnel-Carrier vehicles], we could have completely sealed off that area [Ap Bac]. But we didn't.

"The VC force fought hard. But I think it was only that they were in a position where they thought they *had* to fight. It appeared to them that they were blocked in with the helicopters and the armored personnel carriers, and the troops coming in by boat. They made a determined stand. Then they were able to get the dead and wounded out, probably by sampan. They just disappeared. In the amount of water we had out there, a battalion could be swallowed up.

"And it's hard to identify the VC. All they have to do is grab a hat and a hoe and become a friendly farmer. The problem is much the same as with the police in the U.S.— where you have crooks and bank robbers among the civilian population. You've got to catch the people with the loot, or the tools of their trade."

I could see why Col. Porter is not interested in going home at this time: There are too many vital military problems still to be worked out.

Monday, January 7

This afternoon I managed to promote another T-28 mission, with Vietnamese Air Force (Fighter) Squadron 716, flying out of Tan Son Nhut. No American pilots were flying on this mission. Again, there wasn't an aircraft available for the American who would normally have flown with the mission: Capt. William R. Henderson (30, of Kansas City, Mo.), who already has 25 bombing-strafing missions to his credit with this squadron.

On today's mission, I was reminded of one of the great

obstacles in efficient cooperation between Americans and Vietnamese: the language barrier. My pilot, Lt. Nguyen Huu Bach (27, trained in Corpus Christi, Tex.), proved very hard to understand on the interphone.

Our mission was bombing and strafing a VC concentration in the Tay Ninh vicinity near the Cambodian border. As we circled near an outstanding landmark east of Tay Ninh, called "Black Virgin Mountain," Bach pointed to a road below us and he said to me, "You see whop de road."

I asked if he was talking about a column of smoke rising from the embattled area. He answered, "No, it's lap de vay." He asked again if I saw "halsein road."

"Say again?"

With some irritation he spelled out the critical word: "HAYCHE—O-ELLES-HAYESS," I finally decided he was trying to tell me that there were "holes in the road."

We had another dreadful, neck-snapping, stomach-upsetting 15 minutes over the target, making endless diving passes to rocket and machine-gun several woods and groups of houses—all very evidently VC territory, because the open spaces were filled in with vast spreads of bamboo rotor bumpers, to discourage our helicopters from landing.

Back at Tan Son Nhut, I managed to pull my physical pieces together and get back into Saigon in time to pursue the matter of a Pan American ticket back to the U.S. It seemed about time: time for some real R and R—and time also to go back and work over this book.

Friday, January 11

At 10:50 A.M., sitting in the crowd on Saigon Airport's civilian side, I heard the call that I seem to have been anticipating for several months: "Pan American announces Flight Two for Hong Kong is ready for immediate boarding." I walked out toward the reassuring shape of the Boeing 707 jet with a line of blackheaded, tiny Vietnamese passengers who seemed extraordinarily happy, smiling and waving good-by to the airport crowds. They seemed to feel the same sense of escape, the same lightening of burdens in leaving Vietnam, as I did.

Climbing into the sanitary blue and white interior with rows of fresh white pillows stacked on the shelves over the seats, and pretty American stewardesses in blue caps and white blouses to welcome us, I felt a great sense of release from the mud, the paddies, the entangling jungle, the frightening mountains, and the lurking VC's—and from the multiple gory shocks and sudden surprises of war, set as these things are in Vietnam against the background of misery, filth, parasites, and rampant medieval disease.

The PA system was advising us: "This is your purser, Johnny Blitz, welcoming you aboard Flight Two, for Hong Kong, Tokyo, Honolulu, and San Francisco. Flying time to Hong Kong will be two hours."

At 11:10, we were moving out of the parking area, past a large assemblage of C-47's and C-54's; Caribous; the bulbous, muscular C-123's; a line of H-21's; and a display of Hueys as sharp and sinister as metal dragonflies. There is no escaping the evidence of our American commitment in Vietnam—even now, when we are half anesthetized by the 707's powerful embrace and bound for home.

Usually, I am somewhat cramped in the tourist section of an airliner; the seats are just too small for a six-foot-six frame. But this time I was lucky: there were two empty seats next to me. I could take the armrests out and catch a prone snooze—a fascinating prospect.

At 11:27, we were taking off, and climbing up into the sun, over traces of morning mist still clinging to the green face of Vietnam. The green-brown was fading into a light blue haze, a safe distance away. Even the horrible dense mountain forests were only shades from here. We were getting up into the smooth, high blue, with puffs of white clouds below us; the shadows of clouds were swallowing up the dun-colored land.

Now we are high above a solid bank of white cloud, with nearly solid blue above. Ahead and below, in a break in the white floor of clouds, there is a patch of blue. I hope it's ocean.

It *is* ocean. We're over the blue, cloudless spot now, and I can see the white traceries of waves. We're beginning to put the ocean between us and Vietnam and the Vietnamese war. But I know we can't really get away from it, even in a heavenbound jet. War will be going on in Vietnam, and other countries like Vietnam, for many years, all over the world.

Hawaii, March 9

I had expected to see Capt. Don Toth some time in Hawaii—in fact, we had made elaborate plans for meeting in this Paradise-for-the-Living, when he finished his tour of duty in Vietnam.

But this morning I had very bad news about Don and some other good friends of mine in the Vietnam campaign.

The letter came from Allan Galfund: "In a tragic accident on January 11th 1963 [the day I left], a CH-21 from the 57th Transportation Co. carrying a crew of four plus three passengers fell out of the sky from an altitude of 2500 feet killing all on board. The official report said it was an apparent malfunction of the aircraft controls which made it turn over and fall out of control. The passengers were: 1st Lieut. Lew Stone . . , Capt. Don Toth and 1st Lieut. Charlie Fitts (all of the 93d who were riding up to Saigon with the 57th. The four others, all from the 57th who died were:

CWO (W-2) Lawrence C. Hammond—Biloxi, Miss.

CWO (W-2) Raymond C. Wilde—Daleville, Ala.

Sp/5 James D. Mc Andrew—Santa Ana, Calif.

PFC Boyce E. Lawson—Wise, Va.

Galfund continued:

"As you might easily imagine, I was temporarily demoralized by the simultaneous loss of such good friends. However, as we both realize, they play for keeps out here and we've both been through too many exercises to allow it to get us down."

It was shocking news, so bad that I felt I had been slugged —hard—and I couldn't shake the feeling. I tried to lose myself in work, but the thought kept creeping back across my mind, like a numbing cloud: What injustice that Don, Lew, and Charlie and the others should go so suddenly! They were in their prime, young and fit and alert, in the midst of the dangerous career of risking all they had, and were, for us. What blasted bad luck that they or any of the highly-selected, dedicated American volunteers serving in Vietnam should be killed! It is such a dreadful loss, each time.

I felt particularly numbed by it, that night, because we were obligated to go to a party, a party with booze and supposed merriment, at a suburban house near Koko Head.

I was poor company, kept thinking about Don Toth, Lew, and Charlie. Finally, I explained to Moana and Patti that I had lost some good friends in Vietnam—and that it had been a great shock.

But later a thought came to me which seemed to make it better. I said to Moana:

"At least they died like men, like soldiers—doing their jobs well and bravely—for something bigger than they were. I hope that when I die, I can die as well, and that people will be able to say as much for me."

No matter what happens in Vietnam, nobody can subtract credit from men like Don Toth, who died there valiantly.

Index

Index

Adams, CWO Richard B., 160, 245

Adams, CWO Roy C., 357

Adamson, CWO W. Larry, 32, 41, 59, 68

Albritton, CWO Art M., 176, 182-83

Aldrich, Maj. George Washington, Jr., 338-39, 344

Allen, Lt. James S., 58, 68-69, 137

Allgood, Capt. Frank, 35-42, 110, 118-24, 125-27, 129

Anderson, Lt. Ed, 114, 118-23, 125, 194, 196-97

Anderson, Capt. Paul F., 304-05

Anderson, Cpl. Thomas E., 60

Armstrong, Ken, 305

Arnett, Peter, 241

Athans, Lt. Robert J., 197

Babbs, Lt. Kenneth J., 27, 31, 72, 79, 107, 111

Baird, Capt. John, 340

Baker, CWO George W., 79, 102-03

Baker, Lt. Richard, 103, 105

Baranowski, Lt. Joe, 73, 77, 79, 82-83, 137, 337

Bates, Lt. Austen, 124

Beatty, WO William R., 311

Beauchamp, Maj. Darwin, 177

Beck, Spec/6 Jim, 287

Beebe, Col. John L., 363-69

Bell, Lt. Frank, 40, 123, 126

Bell, CWO Jim, 293

Bellow, Spec/6 Edwin, 249, 299

Benedict, Capt. Chuck, 156, 159, 172, 244-46, 263, 264, 282, 288, 291

Bennett, S/Sgt. William P., 314-15

Bentley, Sgt. Russell, 197-98

Bergdahl, Lt. Harold, 157

Berube, Capt. Joseph R., 301

Betts, Maj. Edward, 294

Beuch, Maj. Bill R., 117, 129

Bitter, Maj. Louise, 348

Blair, Lt. Dorwin T., 29, 126

Blaydes, Maj. Aquilla, 24, 35, 42-43, 81, 84, 88, 89, 97, 111-12, 117, 128, 130-31, 199-200

Bolling, Col. Alexander R., Jr., 222

Bowles, Sgt. 1C William, 325

Boyd, Pfc. Michael, 318-25, 327

Brooks, Lt. Edwin C., 63-64, 79, 134

Burress, Capt. Gene, 236

Butler, Maj. James, 250, 289

Butreaux, Lance Corp. Thonis J., 69

Calhoun, Spec/5 Robert, 188
Callan, Lt. Ida, 350
Calvert, Lt. John, 135-36
Cao, Gen., 177-80, 286, 329, 359
Carr, Sgt. George, 95-99
Carrier, S/Sgt. William, 100
Carter, Pfc. Duncan, 269
Center, Capt. Dick, 92-93
Chaffin, Spec/4 Clyde, 187
Champion, Capt. William, 197
Chapman, Lt. Dick, 126
Chase, Capt. Ambert, 113
Chi, Maj., 316
Chiarenza, Lt. Angelo, 62, 79, 101
Cignotti, Maj. Lew, 81, 88, 131, 200
Clark, Lt. George, 101-02
Clark, Sgt. George M., 308
Coady, Lt. Eric, 35, 124, 126, 127, 336-37
Coggins, Capt. Donald, 340
Compton, Sgt. Alfred, 352-56, 260-63
Compton, Sgt. 1C Marvin, 318, 325-26
Cooney, Warrant/4 John, 185-86
Corrie, Col. Wirt, 148

Dailey, Sgt. James, 117
Dam, Lt., 138-44
Damron, Capt. Herbert C., 225-26, 229-31
Dat, Sgt., 271-80
Deal, Sgt. William L., 358
Deepe, Beverly, 100-01, 106
Deibel, Capt. Robert E., 64-65, 66, 134-35
Delahanty, Capt. Ray, Jr., 164, 245
DeLoune, Spec/3 Sam, 187
Denno, Col. Bryce, 55
Devers, Corp. Darwin L., 69
Dickerson, Pfc. John, 232-34, 288-89

Diem, Pres. Ngo Dinh, 14, 15, 64, 86, 87, 153, 173, 277, 306
Don, Gen., 57
Downing, Capt. John, 355-57, 360
Downs, Sgt. Henry B., 257
Duarte, Sgt. Antonio, 318, 328
Dulaney, Sgt. Jack W., 99-100
Dunlop, Lt. John, 103
Dunnuck, Capt. Robert T., 254-56

Eaves, PRC Kenneth B., 266-67
Ebeling, Corpsman Robert, 62-63
Edwards, Capt. Richard O., 311-12
Eiler, Pfc. Robert, 184-85, 263-64
Eisenhower, Gen. (ret.) Dwight D., 12
Essoyan, Roy, 241
Ewing, Maj. Paul, 173, 185-86, 245, 289, 292-93

Falls, Capt. John, 251, 291
Farner, Sgt./1C Robert N., 105
Farnham, Lt. Donald, 257, 262
Fell, Spec/5 Billie G., 310, 324-25
Felt, Adm. Harry D., 9
Ferroni, Sgt. Danny, 341
Finn, Capt. Bob, 114
Fitts, CWO Charlie M., 299-300, 362, 376
Flippen, WO Carl R., 267
Ford, Capt. Jack, 330-34
Foss, Lt. Col. Don, 23, 67
Frech, Lance Corp. Roland, 35-40
Frickie, Lt. Edmond L., 65-67, 79, 134
Fritzler, Lt. Bob, 82-84

Galfund, Maj. Allan, 17, 149, 155, 160-61, 173, 175, 178, 239-40, 375

INDEX

Ganly, Lt. David, 346, 350-52

Gardner, Capt. William S., 357

Genile, Pfc. Henry, 198

Gilley, Spec/5 Emory, 231

Good, Capt. Kenneth N., 359

Goodson, S/Sgt. William F., 82

Grace, Capt. William R., 308-11, 324, 326-27, 362

Gray, Maj. James E., 54-55

Gressang, CWO Daniel, 339-41

Griffin, Lt. Gerald C., 59-60

Gunter, Lt. Miles Gordon, 79, 99, 135-36

Halberstam, Dave, 215-18, 241-42, 305-06

Hall, Capt. Jim, 296-97

Hamil, Lt. Richard C., 202, 208-09, 248

Hamilton, Sgt. Richard E., 61-63

Hammond, CWO Lawrence C., 375

Hammond, Spec/5 Norris H., 307-08

Hanna, Pfc. Robert, 153, 244-45

Hanson, Capt. Gerald H., 277, 235-36, 243-44, 247, 252-63, 265-68, 283, 287, 290

Harkins, Gen. Paul D., 12, 14, 16

Harp, Capt. Jim, 94-95

Harper, Pfc. James, 176, 183

Harper, Pfc. Jim, 299

Harris, Tom, 93-94

Harrison, Sgt. Alfred, 113-14

Hartenstein, Maj. Paul, 349

Hartsock, Cpl. George, 117-18, 120-23, 124-25

Heathman, Sgt. Howard, 113-14

Heck, CWO Cleatus, 226, 231, 234-35, 253, 265, 288

Hellenga, Capt. Glen, 344

Henderson, Lt. John, 249

Henderson, Capt. William R., 371

Hensley, Spec/6 Arthur, 176-77, 183

Herschberg, Capt. Cy, 24-25, 49, 60-63, 79

Ho, Pres. Chi Minh, 134, 252

Hoa, Father, 245, 292

Hoagland, Sgt. George, III, 319-25, 327

Hoffman, Lt. Col. Robert, 274, 283

Holloway, CWO Charles E., 311, 339-42

Horton, Capt. Sam, 85, 89, 95-98, 121-23, 125

Huang, Lt. Huu-Lac, 73-74

Huy, Lt., 138-44

Hyrowski, Capt. Stanley, 307-08

Ireland, Col. Julius W., 78, 87-88, 101, 106, 132

Jackson, Sen. Henry M., 288-90

Jackson, Lt. Terry, 31

Jenkins, Capt. M. H., 305

Jensen, Pfc. George M., 198-99

Johnson, Cpl. Le Grand, 28

Johnson, Lt. Marshall L., 20-22

Jones, Sgt. Don M., 347

Jones, Sgt. J. D., 114

Jones, Capt. Richard A., 164, 259, 269-82, 283-85

Jordan, Lance Corp. John T., 69

Jordanides, Sam, 93

Josh, Capt. Joseph A., 53-55

Kalin, Lt. Col. Byron, 35, 37, 55-57, 72, 81, 134

Kan, V. C., 195

Keasler, Sgt. Robert T., 131

Kennedy, Pres. John F., 12

Kerr, Lt. Keith K., 131

Khoi, Dung Duc, 353-54

Kibler, CWO Robert, 174-75, 177, 181, 205-06, 244-45

King, Lt. Col. Max, 328, 342-44

Kirchdorfer, Lt. Louis, 20

Kirkpatrick, CWO Joseph, 226, 244, 257

Kleebauer, Lt. Charles, 313, 314
Kleinheinz, Capt. Ernest, 331
Klepsattel, Maj. Don, 72, 107-10, 127
Korman, 79

Lang, Maj. Vincent, 345
Larson, Sgt. Duane, 103
Lawson, Pfc. Boyce E., 375
Lawson, Pfc. Royce, 357
Leach, Capt. Bertram, 246-47, 282
Leary, Lt. Paul, 308-10
Lee, S/Sgt. Johnnie, 152-54, 209, 268
Leek, Maj. Gen. Fred, 336
Lemmons, Maj. Ray, 43, 68-69, 88, 103, 116-17
Leonard, CWO Jess, 286-87
Levreault, Sgt. Lester, 113
Lewis, Lance Corp. Marion W., 69
Lewis, Spec/5 Robert E., 340
Lewis, Capt. Ty, 330-31
Lieberman, Lt. Col. Murray, 349
Lindenmayer, Lt. Comdr. Louie L., 215-18
Linnimeier, Col. George, 190, 200
Loftin, Corp. Bob J., 129-30
Losse, Lt. Col. Bob, 127-28
Lovings, Lt. Wade, 113
Lucas, Sgt. David, 202, 204
Lum, 365-66
Lupu, Spec/5 Robert, 352

MacNevin, Pvt. Donald, 244
MacReynolds, Capt. Sam, 92-93
Madigan, Lt. Ed, 124, 126, 127, 131
Mann, Lt. Col. Herbert R., 138-46
Manning, Sgt. Cyril, 345
Mansfield, Lance Corp. James, 25, 29-30
Marr, Lt. Dave, 71, 87

Martin, Lt. Joe, 45
Marvel, Capt. Jerry, 57-58
Mauser, Maj. Bob, 355
Mc Andrew, Spec/5 James D., 375
McCoy, Capt. Ron, 330-31
McCully, Col. Alton, 25, 67, 123, 132
McDonald, Pfc. Burl, 161, 163-67, 171-73
McDuffie, Lt. Col. David P., 100-01, 138
McElvoy, Tech/Sgt. Herbert W., 300
McFall, Lt. William T., 80, 85
McGee, Corpsman Larry, 62-63
McNamara, Robert, 9, 13
Mecklin, John, 333, 344, 353
Messick, Capt. Thomas R., 316
Mitchell, Sgt. Dale T., 27, 72
Mills, Capt. Lew, 48, 51
Monia, Spec/4 Joe, 316
Mooney, Spec/6 James, 340-41
Moore, Capt. David J., 58
Moorer, Vice-Adml., 336
Morgan, Airman/1C Jerry, 19, 21
Morton, Sgt. Harvey L., 73-78, 124
Murley, Lt. Col. Myron, 303
Murphy, Capt. Galen, 93

Nantz, Sgt. 1C Hobart T., Jr., 60-61
Naylor, Lt. Don, 352
Ng Huy-Cuong, Lt., 138-44
Nguyen Huu Bach, Lt., 372
Nguyen Ngoc-Minh, 113
Nguyen Tuyen, Lt., 35, 37
Nguyen van Dai, 365
Nguyen van Hieu, Maj., 133, 137
Nguyen van Ngoc, 366-67
Nguyen van Thanh, 366-67
Nhu, Mme., 242, 351
Nolting, Frederick E., 13-14

INDEX

Norton, Corpsman Gerald O., 60-63

Nysewander, CWO Carlton, 269

Obleman, Pfc. William, 198

O'Connor, Capt. Henry James, 202-05, 208-09

O'Neil, Lt. Lew, 115, 126

Parnell, Sgt. Charles, 21

Parry, S/Sgt. D. T., 199

Patterson, John, 93-94

Payne, S/Sgt. Chuck, 199

Peart, M/Sgt. George J., 85

Pendell, Sgt. Herald W., 60

Perry, Mert, 179-80, 241

Peters, Maj. George A., 302-05, 311-12, 328

Phan-Tien, Lt. Huc, 73

Phillips, Cpl. Daniel P., 45

Phipps, Capt. John, 334

Phuoc, Father, 294

Picou, Maj. Lloyd, 302-03

Porter, Col. Daniel Boone, 249-50, 335, 357, 371

Prather, Capt. Jay, 27-31, 79, 94-95, 115

Purcell, Tech/4C James, 93

Rathbun, Lt. Col. Robert L., 25, 31, 33-34, 41-42, 44-47, 48-51, 59, 68-70, 72-73, 78-79, 81, 86-87, 94-95, 106, 114-15, 117, 119-24, 127-28, 131, 132, 199, 335

Reed, Spec/6 Joseph, 226, 228, 230

Renaldi, Lt. Frank, 353

Renard, Michel, 215, 218, 330

Rick, Maj. Bob, 88, 337-38

Roberts, Spec/5 Bobby L., 248

Robinson, Sgt. 1C Frank, 350-52

Robinson, Jim, 242

Robinson, Maj. Lewis H., 350

Rogers, Capt. Betty, 347-48

Rosane, Lt. Ed, 21-22

Ross, Lt. Dave, 31

Rowland, Spec/5 Charles, 359-60

Ruf, CWO Willie, 155-56

Runkle, Maj. Robert E., 150-51, 153, 190

Sandvoss, Lt. Bert E. G., 29

Savage, Capt. Derrell J., 211-213

Scofield, Capt. Bob, 154-55, 334-35

Serong, Col. Francis P., 207

Shows, CWO Sidney B., 176, 182-83

Shrouf, Cpl. Michael R., 40-41, 337

Si, Lt., 342-43

Siegal, Stan, 215, 218, 242

Sinnott, Lt. William Thomas, 30-31, 60-63

Slavich, Maj. Ivan, 151, 200-02, 205, 207-10, 236-38, 243-44

Smith, Sgt. Francis A., 202

Smith, Lt. Col. Jim, 13, 16, 19, 69, 94, 149

Sooto, Cpl. Vitale, 80-81

Spellman, Francis Cardinal, 337

Sprague, Lt. Billy, 255-56, 229-31, 249, 252-58, 287-88

Stafford, Dental Tech/3C Robert, 25, 59-63

Starboard, Capt. Earl D., 154-55, 334-35

Steelman, CWO Jim, 293

Steine, Capt. Joel R., 151-52, 243

Stewart, Pfc. Edward L., 244

Stonaker, Spec/5 Jim, 234, 286

Stone, Lt. James E., 358

Stone, Lt. Lewis, 54-55, 245, 252, 360-62, 375-76

Streever, Capt. Karl, 358

Sully, François, 242

Tate, Irving, 228, 230

Taylor, Gen. Maxwell D., 12

Taylor, Spec/5 Ted, 161, 163, 166, 170
Tham, Lt., 342-43
Thompson, Spec/5 Mervyn, 317
Thurman, Capt. Maxwell R., 136
Tiemann, Capt. Floyd J., 312
Timmes, Maj. Gen. Charles F., 211
Tomlinson, CWO Barney, 316
Toth, Capt. Don, 156-59, 160-72, 244-45, 247, 268-69, 283, 294-96, 299-300, 357-58, 359, 375-76
Trumbull, Bob, 196
Tucker, Maj. Gen. Reuben, 219-22
Tunney, Lt. Michael J., 60
Tuten, Capt. Jeff, 274

Vaccero, Sgt. Joseph, 317, 325
Valentin, Lance Corp. Miguel A., Jr., 60-61
Van, Lt., 271-81
Vann, Col., 177, 286, 359, 370-71
Vernon, Capt. Graham, 222, 223
Vining, Capt. Ray, 53-55
Vinson, Lt. Richard P., 32, 48, 69-70, 88, 147
Vizena, Sgt. 1C Alex, 307
Vo, Capt. Van Hai, 364-69

Wadlack, CWO Dick, 247, 265, 268, 358

Wagner, Maj. Robert S., 52-53, 132-34, 136
Walsh, CWO John, 160-71, 231-32, 300
Walsworth, Lt. William A., 57-58
Walton, Maj. Spencer, 348
Washington, Sgt. Willie, 22
Watson, Cpl. Billy, 25-26, 46-48, 58
Webb, Sgt. Ray F., 191, 200
Webster, Capt. Bob, 288, 291
Webster, Maj. Dave, 42, 70, 73, 78, 114-15, 131
Weiner, Capt. Louis, 103-04
Weiss, Pfc. David, 21
West, Lt. Bill, 45-46
West, Capt. Tom W., 164
Whitmore, Spec/4 Arthur M., 340-41
Wibblesman, Lt. Fred, 45
Wilde, CWO Raymond C., 375
Wilkerson, CWO Gary, 249
Will, Maj. Clement, 312, 314-15
Wilson, Col. Wilbur, 301-02
Wirkus, Lt. Faustin, 95-99, 194
Woelfel, SFC Lou, 317
Wolford, Sgt. Donald, 310, 325
Wood, Capt. Ernest, 237, 244
Wright, CWO Richard H., 152-53

Young, Carl, 314

Zornow, Comdr. Gerald, 17, 79, 190, 210